THE ESSENTIAL SHAKESPEARE COMEDIES COLLECTION

A Midsummer Night's Dream, The Merchant of Venice, Much Ado About Nothing, The Taming of the Shrew, The Tempest, Twelfth Night

WILLIAM SHAKESPEARE

CONTENTS

THE TEMPEST

TWELFTH NIGHT

A MIDSUMMER NIGHT'S
DREAM

DRAMATIS PERSONÆ

THESEUS, Duke of Athens.
EGEUS, father to Hermia.
LYSANDER, in love with Hermia.
DEMETRIUS, " " " "
PHILOSTRATE, master of the revels to Theseus
QUINCE, a carpenter.
SNUG, a joiner.
BOTTOM, a weaver.
FLUTE, a bellows-mender.
SNOUT, a tinker.
STARVELING, a tailor.
HIPPOLYTA, queen of the Amazons, betrothed to
    Theseus.
HERMIA, daughter to Egeus, in love with Lysander.
HELENA, in love with Demetrius.
OBERON, king of the fairies.
TITANIA, queen of the fairies.
PUCK, or Robin Goodfellow.
PEASEBLOSSOM, FAIRY.
COBWEB, "
MOTH, "
MUSTARDSEED, "
Other fairies attending their King and Queen. Atten-
    dants on Theseus and Hippolyta.
SCENE — *Athens, and a wood near it.*

3

ACT I

(Enter Theseus, Hippolyta, Philostrate, and Attendants.)

The. Now, fair Hippolyta, our nuptial hour
Draws on apace; four happy days bring in
Another moon: but, O, methinks, how slow
This old moon wanes! she lingers my desires,
Like to a step-dame, or a dowager,
Long withering out a young man's revenue.
Hip. Four days will quickly steep themselves in night;
Four nights will quickly dream away the time;
And then the moon, like to a silver bow
New-bent in heaven, shall behold the night
Of our solemnities.
The. Go, Philostrate,
Stir up the Athenian youth to merriments;
Awake the pert and nimble spirit of mirth:
Turn melancholy forth to funerals;
The pale companion is not for our pomp. *(Exit Philostrate.)*
Hippolyta, I woo'd thee with my sword,
And won thy love, doing thee injuries;
But I will wed thee in another key,
With pomp, with triumph and with revelling.

(Enter Egeus, Hermia, Lysander, and Demetrius.)

5

Ege. Happy be Theseus, our renowned duke!

The. Thanks, good Egeus: what's the news with thee?

Ege. Full of vexation come I, with complaint
Against my child, my daughter Hermia.
Stand forth, Demetrius. My noble lord,
This man hath my consent to marry her.
Stand forth, Lysander: and, my gracious duke,
This man hath bewitch'd the bosom of my child:
Thou, thou, Lysander, thou hast given her rhymes,
And interchanged love-tokens with my child:
Thou hast by moonlight at her window sung,
With feigning voice, verses of feigning love;
And stolen the impression of her fantasy
With bracelets of thy hair, rings, gawds, conceits,
Knacks, trifles, nosegays, sweetmeats, messengers
Of strong prevailment in unharden'd youth:
With cunning hast thou filch'd my daughter's heart;
Turn'd her obedience, which is due to me,
To stubborn harshness: and, my gracious duke,
Be it so she will not here before your Grace
Consent to marry with Demetrius,
I beg the ancient privilege of Athens,
As she is mine, I may dispose of her:
Which shall be either to this gentleman
Or to her death, according to our law
Immediately provided in that case.

The. What say you, Hermia? be advised, fair maid:
To you your father should be as a god;
One that composed your beauties; yea, and one
To whom you are but as a form in wax
By him imprinted and within his power
To leave the figure or disfigure it.
Demetrius is a worthy gentleman.

Her. So is Lysander.

The. In himself he is;
But in this kind, wanting your father's voice,
The other must be held the worthier.

Her. I would my father look'd but with my eyes.

The. Rather your eyes must with his judgement look.

Her. I do entreat your Grace to pardon me.
I know not by what power I am made bold,
Nor how it may concern my modesty,
In such a presence here to plead my thoughts;

That, in a spleen, unfolds both heaven and earth,
And ere a man hath power to say 'Behold!'
The jaws of darkness do devour it up:
So quick bright things come to confusion.
150 *Her.* If then true lovers have been ever cross'd,
It stands as an edict in destiny:
Then let us teach our trial patience,
Because it is a customary cross,
As due to love as thoughts and dreams and sighs,
155 Wishes and tears, poor fancy's followers.
Lys. A good persuasion: therefore, hear me, Hermia.
I have a widow aunt, a dowager
Of great revenue, and she hath no child:
From Athens is her house remote seven leagues;
160 And she respects me as her only son.
There, gentle Hermia, may I marry thee;
And to that place the sharp Athenian law
Cannot pursue us. If thou lovest me, then,
Steal forth thy father's house to-morrow night;
165 And in the wood, a league without the town,
Where I did meet thee once with Helena,
To do observance to a morn of May,
There will I stay for thee.
Her. My good Lysander!
I swear to thee, by Cupid's strongest bow,
170 By his best arrow with the golden head,
By the simplicity of Venus' doves,
By that which knitteth souls and prospers loves,
And by that fire which burn'd the Carthage queen,
When the false Troyan under sail was seen,
175 By all the vows that ever men have broke,
In number more than ever women spoke,
In that same place thou hast appointed me,
To-morrow truly will I meet with thee.
Lys. Keep promise, love. Look, here comes Helena.

(*Enter Helena.*)

180 *Her.* God speed fair Helena! whither away?
Hel. Call you me fair? that fair again unsay.
Demetrius loves your fair: O happy fair!
Your eyes are lode-stars; and your tongue's sweet air
More tuneable than lark to shepherd's ear.

185 When wheat is green, when hawthorn buds appear.
Sickness is catching: O, were favour so,
Yours would I catch, fair Hermia, ere I go;
My ear should catch your voice, my eye your eye,
My tongue should catch your tongue's sweet melody.
190 Were the world mine, Demetrius being bated,
The rest I'd give to be to you translated.
O, teach me how you look; and with what art
You sway the motion of Demetrius' heart!

Her. I frown upon him, *yet* he loves me still.

195 *Hel.* O that your frowns would teach my smiles
such skill!

Her. I give him curses, yet he gives me love.

Hel. O that my prayers could such affection move!

Her. The more I hate, the more he follows me.

Hel. The more I love, the more he hateth me.

200 *Her.* His folly, Helena, is no fault of mine.

Hel. None, but your beauty: would that fault were
mine!

Her. Take comfort: he no more shall see my face;
Lysander and myself will fly this place.
Before the time I did Lysander see,
205 Seem'd Athens as a paradise to me:
O, then, what graces in my love do dwell,
That he hath turn'd a heaven unto a hell!

Lys. Helen, to you our minds we will unfold:
To-morrow night, when Phœbe doth behold
210 Her silver visage in the watery glass,
Decking with liquid pearl the bladed grass,
A time that lovers' flights doth still conceal,
Through Athens' gates have we devised to steal.

Her. And in the wood, where often you and I
215 Upon faint primrose-beds were wont to lie,
Emptying our bosoms of their counsel sweet,
There my Lysander and myself shall meet;
And thence from Athens turn away our eyes,
To seek new friends and stranger companies.
220 Farewell, sweet playfellow: pray thou for us;
And good luck grant thee thy Demetrius!
Keep word, Lysander: we must starve our sight
From lovers' food till morrow deep midnight.

Lys. I will, my Hermia. *(Exit Herm.)*

Helena, adieu:

$_{225}$ As you on him, Demetrius dote on you! *(Exit.)*

Hel. How happy some o'er other some can be!

Through Athens I am thought as fair as she.

But what of that? Demetrius thinks not so;

He will not know what all but he do know:

$_{230}$ And as he errs, doting on Hermia's eyes,

So I, admiring of his qualities:

Things base and vile, holding no quantity,

Love can transpose to form and dignity:

Love looks not with the eyes, but with the mind;

$_{235}$ And therefore is wing'd Cupid painted blind:

Nor hath Love's mind of any judgement taste;

Wings, and no eyes, figure unheedy haste:

And therefore is Love said to be a child,

Because in choice he is so oft beguiled.

$_{240}$ As waggish boys in game themselves forswear,

So the boy Love is perjured every where:

For ere Demetrius look'd on Hermia's eyne,

He hail'd down oaths that he was only mine;

And when this hail some heat from Hermia felt,

$_{245}$ So he dissolved, and showers of oaths did melt.

I will go tell him of fair Hermia's flight:

Then to the wood will he to-morrow night

Pursue her; and for this intelligence

If I have thanks, it is a dear expense:

$_{250}$ But herein mean I to enrich my pain,

To have his sight thither and back again. *(Exit.)*

SCENE II. THE SAME. QUINCE'S HOUSE.

(Enter Quince, Snug, Bottom, Flute, Snout, and Starveling.)

Quin. Is all our company here?

Bot. You were best to call them generally, man by man, according to the scrip.

Quin. Here is the scroll of every man's name, which is

$_{005}$ thought fit, through all Athens, to play in our interlude before

fore the duke and the duchess, on his wedding-day at
night.

Bot. First, good Peter Quince, say what the play
treats

on; then read the names of the actors; and so grow to
a point.

010 *Quin.* Marry, our play is, The most lamentable
comedy, and most cruel death of Pyramus and
Thisby.

Bot. A very good piece of work, I assure you, and a
merry. Now, good Peter Quince, call forth your actors by the scroll. Masters, spread yourselves.

015 *Quin.* Answer as I call you. Nick Bottom, the
weaver.

Bot. Ready. Name what part I am for, and proceed.

Quin. You, Nick Bottom, are set down for Pyramus.

Bot. What is Pyramus? a lover, or a tyrant?

Quin. A lover, that kills himself most gallant for
love.

020 *Bot.* That will ask some tears in the true per-
forming of it: if I do it, let the audience look to
their eyes; I will move storms, I will condole in
some measure. To the rest: yet my chief humour is
for a tyrant: I could play Ercles rarely, or a part to
tear a cat in, to make all split.

025 The raging rocks
And shivering shocks
Shall break the locks
Of prison-gates;
And Phibbus' car
030 Shall shine from far,
And make and mar
The foolish Fates.

This was lofty! Now name the rest of the players. This
is Ercles' vein, a tyrant's vein; a lover is more
condoling.

035 *Quin.* Francis Flute, the bellows-mender.

Flu. Here, Peter Quince.

Quin. Flute, you must take Thisby on you.

Flu. What is Thisby? a wandering knight?

Quin. It is the lady that Pyramus must love.

040 *Flu.* Nay, faith, let not me play a woman; I have a
beard coming.

Quin. That's all one: you shall play it in a mask, and
you may speak as small as you will.

Bot. An I may hide my face, let me play Thisby too,
I'll $_{045}$ speak in a monstrous little voice, 'Thisne,
Thisne;' 'Ah Pyramus, my lover dear! thy Thisby
dear, and lady dear!'

Quin. No, no; you must play Pyramus: and, Flute,
you Thisby.

Bot. Well, proceed.

$_{050}$ *Quin.* Robin Starveling, the tailor.

Star. Here, Peter Quince.

Quin. Robin Starveling, you must play Thisby's
mother. Tom Snout, the tinker.

Snout. Here, Peter Quince.

$_{055}$ *Quin.* You, Pyramus' father: myself, Thisby's father: Snug, the joiner; you, the lion's part: and, I
hope, here is a play fitted.

Snug. Have you the lion's part written? pray you, if it
be, give it me, for I am slow of study.

$_{060}$ *Quin.* You may do it extempore, for it is nothing
but roaring.

Bot. Let me play the lion too: I will roar, that I will do
any man's heart good to hear me; I will roar, that I
will make the duke say, 'Let him roar again, let
him roar $_{065}$ again.'

Quin. An you should do it too terribly, you would
fright the duchess and the ladies, that they would
shriek; and that were enough to hang us all.

All. That would hang us, every mother's son.

$_{070}$ *Bot.* I grant you, friends, if that you should fright
the ladies out of their wits, they would have no
more discretion but to hang us: but I will aggra-
vate my voice so, that I will roar you as gently as
any sucking dove; I will roar you an 'twere any
nightingale.

$_{075}$ *Quin.* You can play no part but Pyramus; for
Pyramus is a sweet-faced man; a proper man, as
one shall see in a summer's day; a most lovely,
gentleman-like man: therefore you must needs
play Pyramus.

Bot. Well, I will undertake it. What beard were I $_{080}$
best to play it in?

Quin. Why, what you will.

Bot. I will discharge it in either your straw colour
 beard, your orange-tawny beard, your purple-in-
 grain beard, or your French crown colour beard,
 your perfect $_{085}$ yellow.
Quin. Some of your French crowns have no hair at
 all, and then you will play barefaced. But, masters,
 here are your parts: and I am to entreat you, request you, and desire you, to con them by to-
 morrow night; and meet me $_{090}$ in the palace
 wood, a mile without the town, by moonlight;
 there will we rehearse, for if we meet in the city,
 we shall be dogged with company, and our de-
 vices known. In the meantime I will draw a bill of
 properties, such as our play wants. I pray you, fail
 me not.
$_{095}$ Bot. We will meet; and there we may rehearse
 most obscenely and courageously. Take pains; be
 perfect: adieu.
Quin. At the duke's oak we meet.
Bot. Enough; hold or cut bow-strings. (Exeunt.)

ACT II

SCENE I. A WOOD NEAR ATHENS.

(Enter, from opposite sides, a Fairy, and Puck.)

Puck. How now, spirit! whither wander you?
Fai.
Over hill, over dale,
Thorough bush, thorough brier,
Over park, over pale,
005 Thorough flood, thorough fire,
I do wander every where,
Swifter than the moon's sphere;
And I serve the fairy queen,
To dew her orbs upon the green.
010 The cowslips tall her pensioners be:
In their gold coats spots you see;
Those be rubies, fairy favours,
In those freckles live their savours:
I must go seek some dewdrops here,
015 And hang a pearl in every cowslip's ear.
Farewell, thou lob of spirits; I'll be gone:
Our queen and all her elves come here anon.
Puck. The king doth keep his revels here to-night:
Take heed the queen come not within his sight;
020 For Oberon is passing fell and wrath,
Because that she as her attendant hath
A lovely boy, stolen from an Indian king;

She never had so sweet a changeling:
And jealous Oberon would have the child
025 Knight of his train, to trace the forests wild;
But she perforce withholds the loved boy,
Crowns him with flowers, and makes him all her joy:
And now they never meet in grove or green,
By fountain clear, or spangled starlight sheen,
030 But they do square, that all their elves for fear
Creep into acorn-cups and hide them there.

Fai. Either I mistake your shape and making quite,
Or else you are that shrewd and knavish sprite
Call'd Robin Goodfellow: are not you he
035 That frights the maidens of the villagery;
Skim milk, and sometimes labour in the quern,
And bootless make the breathless housewife churn;
And sometime make the drink to bear no barm;
Mislead night-wanderers, laughing at their harm?
040 Those that Hobgoblin call you, and sweet Puck,
You do their work, and they shall have good luck:
Are not you he?

Puck.
Thou speak'st aright;
I am that merry wanderer of the night.
I jest to Oberon, and make him smile,
045 When I a fat and bean-fed horse beguile,
Neighing in likeness of a filly foal:
And sometime lurk I in a gossip's bowl,
In very likeness of a roasted crab;
And when she drinks, against her lips I bob
050 And on her wither'd dewlap pour the ale.
The wisest aunt, telling the saddest tale,
Sometime for three-foot stool mistaketh me;
Then slip I from her bum, down topples she,
And 'tailor' cries, and falls into a cough;
055 And then the whole quire hold their hips and
   laugh;
And waxen in their mirth, and neeze, and swear
A merrier hour was never wasted there.
But, room, fairy! here comes Oberon.

Fai. And here my mistress. Would that he were gone!

*(Enter, from one side, OBERON, with his train; from the other,
TITANIA, with hers.)*

060 *Obe.* Ill met by moonlight, proud Titania.
Tita. What, jealous Oberon! Fairies, skip hence:
I have forsworn his bed and company.
Obe. Tarry, rash wanton: am not I thy lord?
Tita. Then I must be thy lady: but I know
065 When thou hast stolen away from fairy land,
And in the shape of Corin sat all day,
Playing on pipes of corn, and versing love
To amorous Phillida. Why art thou here,
Come from the farthest steppe of India?
070 But that, forsooth, the bouncing Amazon,
Your buskin'd mistress and your warrior love,
To Theseus must be wedded, and you come
To give their bed joy and prosperity.
Obe. How canst thou thus for shame, Titania,
075 Glance at my credit with Hippolyta,
Knowing I know thy love to Theseus?
Didst thou not lead him through the glimmering
 night
From Perigenia, whom he ravished?
And make him with fair Ægle break his faith,
080 With Ariadne and Antiopa?
Tita. These are the forgeries of jealousy:
And never, since the middle summer's spring,
Met we on hill, in dale, forest, or mead,
By paved fountain or by rushy brook,
085 Or in the beached margent of the sea,
To dance our ringlets to the whistling wind,
But with thy brawls thou hast disturb'd our sport.
Therefore the winds, piping to us in vain,
As in revenge, have suck'd up from the sea
090 Contagious fogs; which falling in the land,
Have every pelting river made so proud,
That they have overborne their continents:
The ox hath therefore stretch'd his yoke in vain,
The ploughman lost his sweat; and the green corn
095 Hath rotted ere his youth attain'd a beard:
The fold stands empty in the drowned field,
And crows are fatted with the murrion flock;
The nine men's morris is fill'd up with mud;
And the quaint mazes in the wanton green,
100 For lack of tread, are undistinguishable:
The human mortals want their winter here;

No night is now with hymn or carol blest:
Therefore the moon, the governess of floods,
Pale in her anger, washes all the air,
105 That rheumatic diseases do abound:
And thorough this distemperature we see
The seasons alter: hoary-headed frosts
Fall in the fresh lap of the crimson rose;
And on old Hiems' thin and icy crown
110 An odorous chaplet of sweet summer buds
Is, as in mockery, set: the spring, the summer,
The childing autumn, angry winter, change
Their wonted liveries; and the mazed world,
By their increase, now knows not which is which:
115 And this same progeny of evils comes
From our debate, from our dissension;
We are their parents and original.
Obe. Do you amend it, then; it lies in you:
Why should Titania cross her Oberon?
120 I do but beg a little changeling boy,
To be my henchman.
Tita.
Set your heart at rest:
The fairy land buys not the child of me.
His mother was a votaress of my order:
And, in the spiced Indian air, by night,
125 Full often hath she gossip'd by my side;
And sat with me on Neptune's yellow sands,
Marking the embarked traders on the flood;
When we have laugh'd to see the sails conceive
And grow big-bellied with the wanton wind;
130 Which she, with pretty and with swimming gait
Following,—her womb then rich with my young
    squire,—
Would imitate, and sail upon the land,
To fetch me trifles, and return again,
As from a voyage, rich with merchandise.
135 But she, being mortal, of that boy did die;
And for her sake do I rear up her boy;
And for her sake I will not part with him.
Obe. How long within this wood intend you stay?
Tita. Perchance till after Theseus' wedding-day.
140 If you will patiently dance in our round,
And see our moonlight revels, go with us;

If not, shun me, and I will spare your haunts.
Obe. Give me that boy, and I will go with thee.
Tita. Not for thy fairy kingdom. Fairies, away!
145 We shall chide downright, if I longer stay. *(Exit Ti-
tania with her train.)*
Obe. Well, go thy way: thou shalt not from this grove
Till I torment thee for this injury.
My gentle Puck, come hither. Thou rememberest
Since once I sat upon a promontory,
150 And heard a mermaid, on a dolphin's back,
Uttering such dulcet and harmonious breath,
That the rude sea grew civil at her song,
And certain stars shot madly from their spheres,
To hear the sea-maid's music.
Puck. I remember.
155 *Obe.* That very time I saw, but thou couldst not,
Flying between the cold moon and the earth,
Cupid all arm'd: a certain aim he took
At a fair vestal throned by the west,
And loosed his love-shaft smartly from his bow,
160 As it should pierce a hundred thousand hearts:
But I might see young Cupid's fiery shaft
Quench'd in the chaste beams of the watery moon,
And the imperial votaress passed on,
In maiden meditation, fancy-free.
165 Yet mark'd I where the bolt of Cupid fell:
It fell upon a little western flower,
Before milk-white, now purple with love's wound,
And maidens call it love-in-idleness.
Fetch me that flower; the herb I shew'd thee once:
170 The juice of it on sleeping eye-lids laid
Will make or man or woman madly dote
Upon the next live creature that it sees.
Fetch me this herb; and be thou here again
Ere the leviathan can swim a league.
175 *Puck.* I'll put a girdle round about the earth
In forty minutes. *(Exit.)*
Obe. Having once this juice,
I'll watch Titania when she is asleep,
And drop the liquor of it in her eyes.
The next thing then she waking looks upon,
180 Be it on lion, bear, or wolf, or bull,
On meddling monkey, or on busy ape,

She shall pursue it with the soul of love:
And ere I take this charm from off her sight,
As I can take it with another herb,
185 I'll make her render up her page to me.
But who comes here? I am invisible;
And I will overhear their conference.

(Enter DEMETRIUS, HELENA *following him.)*

DEM. I love thee not, therefore pursue me not.
Where is Lysander and fair Hermia?
190 The one I'll slay, the other slayeth me.
Thou told'st me they were stolen unto this wood;
And here am I, and wode within this wood,
Because I cannot meet my Hermia.
Hence, get thee gone, and follow me no more.
195 HEL. You draw me, you hard-hearted adamant;
But yet you draw not iron, for my heart
Is true as steel: leave you your power to draw,
And I shall have no power to follow you.
DEM. Do I entice you? do I speak you fair?
200 Or, rather, do I not in plainest truth
Tell you, I do not nor I cannot love you?
HEL. And even for that do I love you the more.
I am your spaniel; and, Demetrius,
The more you beat me, I will fawn on you:
205 Use me but as your spaniel, spurn me, strike me,
Neglect me, lose me; only give me leave,
Unworthy as I am, to follow you.
What worser place can I beg in your love,—
And yet a place of high respect with me,—
210 Than to be used as you use your dog?
DEM. Tempt not too much the hatred of my spirit;
For I am sick when I do look on thee.
HEL. And I am sick when I look not on you.
DEM. You do impeach your modesty too much,
215 To leave the city, and commit yourself
Into the hands of one that loves you not;
To trust the opportunity of night
And the ill counsel of a desert place
With the rich worth of your virginity.
220 HEL. Your virtue is my privilege: for that
It is not night when I do see your face,

Therefore I think I am not in the night;
Nor doth this wood lack worlds of company,
For you in my respect are all the world:
225 Then how can it be said I am alone,
When all the world is here to look on me?
DEM. I'll run from thee and hide me in the brakes,
And leave thee to the mercy of wild beasts.
HEL. The wildest hath not such a heart as you.
230 Run when you will, the story shall be changed:
Apollo flies, and Daphne holds the chase;
The dove pursues the griffin; the mild hind
Makes speed to catch the tiger; bootless speed,
When cowardice pursues, and valour flies.
235 *DEM.* I will not stay thy questions; let me go:
Or, if thou follow me, do not believe
But I shall do thee mischief in the wood.
HEL. Ay, in the temple, in the town, the field,
You do me mischief. Fie, Demetrius!
240 Your wrongs do set a scandal on my sex:
We cannot fight for love, as men may do;
We should be woo'd, and were not made to woo. *(Exit
Dem.)*
I'll follow thee, and make a heaven of hell,
To die upon the hand I love so well. *(Exit.)*
245 *OBE.* Fare thee well, nymph: ere he do leave this
grove,
Thou shalt fly him, and he shall seek thy love.

(Re-enter PUCK.)

Hast thou the flower there? Welcome, wanderer.
PUCK. Ay, there it is.
OBE. I pray thee, give it me.
I know a bank where the wild thyme blows,
250 Where oxlips and the nodding violet grows;
Quite over-canopied with luscious woodbine,
With sweet musk-roses, and with eglantine:
There sleeps Titania sometime of the night,
Lull'd in these flowers with dances and delight;
255 And there the snake throws her enamell'd skin,
Weed wide enough to wrap a fairy in:
And with the juice of this I'll streak her eyes,
And make her full of hateful fantasies.

Take thou some of it, and seek through this grove:
260 A sweet Athenian lady is in love
With a disdainful youth: anoint his eyes;
But do it when the next thing he espies
May be the lady: thou shalt know the man
By the Athenian garments he hath on.
265 Effect it with some care that he may prove
More fond on her than she upon her love:
And look thou meet me ere the first cock crow.
Puck. Fear not, my lord, your servant shall do so.
(*Exeunt.*)

SCENE II. ANOTHER PART OF THE WOOD.

(*Enter Titania, with her train.*)

Tita. Come, now a roundel and a fairy song;
Then, for the third part of a minute, hence;
Some to kill cankers in the musk-rose buds;
Some war with rere-mice for their leathern wings,
005 To make my small elves coats; and some keep back
The clamorous owl, that nightly hoots and wonders
At our quaint spirits. Sing me now asleep;
Then to your offices, and let me rest.

(*Song.*)

Fir. Fairy.
You spotted snakes with double tongue.
010 Thorny hedgehogs, be not seen;
Newts and blind-worms, do no wrong,
Come not near our fairy queen.
Chorus.
Philomel, with melody
Sing in our sweet lullaby;
015 Lulla, lulla, lullaby, lulla, lulla, lullaby:
Never harm,
Nor spell, nor charm,
Come our lovely lady nigh;
So, good night, with lullaby.
Fir. Fairy.
020 Weaving spiders, come not here;

22

Hence, you long-legg'd spinners, hence!
Beetles black, approach not near;
Worm nor snail, do no offence.
CHORUS.
Philomel, with melody, &c.
SEC. FAIRY.
025 Hence, away! now all is well:
One aloof stand sentinel. (Exeunt Fairies. Titania sleeps.)

(Enter OBERON, and squeezes the flower on Titania's eyelids.)

OBE. What thou seest when thou dost wake,
Do it for thy true-love take;
Love and languish for his sake:
030 Be it ounce, or cat, or bear,
Pard, or boar with bristled hair,
In thy eye that shall appear
When thou wakest, it is thy dear:
Wake when some vile thing is near. *(Exit.)*

(ENTER LYSANDER AND HERMIA.)

035 *LYS.* Fair love, you faint with wandering in the
    wood;
And to speak troth, I have forgot our way:
We'll rest us, Hermia, if you think it good,
And tarry for the comfort of the day.
HER. Be it so, Lysander: find you out a bed;
040 For I upon this bank will rest my head.
LYS. One turf shall serve as pillow for us both;
One heart, one bed, two bosoms, and one troth.
HER. Nay, good Lysander; for my sake, my dear,
Lie further off yet, do not lie so near.
045 *LYS.* O, take the sense, sweet, of my innocence!
Love takes the meaning in love's conference.
I mean, that my heart unto yours is knit,
So that but one heart we can make of it:
Two bosoms interchained with an oath;
050 So then two bosoms and a single troth.
Then by your side no bed-room me deny;
For lying so, Hermia, I do not lie.
HER. Lysander riddles very prettily:
Now much beshrew my manners and my pride,

23

055 If Hermia meant to say Lysander lied.
But, gentle friend, for love and courtesy
Lie further off; in human modesty,
Such separation as may well be said
Becomes a virtuous bachelor and a maid,
060 So far be distant; and, good night, sweet friend:
Thy love ne'er alter till thy sweet life end!
Lys. Amen, amen, to that fair prayer, say I;
And then end life when I end loyalty!
Here is my bed: sleep give thee all his rest!
065 *Her.* With half that wish the wisher's eyes be
press'd! *(They sleep.)*

(Enter Puck.)

Puck. Through the forest have I gone,
But Athenian found I none,
On whose eyes I might approve
This flower's force in stirring love.
070 Night and silence.—Who is here?
Weeds of Athens he doth wear:
This is he, my master said,
Despised the Athenian maid;
And here the maiden, sleeping sound,
075 On the dank and dirty ground.
Pretty soul! she durst not lie
Near this lack-love, this kill-courtesy.
Churl, upon thy eyes I throw
All the power this charm doth owe.
080 When thou wakest, let love forbid
Sleep his seat on thy eyelid:
So awake when I am gone;
For I must now to Oberon. *(Exit.)*

(Enter Demetrius and Helena, running.)

Hel. Stay, though thou kill me, sweet Demetrius.
085 *Dem.* I charge thee, hence, and do not haunt me
thus.
Hel. O, wilt thou darkling leave me? do not so.
Dem. Stay, on thy peril: I alone will go. *(Exit.)*
Hel. O, I am out of breath in this fond chase!
The more my prayer, the lesser is my grace.

$_{090}$ Happy is Hermia, wheresoe'er she lies;
For she hath blessed and attractive eyes.
How came her eyes so bright? Not with salt tears:
If so, my eyes are oftener wash'd than hers.
No, no, I am as ugly as a bear;
$_{095}$ For beasts that meet me run away for fear:
Therefore no marvel though Demetrius
Do, as a monster, fly my presence thus.
What wicked and dissembling glass of mine
Made me compare with Hermia's sphery eyne?
$_{100}$ But who is here? Lysander! on the ground!
Dead? or asleep? I see no blood, no wound.
Lysander, if you live, good sir, awake.
Lys. (Awaking) And run through fire I will for thy
    sweet sake.
Transparent Helena! Nature shows art,
$_{105}$ That through thy bosom makes me see thy heart.
Where is Demetrius? O, how fit a word
Is that vile name to perish on my sword!
Hel. Do not say so, Lysander; say not so.
What though he love your Hermia? Lord, what
    though?
$_{110}$ Yet Hermia still loves you: then be content.
Lys. Content with Hermia! No; I do repent
The tedious minutes I with her have spent.
Not Hermia but Helena I love:
Who will not change a raven for a dove?
$_{115}$ The will of man is by his reason sway'd;
And reason says you are the worthier maid.
Things growing are not ripe until their season:
So I, being young, till now ripe not to reason;
And touching now the point of human skill,
$_{120}$ Reason becomes the marshal to my will,
And leads me to your eyes; where I o'erlook
Love's stories, written in love's richest book.
Hel. Wherefore was I to this keen mockery born?
When at your hands did I deserve this scorn?
$_{125}$ Is't not enough, is't not enough, young man,
That I did never, no, nor never can,
Deserve a sweet look from Demetrius' eye,
But you must flout my insufficiency?
Good troth, you do me wrong, good sooth, you do,
$_{130}$ In such disdainful manner me to woo.

But fare you well: perforce I must confess
I thought you lord of more true gentleness.
O, that a lady, of one man refused,
Should of another therefore be abused! *(Exit)*.
135 *Lys.* She sees not Hermia. Hermia, sleep thou
    there:
And never mayst thou come Lysander near!
For as a surfeit of the sweetest things
The deepest loathing to the stomach brings,
Or as the heresies that men do leave
140 Are hated most of those they did deceive,
So thou, my surfeit and my heresy,
Of all be hated, but the most of me!
And, all my powers, address your love and might
To honour Helen and to be her knight! *(Exit.)*
145 *Her.* *(Awaking)* Help me, Lysander, help me! do
    thy best
To pluck this crawling serpent from my breast!
Ay me, for pity! what a dream was here!
Lysander, look how I do quake with fear:
Methought a serpent eat my heart away,
150 And you sat smiling at his cruel prey.
Lysander! what, removed? Lysander! lord!
What, out of hearing? gone? no sound, no word?
Alack, where are you? speak, an if you hear;
Speak, of all loves! I swoon almost with fear.
155 No? then I well perceive you are not nigh:
Either death or you I'll find immediately. *(Exit.)*

ACT III

SCENE I. THE WOOD. TITANIA LYING ASLEEP.

(ENTER QUINCE, SNUG, BOTTOM, FLUTE, SNOUT, AND STARVELING.)

Bot. Are we all met?

Quin. Pat, pat; and here's a marvellous convenient place for our rehearsal. This green plot shall be our stage, this hawthorn-brake our tiring-house; and we will do it in $_{005}$ action as we will do it before the duke.

Bot. Peter Quince,—

Quin. What sayest thou, bully Bottom?

Bot. There are things in this comedy of Pyramus and Thisby that will never please. First, Pyramus must draw $_{010}$ a sword to kill himself; which the ladies cannot abide. How answer you that?

Snout. By'r lakin, a parlous fear.

Star. I believe we must leave the killing out, when all is done.

$_{015}$ *Bot.* Not a whit: I have a device to make all well. Write me a prologue; and let the prologue seem to say, we will do no harm with our swords, and that Pyramus is not killed indeed; and, for the more better assurance, tell them that I Pyramus am not Pyramus, but Bottom the weaver: $_{020}$ this will put them out of fear.

Quin. Well, we will have such a prologue; and it shall be written in eight and six.

Bot. No, make it two more; let it be written in eight and eight.

025 *Snout.* Will not the ladies be afeard of the lion?

Star. I fear it, I promise you.

Bot. Masters, you ought to consider with yourselves: to bring in,—God shield us!—a lion among ladies, is a most dreadful thing; for there is not a more fearful wild-fowl 030 than your lion living; and we ought to look to 't.

Snout. Therefore another prologue must tell he is not a lion.

Bot. Nay, you must name his name, and half his face must be seen through the lion's neck; and he himself must 035 speak through, saying thus, or to the same defect,—'Ladies,' —or, 'Fair ladies,—I would wish you,'—or, 'I would request you,'—or, 'I would entreat you,—not to fear, not to tremble: my life for yours. If you think I come hither as a lion, it were pity of my life: no, I am no such thing; I 040 am a man as other men are:' and there indeed let him name his name, and tell them plainly, he is Snug the joiner.

Quin. Well, it shall be so. But there is two hard things; that is, to bring the moonlight into a chamber; for, you know, Pyramus and Thisby meet by moonlight.

045 *Snout.* Doth the moon shine that night we play our play?

Bot. A calendar, a calendar! look in the almanac; find out moonshine, find out moonshine.

Quin. Yes, it doth shine that night.

Bot. Why, then may you leave a casement of the great 050 chamber window, where we play, open, and the moon may shine in at the casement.

Quin. Ay; or else one must come in with a bush of thorns and a lantern, and say he comes to disfigure, or to present, the person of moonshine. Then, there is another 055 thing: we must have a wall in the great chamber; for Pyramus and Thisby, says the story, did talk through the chink of a wall.

28

Snout. You can never bring in a wall. What say you, Bottom?

060 *Bot.* Some man or other must present wall: and let him have some plaster, or some loam, or some rough-cast about him, to signify wall; and let him hold his fingers thus, and through that cranny shall Pyramus and Thisby whisper.

Quin. If that may be, then all is well. Come, sit 065 down, every mother's son, and rehearse your parts. Pyramus, you begin: when you have spoken your speech, enter into that brake: and so every one according to his cue.

(Enter PUCK behind.)

Puck. What hempen home-spuns have we swaggering here,
So near the cradle of the fairy queen?
070 What, a play toward! I'll be an auditor;
An actor too perhaps, if I see cause.
Quin. Speak, Pyramus. Thisby, stand forth.
Bot. Thisby, the flowers of odious savours sweet,—
Quin. Odours, odours.
075 *Bot.* —— odours savours sweet:
So hath thy breath, my dearest Thisby dear.
But hark, a voice! stay thou but here awhile,
And by and by I will to thee appear. *(Exit.)*
Puck. A stranger Pyramus than e'er play'd here.
(Exit.)
080 *Flu.* Must I speak now?
Quin. Ay, marry, must you; for you must understand he
goes but to see a noise that he heard, and is to come again.
Flu. Most radiant Pyramus, most lily-white of hue,
Of colour like the red rose on triumphant brier,
085 Most brisky juvenal, and eke most lovely Jew,
As true as truest horse, that yet would never tire,
I'll meet thee, Pyramus, at Ninny's tomb.
Quin. 'Ninus' tomb,' man: why, you must not speak that yet; that you answer to Pyramus: you speak all your 090 part at once, cues and all. Pyramus enter: your cue is past; it is, 'never tire.'

Flu. O,—As true as truest horse, that yet would never tire.

(Re-enter PUCK, and BOTTOM with an ass's head.)

Bot. If I were fair, Thisby, I were only thine.
Quin. O monstrous! O strange! we are haunted. Pray, 095 masters! fly, masters! Help! *(Exeunt Quince, Snug, Flute, Snout, and Starveling.)*
Puck. I'll follow you, I'll lead you about a round,
Through bog, through bush, through brake, through brier:
Sometime a horse I'll be, sometime a hound,
A hog, a headless bear, sometime a fire;
100 And neigh, and bark, and grunt, and roar, and burn,
Like horse, hound, hog, bear, fire, at every turn. *(Exit.)*
Bot. Why do they run away? this is a knavery of them to make me afeard.

(Re-enter SNOUT.)

Snout. O bottom, thou art changed! what do I see on 105 thee?
Bot. What do you see? you see an ass-head of your own, do you? *(Exit Snout.)*

(Re-enter QUINCE.)

Quin. Bless thee, Bottom! bless thee! thou art trans-lated. *(Exit.)*
110 *Bot.* I see their knavery: this is to make an ass of me; to fright me, if they could. But I will not stir from this place, do what they can: I will walk up and down here, and I will sing, that they shall hear I am not afraid. *(Sings.)*
The ousel cock so black of hue,
115 With orange-tawny bill,
The throstle with his note so true,
The wren with little quill;
Tita. *(Awaking)* What angel wakes me from my flowery bed?
Bot. *(Sings)*

The finch, the sparrow, and the lark,
120 The plain-song cuckoo gray,
Whose note full many a man doth mark,
And dares not answer nay;—
for, indeed, who would set his wit to so foolish a
    bird? who would give a bird the lie, though he cry
    'cuckoo' never so?

125 *Tita.* I pray thee, gentle mortal, sing again:
Mine ear is much enamour'd of thy note;
So is mine eye enthralled to thy shape;
And thy fair virtue's force perforce doth move me
On the first view to say, to swear, I love thee.

130 *Bot.* Methinks, mistress, you should have little
    reason for that: and yet, to say the truth, reason
    and love keep little company together now-a-
    days; the more the pity, that some honest neigh-
    bours will not make them friends. Nay, I can gleek
    upon occasion.

135 *Tita.* Thou art as wise as thou art beautiful.

Bot. Not so, neither: but if I had wit enough to get
    out of this wood, I have enough to serve mine
    own turn.

Tita. Out of this wood do not desire to go:
Thou shalt remain here, whether thou wilt or no.
140 I am a spirit of no common rate:
The summer still doth tend upon my state;
And I do love thee: therefore, go with me;
I'll give thee fairies to attend on thee;
And they shall fetch thee jewels from the deep,
145 And sing, while thou on pressed flowers dost
    sleep:
And I will purge thy mortal grossness so,
That thou shalt like an airy spirit go.
Peaseblossom! Cobweb! Moth! and Mustardseed!

(*Enter Peaseblossom, Cobweb, Moth, and Mustardseed.*)

First Fai. Ready.
Sec. Fai. And I.
Third Fai. And I.
Fourth Fai. And I.
All. Where shall we go?
150 *Tita.* Be kind and courteous to this gentleman;

Hop in his walks, and gambol in his eyes;
Feed him with apricocks and dewberries,
With purple grapes, green figs, and mulberries;
The honey-bags steal from the humble-bees,
155 And for night-tapers crop their waxen thighs,
And light them at the fiery glow-worm's eyes,
To have my love to bed and to arise;
And pluck the wings from painted butterflies
To fan the moonbeams from his sleeping eyes:
160 Nod to him, elves, and do him courtesies.

First Fai. Hail, mortal!

Sec. Fai. Hail!

Third Fai. Hail!

Fourth Fai. Hail!

165 *Bot.* I cry your worships mercy, heartily: I beseech
your worship's name.

Cob. Cobweb.

Bot. I shall desire you of more acquaintance, good
Master Cobweb: if I cut my finger, I shall make
bold with 170 you. Your name, honest gentleman?

Peas. Peaseblossom.

Bot. I pray you, commend me to Mistress Squash,
your mother, and to Master Peascod, your father.
Good Master Peaseblossom, I shall desire you of
more acquaintance 175 too. Your name, I beseech
you, sir?

Mus. Mustardseed.

Bot. Good Master Mustardseed, I know your patience well: that same cowardly, giant-like ox-beef
hath devoured many a gentleman of your house: I
promise you 180 your kindred hath made my eyes
water ere now. I desire your more acquaintance,
good Master Mustardseed.

Tita. Come, wait upon him; lead him to my bower.
The moon methinks looks with a watery eye;
And when she weeps, weeps every little flower,
185 Lamenting some enforced chastity.
Tie up my love's tongue, bring him silently. *(Exeunt.)*

SCENE II. ANOTHER PART OF THE WOOD.

(Enter Oberon.)

OBE. I wonder if Titania be awaked;
Then, what it was that next came in her eye,
Which she must dote on in extremity.

(Enter PUCK.)

Here comes my messenger.
How now, mad spirit!
005 What night-rule now about this haunted grove?
PUCK. My mistress with a monster is in love.
Near to her close and consecrated bower,
While she was in her dull and sleeping hour,
A crew of patches, rude mechanicals,
010 That work for bread upon Athenian stalls,
Were met together to rehearse a play,
Intended for great Theseus' nuptial-day.
The shallowest thick-skin of that barren sort,
Who Pyramus presented, in their sport
015 Forsook his scene, and enter'd in a brake:
When I did him at this advantage take,
An ass's nole I fixed on his head:
Anon his Thisbe must be answered,
And forth my mimic comes. When they him spy,
020 As wild geese that the creeping fowler eye,
Or russet-pated choughs, many in sort,
Rising and cawing at the gun's report,
Sever themselves and madly sweep the sky,
So, at his sight, away his fellows fly;
025 And, at our stamp, here o'er and o'er one falls;
He murder cries, and help from Athens calls.
Their sense thus weak, lost with their fears thus
    strong,
Made senseless things begin to do them wrong;
For briers and thorns at their apparel snatch;
030 Some sleeves, some hats, from yielders all things
    catch.
I led them on in this distracted fear,
And left sweet Pyramus translated there:
When in that moment, so it came to pass,
Titania waked, and straightway loved an ass.
035 *OBE.* This falls out better than I could devise.
But hast thou yet latch'd the Athenian's eyes
With the love-juice, as I did bid thee do?

Puck. I took him sleeping,—that is finish'd too,—
And the Athenian woman by his side;
₀₄₀ That, when he waked, of force she must be eyed.

(ENTER HERMIA AND DEMETRIUS.)

Obe. Stand close: this is the same Athenian.
Puck. This is the woman, but not this the man.
Dem. O, why rebuke you him that loves you so?
Lay breath so bitter on your bitter foe.
₀₄₅ *Her.* Now I but chide; but I should use thee worse,
For thou, I fear, hast given me cause to curse.
If thou hast slain Lysander in his sleep,
Being o'er shoes in blood, plunge in the deep,
And kill me too.
₀₅₀ The sun was not so true unto the day
As he to me: would he have stolen away
From sleeping Hermia? I'll believe as soon
This whole earth may be bored, and that the moon
May through the centre creep, and so displease
₀₅₅ Her brother's noontide with the Antipodes.
It cannot be but thou hast murder'd him;
So should a murderer look, so dead, so grim.
Dem. So should the murder'd look; and so should I,
Pierced through the heart with your stern cruelty:
₀₆₀ Yet you, the murderer, look as bright, as clear,
As yonder Venus in her glimmering sphere.
Her. What's this to my Lysander? where is he?
Ah, good Demetrius, wilt thou give him me?
Dem. I had rather give his carcass to my hounds.
₀₆₅ *Her.* Out, dog! out, cur! thou drivest me past the
   bounds
Of maiden's patience. Hast thou slain him, then?
Henceforth be never number'd among men!
O, once tell true, tell true, even for my sake!
Durst thou have look'd upon him being awake,
₀₇₀ And hast thou kill'd him sleeping? O brave touch!
Could not a worm, an adder, do so much?
An adder did it; for with doubler tongue
Than thine, thou serpent, never adder stung.
Dem. You spend your passion on a misprised mood:
₀₇₅ I am not guilty of Lysander's blood;
Nor is he dead, for aught that I can tell.

Her. I pray thee, tell me then that he is well.

Dem. An if I could, what should I get therefore?

Her. A privilege, never to see me more.

080 And from thy hated presence part I so:
See me no more, whether he be dead or no. *(Exit.)*

Dem. There is no following her in this fierce vein:
Here therefore for a while I will remain.
So sorrow's heaviness doth heavier grow
085 For debt that bankrupt sleep doth sorrow owe;
Which now in some slight measure it will pay,
If for his tender here I make some stay. *(Lies down and
    sleeps.)*

Obe. What hast thou done? thou hast mistaken quite,
And laid the love-juice on some true-love's sight:
090 Of thy misprision must perforce ensue
Some true love turn'd, and not a false turn'd true.

Puck. Then fate o'er-rules, that, one man holding
    troth,
A million fail, confounding oath on oath.

Obe. About the wood go swifter than the wind,
095 And Helena of Athens look thou find:
All fancy-sick she is and pale of cheer,
With sighs of love, that costs the fresh blood dear:
By some illusion see thou bring her here:
I'll charm his eyes against she do appear.

100 *Puck.* I go, I go; look how I go,
Swifter than arrow from the Tartar's bow. *(Exit.)*

Obe. Flower of this purple dye,
Hit with Cupid's archery,
Sink in apple of his eye.
105 When his love he doth espy,
Let her shine as gloriously
As the Venus of the sky.
When thou wakest, if she be by,
Beg of her for remedy.

(Re-enter Puck.)

Puck. 110 Captain of our fairy band,
Helena is here at hand;
And the youth, mistook by me,
Pleading for a lover's fee.
Shall we their fond pageant see?

115 Lord, what fools these mortals be!
OBE. Stand aside: the noise they make
Will cause Demetrius to awake.
PUCK. Then will two at once woo one;
That must needs be sport alone;
120 And those things do best please me
That befal preposterously.

(*ENTER LYSANDER AND HELENA.*)

LYS. Why should you think that I should woo in
      scorn?
Scorn and derision never come in tears:
Look, when I vow, I weep; and vows so born,
125 In their nativity all truth appears.
How can these things in me seem scorn to you,
Bearing the badge of faith, to prove them true?
HEL. You do advance your cunning more and more.
When truth kills truth, O devilish-holy fray!
130 These vows are Hermia's: will you give her o'er?
Weigh oath with oath, and you will nothing weigh:
Your vows to her and me, put in two scales,
Will even weigh; and both as light as tales.
LYS. I had no judgement when to her I swore.
135 *HEL.* Nor none, in my mind, now you give her
      o'er.
LYS. Demetrius loves her, and he loves not you.
DEM. (Awaking) O Helen, goddess, nymph, perfect,
      divine!
To what, my love, shall I compare thine eyne?
Crystal is muddy. O, how ripe in show
140 Thy lips, those kissing cherries, tempting grow!
That pure congealed white, high Taurus' snow,
Fann'd with the eastern wind, turns to a crow
When thou hold'st up thy hand: O, let me kiss
This princess of pure white, this seal of bliss!
145 *HEL.* O spite! O hell! I see you all are bent
To set against me for your merriment:
If you were civil and knew courtesy,
You would not do me thus much injury.
Can you not hate me, as I know you do,
150 But you must join in souls to mock me too?
If you were men, as men you are in show,

You would not use a gentle lady so;
To vow, and swear, and superpraise my parts,
When I am sure you hate me with your hearts.
₁₅₅ You both are rivals, and love Hermia;
And now both rivals, to mock Helena:
A trim exploit, a manly enterprise,
To conjure tears up in a poor maid's eyes
With your derision! none of noble sort
₁₆₀ Would so offend a virgin, and extort
A poor soul's patience, all to make you sport.
Lys. You are unkind, Demetrius; be not so;
For you love Hermia; this you know I know:
And here, with all good will, with all my heart,
₁₆₅ In Hermia's love I yield you up my part;
And yours of Helena to me bequeath,
Whom I do love, and will do till my death.
Hel. Never did mockers waste more idle breath.
Dem. Lysander, keep thy Hermia; I will none:
₁₇₀ If e'er I loved her, all that love is gone.
My heart to her but as guest-wise sojourn'd,
And now to Helen is it home return'd,
There to remain.
Lys. Helen, it is not so.
Dem. Disparage not the faith thou dost not know,
₁₇₅ Lest, to thy peril, thou aby it dear.
Look, where thy love comes; yonder is thy dear.

(Re-enter HERMIA.)

Her. Dark night, that from the eye his function takes,
The ear more quick of apprehension makes;
Wherein it doth impair the seeing sense,
₁₈₀ It pays the hearing double recompense.
Thou art not by mine eye, Lysander, found;
Mine ear, I thank it, brought me to thy sound.
But why unkindly didst thou leave me so?
Lys. Why should he stay, whom love doth press
  to go?
₁₈₅ *Her.* What love could press Lysander from my
  side?
Lys. Lysander's love, that would not let him bide,
Fair Helena, who more engilds the night
Than all yon fiery oes and eyes of light.

Why seek'st thou me? could not this make thee know,
190 The hate I bear thee made me leave thee so?
HER. You speak not as you think: it cannot be.
HEL. Lo, she is one of this confederacy!
Now I perceive they have conjoin'd all three
To fashion this false sport, in spite of me.
195 Injurious Hermia! most ungrateful maid!
Have you conspired, have you with these contrived
To bait me with this foul derision?
Is all the counsel that we two have shared,
The sisters' vows, the hours that we have spent,
200 When we have chid the hasty-footed time
For parting us,—O, is all forgot?
All school-days' friendship, childhood innocence?
We, Hermia, like two artificial gods,
Have with our needles created both one flower,
205 Both on one sampler, sitting on one cushion,
Both warbling of one song, both in one key;
As if our hands, our sides, voices, and minds,
Had been incorporate. So we grew together,
Like to a double cherry, seeming parted;
210 But yet an union in partition,
Two lovely berries moulded on one stem;
So, with two seeming bodies, but one heart;
Two of the first, like coats in heraldry,
Due but to one, and crowned with one crest.
215 And will you rent our ancient love asunder,
To join with men in scorning your poor friend?
It is not friendly, 'tis not maidenly:
Our sex, as well as I, may chide you for it,
Though I alone do feel the injury.
220 *HER.* I am amazed at your passionate words.
I scorn you not: it seems that you scorn me.
HEL. Have you not set Lysander, as in scorn,
To follow me and praise my eyes and face?
And made your other love, Demetrius,
225 Who even but now did spurn me with his foot,
To call me goddess, nymph, divine and rare,
Precious, celestial? Wherefore speaks he this
To her he hates? and wherefore doth Lysander
Deny your love, so rich within his soul,
230 And tender me, forsooth, affection,
But by your setting on, by your consent?

What though I be not so in grace as you,
So hung upon with love, so fortunate,
But miserable most, to love unloved?
235 This you should pity rather than despise.
Her. I understand not what you mean by this.
Hel. Ay, do, persever, counterfeit sad looks,
Make mouths upon me when I turn my back;
Wink each at other; hold the sweet jest up:
240 This sport, well carried, shall be chronicled.
If you have any pity, grace, or manners,
You would not make me such an argument.
But fare ye well: 'tis partly my own fault;
Which death or absence soon shall remedy.
245 *Lys.* Stay, gentle Helena; hear my excuse:
My love, my life, my soul, fair Helena!
Hel. O excellent!
Her. Sweet, do not scorn her so.
Dem. If she cannot entreat, I can compel.
Lys. Thou canst compel no more than she entreat:
250 Thy threats have no more strength than her weak
    prayers.
Helen, I love thee; by my life, I do:
I swear by that which I will lose for thee,
To prove him false that says I love thee not.
Dem. I say I love thee more than he can do.
255 *Lys.* If thou say so, withdraw, and prove it too.
Dem. Quick, come!
Her. Lysander, whereto tends all this?
Lys. Away, you Ethiope!
Dem. No, no; he'll . . .
Seem to break loose; take on as you would follow,
But yet come not: you are a tame man, go!
260 *Lys.* Hang off, thou cat, thou burr! vile thing, let
    loose,
Or I will shake thee from me like a serpent!
Her. Why are you grown so rude? what change is
    this?
Sweet love,—
Lys. Thy love! out, tawny Tartar, out!
Out, loathed medicine! hated potion, hence!
Her. Do you not jest?
Hel.
265 Yes, sooth; and so do you.

39

Lys. Demetrius, I will keep my word with thee.
Dem. I would I had your bond, for I perceive
A weak bond holds you: I'll not trust your word.
Lys. What, should I hurt her, strike her, kill her dead?
270 Although I hate her, I'll not harm her so.
Her. What, can you do me greater harm than hate?
Hate me! wherefore? O me! what news, my love!
Am not I Hermia? are not you Lysander?
I am as fair now as I was erewhile.
275 Since night you loved me; yet since night you
 left me:
Why, then you left me,—O, the gods forbid!—
In earnest, shall I say?
Lys. Ay, by my life;
And never did desire to see thee more.
Therefore be out of hope, of question, of doubt;
280 Be certain, nothing truer; 'tis no jest
That I do hate thee, and love Helena.
Her. O me! you juggler! you canker-blossom!
You thief of love! what, have you come by night
And stolen my love's heart from him?
Hel. Fine, i'faith!
285 Have you no modesty, no maiden shame,
No touch of bashfulness? What, will you tear
Impatient answers from my gentle tongue?
Fie, fie! you counterfeit, you puppet, you!
Her. Puppet? why so? ay, that way goes the game.
290 Now I perceive that she hath made compare
Between our statures; she hath urged her height;
And with her personage, her tall personage,
Her height, forsooth, she hath prevail'd with him.
And are you grown so high in his esteem,
295 Because I am so dwarfish and so low?
How low am I, thou painted maypole? speak;
How low am I? I am not yet so low
But that my nails can reach unto thine eyes.
Hel. I pray you, though you mock me, gentlemen,
300 Let her not hurt me: I was never curst;
I have no gift at all in shrewishness;
I am a right maid for my cowardice:
Let her not strike me. You perhaps may think,
Because she is something lower than myself,
That I can match her.

Her. ₃₀₅ Lower! hark, again.
Hel. Good Hermia, do not be so bitter with me
I evermore did love you, Hermia,
Did ever keep your counsels, never wrong'd you;
Save that, in love unto Demetrius,
₃₁₀ I told him of your stealth unto this wood.
He follow'd you; for love I follow'd him;
But he hath chid me hence, and threaten'd me
To strike me, spurn me, nay, to kill me too:
And now, so you will let me quiet go,
₃₁₅ To Athens will I bear my folly back,
And follow you no further: let me go:
You see how simple and how fond I am.
Her. Why, get you gone: who is't that hinders you?
Hel. A foolish heart, that I leave here behind.
Her. What, with Lysander?
Hel. ₃₂₀ With Demetrius.
Lys. Be not afraid; she shall not harm thee, Helena.
Dem. No, sir, she shall not, though you take her part.
Hel. O, when she's angry, she is keen and shrewd!
She was a vixen when she went to school;
₃₂₅ And though she be but little, she is fierce.
Her. Little again! nothing but low and little!
Why will you suffer her to flout me thus?
Let me come to her.
Lys. Get you gone, you dwarf;
You minimus, of hindering knot-grass made;
You bead, you acorn.
Dem. ₃₃₀ You are too officious
In her behalf that scorns your services.
Let her alone: speak not of Helena;
Take not her part; for, if thou dost intend
Never so little show of love to her,
₃₃₅ Thou shalt aby it.
Lys. Now she holds me not;
Now follow, if thou darest, to try whose right,
Of thine or mine, is most in Helena.
Dem. Follow! nay, I'll go with thee, cheek by jole.
(Exeunt Lysander and Demetrius.)
Her. You, mistress, all this coil is 'long of you:
Nay, go not back.
Hel. ₃₄₀ I will not trust you, I,
Nor longer stay in your curst company.

Your hands than mine are quicker for a fray,
My legs are longer though, to run away. *(Exit.)*
HER. I am amazed, and know not what to say. *(Exit.)*
345 OBE. This is thy negligence: still thou mistakest,
Or else committ'st thy knaveries wilfully.
PUCK. Believe me, king of shadows, I mistook.
Did not you tell me I should know the man
By the Athenian garments he had on?
350 And so far blameless proves my enterprise,
That I have 'nointed an Athenian's eyes;
And so far am I glad it so did sort,
As this their jangling I esteem a sport.
OBE. Thou see'st these lovers seek a place to fight:
355 Hie therefore, Robin, overcast the night;
The starry welkin cover thou anon
With drooping fog, as black as Acheron;
And lead these testy rivals so astray,
As one come not within another's way.
360 Like to Lysander sometime frame thy tongue,
Then stir Demetrius up with bitter wrong;
And sometime rail thou like Demetrius;
And from each other look thou lead them thus.
Till o'er their brows death-counterfeiting sleep
365 With leaden legs and batty wings doth creep:
Then crush this herb into Lysander's eye;
Whose liquor hath this virtuous property,
To take from thence all error with his might,
And make his eyeballs roll with wonted sight.
370 When they next wake, all this derision
Shall seem a dream and fruitless vision;
And back to Athens shall the lovers wend,
With league whose date till death shall never end.
Whiles I in this affair do thee employ,
375 I'll to my queen and beg her Indian boy;
And then I will her charmed eye release
From monster's view, and all things shall be peace.
PUCK. My fairy lord, this must be done with haste,
For night's swift dragons cut the clouds full fast,
380 And yonder shines Aurora's harbinger;
At whose approach, ghosts, wandering here and
    there,
Troop home to churchyards: damned spirits all,
That in crossways and floods have burial,

Already to their wormy beds are gone;
₃₈₅ For fear lest day should look their shames upon,
They wilfully themselves exile from light,
And must for aye consort with black-brow'd night.
Obe. But we are spirits of another sort:
I with the morning's love have oft made sport;
₃₉₀ And, like a forester, the groves may tread,
Even till the eastern gate, all fiery-red,
Opening on Neptune with fair blessed beams,
Turns into yellow gold his salt green streams.
But, notwithstanding, haste; make no delay:
₃₉₅ We may effect this business yet ere day. (Exit.)
Puck. Up and down, up and down,
I will lead them up and down:
I am fear'd in field and town:
Goblin, lead them up and down.
₄₀₀ Here comes one.

(Re-enter LYSANDER.)

Lys. Where art thou, proud Demetrius? speak
    thou now.
Puck. Here, villain; drawn and ready. Where art
    thou?
Lys. I will be with thee straight.
Puck.
Follow me, then,
To plainer ground. (Exit Lysander, as following the
    voice.)

(RE-ENTER DEMETRIUS.)

Dem. Lysander! speak again:
₄₀₅ Thou runaway, thou coward, art thou fled?
Speak! In some bush? Where dost thou hide thy
    head?
Puck. Thou coward, art thou bragging to the stars,
Telling the bushes that thou look'st for wars,
And wilt not come? Come, recreant; come, thou
    child;
₄₁₀ I'll whip thee with a rod: he is defiled
That draws a sword on thee.
Dem. Yea, art thou there?

43

Puck. Follow my voice: we'll try no manhood here.
   (Exeunt.)

(Re-enter LYSANDER.)

Lys. He goes before me and still dares me on:
When I come where he calls, then he is gone.
415 The villain is much lighter-heel'd than I:
I follow'd fast, but faster he did fly;
That fallen am I in dark uneven way,
And here will rest me. *(Lies down.)* Come, thou
   gentle day!
For if but once thou show me thy grey light,
420 I'll find Demetrius, and revenge this spite. *(Sleeps.)*

(RE-ENTER PUCK AND DEMETRIUS.)

Puck. Ho, ho, ho! Coward, why comest thou not?
Dem. Abide me, if thou darest; for well I wot
Thou runn'st before me, shifting every place,
And darest not stand, nor look me in the face.
425 Where art thou now?
Puck.
425 Come hither: I am here.
Dem. Nay, then, thou mock'st me. Thou shalt buy this
   dear,
If ever I thy face by daylight see:
Now, go thy way. Faintness constraineth me
To measure out my length on this cold bed.
430 By day's approach look to be visited. *(Lies down
   and sleeps.)*

(Re-enter HELENA.)

Hel. O weary night, O long and tedious night,
Abate thy hours! Shine comforts from the east,
That I may back to Athens by daylight,
From these that my poor company detest:
435 And sleep, that sometimes shuts up sorrow's eye,
Steal me awhile from mine own company. *(Lies down
   and sleeps.)*
Puck. Yet but three? Come one more;
Two of both kinds makes up four.

Here she comes, curst and sad:
440 Cupid is a knavish lad,
Thus to make poor females mad.

(Re-enter HERMIA.)

HER. Never so weary, never so in woe;
Bedabbled with the dew, and torn with briers;
I can no further crawl, no further go;
445 My legs can keep no pace with my desires.
Here will I rest me till the break of day.
Heavens shield Lysander, if they mean a fray! *(Lies
down and sleeps.)*
PUCK.
On the ground
Sleep sound:
450 I'll apply
To your eye,
Gentle lover, remedy. *(Squeezing the juice on Lysander's
eyes.)*
When thou wakest,
Thou takest
455 True delight
In the sight
Of thy former lady's eye:
And the country proverb known,
That every man should take his own,
460 In your waking shall be shown:
Jack shall have Jill;
Nought shall go ill;
The man shall have his mare again, and all shall be
well. *(Exit.)*

ACT IV

SCENE I. *THE SAME.* LYSANDER, DEMETRIUS,
HELENA, *AND* HERMIA *LYING ASLEEP.*

(*ENTER TITANIA AND BOTTOM; PEASEBLOSSOM, COBWEB, MOTH,
MUSTARDSEED, AND OTHER FAIRIES ATTENDING; OBERON BEHIND
UNSEEN.*)

TITA. Come, sit thee down upon this flowery bed,
While I thy amiable cheeks do coy,
And stick musk-roses in thy sleek smooth head,
And kiss thy fair large ears, my gentle joy.
005 *BOT.* Where's Peaseblossom?
PEAS. Ready.
BOT. Scratch my head, Peaseblossom. Where's Mounsieur Cobweb?
COB. Ready.
010 *BOT.* Mounsieur Cobweb, good mounsieur, get
you your weapons in your hand, and kill me a
red-hipped humble-bee on the top of a thistle;
and, good mounsieur, bring me the honey-bag. Do
not fret yourself too much in the action, mounsieur; and, good mounsieur, have a care the
honey-bag 015 break not; I would be loth to have
you overflown with a honey-bag, signior. Where's
Mounsieur Mustardseed.
MUS. Ready.

Bot. Give me your neaf, Mounsieur Mustardseed.
Pray you, leave your courtesy, good mounsieur.
020 *Mus.* What's your will?
Bot. Nothing, good mounsieur, but to help Cavalery
Cobweb to scratch. I must to the barber's, mounsieur; for methinks I am marvellous hairy about
the face; and I am such a tender ass, if my hair do
but tickle me, I must scratch.
025 *Tita.* What, wilt thou hear some music, my sweet
love?
Bot. I have a reasonable good ear in music. Let's have
the tongs and the bones.
Tita. Or say, sweet love, what thou desirest to eat.
Bot. Truly, a peck of provender: I could munch your
030 good dry oats. Methinks I have a great desire to
a bottle of hay: good hay, sweet hay, hath no
fellow.
Tita. I have a venturous fairy that shall seek
The squirrel's hoard, and fetch thee new nuts.
Bot. I had rather have a handful or two of dried peas.
035 But, I pray you, let none of your people stir me:
I have an exposition of sleep come upon me.
Tita. Sleep thou, and I will wind thee in my arms.
Fairies, be gone, and be all ways away. *(Exeunt
Fairies.)*
So doth the woodbine the sweet honeysuckle
040 Gently entwist; the female ivy so
Enrings the barky fingers of the elm.
O, how I love thee! how I dote on thee! *(They sleep.)*

(Enter Puck.)

Obe. *(Advancing)* Welcome, good Robin. See'st thou
this sweet sight?
Her dotage now I do begin to pity:
045 For, meeting her of late behind the wood,
Seeking sweet favours for this hateful fool,
I did upbraid her, and fall out with her;
For she his hairy temples then had rounded
With coronet of fresh and fragrant flowers;
050 And that same dew, which sometime on the buds
Was wont to swell, like round and orient pearls,
Stood now within the pretty flowerets' eyes,

Like tears, that did their own disgrace bewail.
When I had at my pleasure taunted her,
55 And she in mild terms begg'd my patience,
I then did ask of her her changeling child;
Which straight she gave me, and her fairy sent
To bear him to my bower in fairy land.
And now I have the boy, I will undo
60 This hateful imperfection of her eyes:
And, gentle Puck, take this transformed scalp
From off the head of this Athenian swain;
That, he awaking when the other do,
May all to Athens back again repair,
65 And think no more of this night's accidents,
But as the fierce vexation of a dream.
But first I will release the fairy queen.
Be as thou wast wont to be;
See as thou wast wont to see:
70 Dian's bud o'er Cupid's flower
Hath such force and blessed power.
Now, my Titania; wake you, my sweet queen.
TITA. My Oberon! what visions have I seen!
Methought I was enamour'd of an ass.
OBE. There lies your love.
TITA.
75 How came these things to pass?
O, how mine eyes do loathe his visage now!
OBE. Silence awhile. Robin, take off this head.
Titania, music call; and strike more dead
Than common sleep of all these five the sense.
80 *TITA.* Music, ho! music, such as charmeth sleep!
(*Music, still.*)
PUCK. Now, when thou wakest, with thine own fool's
eyes peep.
OBE. Sound, music! Come, my queen, take hands
with me,
And rock the ground whereon these sleepers be.
Now thou and I are new in amity,
85 And will to-morrow midnight solemnly
Dance in Duke Theseus' house triumphantly,
And bless it to all fair prosperity:
There shall the pairs of faithful lovers be
Wedded, with Theseus, all in jollity.
PUCK.

090 Fairy king, attend, and mark:
I do hear the morning lark.
OBE.
Then, my queen, in silence sad,
Trip we after the night's shade:
We the globe can compass soon,
095 Swifter than the wandering moon.
TITA.
Come, my lord; and in our flight,
Tell me how it came this night,
That I sleeping here was found
With these mortals on the ground. (*Horns winded with-
in.*) (*Exeunt.*)

(*ENTER THESEUS, HIPPOLYTA, EGEUS, AND TRAIN.*)

100 *THE.* Go, one of you, find out the forester;
For now our observation is perform'd;
And since we have the vaward of the day,
My love shall hear the music of my hounds.
Uncouple in the western valley; let them go:
105 Dispatch, I say, and find the forester. (*Exit an
Attend.*)
We will, fair queen, up to the mountain's top,
And mark the musical confusion
Of hounds and echo in conjunction.
HIP. I was with Hercules and Cadmus once,
110 When in a wood of Crete they bay'd the bear
With hounds of Sparta: never did I hear
Such gallant chiding; for, besides the groves,
The skies, the fountains, every region near
Seem'd all one mutual cry: I never heard
115 So musical a discord, such sweet thunder.
THE. My hounds are bred out of the Spartan kind,
So flew'd, so sanded; and their heads are hung
With ears that sweep away the morning dew;
Crook-knee'd, and dew-lapp'd like Thessalian bulls;
120 Slow in pursuit, but match'd in mouth like bells,
Each under each. A cry more tuneable
Was never holla'd to, nor cheer'd with horn,
In Crete, in Sparta, nor in Thessaly:
Judge when you hear. But, soft! what nymphs are
these?

125 *Ege.* My lord, this is my daughter here asleep;
And this, Lysander; this Demetrius is;
This Helena, old Nedar's Helena:
I wonder of their being here together.
The. No doubt they rose up early to observe
130 The rite of May; and, hearing our intent,
Came here in grace of our solemnity.
But speak, Egeus; is not this the day
That Hermia should give answer of her choice?
Ege. It is, my lord.
135 *The.* Go, bid the huntsmen wake them with their
  horns. *(Horns and shout within.) (Lys., Dem., Hel.,
  and Her., wake and start up.)*
Good morrow, friends. Saint Valentine is past:
Begin these wood-birds but to couple now?
Lys. Pardon, my lord.
The. I pray you all, stand up.
I know you two are rival enemies:
140 How comes this gentle concord in the world,
That hatred is so far from jealousy,
To sleep by hate, and fear no enmity?
Lys. My lord, I shall reply amazedly,
Half sleep, half waking: but as yet, I swear,
145 I cannot truly say how I came here;
But, as I think,—for truly would I speak,
And now I do bethink me, so it is,—
I came with Hermia hither: our intent
Was to be gone from Athens, where we might,
150 Without the peril of the Athenian law.
Ege. Enough, enough, my lord; you have enough:
I beg the law, the law, upon his head.
They would have stolen away; they would,
    Demetrius,
Thereby to have defeated you and me,
155 You of your wife and me of my consent,
Of my consent that she should be your wife.
Dem. My lord, fair Helen told me of their stealth,
Of this their purpose hither to this wood;
And I in fury hither follow'd them,
160 Fair Helena in fancy following me.
But, my good lord, I wot not by what power,—
But by some power it is,—my love to Hermia,
Melted as the snow, seems to me now

As the remembrance of an idle gaud,
165 Which in my childhood I did dote upon;
And all the faith, the virtue of my heart,
The object and the pleasure of mine eye,
Is only Helena. To her, my lord,
Was I betroth'd ere I saw Hermia:
170 But, like in sickness, did I loathe this food;
But, as in health, come to my natural taste,
Now I do wish it, love it, long for it,
And will for evermore be true to it.
The. Fair lovers, you are fortunately met:
175 Of this discourse we more will hear anon.
Egeus, I will overbear your will;
For in the temple, by and by, with us
These couples shall eternally be knit:
And, for the morning now is something worn,
180 Our purposed hunting shall be set aside.
Away with us to Athens! three and three,
We'll hold a feast in great solemnity.
Come, Hippolyta. *(Exeunt The., Hip., Ege., and train.)*
Dem. These things seem small and undistinguishable,
185 Like far-off mountains turned into clouds.
Her. Methinks I see these things with parted eye,
When every thing seems double.
Hel. So methinks:
And I have found Demetrius like a jewel,
Mine own, and not mine own.
Dem.
Are you sure
190 That we are awake? It seems to me
That yet we sleep, we dream. Do not you think
The Duke was here, and bid us follow him?
Her. Yea; and my father.
Hel. And Hippolyta.
Lys. And he did bid us follow to the temple.
195 *Dem.* Why, then, we are awake: let's follow him;
And by the way let us recount our dreams. *(Exeunt.)*
Bot. (Awaking) When my cue comes, call me, and I
   will answer: my next is, 'Most fair Pyramus.'
   Heigh-ho! Peter Quince! Flute, the bellows-
   mender! Snout, the 200 tinker! Starveling! God's
   my life, stolen hence, and left me asleep! I have
   had a most rare vision. I have had a dream, past

the wit of man to say what dream it was: man is but an ass, if he go about to expound this dream. Methought I was—there is no man can tell what. Methought I was,—and methought I had,—but man is but a patched 205 fool, if he will offer to say what methought I had. The eye of man hath not heard, the ear of man hath not seen, man's hand is not able to taste, his tongue to conceive, nor his heart to report, what my dream was. I will get Peter Quince 210 to write a ballad of this dream: it shall be called Bottom's Dream, because it hath no bottom; and I will sing it in the latter end of a play, before the Duke: peradventure, to make it the more gracious, I shall sing it at her death. *(Exit.)*

SCENE II. ATHENS. QUINCE'S HOUSE.

(ENTER QUINCE, FLUTE, SNOUT, AND STARVELING.)

QUIN. Have you sent to Bottom's house? is he come home yet?

STAR. He cannot be heard of. Out of doubt he is transported.

005 *FLU.* If he come not, then the play is marred: it goes not forward, doth it?

QUIN. It is not possible: you have not a man in all Athens able to discharge Pyramus but he.

FLU. No, he hath simply the best wit of any handicraft 010 man in Athens.

QUIN. Yea, and the best person too; and he is a very paramour for a sweet voice.

FLU. You must say 'paragon': a paramour is, God bless us, a thing of naught.

(Enter SNUG.)

015 *SNUG.* Masters, the Duke is coming from the temple, and there is two or three lords and ladies more married: if our sport had gone forward, we had all been made men.

FLU. O sweet bully Bottom! Thus hath he lost sixpence a day during his life; he could not have scaped sixpence $_{020}$ a day: an the Duke had not given him sixpence a day for playing Pyramus, I'll be hanged; he would have deserved it: sixpence a day in Pyramus, or nothing.

(ENTER BOTTOM.)

BOT. Where are these lads? where are these hearts?

QUIN. Bottom! O most courageous day! O most $_{025}$ happy hour!

BOT. Masters, I am to discourse wonders: but ask me not what; for if I tell you, I am no true Athenian. I will tell you every thing, right as it fell out.

QUIN. Let us hear, sweet Bottom.

$_{030}$ *BOT.* Not a word of me. All that I will tell you is, that the Duke hath dined. Get your apparel together, good strings to your beards, new ribbons to your pumps; meet presently at the palace; every man look o'er his part; for the short and the long is, our play is preferred. In any $_{035}$ case, let Thisby have clean linen; and let not him that plays the lion pare his nails, for they shall hang out for the lion's claws. And, most dear actors, eat no onions nor garlic, for we are to utter sweet breath; and I do not doubt but to hear them say, it is a sweet comedy. No more $_{040}$ words: away! go, away! *(Exeunt.)*

ACT V

SCENE I. ATHENS. THE PALACE OF THESEUS.

(Enter THESEUS, HIPPOLYTA, PHILOSTRATE, Lords, and Attendants.)

HIP. 'Tis strange, my Theseus, that these lovers
    speak of.
THE. More strange than true: I never may believe
These antique fables, nor these fairy toys.
Lovers and madmen have such seething brains,
005 Such shaping fantasies, that apprehend
More than cool reason ever comprehends.
The lunatic, the lover and the poet
Are of imagination all compact:
One sees more devils than vast hell can hold,
010 That is, the madman: the lover, all as frantic,
Sees Helen's beauty in a brow of Egypt:
The poet's eye, in a fine frenzy rolling,
Doth glance from heaven to earth, from earth to
    heaven;
And as imagination bodies forth
015 The forms of things unknown, the poet's pen
Turns them to shapes, and gives to airy nothing
A local habitation and a name.
Such tricks hath strong imagination,
That, if it would but apprehend some joy,
020 It comprehends some bringer of that joy;
Or in the night, imagining some fear,
How easy is a bush supposed a bear!
HIP. But all the story of the night told over,

And all their minds transfigured so together,
025 More witnesseth than fancy's images,
And grows to something of great constancy;
But, howsoever, strange and admirable.
THE. Here come the lovers, full of joy and mirth.

(ENTER LYSANDER, DEMETRIUS, HERMIA, AND HELENA.)

Joy, gentle friends! joy and fresh days of love
Accompany your hearts!
LYS. 030 More than to us
Wait in your royal walks, your board, your bed!
THE. Come now; what masques, what dances shall we
   have,
To wear away this long age of three hours
Between our after-supper and bed-time?
035 Where is our usual manager of mirth?
What revels are in hand? Is there no play,
To ease the anguish of a torturing hour?
Call Philostrate.
PHIL. Here, mighty Theseus.
THE. Say, what abridgement have you for this
   evening?
040 What masque? what music? How shall we beguile
The lazy time, if not with some delight?
PHIL. There is a brief how many sports are ripe:
Make choice of which your highness will see first.
   (Giving a paper.)
THE. (reads) The battle with the Centaurs, to be sung
045 By an Athenian eunuch to the harp.
We'll none of that: that have I told my love,
In glory of my kinsman Hercules.
(Reads) The riot of the tipsy Bacchanals,
Tearing the Thracian singer in their rage.
050 That is an old device; and it was play'd
When I from Thebes came last a conqueror.
(Reads) The thrice three Muses mourning for the
   death
Of Learning, late deceased in beggary.
That is some satire, keen and critical,
055 Not sorting with a nuptial ceremony.
(Reads) A tedious brief scene of young Pyramus
And his love Thisbe; very tragical mirth.

Merry and tragical! tedious and brief!
That is, hot ice and wondrous strange snow.
060 How shall we find the concord of this discord?
PHIL. A play there is, my lord, some ten words long,
Which is as brief as I have known a play;
But by ten words, my lord, it is too long,
Which makes it tedious; for in all the play
065 There is not one word apt, one player fitted:
And tragical, my noble lord, it is;
For Pyramus therein doth kill himself.
Which, when I saw rehearsed, I must confess,
Made mine eyes water; but more merry tears
070 The passion of loud laughter never shed.
THE. What are they that do play it?
PHIL. Hard-handed men, that work in Athens here,
Which never labour'd in their minds till now;
And now have toil'd their unbreathed memories
075 With this same play, against your nuptial.
THE. And we will hear it.
PHIL. No, my noble lord;
It is not for you: I have heard it over,
And it is nothing, nothing in the world;
Unless you can find sport in their intents,
080 Extremely stretch'd and conn'd with cruel pain,
To do you service.
THE. I will hear that play;
For never any thing can be amiss,
When simpleness and duty tender it.
Go, bring them in: and take your places, ladies. *(Exit
     Philostrate.)*
085 *HIP.* I love not to see wretchedness o'ercharged,
And duty in his service perishing.
THE. Why, gentle sweet, you shall see no such thing.
HIP. He says they can do nothing in this kind.
THE. The kinder we, to give them thanks for nothing.
090 Our sport shall be to take what they mistake:
And what poor duty cannot do, noble respect
Takes it in might, not merit.
Where I have come, great clerks have purposed
To greet me with premeditated welcomes;
095 Where I have seen them shiver and look pale,
Make periods in the midst of sentences,
Throttle their practised accent in their fears,

And, in conclusion, dumbly have broke off,
Not paying me a welcome. Trust me, sweet,
100 Out of this silence yet I pick'd a welcome;
And in the modesty of fearful duty
I read as much as from the rattling tongue
Of saucy and audacious eloquence.
Love, therefore, and tongue-tied simplicity
105 In least speak most, to my capacity.

(RE-ENTER PHILOSTRATE.)

PHIL. So please your Grace, the Prologue is address'd.
THE. Let him approach. *(Flourish of trumpets.)*

(Enter QUINCE for the Prologue.)

PRO. If we offend, it is with our good will.
That you should think, we come not to offend,
110 But with good will. To show our simple skill,
That is the true beginning of our end.
Consider, then, we come but in despite.
We do not come as minding to content you,
Our true intent is. All for your delight,
115 We are not here. That you should here repent you,
The actors are at hand; and, by their show,
You shall know all, that you are like to know.
THE. This fellow doth not stand upon points.
LYS. He hath rid his prologue like a rough colt; he
knows not the stop. A good moral, my lord: it is
not 120 enough to speak, but to speak true.
HIP. Indeed he hath played on his prologue like a
child on a recorder; a sound, but not in gov-
ernment.
THE. His speech was like a tangled chain; nothing im-
paired, 125 but all disordered. Who is next?

(ENTER PYRAMUS AND THISBE, WALL, MOONSHINE, AND LION.)

PRO. Gentles, perchance you wonder at this show;
But wonder on, till truth make all things plain.
This man is Pyramus, if you would know;
This beauteous lady Thisby is certain.
130 This man, with lime and rough-cast, doth present

Wall, that vile Wall which did these lovers sunder;
And through Wall's chink, poor souls, they are
   content
To whisper. At the which let no man wonder.
This man, with lanthorn, dog, and bush of thorn,
135 Presenteth Moonshine; for, if you will know,
By moonshine did these lovers think no scorn
To meet at Ninus' tomb, there, there to woo.
This grisly beast, which Lion hight by name,
The trusty Thisby, coming first by night,
140 Did scare away, or rather did affright;
And, as she fled, her mantle she did fall,
Which Lion vile with bloody mouth did stain.
Anon comes Pyramus, sweet youth and tall,
And finds his trusty Thisby's mantle slain:
145 Whereat, with blade, with bloody blameful blade,
He bravely broach'd his boiling bloody breast;
And Thisby, tarrying in mulberry shade,
His dagger drew, and died. For all the rest,
Let Lion, Moonshine, Wall, and lovers twain
150 At large discourse, while here they do remain.
   (Exeunt Prologue, Thisbe, Lion, and Moonshine.)
THE. I wonder if the lion be to speak.
DEM. No wonder, my lord: one lion may, when many
asses do.
WALL. In this same interlude it doth befall
155 That I, one Snout by name, present a wall;
And such a wall, as I would have you think,
That had in it a crannied hole or chink,
Through which the lovers, Pyramus and Thisby,
Did whisper often very secretly.
160 This loam, this rough-cast, and this stone,
   doth show
That I am that same wall; the truth is so:
And this the cranny is, right and sinister,
Through which the fearful lovers are to whisper.
THE. Would you desire lime and hair to speak better?
165 *DEM.* It is the wittiest partition that ever I heard
   discourse, my lord.
THE. Pyramus draws near the wall: silence!

(ENTER PYRAMUS.)

Pyr. O grim-look'd night! O night with hue so black!
O night, which ever art when day is not!
170 O night, O night! alack, alack, alack,
I fear my Thisby's promise is forgot!
And them, O wall, O sweet, O lovely wall,
That stand'st between her father's ground and mine!
Thou wall, O wall, O sweet and lovely wall,
175 Show me thy chink, to blink through with mine
eyne! *(Wall holds up his fingers.)*
Thanks, courteous wall: Jove shield thee well for this!
But what see I? No Thisby do I see.
O wicked wall, through whom I see no bliss!
Cursed be thy stones for thus deceiving me!
The. The wall, methinks, being sensible, should curse
180 again.
Pyr. No, in truth, sir, he should not. 'Deceiving me' is
Thisby's cue: she is to enter now, and I am to spy
her through the wall. You shall see, it will fall pat
as I told 185 you. Yonder she comes.

(ENTER THISBE.)

This. O wall, full often hast thou heard my moans,
For parting my fair Pyramus and me!
My cherry lips have often kiss'd thy stones,
Thy stones with lime and hair knit up in thee.
190 *Pyr.* I see a voice: now will I to the chink,
To spy an I can hear my Thisby's face.
Thisby!
This. My love thou art, my love I think.
Pyr. Think what thou wilt, I am thy lover's grace;
195 And, like Limander, am I trusty still.
This. And I like Helen, till the Fates me kill.
Pyr. Not Shafalus to Procrus was so true.
This. As Shafalus to Procrus, I to you.
Pyr. O, kiss me through the hole of this vile wall!
200 *This.* I kiss the wall's hole, not your lips at all.
Pyr. Wilt thou at Ninny's tomb meet me
straightway?
This. 'Tide life, 'tide death, I come without delay.
(Exeunt Pyramus and Thisbe.)
Wall. Thus have I, wall, my part discharged so;
And, being done, thus wall away doth go. *(Exit.)*

205 *THE.* Now is the mural down between the two
   neighbours.

DEM. No remedy, my lord, when walls are so wilful to
hear without warning.

HIP. This is the silliest stuff that ever I heard.

210 *THE.* The best in this kind are but shadows;
   and the

worst are no worse, if imagination amend them.

HIP. It must be your imagination then, and not theirs.

THE. If we imagine no worse of them than they of
themselves, they may pass for excellent men.

   Here come

215 two noble beasts in a man and a lion.

(*ENTER LION AND MOONSHINE.*)

LION. You, ladies, you, whose gentle hearts do fear
The smallest monstrous mouse that creeps on floor,
May now perchance both quake and tremble here,
When lion rough in wildest rage doth roar.

220 Then know that I, one Snug the joiner, am
A lion-fell, nor else no lion's dam;
For, if I should as lion come in strife
Into this place, 'twere pity on my life.

THE. A very gentle beast, and of a good conscience.

225 *DEM.* The very best at a beast, my lord, that e'er
   I saw.

LYS. This lion is a very fox for his valour.

THE. True; and a goose for his discretion.

DEM. Not so, my lord; for his valour cannot carry his
discretion; and the fox carries the goose.

230 *THE.* His discretion, I am sure, cannot carry his valour; for the goose carries not the fox. It is well:
leave it to his discretion, and let us listen to the
moon.

MOON. This lanthorn doth the horned moon present;
   —

DEM. He should have worn the horns on his head.

235 *THE.* He is no crescent, and his horns are invisible
within the circumference.

MOON. This lanthorn doth the horned moon present;
Myself the man i' the moon do seem to be.

THE. This is the greatest error of all the rest: the man

$_{240}$ should be put into the lantern. How is it else
the man i' the moon?

DEM. He dares not come there for the candle; for, you
see, it is already in snuff.

HIP. I am aweary of this moon: would he would $_{245}$
change!

THE. It appears, by his small light of discretion, that
he is in the wane; but yet, in courtesy, in all reason,
we must stay the time.

LYS. Proceed, Moon.

$_{250}$ *MOON.* All that I have to say, is, to tell you that the
lanthorn is the moon; I, the man in the moon; this
thorn-bush, my thorn-bush; and this dog, my dog.

DEM. Why, all these should be in the lantern; for all
these are in the moon. But, silence! here comes
Thisbe.

(ENTER THISBE.)

$_{255}$ *THIS.* This is old Ninny's tomb. Where is my love?

LION. (*Roaring*) Oh — — (*Thisbe runs off.*)

DEM. Well roared, Lion.

THE. Well run, Thisbe.

HIP. Well shone, Moon. Truly, the moon shines with $_{260}$ a
good grace. (*The Lion shakes Thisbe's mantle, and exit.*)

THE. Well moused, Lion.

DEM. And then came Pyramus.

LYS. And so the lion vanished.

(ENTER PYRAMUS.)

PYR. Sweet Moon, I thank thee for thy sunny beams;
$_{265}$ I thank thee, Moon, for shining now so bright;
For, by thy gracious, golden, glittering gleams,
I trust to take of truest Thisby sight.
But stay, O spite!
But mark, poor knight,
$_{270}$ What dreadful dole is here!
Eyes, do you see?
How can it be?
O dainty duck! O dear!
Thy mantle good,

275 What, stain'd with blood!
Approach, ye Furies fell!
O Fates, come, come,
Cut thread and thrum;
Quail, crush, conclude, and quell!
280 *THE.* This passion, and the death of a dear friend,
would go near to make a man look sad.
HIP. Beshrew my heart, but I pity the man.
PYR. O wherefore, Nature, didst thou lions frame?
Since lion vile hath here deflower'd my dear:
285 Which is—no, no—which was the fairest dame
That lived, that loved, that liked, that look'd with
cheer.
Come, tears, confound;
Out, sword, and wound
The pap of Pyramus;
290 Ay, that left pap,
Where heart doth hop: *(Stabs himself.)*
Thus die I, thus, thus, thus.
Now am I dead,
Now am I fled;
295 My soul is in the sky:
Tongue, lose thy light;
Moon, take thy flight: *(Exit Moonshine.)*
Now die, die, die, die, die. *(Dies.)*
DEM. No die, but an ace, for him; for he is but one.
300 *LYS.* Less than an ace, man; for he is dead; he is
nothing.
THE. With the help of a surgeon he might yet recover,
and prove an ass.
HIP. How chance Moonshine is gone before Thisbe 305
comes back and finds her lover?
THE. She will find him by starlight. Here she comes;
and her passion ends the play.

(Re-enter THISBE.)

HIP. Methinks she should not use a long one for such
a Pyramus: I hope she will be brief.
310 *DEM.* A mote will turn the balance, which Pyramus, which Thisbe, is the better; he for a man,
God warrant us; she for a woman, God bless us.

Lys. She hath spied him already with those sweet
    eyes.

Dem. And thus she means, videlicet:—

This. 315 Asleep, my love?
What, dead, my dove?
O Pyramus, arise!
Speak, speak. Quite dumb?
Dead, dead? A tomb
320 Must cover thy sweet eyes.
These lily lips,
This cherry nose,
These yellow cowslip cheeks,
Are gone, are gone:
325 Lovers, make moan:
His eyes were green as leeks.
O Sisters Three,
Come, come to me,
With hands as pale as milk;
330 Lay them in gore,
Since you have shore
With shears his thread of silk.
Tongue, not a word:
Come, trusty sword;
335 Come, blade, my breast imbrue: *(Stabs herself.)*
And, farewell, friends;
Thus Thisby ends:
Adieu, adieu, adieu. *(Dies.)*

The. Moonshine and Lion are left to bury the dead.

340 *Dem.* Ay, and Wall too.

Bot. (Starting up) No, I assure you; the wall is down
    that parted their fathers. Will it please you to see
    the epilogue, or to hear a Bergomask dance be-
    tween two of our company?

345 *The.* No epilogue, I pray you; for your play needs
    no excuse. Never excuse; for when the players are
    all dead, there need none to be blamed. Marry, if
    he that writ it had played Pyramus and hanged
    himself in Thisbe's garter, it would have been a
    fine tragedy: and so it is, truly; and 350 very no-
    tably discharged. But, come, your Bergomask: let
    your epilogue alone. *(A dance.)*

The iron tongue of midnight hath told twelve:
Lovers, to bed; 'tis almost fairy time.

I fear we shall out-sleep the coming morn,
355 As much as we this night have overwatch'd.
This palpable-gross play hath well beguiled
The heavy gait of night. Sweet friends, to bed.
A fortnight hold we this solemnity,
In nightly revels and new jollity. *(Exeunt.)*

(Enter Puck.)

360 **Puck.** Now the hungry lion roars,
And the wolf behowls the moon;
Whilst the heavy ploughman snores,
All with weary task fordone.
Now the wasted brands do glow,
365 Whilst the screech-owl, screeching loud,
Puts the wretch that lies in woe
In remembrance of a shroud.
Now it is the time of night,
That the graves, all gaping wide,
370 Every one lets forth his sprite,
In the church-way paths to glide:
And we fairies, that do run
By the triple Hecate's team,
From the presence of the sun,
375 Following darkness like a dream,
Now are frolic: not a mouse
Shall disturb this hallow'd house:
I am sent with broom before,
To sweep the dust behind the door.

(Enter Oberon and Titania with their train.)

380 **Obe.** Through the house give glimmering light,
By the dead and drowsy fire:
Every elf and fairy sprite
Hop as light as bird from brier;
And this ditty, after me,
385 Sing, and dance it trippingly.
Tita. First, rehearse your song by rote,
To each word a warbling note:
Hand in hand, with fairy grace,
Will we sing, and bless this place. *(Song and dance.)*
390 **Obe.** Now, until the break of day,

Through this house each fairy stray.
To the best bride-bed will we,
Which by us shall blessed be;
And the issue there create
395 Ever shall be fortunate.
So shall all the couples three
Ever true in loving be;
And the blots of Nature's hand
Shall not in their issue stand;
400 Never mole, hare lip, nor scar,
Nor mark prodigious, such as are
Despised in nativity,
Shall upon their children be.
With this field-dew consecrate,
405 Every fairy take his gait;
And each several chamber bless,
Through this palace, with sweet peace,
Ever shall in safety rest,
And the owner of it blest.
410 Trip away; make no stay;
Meet me all by break of day. *(Exeunt Oberon, Titania, and train.)*
Puck. If we shadows have offended,
Think but this, and all is mended,
That you have but slumber'd here,
415 While these visions did appear.
And this weak and idle theme,
No more yielding but a dream,
Gentles, do not reprehend:
If you pardon, we will mend.
420 And, as I am an honest Puck,
If we have unearned luck
Now to scape the serpent's tongue,
We will make amends ere long;
Else the Puck a liar call:
425 So, good night unto you all.
Give me your hands, if we be friends,
And Robin shall restore amends. *(Exit.)*

THE MERCHANT OF
VENICE

DRAMATIS PERSONÆ

THE DUKE OF VENICE.
The PRINCE OF MOROCCO, suitor to Portia.
THE PRINCE OF ARRAGON, " "
ANTONIO, a merchant of Venice.
BASSANIO, his friend, suitor likewise to Portia.
SALANIO, SALARINO, GRATIANO, & SALERIO, friends to
    Antonio and Bassanio.
LORENZO, in love with Jessica.
SHYLOCK, a rich Jew.
TUBAL, a Jew, his friend.
LAUNCELOT GOBBO, the clown, servant to Shylock.
OLD GOBBO, father to Launcelot.
LEONARDO, servant to Bassanio.
BALTHASAR, servant to Portia.
STEPHANO, " "
PORTIA, a rich heiress.
NERISSA, her waiting-maid.
JESSICA, daughter to Shylock.
Magnificoes of Venice, Officers of the Court of Justice,
    Gaoler, Servants to Portia, and other Attendants.
*SCENE — Partly at Venice, and partly at Belmont, the seat
    of Portia, on the Continent.*

ACT I

SCENE I. VENICE. A STREET.

ENTER ANTONIO, SALARINO, *AND* SALANIO.

ANT. In sooth, I know not why I am so sad:
It wearies me; you say it wearies you;
But how I caught it, found it, or came by it,
What stuff 'tis made of, whereof it is born,
005 I am to learn;
And such a want-wit sadness makes of me,
That I have much ado to know myself.
SALAR. Your mind is tossing on the ocean;
There, where your argosies with portly sail,
010 Like signiors and rich burghers on the flood,
Or, as it were, the pageants of the sea,
Do overpeer the petty traffickers,
That curt'sy to them, do them reverence,
As they fly by them with their woven wings.
015 SALAN. Believe me, sir, had I such venture forth,
The better part of my affections would
Be with my hopes abroad. I should be still
Plucking the grass, to know where sits the wind;
Peering in maps for ports, and piers, and roads;
020 And every object that might make me fear
Misfortune to my ventures, out of doubt
Would make me sad.
SALAR. My wind, cooling my broth,

Would blow me to an ague, when I thought
What harm a wind too great at sea might do.
025 I should not see the sandy hour-glass run,
But I should think of shallows and of flats,
And see my wealthy Andrew dock'd in sand
Vailing her high-top lower than her ribs
To kiss her burial. Should I go to church
030 And see the holy edifice of stone,
And not bethink me straight of dangerous rocks,
Which touching but my gentle vessel's side,
Would scatter all her spices on the stream;
Enrobe the roaring waters with my silks;
035 And, in a word, but even now worth this,
And now worth nothing? Shall I have the thought
To think on this; and shall I lack the thought,
That such a thing bechanced would make me sad?
But tell not me; I know, Antonio
040 Is sad to think upon his merchandise.
ANT. Believe me, no: I thank my fortune for it,
My ventures are not in one bottom trusted,
Nor to one place; nor is my whole estate
Upon the fortune of this present year:
045 Therefore my merchandise makes me not sad.
SALAR. Why, then you are in love.
ANT. Fie, fie!
SALAR. Not in love neither? Then let us say you
        are sad,
Because you are not merry: and 'twere as easy
For you to laugh, and leap, and say you are merry,
050 Because you are not sad. Now, by two-headed
        Janus,
Nature hath framed strange fellows in her time:
Some that will evermore peep through their eyes,
And laugh like parrots at a bag-piper;
And other of such vinegar aspect,
055 That they'll not show their teeth in way of smile,
Though Nestor swear the jest be laughable.

ENTER BASSANIO, LORENZO, *AND* GRATIANO.

SALAN. Here comes Bassanio, your most noble
        kinsman,
Gratiano, and Lorenzo. Fare ye well:

We leave you now with better company.

SALAR. I would have stay'd till I had made you merry,
If worthier friends had not prevented me.

ANT. Your worth is very dear in my regard.
I take it, your own business calls on you,
And you embrace the occasion to depart.

SALAR. Good morrow, my good lords.

BASS. Good signiors both, when shall we laugh? say, when?
You grow exceeding strange: must it be so?

SALAR. We'll make our leisures to attend on yours.

[*Exeunt Salarino and Salanio.*

LOR. My Lord Bassanio, since you have found Antonio,
We two will leave you: but, at dinner-time,
I pray you, have in mind where we must meet.

BASS. I will not fail you.

GRA. You look not well, Signior Antonio;
You have too much respect upon the world:
They lose it that do buy it with much care:
Believe me, you are marvellously changed.

ANT. I hold the world but as the world, Gratiano;
A stage, where every man must play a part,
And mine a sad one.

GRA. Let me play the fool:
With mirth and laughter let old wrinkles come;
And let my liver rather heat with wine
Than my heart cool with mortifying groans.
Why should a man, whose blood is warm within,
Sit like his grandsire cut in alabaster?
Sleep when he wakes, and creep into the jaundice
By being peevish? I tell thee what, Antonio—,
I love thee, and it is my love that speaks,—
There are a sort of men, whose visages
Do cream and mantle like a standing pond;
And do a wilful stillness entertain,
With purpose to be dress'd in an opinion
Of wisdom, gravity, profound conceit;
As who should say, 'I am Sir Oracle,
And, when I ope my lips, let no dog bark!'
O my Antonio, I do know of these,
That therefore only are reputed wise

73

For saying nothing; when, I am very sure,
If they should speak, would almost damn those ears,
Which, hearing them, would call their brothers fools.
100 I'll tell thee more of this another time:
But fish not, with this melancholy bait,
For this fool gudgeon, this opinion.
Come, good Lorenzo. Fare ye well awhile:
I'll end my exhortation after dinner.
105 *LOR.* Well, we will leave you, then, till dinner-time:
I must be one of these same dumb wise men,
For Gratiano never lets me speak.
GRA. Well, keep me company but two years moe,
Thou shalt not know the sound of thine own tongue.
110 *ANT.* Farewell: I'll grow a talker for this gear.
GRA. Thanks, i'faith; for silence is only commendable
In a neat's tongue dried, and a maid not vendible.
    [*Exeunt Gratiano and Lorenzo.*
ANT. Is that any thing now?
BASS. Gratiano speaks an infinite deal of nothing, more
115 than any man in all Venice. His reasons are as two grains
of wheat hid in two bushels of chaff: you shall seek all day
ere you find them: and when you have them, they are not
worth the search.
ANT. Well, tell me now, what lady is the same
120 To whom you swore a secret pilgrimage,
That you to-day promised to tell me of?
BASS. 'Tis not unknown to you, Antonio,
How much I have disabled mine estate,
By something showing a more swelling port
125 Than my faint means would grant continuance:
Nor do I now make moan to be abridged
From such a noble rate; but my chief care
Is, to come fairly off from the great debts,
Wherein my time, something too prodigal,
130 Hath left me gaged. To you, Antonio,
I owe the most, in money and in love;
And from your love I have a warranty
To unburden all my plots and purposes
How to get clear of all the debts I owe.

135 *ANT.* I pray you, good Bassanio, let me know it;
And if it stand, as you yourself still do,
Within the eye of honour, be assured,
My purse, my person, my extremest means,
Lie all unlock'd to your occasions.
140 *BASS.* In my school-days, when I had lost one
    shaft,
I shot his fellow of the self-same flight
The self-same way with more advised watch,
To find the other forth; and by adventuring both,
I oft found both: I urge this childhood proof,
145 Because what follows is pure innocence.
I owe you much; and, like a wilful youth,
That which I owe is lost: but if you please
To shoot another arrow that self way
Which you did shoot the first, I do not doubt,
150 As I will watch the aim, or to find both,
Or bring your latter hazard back again,
And thankfully rest debtor for the first.
ANT. You know me well; and herein spend but time
To wind about my love with circumstance;
155 And out of doubt you do me now more wrong
In making question of my uttermost,
Than if you had made waste of all I have:
Then do but say to me what I should do,
That in your knowledge may by me be done,
160 And I am prest unto it: therefore, speak.
BASS. In Belmont is a lady richly left;
And she is fair, and, fairer than that word,
Of wondrous virtues: sometimes from her eyes
I did receive fair speechless messages:
165 Her name is Portia; nothing undervalued
To Cato's daughter, Brutus' Portia:
Nor is the wide world ignorant of her worth;
For the four winds blow in from every coast
Renowned suitors: and her sunny locks
170 Hang on her temples like a golden fleece;
Which makes her seat of Belmont Colchos' strond,
And many Jasons come in quest of her.
O my Antonio, had I but the means
To hold a rival place with one of them,
175 I have a mind presages me such thrift,
That I should questionless be fortunate!

Ant. Thou know'st that all my fortunes are at sea;
Neither have I money, nor commodity
To raise a present sum: therefore go forth;
180 Try what my credit can in Venice do:
That shall be rack'd, even to the uttermost,
To furnish thee to Belmont, to fair Portia.
Go, presently inquire, and so will I,
Where money is; and I no question make,
185 To have it of my trust, or for my sake. [*Exeunt.*

SCENE II. BELMONT. A ROOM IN PORTIA'S HOUSE.

Enter Portia *and* Nerissa.

Por. By my troth, Nerissa, my little body is aweary of
  this great world.
Ner. You would be, sweet madam, if your miseries
  were in the same abundance as your good fortunes are: and 005 yet, for aught I see, they are as
  sick that surfeit with too much, as they that starve
  with nothing. It is no mean happiness, therefore,
  to be seated in the mean: superfluity comes sooner
  by white hairs; but competency lives longer.
Por. Good sentences, and well pronounced.
010 *Ner.* They would be better, if well followed.
Por. If to do were as easy as to know what were good
  to do, chapels had been churches, and poor men's
  cottages princes' palaces. It is a good divine that
  follows his own instructions: I can easier teach
  twenty what were good to be 015 done, than be one
  of the twenty to follow mine own teaching. The
  brain may devise laws for the blood; but a hot
  temper leaps o'er a cold decree: such a hare is
  madness the youth, to skip o'er the meshes of
  good counsel the cripple. But this reasoning is not
  in the fashion to choose me a husband. 020 O me,
  the word 'choose'! I may neither choose whom I
  would, nor refuse whom I dislike; so is the will of
  a living daughter curbed by the will of a dead father. Is it not hard, Nerissa, that I cannot choose
  one, nor refuse none?
Ner. Your father was ever virtuous; and holy men, at

$_{025}$ their death, have good inspirations: therefore,
the lottery, that he hath devised in these three
chests of gold, silver, and lead,—whereof who
chooses his meaning chooses you,— will, no
doubt, never be chosen by any rightly, but one
who shall rightly love. But what warmth is there
in your $_{030}$ affection towards any of these princely
suitors that are already come?

Por. I pray thee, over-name them; and as thou
namest them, I will describe them; and, according
to my description, level at my affection.

$_{035}$ *Ner.* First, there is the Neapolitan prince.

Por. Ay, that's a colt indeed, for he doth nothing but
talk of his horse; and he makes it a great appropri-
ation to his own good parts, that he can shoe him
himself. I am much afeard my lady his mother
played false with a smith.

$_{040}$ *Ner.* $_{040}$ Then there is the County Palatine.

Por. He doth nothing but frown; as who should say,
'if you will not have me, choose:' he hears merry
tales, and smiles not: I fear he will prove the
weeping philosopher when he grows old, being so
full of unmannerly sadness in $_{045}$ his youth. I had
rather be married to a death's-head with a bone in
his mouth than to either of these. God defend me
from these two!

Ner. How say you by the French lord, Monsieur
Le Bon?

$_{050}$ *Por.* God made him, and therefore let him pass for
a man. In truth, I know it is a sin to be a mocker:
but, he! —why, he hath a horse better than the
Neapolitan's; a better bad habit of frowning than
the Count Palatine: he is every man in no man; if a
throstle sing, he falls straight a $_{055}$ capering: he
will fence with his own shadow: if I should marry
him, I should marry twenty husbands. If he would
despise me, I would forgive him; for if he love me
to madness, I shall never requite him.

Ner. What say you, then, to Falconbridge, the young
$_{060}$ baron of England?

Por. You know I say nothing to him; for he under-
stands not me, nor I him: he hath neither Latin,
French, nor Italian; and you will come into the

court and swear that I have a poor pennyworth
in the English. He is a _065_ proper man's picture;
but, alas, who can converse with a dumbshow?
How oddly he is suited! I think he bought his
doublet in Italy, his round hose in France, his
bonnet in Germany, and his behaviour every
where.

NER. What think you of the Scottish lord, his
neighbour?

_070_ *POR.* That he hath a neighbourly charity in him;
for he borrowed a box of the ear of the English-
man, and swore he would pay him again when he
was able: I think the Frenchman became his surety,
and sealed under for another.

_075_ *NER.* How like you the young German, the Duke
of Saxony's nephew?

POR. Very vilely in the morning, when he is sober;
and most vilely in the afternoon, when he is
drunk: when he is best, he is a little worse than a
man; and when he is worst, he is little better than
a beast: an worst fall that ever _080_ fell, I hope I
shall make shift to go without him.

NER. If he should offer to choose, and choose the right
casket, you should refuse to perform your father's
will, if you should refuse to accept him.

POR. Therefore, for fear of the worst, I pray thee, set a
_085_ deep glass of Rhenish wine on the contrary casket; for, if the devil be within and that temptation
without, I know he will choose it. I will do any
thing, Nerissa, ere I'll be married to a sponge.

NER. You need not fear, lady, the having any of these
_090_ lords: they have acquainted me with their de-
terminations; which is, indeed, to return to their
home, and to trouble you with no more suit, unless you may be won by some other sort than your
father's imposition, depending on the caskets.

_095_ *POR.* If I live to be as old as Sibylla, I will die as
chaste as Diana, unless I be obtained by the
manner of my father's will. I am glad this parcel
of wooers are so reasonable; for there is not one
among them but I dote on his very absence; and I
pray God grant them a fair departure.

_100_ *NER.* Do you not remember, lady, in your father's

time, a Venetian, a scholar, and a soldier, that came
hither in company of the Marquis of Montferrat?

Por. Yes, yes, it was Bassanio; as I think he was so
called.

105 *Ner.* True, madam: he, of all the men that ever my
foolish eyes looked upon, was the best deserving a
fair lady.

Por. I remember him well; and I remember him
worthy of thy praise.

Enter a Serving-man.

How now! what news?

110 *Serv.* The four strangers seek for you, madam, to
take their leave: and there is a forerunner come
from a fifth, the Prince of Morocco; who brings
word, the prince his master will be here to-night.

Por. If I could bid the fifth welcome with so good a
115 heart as I can bid the other four farewell, I
should be glad of his approach: if he have the condition of a saint and the complexion of a devil, I
had rather he should shrive me than wive me.
Come, Nerissa. Sirrah, go before.
Whiles we shut the gates upon one wooer, another
knocks 120 at the door. [*Exeunt.*

SCENE III. VENICE. A PUBLIC PLACE.

Enter Bassanio *and* Shylock.

Shy. Three thousand ducats; well.

Bass. Ay, sir, for three months.

Shy. For three months; well.

Bass. For the which, as I told you, Antonio shall be 005
bound.

Shy. Antonio shall become bound; well.

Bass. May you stead me? will you pleasure me? shall
I know your answer?

Shy. Three thousand ducats for three months, and 010
Antonio bound.

Bass. Your answer to that.

Shy. Antonio is a good man.

Bass. Have you heard any imputation to the
contrary?

Shy. Ho, no, no, no, no: my meaning, in saying he is
015 a good man, is to have you understand me,
that he is sufficient. Yet his means are in supposition: he hath an argosy bound to Tripolis, another
to the Indies; I understand, moreover, upon the Rialto, he hath a third at Mexico, a fourth for England, and other ventures he hath, squandered 020
abroad. But ships are but boards, sailors but men:
there be land-rats and water-rats, water-thieves
and land-thieves, I mean pirates; and then there is
the peril of waters, winds, and rocks. The man is,
notwithstanding, sufficient. Three thousand
ducats; I think I may take his bond.

025 *Bass.* Be assured you may.

Shy. I will be assured I may; and, that I may be assured, I will bethink me. May I speak with
Antonio?

Bass. If it please you to dine with us.

Shy. Yes, to smell pork; to eat of the habitation 030
which your prophet the Nazarite conjured the
devil into. I will buy with you, sell with you, talk
with you, walk with you, and so following; but I
will not eat with you, drink with you, nor pray
with you. What news on the Rialto? Who is he
comes here?

Enter Antonio.

035 *Bass.* This is Signior Antonio.

Shy. [*Aside*] How like a fawning publican he looks!
I hate him for he is a Christian;
But more for that in low simplicity
He lends out money gratis and brings down
040 The rate of usance here with us in Venice.
If I can catch him once upon the hip,
I will feed fat the ancient grudge I bear him.
He hates our sacred nation; and he rails,
Even there where merchants most do congregate,
045 On me, my bargains, and my well-won thrift,
Which he calls interest. Cursed be my tribe,
If I forgive him!

Bass. Shylock, do you hear?

Shy. I am debating of my present store;
And, by the near guess of my memory,
050 I cannot instantly raise up the gross
Of full three thousand ducats. What of that?
Tubal, a wealthy Hebrew of my tribe,
Will furnish me. But soft! how many months
Do you desire? [*To Ant.*] Rest you fair, good signior;
055 Your worship was the last man in our mouths.

Ant. Shylock, although I neither lend nor borrow,
By taking nor by giving of excess,
Yet, to supply the ripe wants of my friend,
I'll break a custom. Is he yet possess'd
How much ye would?

060 *Shy.* Ay, ay, three thousand ducats.

Ant. And for three months.

Shy. I had forgot; three months, you told me so.
Well then, your bond; and let me see; but hear you;
Methought you said you neither lend nor borrow
Upon advantage.

065 *Ant.* I do never use it.

Shy. When Jacob grazed his uncle Laban's sheep,—
This Jacob from our holy Abram was,
As his wise mother wrought in his behalf,
The third possessor; ay, he was the third,—

070 *Ant.* And what of him? did he take interest?

Shy. No, not take interest; not, as you would say,
Directly interest: mark what Jacob did.
When Laban and himself were compromised
That all the eanlings which were streak'd and pied
075 Should fall as Jacob's hire, the ewes, being rank,
In the end of autumn turned to the rams;
And when the work of generation was
Between these woolly breeders in the act,
The skilful shepherd peel'd me certain wands,
080 And, in the doing of the deed of kind,
He stuck them up before the fulsome ewes,
Who, then conceiving, did in eaning time
Fall parti-colour'd lambs, and those were Jacob's.
This was a way to thrive, and he was blest:
085 And thrift is blessing, if men steal it not.

Ant. This was a venture, sir, that Jacob served for;
A thing not in his power to bring to pass,

But sway'd and fashion'd by the hand of heaven.
Was this inserted to make interest good?
090 Or is your gold and silver ewes and rams?
Shy. I cannot tell; I make it breed as fast:
But note me, signior.
Ant. Mark you this, Bassanio,
The devil can cite Scripture for his purpose.
An evil soul, producing holy witness,
095 Is like a villain with a smiling cheek;
A goodly apple rotten at the heart:
O, what a goodly outside falsehood hath!
Shy. Three thousand ducats; 'tis a good round sum.
Three months from twelve; then, let me see; the rate—
100 *Ant.* Well, Shylock, shall we be beholding to you?
Shy. Signior Antonio, many a time and oft
In the Rialto you have rated me
About my moneys and my usances:
Still have I borne it with a patient shrug;
105 For sufferance is the badge of all our tribe.
You call me misbeliever, cut-throat dog,
And spit upon my Jewish gaberdine,
And all for use of that which is mine own.
Well then, it now appears you need my help:
110 Go to, then; you come to me, and you say
'Shylock, we would have moneys:' you say so;
You, that did void your rheum upon my beard,
And foot me as you spurn a stranger cur
Over your threshold: moneys is your suit.
115 What should I say to you? Should I not say
'Hath a dog money? is it possible
A cur can lend three thousand ducats?' or
Shall I bend low and in a bondman's key,
With bated breath and whispering humbleness,
120 Say this,—
'Fair sir, you spit on me on Wednesday last;
You spurn'd me such a day; another time
You call'd me dog; and for these courtesies
I'll lend you thus much moneys'?
125 *Ant.* I am as like to call thee so again,
To spit on thee again, to spurn thee too.
If thou wilt lend this money, lend it not
As to thy friends; for when did friendship take
A breed for barren metal of his friend?

130 But lend it rather to thine enemy;
Who if he break, thou mayst with better face
Exact the penalty.
Shy. Why, look you, how you storm!
I would be friends with you, and have your love,
Forget the shames that you have stain'd me with,
135 Supply your present wants, and take no doit
Of usance for my moneys, and you'll not hear me:
This is kind I offer.
Bass. This were kindness.
Shy. This kindness will I show.
Go with me to a notary, seal me there
140 Your single bond; and, in a merry sport,
If you repay me not on such a day,
In such a place, such sum or sums as are
Express'd in the condition, let the forfeit
Be nominated for an equal pound
145 Of your fair flesh, to be cut off and taken
In what part of your body pleaseth me.
Ant. Content, i'faith: I'll seal to such a bond,
And say there is much kindness in the Jew.
Bass. You shall not seal to such a bond for me:
150 I'll rather dwell in my necessity.
Ant. Why, fear not, man; I will not forfeit it:
Within these two months, that's a month before
This bond expires, I do expect return
Of thrice three times the value of this bond.
155 *Shy.* O father Abram, what these Christians are,
Whose own hard dealings teaches them suspect
The thoughts of others! Pray you, tell me this;
If he should break his day, what should I gain
By the exaction of the forfeiture?
160 A pound of man's flesh taken from a man
Is not so estimable, profitable neither,
As flesh of muttons, beefs, or goats. I say,
To buy his favour, I extend this friendship:
If he will take it, so; if not, adieu;
165 And, for my love, I pray you wrong me not.
Ant. Yes, Shylock, I will seal unto this bond.
Shy. Then meet me forthwith at the notary's;
Give him direction for this merry bond;
And I will go and purse the ducats straight;
170 See to my house, left in the fearful guard

Of an unthrifty knave; and presently
I will be with you.
Ant. Hie thee, gentle Jew. [*Exit Shylock.*
The Hebrew will turn Christian: he grows kind.
Bass. I like not fair terms and a villain's mind.
175 *Ant.* Come on: in this there can be no dismay;
My ships come home a month before the day. [*Exeunt.*

ACT II

SCENE I. BELMONT. A ROOM IN PORTIA'S HOUSE.

*Flourish of cornets. Enter the PRINCE OF MOROCCO and his train:
PORTIA, NERISSA, and others attending.*

MOR. Mislike me not for my complexion,
The shadow'd livery of the burnish'd sun,
To whom I am a neighbour and near bred.
Bring me the fairest creature northward born,
005 Where Phœbus' fire scarce thaws the icicles,
And let us make incision for your love,
To prove whose blood is reddest, his or mine.
I tell thee, lady, this aspect of mine
Hath fear'd the valiant: by my love, I swear
010 The best-regarded virgins of our clime
Have loved it too: I would not change this hue,
Except to steal your thoughts, my gentle queen.
POR. In terms of choice I am not solely led
By nice direction of a maiden's eyes;
015 Besides, the lottery of my destiny
Bars me the right of voluntary choosing:
But if my father had not scanted me
And hedged me by his wit, to yield myself
His wife who wins me by that means I told you,
020 Yourself, renowned prince, then stood as fair
As any comer I have look'd on yet
For my affection.

Mor. Even for that I thank you:
Therefore, I pray you, lead me to the caskets.
To try my fortune. By this scimitar
025 That slew the Sophy and a Persian prince
That won three fields of Sultan Solyman,
I would outstare the sternest eyes that look,
Outbrave the heart most daring on the earth,
Pluck the young sucking cubs from the she-bear,
030 Yea, mock the lion when he roars for prey,
To win thee, lady. But, alas the while!
If Hercules and Lichas play at dice
Which is the better man, the greater throw
May turn by fortune from the weaker hand:
035 So is Alcides beaten by his page;
And so may I, blind fortune leading me,
Miss that which one unworthier may attain,
And die with grieving.
Por. You must take your chance;
And either not attempt to choose at all,
040 Or swear before you choose, if you choose wrong,
Never to speak to lady afterward
In way of marriage: therefore be advised.
Mor. Nor will not. Come, bring me unto my chance.
Por. First, forward to the temple: after dinner
Your hazard shall be made.
045 *Mor.* Good fortune then!
To make me blest or cursed'st among men. [*Cornets,
and exeunt.*

SCENE II. VENICE. A STREET.

Enter LAUNCELOT.

Laun. Certainly my conscience will serve me to run
from this Jew my master. The fiend is at mine elbow, and tempts me, saying to me, 'Gobbo,
Launcelot Gobbo, good Launcelot,' or 'good Gobbo,' or 'good Launcelot Gobbo, 005 use your legs,
take the start, run away.' My conscience says, 'No;
take heed, honest Launcelot; take heed, honest
Gobbo,' or, as aforesaid, 'honest Launcelot Gobbo;
do not run; scorn running with thy heels.' Well,

the most courageous fiend bids me pack: 'Via!'
says the fiend; 'away!' $_{010}$ says the fiend; 'for the
heavens, rouse up a brave mind,' says the fiend,
'and run.' Well, my conscience, hanging about the
neck of my heart, says very wisely to me, 'My
honest friend Launcelot, being an honest man's
son,'—or rather an honest woman's son;—for, indeed, my father did $_{015}$ something smack, something grow to, he had a kind of taste;—well, my
conscience says, 'Launcelot, budge not.' 'Budge,'
says the fiend. 'Budge not,' says my conscience.
'Conscience,' say I, 'you counsel well;' 'Fiend,' say
I, 'you counsel well:' to be ruled by my conscience,
I should stay $_{020}$ with the Jew my master, who,
God bless the mark, is a kind of devil; and, to run
away from the Jew, I should be ruled by the fiend,
who, saving your reverence, is the devil himself.
Certainly the Jew is the very devil incarnal; and,
in my
conscience, my conscience is but a kind of hard $_{025}$
conscience, to offer to counsel me to stay with the
Jew. The fiend gives the more friendly counsel: I
will run, fiend; my heels are at your command; I
will run.

Enter Old GOBBO, with a basket.

GOB. Master young man, you, I pray you, which is
    the way to master Jew's?
$_{030}$ LAUN. [*Aside*] O heavens, this is my true-begotten
    father! who, being more than sand-blind, high-
    gravel blind, knows me not: I will try confusions
    with him.
GOB. Master young gentleman, I pray you, which is
    the way to master Jew's?
$_{035}$ LAUN. Turn up on your right hand at the next turn-
    ing, but, at the next turning of all, on your left;
    marry, at the very next turning, turn of no hand,
    but turn down indirectly to the Jew's house.
GOB. By God's sonties, 'twill be a hard way to hit. $_{040}$
    Can you tell me whether one Launcelot, that
    dwells with him, dwell with him or no?
LAUN. Talk you of young Master Launcelot? [*Aside*]

Mark me now; now will I raise the waters. Talk
you of young Master Launcelot?

045 *Gob.* No master, sir, but a poor man's son: his father, though I say it, is an honest exceeding poor
man, and, God be thanked, well to live.

Laun. Well, let his father be what a' will, we talk of
young Master Launcelot.

050 *Gob.* Your worship's friend, and Launcelot, sir.

Laun. But I pray you, ergo, old man, ergo, I beseech
you, talk you of young Master Launcelot?

Gob. Of Launcelot, an't please your mastership.

Laun. Ergo, Master Launcelot. Talk not of Master 055
Launcelot, father; for the young gentleman, according to Fates and Destinies and such odd sayings, the Sisters Three and such branches of
learning, is indeed deceased; or, as you would say
in plain terms, gone to heaven.

Gob. Marry, God forbid! the boy was the very staff of
060 my age, my very prop.

Laun. Do I look like a cudgel or a hovel-post, a staff
or a prop? Do you know me, father?

Gob. Alack the day, I know you not, young gentleman: but, I pray you, tell me, is my boy, God rest
his 065 soul, alive or dead?

Laun. Do you not know me, father?

Gob. Alack, sir, I am sand-blind; I-know you not.

Laun. Nay, indeed, if you had your eyes, you might
fail of the knowing me: it is a wise father that
knows his own 070 child. Well, old man, I will tell
you news of your son: give me your blessing:
truth will come to light; murder cannot be hid
long; a man's son may; but, at the length, truth
will out.

Gob. Pray you, sir, stand up: I am sure you are not 075
Launcelot, my boy.

Laun. Pray you, let's have no more fooling about it,
but give me your blessing: I am Launcelot, your
boy that was, your son that is, your child that
shall be.

Gob. I cannot think you are my son.

080 *Laun.* I know not what I shall think of that: but I
am Launcelot, the Jew's man; and I am sure
Margery your wife is my mother.

Gob. Her name is Margery, indeed: I'll be sworn, if thou be Launcelot, thou art mine own flesh and blood. $_{085}$ Lord worshipped might he be! what a beard hast thou got! thou hast got more hair on thy chin than Dobbin my fill-horse has on his tail.

Laun. It should seem, then, that Dobbin's tail grows backward: I am sure he had more hair of his tail than $_{090}$ I have of my face when I last saw him.

Gob. Lord, how art thou changed! How dost thou and thy master agree? I have brought him a present. How 'gree you now?

Laun. Well, well: but, for mine own part, as I have $_{095}$ set up my rest to run away, so I will not rest till I have run some ground. My master's a very Jew: give him a present! give him a halter: I am famished in his service; you may tell every finger I have with my ribs. Father, I am glad you are come: give me your present to one $_{100}$ Master Bassanio, who, indeed, gives rare new liveries: if I serve not him, I will run as far as God has any ground. O rare fortune! here comes the man: to him, father; for I am a Jew, if I serve the Jew any longer.

Enter BASSANIO, with LEONARDO and other followers.

Bass. You may do so; but let it be so hasted, that $_{105}$ supper be ready at the farthest by five of the clock. See these letters delivered; put the liveries to making; and desire Gratiano to come anon to my lodging. [*Exit a Servant.*

Laun. To him, father.

Gob. God bless your worship!

$_{110}$ *Bass.* Gramercy! wouldst thou aught with me?

Gob. Here's my son, sir, a poor boy,—

Laun. Not a poor boy, sir, but the rich Jew's man; that would, sir,—as my father shall specify,—

Gob. He hath a great infection, sir, as one would say, $_{115}$ to serve,—

Laun. Indeed, the short and the long is, I serve the Jew, and have a desire,—as my father shall specify,—

Gob. His master and he, saving your worship's reverence, are scarce cater-cousins,—

120 *LAUN.* To be brief, the very truth is that the Jew,
having done me wrong, doth cause me,—as my
father, being, I hope, an old man, shall frutify unto
you,—

GOB. I have here a dish of doves that I would bestow
upon your worship, and my suit is,—

125 *LAUN.* In very brief, the suit is impertinent to myself, as your worship shall know by this honest
old man; and, though I say it, though old man, yet
poor man, my father.

BASS. One speak for both. What would you?

LAUN. Serve you, sir.

130 *GOB.* That is the very defect of the matter, sir.

BASS. I know thee well; thou hast obtain'd thy suit:
Shylock thy master spoke with me this day,
And hath preferr'd thee, if it be preferment
To leave a rich Jew's service, to become

135 The follower of so poor a gentleman.

LAUN. The old proverb is very well parted between
my master Shylock and you, sir: you have the
grace of God, sir, and he hath enough.

BASS. Thou speak'st it well. Go, father, with thy son.

140 Take leave of thy old master and inquire
My lodging out. Give him a livery
More guarded than his fellows': see it done.

LAUN. Father, in. I cannot get a service, no; I have
ne'er a tongue in my head. Well, if any man in
Italy have 145 a fairer table which doth offer to
swear upon a book, I shall have good fortune. Go
to, here's a simple line of life: here's a small trifle
of wives: alas, fifteen wives is nothing! a'leven
widows and nine maids is a simple coming-in for
one man: and then to 'scape drowning thrice, 150
and to be in peril of my life with the edge of a
feather-bed; here are simple scapes. Well, if Fortune be a woman, she's a good wench for this
geAR. Father, come; I'll take my leave of the Jew in
the twinkling of an eye. [*Exeunt Launcelot and Old
Gobbo.*

BASS. I pray thee, good Leonardo, think on this:

155 These things being bought and orderly bestow'd,
Return in haste, for I do feast to-night
My best-esteem'd acquaintance: hie thee, go.

Leon. My best endeavours shall be done herein.

Enter Gratiano.

Gra. Where is your master?
Leon. Yonder, sir, he walks. [*Exit.*
160 *Gra.* Signior Bassanio,—
Bass. Gratiano!
Gra. I have a suit to you.
Bass. You have obtain'd it.
Gra. You must not deny me: I must go with you to
    Belmont.
165 *Bass.* Why, then you must. But hear thee,
    Gratiano:
Thou art too wild, too rude, and bold of voice;
Parts that become thee happily enough,
And in such eyes as ours appear not faults;
But where thou art not known, why, there they show
170 Something too liberal. Pray thee, take pain
To allay with some cold drops of modesty
Thy skipping spirit; lest, through thy wild behaviour,
I be misconstrued in the place I go to,
And lose my hopes.
Gra. Signior Bassanio, hear me:
175 If I do not put on a sober habit,
Talk with respect, and swear but now and then,
Wear prayer-books in my pocket, look demurely;
Nay more, while grace is saying, hood mine eyes
Thus with my hat, and sigh, and say 'amen;'
180 Use all the observance of civility,
Like one well studied in a sad ostent
To please his grandam, never trust me more.
Bass. Well, we shall see your bearing.
Gra. Nay, but I bar to-night: you shall not gauge me
By what we do to-night.
185 *Bass.* No, that were pity:
I would entreat you rather to put on
Your boldest suit of mirth, for we have friends
That purpose merriment. But fare you well:
I have some business.
190 *Gra.* And I must to Lorenzo and the rest:
But we will visit you at supper-time. [*Exeunt.*

SCENE III. THE SAME. A ROOM IN SHYLOCK'S HOUSE.

ENTER JESSICA *AND* LAUNCELOT.

JES. I am sorry thou wilt leave my father so:
Our house is hell; and thou, a merry devil,
Didst rob it of some taste of tediousness.
But fare thee well; there is a ducat for thee:
005 And, Launcelot, soon at supper shalt thou see
Lorenzo, who is thy new master's guest:
Give him this letter; do it secretly;
And so farewell: I would not have my father
See me in talk with thee.
010 *LAUN.* Adieu! tears exhibit my tongue. Most beau-
tiful pagan, most sweet Jew! if a Christian did not
play the knave, and get thee, I am much deceived.
But, adieu: these foolish drops do something
drown my manly spirit: adieu.
015 *JES.* Farewell, good Launcelot. [*Exit Launcelot.*
Alack, what heinous sin is it in me
To be ashamed to be my father's child!
But though I am a daughter to his blood,
I am not to his manners. O Lorenzo,
020 If thou keep promise, I shall end this strife,
Become a Christian, and thy loving wife. [*Exit.*

SCENE IV. THE SAME. A STREET.

ENTER GRATIANO, LORENZO, SALARINO, *AND* SALANIO.

LOR. Nay, we will slink away in supper-time,
Disguise us at my lodging, and return
All in an hour.
GRA. We have not made good preparation.
005 *SALAR.* We have not spoke us yet of torch-bearers.
SALAN. 'Tis vile, unless it may be quaintly order'd,
And better in my mind not undertook.
LOR. 'Tis now but four o'clock: we have two hours
To furnish us.

Enter LAUNCELOT, *with a letter.*

Friend Launcelot, what's the news?

010 *LAUN.* An it shall please you to break up this, it
    shall seem to signify.

LOR. I know the hand: in faith, 'tis a fair hand;
And whiter than the paper it writ on
Is the fair hand that writ.

GRA. Love-news, in faith.

015 *LAUN.* By your leave, sir.

LOR. Whither goest thou?

LAUN. Marry, sir, to bid my old master the Jew to sup
    to-night with my new master the Christian.

LOR. Hold here, take this: tell gentle Jessica
020 I will not fail her; speak it privately.
Go, gentlemen, [*Exit Launcelot.*
Will you prepare you for this masque to-night?
I am provided of a torch-bearer.

SALAR. Ay, marry, I'll be gone about it straight.

SALAN. And so will I.

025 *LOR.* Meet me and Gratiano
At Gratiano's lodging some hour hence.

SALAR. 'Tis good we do so. [*Exeunt Salar. and Salan.*

GRA. Was not that letter from fair Jessica?

LOR. I must needs tell thee all. She hath directed
030 How I shall take her from her father's house;
What gold and jewels she is furnish'd with;
What page's suit she hath in readiness.
If e'er the Jew her father come to heaven,
It will be for his gentle daughter's sake:
035 And never dare misfortune cross her foot,
Unless she do it under this excuse,
That she is issue to a faithless Jew.
Come, go with me; peruse this as thou goest:
Fair Jessica shall be my torch-bearer. [*Exeunt.*

SCENE V. THE SAME. BEFORE SHYLOCK'S HOUSE.

ENTER SHYLOCK *AND* LAUNCELOT.

SHY. Well, thou shalt see, thy eyes shall be thy judge,
The difference of old Shylock and Bassanio:—
What, Jessica!—thou shalt not gormandise,
As thou hast done with me:—What, Jessica!—

005 And sleep and snore, and rend apparel out;—
Why, Jessica, I say!
Laun. Why, Jessica!
Shy. Who bids thee call? I do not bid thee call.
Laun. Your worship was wont to tell me that I could
do nothing without bidding.

Enter Jessica.

010 *Jes.* Call you? what is your will?
Shy. I am bid forth to supper, Jessica:
There are my keys. But wherefore should I go?
I am not bid for love; they flatter me:
But yet I'll go in hate, to feed upon
015 The prodigal Christian. Jessica, my girl,
Look to my house. I am right loath to go:
There is some ill a-brewing towards my rest,
For I did dream of money-bags to-night.
Laun. I beseech you, sir, go: my young master doth
020 expect your reproach.
Shy. So do I his.
Laun. And they have conspired together, I will not
say you shall see a masque; but if you do, then it
was not for nothing that my nose fell a-bleeding
on Black-Monday 025 last at six o'clock i' the morn-
ing, falling out that year on Ash-Wednesday was
four year, in the afternoon.
Shy. What, are there masques? Hear you me, Jessica:
Lock up my doors; and when you hear the drum,
And the vile squealing of the wry-neck'd fife,
030 Clamber not you up to the casements then,
Nor thrust your head into the public street
To gaze on Christian fools with varnish'd faces;
But stop my house's ears, I mean my casements:
Let not the sound of shallow foppery enter
035 My sober house. By Jacob's staff, I swear
I have no mind of feasting forth to-night:
But I will go. Go you before me, sirrah;
Say I will come.
Laun. I will go before, sir. Mistress, look out at 040
window, for all this;
There will come a Christian by,
Will be worth a Jewess' eye. [*Exit.*

SHY. What says that fool of Hagar's offspring, ha?
JES. His words were, 'Farewell, mistress;' nothing
  else.
045 SHY. The patch is kind enough, but a huge feeder;
Snail-slow in profit, and he sleeps by day
More than the wild-cat: drones hive not with me;
Therefore I part with him; and part with him
To one that I would have him help to waste
050 His borrow'd purse. Well, Jessica, go in:
Perhaps I will return immediately:
Do as I bid you; shut doors after you:
Fast bind, fast find,
A proverb never stale in thrifty mind. [*Exit.*
055 JES. Farewell; and if my fortune be not crost,
I have a father, you a daughter, lost. [*Exit.*

SCENE VI. THE SAME.

ENTER GRATIANO *AND* SALARINO, *MASQUED.*

GRA. This is the pent-house under which Lorenzo
Desired us to make stand.
SALAR. His hour is almost past.
GRA. And it is marvel he out-dwells his hour,
For lovers ever run before the clock.
005 SALAR. O, ten times faster Venus' pigeons fly
To seal love's bonds new-made, than they are wont
To keep obliged faith unforfeited!
GRA. That ever holds: who riseth from a feast
With that keen appetite that he sits down?
010 Where is the horse that doth untread again
His tedious measures with the unbated fire
That he did pace them first? All things that are,
Are with more spirit chased than enjoy'd.
How like a younker or a prodigal
015 The scarfed bark puts from her native bay,
Hugg'd and embraced by the strumpet wind!
How like the prodigal doth she return,
With over-weather'd ribs and ragged sails,
Lean, rent, and beggar'd by the strumpet wind!
020 SALAR. Here comes Lorenzo: more of this hereafter.

Enter Lorenzo.

Lor. Sweet friends, your patience for my long abode;
Not I, but my affairs, have made you wait:
When you shall please to play the thieves for wives,
I'll watch as long for you then. Approach;
025 Here dwells my father Jew. Ho! who's within?

Enter Jessica, *above, in boy's clothes.*

Jes. Who are you? Tell me, for more certainty,
Albeit I'll swear that I do know your tongue.
Lor. Lorenzo, and thy love.
Jes. Lorenzo, certain; and my love, indeed,
030 For who love I so much? And now who knows
But you, Lorenzo, whether I am yours?
Lor. Heaven and thy thoughts are witness that
        thou art.
Jes. Here, catch this casket; it is worth the pains.
I am glad 'tis night, you do not look on me,
For I am much ashamed of my exchange:
But love is blind, and lovers cannot see
The pretty follies that themselves commit;
For if they could, Cupid himself would blush
To see me thus transformed to a boy.
040 Lor. Descend, for you must be my torch-bearer.
Jes. What, must I hold a candle to my shames?
They in themselves, good sooth, are too too light.
Why, 'tis an office of discovery, love;
And I should be obscured.
Lor. So are you, sweet,
045 Even in the lovely garnish of a boy.
But come at once;
For the close night doth play the runaway,
And we are stay'd for at Bassanio's feast.
Jes. I will make fast the doors, and gild myself
050 With some more ducats, and be with you straight.
        [*Exit above.*
Gra. Now, by my hood, a Gentile, and no Jew.
Lor. Beshrew me but I love her heartily;
For she is wise, if I can judge of her;
And fair she is, if that mine eyes be true;
055 And true she is, as she hath proved herself;

And therefore, like herself, wise, fair, and true,
Shall she be placed in my constant soul.

Enter JESSICA, below.

What, art thou come? On, gentlemen; away!
Our masquing mates by this time for us stay. [*Exit
    with Jessica and Salarino.*

ENTER ANTONIO.

060 *ANT.* Who's there?
GRA. Signior Antonio!
ANT. Fie, fie, Gratiano! where are all the rest?
'Tis nine o'clock: our friends all stay for you.
No masque to-night: the wind is come about;
065 Bassanio presently will go aboard:
I have sent twenty out to seek for you.
GRA. I am glad on't: I desire no more delight
Than to be under sail and gone to-night. [*Exeunt.*

SCENE VII. BELMONT. A ROOM IN PORTIA'S HOUSE.

*Flourish of cornets. Enter PORTIA, with the PRINCE OF MOROCCO,
and their trains.*

POR. Go draw aside the curtains, and discover
The several caskets to this noble prince.
Now make your choice.
MOR. The first, of gold, who this inscription bears,
005 'Who chooseth me shall gain what many men
    desire;'
The second, silver, which this promise carries,
'Who chooseth me shall get as much as he deserves;'
This third, dull lead, with warning all as blunt,
'Who chooseth me must give and hazard all he hath.'
010 How shall I know if I do choose the right?
POR. The one of them contains my picture, prince:
If you choose that, then I am yours withal.
MOR. Some god direct my judgment! Let me see;
I will survey the inscriptions back again.
015 What says this leaden casket?

'Who chooseth me must give and hazard all he hath.'
Must give,—for what? for lead? hazard for lead?
This casket threatens. Men that hazard all
Do it in hope of fair advantages:
020 A golden mind stoops not to shows of dross;
I'll then nor give nor hazard aught for lead.
What says the silver with her virgin hue?
'Who chooseth me shall get as much as he deserves.'
As much as he deserves! Pause there, Morocco,
025 And weigh thy value with an even hand:
If thou be'st rated by thy estimation,
Thou dost deserve enough; and yet enough
May not extend so far as to the lady:
And yet to be afeard of my deserving
030 Were but a weak disabling of myself.
As much as I deserve! Why, that's the lady:
I do in birth deserve her, and in fortunes,
In graces and in qualities of breeding;
But more than these, in love I do deserve.
035 What if I stray'd no further, but chose here?
Let's see once more this saying graved in gold;
'Who chooseth me shall gain what many men desire.'
Why, that's the lady; all the world desires her;
From the four corners of the earth they come,
040 To kiss this shrine, this mortal-breathing saint:
The Hyrcanian deserts and the vasty wilds
Of wide Arabia are as throughfares now
For princes to come view fair Portia:
The watery kingdom, whose ambitious head
045 Spits in the face of heaven, is no bar
To stop the foreign spirits; but they come,
As o'er a brook, to see fair Portia.
One of these three contains her heavenly picture.
Is't like that lead contains her? 'Twere damnation
050 To think so base a thought: it were too gross
To rib her cerecloth in the obscure grave.
Or shall I think in silver she's immured,
Being ten times undervalued to tried gold?
O sinful thought! Never so rich a gem
055 Was set in worse than gold. They have in England
A coin that bears the figure of an angel
Stamped in gold, but that's insculp'd upon;
But here an angel in a golden bed

Lies all within. Deliver me the key:
060 Here do I choose, and thrive I as I may!
Por. There, take it, prince; and if my form lie there,
Then I am yours. [He unlocks the golden casket.
Mor. O hell! what have we here?
A carrion Death, within whose empty eye
There is a written scroll! I'll read the writing. [*Reads.*
065 All that glisters is not gold;
Often have you heard that told:
Many a man his life hath sold
But my outside to behold:
Gilded tombs do worms infold.
070 Had you been as wise as bold,
Young in limbs, in judgment old,
Your answer had not been inscroll'd:
Fare you well; your suit is cold.
Cold, indeed; and labour lost:
075 Then, farewell, heat, and welcome, frost!
Portia, adieu. I have too grieved a heart
To take a tedious leave: thus losers part. [*Exit with his
    train. Flourish of cornets.*
Por. A gentle riddance. Draw the curtains, go.
Let all of his complexion choose me so. [*Exeunt.*

SCENE VIII. VENICE. A STREET.

Enter Salarino *and* Salanio.

Salar. Why, man, I saw Bassanio under sail:
With him is Gratiano gone along;
And in their ship I am sure Lorenzo is not.
Salan. The villain Jew with outcries raised the Duke,
005 Who went with him to search Bassanio's ship.
Salar. He came too late, the ship was under sail:
But there the Duke was given to understand
That in a gondola were seen together
Lorenzo and his amorous Jessica:
010 Besides, Antonio certified the Duke
They were not with Bassanio in his ship.
Salan. I never heard a passion so confused,
So strange, outrageous, and so variable,
As the dog Jew did utter in the streets:

015 'My daughter! O my ducats! O my daughter!
Fled with a Christian! O my Christian ducats!
Justice! the law! my ducats, and my daughter!
A sealed bag, two sealed bags of ducats,
Of double ducats, stolen from me by my daughter!
020 And jewels, two stones, two rich and precious
    stones,
Stolen by my daughter! Justice! find the girl!
She hath the stones upon her, and the ducats!'
SALAR. Why, all the boys in Venice follow him,
Crying, his stones, his daughter, and his ducats.
025 *SALAN.* Let good Antonio look he keep his day,
Or he shall pay for this.
SALAR. Marry, well remember'd.
I reason'd with a Frenchman yesterday,
Who told me, in the narrow seas that part
The French and English, there miscarried
030 A vessel of our country richly fraught:
I thought upon Antonio when he told me;
And wish'd in silence that it were not his.
SALAN. You were best to tell Antonio what you hear;
Yet do not suddenly, for it may grieve him.
035 *SALAR.* A kinder gentleman treads not the earth.
I saw Bassanio and Antonio part:
Bassanio told him he would make some speed
Of his return: he answer'd, 'Do not so;
Slubber not business for my sake, Bassanio,
040 But stay the very riping of the time;
And for the Jew's bond which he hath of me,
Let it not enter in your mind of love:
Be merry; and employ your chiefest thoughts
To courtship, and such fair ostents of love
045 As shall conveniently become you there:'
And even there, his eye being big with tears,
Turning his face, he put his hand behind him,
And with affection wondrous sensible
He wrung Bassanio's hand; and so they parted.
050 *SALAN.* I think he only loves the world for him.
I pray thee, let us go and find him out,
And quicken his embraced heaviness
With some delight or other.
SALAR. Do we so. [*Exeunt.*

SCENE IX. BELMONT. A ROOM IN PORTIA'S HOUSE.

Enter Nerissa *with a* Servitor.

Ner. Quick, quick, I pray thee; draw the curtain
    straight:
The Prince of Arragon hath ta'en his oath,
And comes to his election presently.

Flourish of cornets. Enter the Prince of Arragon, Portia, *and
their trains.*

Por. Behold, there stand the caskets, noble prince:
005 If you choose that wherein I am contain'd,
Straight shall our nuptial rites be solemnized:
But if you fail, without more speech, my lord,
You must be gone from hence immediately.
Ar. I am enjoin'd by oath to observe three things:
010 First, never to unfold to any one
Which casket 'twas I chose; next, if I fail
Of the right casket, never in my life
To woo a maid in way of marriage:
Lastly,
015 If I do fail in fortune of my choice,
Immediately to leave you and be gone.
Por. To these injunctions every one doth swear
That comes to hazard for my worthless self.
Ar. And so have I address'd me. Fortune now
020 To my heart's hope! Gold; silver; and base lead.
'Who chooseth me must give and hazard all he hath.'
You shall look fairer, ere I give or hazard.
What says the golden chest? ha! let me see:
'Who chooseth me shall gain what many men desire.'
025 What many men desire! that 'many' may be meant
By the fool multitude, that choose by show,
Not learning more than the fond eye doth teach;
Which pries not to the interior, but, like the martlet,
Builds in the weather on the outward wall,
030 Even in the force and road of casualty.
I will not choose what many men desire,
Because I will not jump with common spirits,
And rank me with the barbarous multitudes.

Why, then to thee, thou silver treasure-house;
035 Tell me once more what title thou dost bear:
'Who chooseth me shall get as much as he deserves:'
And well said too; for who shall go about
To cozen fortune, and be honourable
Without the stamp of merit? Let none presume
040 To wear an undeserved dignity.
O, that estates, degrees and offices
Were not derived corruptly, and that clear honour
Were purchased by the merit of the wearer!
How many then should cover that stand bare!
045 How many be commanded that command!
How much low peasantry would then be glean'd
From the true seed of honour! and how much honour
Pick'd from the chaff and ruin of the times,
To be new-varnish'd! Well, but to my choice:
050 'Who chooseth me shall get as much as he
    deserves.'
I will assume desert. Give me a key for this,
And instantly unlock my fortunes here. [*He opens the
    silver casket.*
Por. Too long a pause for that which you find there.
Ar. What's here? the portrait of a blinking idiot,
055 Presenting me a schedule! I will read it.
How much unlike art thou to Portia!
How much unlike my hopes and my deservings!
'Who chooseth me shall have as much as he
    deserves.'
Did I deserve no more than a fool's head?
060 Is that my prize? are my deserts no better?
Por. To offend, and judge, are distinct offices,
And of opposed natures.
Ar. What is here? [*Reads*]
The fire seven times tried this;
Seven times tried that judgement is,
065 That did never choose amiss.
Some there be that shadows kiss;
Such have but a shadow's bliss:
There be fools alive, I wis,
Silver'd o'er; and so was this.
070 Take what wife you will to bed,
I will ever be your head:
So be gone: you are sped.

Still more fool I shall appear
By the time I linger here:
075 With one fool's head I came to woo,
But I go away with two.
Sweet, adieu. I'll keep my oath,
Patiently to bear my wroth. [*Exeunt Arragon and train.*
Por. Thus hath the candle singed the moth.
080 O, these deliberate fools! when they do choose,
They have the wisdom by their wit to lose.
Ner. The ancient saying is no heresy,
Hanging and wiving goes by destiny.
Por. Come, draw the curtain, Nerissa.

Enter a Servant.

Serv. Where is my lady?
085 *Por.* Here: what would my lord?
Serv. Madam, there is alighted at your gate
A young Venetian, one that comes before
To signify the approaching of his lord;
From whom he bringeth sensible regreets,
090 To wit, besides commends and courteous breath,
Gifts of rich value. Yet I have not seen
So likely an ambassador of love:
A day in April never came so sweet,
To show how costly summer was at hand,
095 As this fore-spurrer comes before his lord.
Por. No more, I pray thee: I am half afeard
Thou wilt say anon he is some kin to thee,
Thou spend'st such high-day wit in praising him.
Come, come, Nerissa; for I long to see
100 Quick Cupid's post that comes so mannerly.
Ner. Bassanio, lord Love, if thy will it be! [*Exeunt.*

ACT III

ENTER SALANIO *AND* SALARINO.

SALAN. Now, what news on the Rialto?

SALAR. Why, yet it lives there unchecked, that Antonio hath a ship of rich lading wrecked on the narrow seas; the Goodwins, I think they call the place; a very dangerous flat $_{005}$ and fatal, where the carcases of many a tall ship lie buried, as they say, if my gossip Report be an honest woman of her word.

SALAN. I would she were as lying a gossip in that as ever knapped ginger, or made her neighbours believe she wept $_{010}$ for the death of a third husband. But it is true, without any slips of prolixity, or crossing the plain highway of talk, that the good Antonio, the honest Antonio,——O that I had a title good enough to keep his name company!—

SALAR. Come, the full stop.

$_{015}$ **SALAN.** Ha! what sayest thou? Why, the end is, he hath lost a ship.

SALAR. I would it might prove the end of his losses.

SALAN. Let me say 'amen' betimes, lest the devil cross my prayer, for here he comes in the likeness of a Jew.

Enter Shylock.

020 How now, Shylock! what news among the
merchants?

Shy. You knew, none so well, none so well as you, of
my daughter's flight.

Salar. That's certain: I, for my part, knew the tailor
that made the wings she flew withal.

025 Salan. And Shylock, for his own part, knew the
bird was fledged; and then it is the complexion of
them all to leave the dam.

Shy. She is damned for it.

Salar. That's certain, if the devil may be her judge.

030 Shy. My own flesh and blood to rebel!

Salar. Out upon it, old carrion! rebels it at these
years?

Shy. I say, my daughter is my flesh and blood.

Salar. There is more difference between thy flesh and
hers than between jet and ivory; more between
your bloods 035 than there is between red wine
and rhenish. But tell us, do you hear whether Antonio have had any loss at sea or no?

Shy. There I have another bad match: a bankrupt, a
prodigal, who dare scarce show his head on the
Rialto; a beggar, that was used to come so smug
upon the mart; let 040 him look to his bond: he was
wont to call me usurer; let him look to his bond:
he was wont to lend money for a Christian courtesy; let him look to his bond.

Salar. Why, I am sure, if he forfeit, thou wilt not take
his flesh: what's that good for?

045 Shy. To bait fish withal: if it will feed nothing else,
it will feed my revenge. He hath disgraced me,
and hindered me half a million; laughed at my
losses, mocked at my gains, scorned my nation,
thwarted my bargains, cooled my friends, heated
mine enemies; and what's his reason? I am 050 a
Jew. Hath not a Jew eyes? hath not a Jew hands,
organs, dimensions, senses, affections, passions?
fed with the same food, hurt with the same
weapons, subject to the same diseases, healed by
the same means, warmed and cooled by the same
winter and summer, as a Christian is? If you prick

us, do we not bleed? if you tickle us, do we not
laugh? if you poison us, do we not die? and if you
wrong us, shall we not revenge? if we are like you
in the rest, we will resemble you in that. If a Jew
wrong a Christian, what is his humility? Revenge.
If a Christian wrong a Jew, what should his sufferance be by Christian example? Why, revenge.
The villany you teach me, I will execute; and it
shall go hard but I will better the instruction.

Enter a Servant.

SERV. Gentlemen, my master Antonio is at his house,
and desires to speak with you both.
SALAR. We have been up and down to seek him.

Enter TUBAL.

SALAN. Here comes another of the tribe: a third cannot
be matched, unless the devil himself turn Jew.
[*Exeunt* SALAN. SALAR. *and Servant.*
SHY. How now, Tubal! what news from Genoa? hast
thou found my daughter?
TUB. I often came where I did hear of her, but
cannot find her.
SHY. Why, there, there, there, there! a diamond gone,
cost me two thousand ducats in Frankfort! The
curse never fell upon our nation till now; I never
felt it till now: two thousand ducats in that; and
other precious, precious jewels. I would my
daughter were dead at my foot, and the jewels in
her ear! would she were hearsed at my foot, and
the ducats in her coffin! No news of them? Why,
so:— and I know not what's spent in the search:
why, thou loss upon loss! the thief gone with so
much, and so much to find the thief; and no satisfaction, no revenge: nor no ill luck stirring but
what lights on my shoulders; no sighs but of my
breathing; no tears but of my shedding.
TUB. Yes, other men have ill luck too: Antonio, as I
heard in Genoa,—
SHY. What, what, what? ill luck, ill luck?
TUB. Hath an argosy cast away, coming from Tripolis.

Shy. I thank God, I thank God! Is't true, is't true?

Tub. I spoke with some of the sailors that escaped the 090 wreck.

Shy. I thank thee, good Tubal: good news, good news! ha, ha! where? in Genoa?

Tub. Your daughter spent in Genoa, as I heard, in one night fourscore ducats.

095 *Shy.* Thou stickest a dagger in me: I shall never see my gold again: fourscore ducats at a sitting! fourscore ducats.

Tub. There came divers of Antonio's creditors in my company to Venice, that swear he cannot choose but break.

100 *Shy.* I am very glad of it: I'll plague him; I'll torture him: I am glad of it.

Tub. One of them showed me a ring that he had of your daughter for a monkey.

Shy. Out upon her! Thou torturest me, Tubal: it 105 was my turquoise; I had it of Leah when I was a bachelor: I would not have given it for a wilderness of monkeys.

Tub. But Antonio is certainly undone.

Shy. Nay, that's true, that's very true. Go, Tubal, fee me an officer; bespeak him a fortnight before. I will 110 have the heart of him, if he forfeit; for, were he out of Venice, I can make what merchandise I will. Go, go, Tubal, and meet me at our synagogue; go, good Tubal; at our synagogue, Tubal. [*Exeunt.*

SCENE II. BELMONT. A ROOM IN PORTIA'S HOUSE.

Enter Bassanio, Portia, Gratiano, Nerissa, *and* Attendants.

Por. I pray you, tarry: pause a day or two
Before you hazard; for, in choosing wrong,
I lose your company: therefore forbear awhile.
There's something tells me, but it is not love,
005 I would not lose you; and you know yourself,
Hate counsels not in such a quality.
But lest you should not understand me well,—

And yet a maiden hath no tongue but thought,—
I would detain you here some month or two
$_{010}$ Before you venture for me. I could teach you
How to choose right, but I am then forsworn;
So will I never be: so may you miss me;
But if you do, you'll make me wish a sin,
That I had been forsworn. Beshrew your eyes,
$_{015}$ They have o'er-look'd me, and divided me;
One half of me is yours, the other half yours.
Mine own, I would say; but if mine, then yours,
And so all yours! O, these naughty times
Put bars between the owners and their rights!
$_{020}$ And so, though yours, not yours. Prove it so,
Let fortune go to hell for it, not I.
I speak too long; but 'tis to peize the time,
To eke it and to draw it out in length,
To stay you from election.
Bass. Let me choose;
$_{025}$ For as I am, I live upon the rack.
Por. Upon the rack, Bassanio! then confess
What treason there is mingled with your love.
Bass. None but that ugly treason of mistrust,
Which makes me fear the enjoying of my love:
$_{030}$ There may as well be amity and life
'Tween snow and fire, as treason and my love.
Por. Ay, but I fear you speak upon the rack,
Where men enforced do speak any thing.
Bass. Promise me life, and I'll confess the truth.
Por. Well then, confess and live.
$_{035}$ *Bass.* 'Confess,' and 'love,'
Had been the very sum of my confession:
O happy torment, when my torturer
Doth teach me answers for deliverance!
But let me to my fortune and the caskets.
$_{040}$ *Por.* Away, then! I am lock'd in one of them:
If you do love me, you will find me out.
Nerissa and the rest, stand all aloof.
Let music sound while he doth make his choice;
Then, if he lose, he makes a swan-like end,
$_{045}$ Fading in music: that the comparison
May stand more proper, my eye shall be the stream,
And watery death-bed for him. He may win;
And what is music then? Then music is

Even as the flourish when true subjects bow
050 To a new-crowned monarch: such it is
As are those dulcet sounds in break of day
That creep into the dreaming bridegroom's ear,
And summon him to marriage. Now he goes,
With no less presence, but with much more love,
055 Than young Alcides, when he did redeem
The virgin tribute paid by howling Troy
To the sea-monster: I stand for sacrifice;
The rest aloof are the Dardanian wives,
With bleared visages, come forth to view
060 The issue of the exploit. Go, Hercules!
Live thou, I live: with much much more dismay
I view the fight than thou that makest the fray.

Music, whilst Bassanio *comments on the caskets to himself.*
Song.

Tell me where is fancy bred,
Or in the heart or in the head?
065 How begot, how nourished?
Reply, reply.
It is engender'd in the eye,
With gazing fed; and fancy dies
In the cradle where it lies.
070 Let us all ring fancy's knell;
I'll begin it,—Ding, dong, bell.
All. Ding, dong, bell.
Bass. So may the outward shows be least themselves:
The world is still deceived with ornament.
075 In law, what plea so tainted and corrupt,
But, being seasoned with a gracious voice,
Obscures the show of evil? In religion,
What damned error, but some sober brow
Will bless it, and approve it with a text,
080 Hiding the grossness with fair ornament?
There is no vice so simple, but assumes
Some mark of virtue on his outward parts:
How many cowards, whose hearts are all as false
As stairs of sand, wear yet upon their chins
085 The beards of Hercules and frowning Mars;
Who, inward search'd, have livers white as milk;
And these assume but valour's excrement

To render them redoubted! Look on beauty,
And you shall see 'tis purchased by the weight;
090 Which therein works a miracle in nature,
Making them lightest that wear most of it:
So are those crisped snaky golden locks
Which make such wanton gambols with the wind,
Upon supposed fairness, often known
095 To be the dowry of a second head,
The skull that bred them in the sepulchre.
Thus ornament is but the guiled shore
To a most dangerous sea; the beauteous scarf
Veiling an Indian beauty; in a word,
100 The seeming truth which cunning times put on
To entrap the wisest. Therefore, thou gaudy gold,
Hard food for Midas, I will none of thee;
Nor none of thee, thou pale and common drudge
'Tween man and man: but thou, thou meagre lead,
105 Which rather threatenest than dost promise aught,
Thy paleness moves me more than eloquence;
And here choose I: joy be the consequence!
Por. [*Aside*] How all the other passions fleet to air,
As doubtful thoughts, and rash-embraced despair,
110 And shuddering fear, and green-eyed jealousy!
O love, be moderate; allay thy ecstasy;
In measure rein thy joy; scant this excess!
I feel too much thy blessing: make it less,
For fear I surfeit!
Bass. What find I here? [*Opening the leaden casket.*
115 Fair Portia's counterfeit! What demi-god
Hath come so near creation? Move these eyes?
Or whether, riding on the balls of mine,
Seem they in motion? Here are sever'd lips,
Parted with sugar breath: so sweet a bar
120 Should sunder such sweet friends. Here in her hairs
The painter plays the spider, and hath woven
A golden mesh to entrap the hearts of men,
Faster than gnats in cobwebs: but her eyes,—
How could he see to do them? having made one,
125 Methinks it should have power to steal both his
And leave itself unfurnish'd. Yet look, how far
The substance of my praise doth wrong this shadow
In underprizing it, so far this shadow

Doth limp behind the substance. Here's the scroll,
130 The continent and summary of my fortune.
[*Reads*]
You that choose not by the view,
Chance as fair, and choose as true!
Since this fortune falls to you,
Be content and seek no new.
135 If you be well pleased with this,
And hold your fortune for your bliss,
Turn you where your lady is,
And claim her with a loving kiss.
A gentle scroll. Fair lady, by your leave;
140 I come by note, to give and to receive.
Like one of two contending in a prize,
That thinks he hath done well in people's eyes,
Hearing applause and universal shout,
Giddy in spirit, still gazing in a doubt
145 Whether those peals of praise be his or no;
So, thrice-fair lady, stand I, even so;
As doubtful whether what I see be true,
Until confirm'd, sign'd, ratified by you.
Por. You see me, Lord Bassanio, where I stand,
150 Such as I am: though for myself alone
I would not be ambitious in my wish,
To wish myself much better; yet, for you
I would be trebled twenty times myself;
A thousand times more fair, ten thousand times
155 More rich;
That only to stand high in your account,
I might in virtues, beauties, livings, friends,
Exceed account; but the full sum of me
Is sum of something, which, to term in gross,
160 Is an unlesson'd girl, unschool'd, unpractised;
Happy in this, she is not yet so old
But she may learn; happier than this,
She is not bred so dull but she can learn;
Happiest of all is that her gentle spirit
165 Commits itself to yours to be directed,
As from her lord, her governor, her king.
Myself and what is mine to you and yours
Is now converted: but now I was the lord
Of this fair mansion, master of my servants,
170 Queen o'er myself; and even now, but now,

This house, these servants, and this same myself,
Are yours, my lord: I give them with this ring;
Which when you part from, lose, or give away,
Let it presage the ruin of your love,
175 And be my vantage to exclaim on you.
Bass. Madam, you have bereft me of all words,
Only my blood speaks to you in my veins;
And there is such confusion in my powers,
As, after some oration fairly spoke
180 By a beloved prince, there doth appear
Among the buzzing pleased multitude;
Where every something, being blent together,
Turns to a wild of nothing, save of joy,
Express'd and not express'd. But when this ring
185 Parts from this finger, then parts life from hence:
O, then be bold to say Bassanio's dead!
Ner. My lord and lady, it is now our time,
That have stood by and seen our wishes prosper,
To cry, good joy: good joy, my lord and lady!
190 *Gra.* My Lord Bassanio and my gentle lady,
I wish you all the joy that you can wish;
For I am sure you can wish none from me:
And when your honours mean to solemnize
The bargain of your faith, I do beseech you,
195 Even at that time I may be married too.
Bass. With all my heart, so thou canst get a wife.
Gra. I thank your lordship, you have got me one.
My eyes, my lord, can look as swift as yours:
You saw the mistress, I beheld the maid;
200 You loved, I loved for intermission.
No more pertains to me, my lord, than you.
Your fortune stood upon the casket there,
And so did mine too, as the matter falls;
For wooing here until I sweat again,
205 And swearing till my very roof was dry
With oaths of love, at last, if promise last,
I got a promise of this fair one here
To have her love, provided that your fortune
Achieved her mistress.
Por. Is this true, Nerissa?
210 *Ner.* Madam, it is, so you stand pleased withal.
Bass. And do you, Gratiano, mean good faith?
Gra. Yes, faith, my lord.

Bass. Our feast shall be much honour'd in your
   marriage.
Gra. We'll play with them the first boy for a thousand
   215 ducats.
Ner. What, and stake down?
Gra. No; we shall ne'er win at that sport, and stake
   down.
   220 But who comes here? Lorenzo and his infidel?
What, and my old Venetian friend Salerio?

Enter LORENZO, JESSICA, *and* SALERIO, *a Messenger from Venice.*

Bass. Lorenzo and Salerio, welcome hither;
If that the youth of my new interest here
Have power to bid you welcome. By your leave,
   225 I bid my very friends and countrymen,
Sweet Portia, welcome.
Por. So do I, my lord:
They are entirely welcome.
Lor. I thank your honour. For my part, my lord,
My purpose was not to have seen you here;
   230 But meeting with Salerio by the way,
He did entreat me, past all saying nay,
To come with him along.
Saler. I did, my lord;
And I have reason for it. Signior Antonio
Commends him to you. [Gives Bassanio a letter.
Bass. Ere I ope his letter,
   235 I pray you, tell me how my good friend doth.
Saler. Not sick, my lord, unless it be in mind;
Nor well, unless in mind: his letter there
Will show you his estate.
Gra. Nerissa, cheer yon stranger; bid her welcome.
   240 Your hand, Salerio: what's the news from Venice?
How doth that royal merchant, good Antonio?
I know he will be glad of our success;
We are the Jasons, we have won the fleece.
Saler. I would you had won the fleece that he hath
   lost.
   245 *Por.* There are some shrewd contents in yon same
   paper,
That steals the colour from Bassanio's cheek:
Some dear friend dead; else nothing in the world

Could turn so much the constitution
Of any constant man. What, worse and worse!
250 With leave, Bassanio; I am half yourself,
And I must freely have the half of any thing
That this same paper brings you.
Bass. O sweet Portia,
Here are a few of the unpleasant'st words
That ever blotted paper! Gentle lady,
255 When I did first impart my love to you,
I freely told you, all the wealth I had
Ran in my veins, I was a gentleman;
And then I told you true: and yet, dear lady,
Rating myself at nothing, you shall see
260 How much I was a braggart. When I told you
My state was nothing, I should then have told you
That I was worse than nothing; for, indeed,
I have engaged myself to a dear friend,
Engaged my friend to his mere enemy,
265 To feed my means. Here is a letter, lady;
The paper as the body of my friend,
And every word in it a gaping wound,
Issuing life-blood. But is it true, Salerio?
Have all his ventures fail'd? What, not one hit?
270 From Tripolis, from Mexico, and England,
From Lisbon, Barbary, and India?
And not one vessel scape the dreadful touch
Of merchant-marring rocks?
Saler. Not one, my lord.
Besides, it should appear, that if he had
275 The present money to discharge the Jew,
He would not take it. Never did I know
A creature, that did bear the shape of man,
So keen and greedy to confound a man:
He plies the Duke at morning and at night;
280 And doth impeach the freedom of the state,
If they deny him justice: twenty merchants,
The Duke himself, and the magnificoes
Of greatest port, have all persuaded with him;
But none can drive him from the envious plea
285 Of forfeiture, of justice, and his bond.
Jes. When I was with him I have heard him swear
To Tubal and to Chus, his countrymen,
That he would rather have Antonio's flesh

Than twenty times the value of the sum
290 That he did owe him: and I know, my lord,
If law, authority and power deny not,
It will go hard with poor Antonio.

Por. Is it your dear friend that is thus in trouble?

Bass. The dearest friend to me, the kindest man,
295 The best-condition'd and unwearied spirit
In doing courtesies; and one in whom
The ancient Roman honour more appears
Than any that draws breath in Italy.

Por. What sum owes he the Jew?

Bass. For me three thousand ducats.

300 *Por.* What, no more?
Pay him six thousand, and deface the bond;
Double six thousand, and then treble that,
Before a friend of this description
Shall lose a hair through Bassanio's fault.
305 First go with me to church and call me wife,
And then away to Venice to your friend;
For never shall you lie by Portia's side
With an unquiet soul. You shall have gold
To pay the petty debt twenty times over:
310 When it is paid, bring your true friend along.
My maid Nerissa and myself meantime
Will live as maids and widows. Come, away!
For you shall hence upon your wedding-day:
Bid your friends welcome, show a merry cheer:
315 Since you are dear bought, I will love you de*ar*.
But let me hear the letter of your friend.

Bass. [*reads*] Sweet Bassanio, my ships have all miscarried, my creditors grow cruel, my estate is very
low, my bond to the Jew is forfeit; and since in
paying it, it is impossible I should live, all 320 debts
are cleared between you and I, if I might but see
you at my death. Notwithstanding, use your pleasure: if your love do not persuade you to come, let
not my letter.

Por. O love, dispatch all business, and be gone!

Bass. Since I have your good leave to go away,
325 I will make haste: but, till I come again,
No bed shall e'er be guilty of my stay,
No rest be interposer 'twixt us twain. [*Exeunt.*

SCENE III. VENICE. A STREET.

ENTER SHYLOCK, SALARINO, ANTONIO, *AND* GAOLER.

SHY. Gaoler, look to him: tell not me of mercy;
This is the fool that lent out money gratis:
Gaoler, look to him.
ANT. Hear me yet, good Shylock.
SHY. I'll have my bond; speak not against my bond:
005 I have sworn an oath that I will have my bond.
Thou call'dst me dog before thou hadst a cause;
But, since I am a dog, beware my fangs:
The Duke shall grant me justice. I do wonder,
Thou naughty gaoler, that thou art so fond
010 To come abroad with him at his request.
ANT. I pray thee, hear me speak.
SHY. I'll have my bond; I will not hear thee speak:
I'll have my bond; and therefore speak no more.
I'll not be made a soft and dull-eyed fool,
015 To shake the head, relent, and sigh, and yield
To Christian intercessors. Follow not;
I'll have no speaking: I will have my bond. [*Exit.*
SALAR. It is the most impenetrable cur
That ever kept with men.
ANT. Let him alone:
020 I'll follow him no more with bootless prayers.
He seeks my life; his reason well I know:
I oft deliver'd from his forfeitures
Many that have at times made moan to me;
Therefore he hates me.
SALAR. I am sure the Duke
025 Will never grant this forfeiture to hold.
ANT. The Duke cannot deny the course of law:
For the commodity that strangers have
With us in Venice, if it be denied,
Will much impeach the justice of his state;
030 Since that the trade and profit of the city
Consisteth of all nations. Therefore, go:
These griefs and losses have so bated me,
That I shall hardly spare a pound of flesh
To-morrow to my bloody creditor.
035 Well, gaoler, on. Pray God, Bassanio come

To see me pay his debt, and then I care not! [*Exeunt.*

SCENE IV. BELMONT. A ROOM IN PORTIA'S HOUSE

ENTER PORTIA, NERISSA, LORENZO, JESSICA, *AND* BALTHASAR.

LOR. Madam, although I speak it in your presence,
You have a noble and a true conceit
Of god-like amity; which appears most strongly
In bearing thus the absence of your lord.
005 But if you knew to whom you show this honour.
How true a gentleman you send relief,
How dear a lover of my lord your husband,
I know you would be prouder of the work
Than customary bounty can enforce you.
010 POR. I never did repent for doing good,
Nor shall not now: for in companions
That do converse and waste the time together,
Whose souls do bear an equal yoke of love,
There must be needs a like proportion
015 Of lineaments, of manners and of spirit;
Which makes me think that this Antonio,
Being the bosom lover of my lord,
Must needs be like my lord. If it be so,
How little is the cost I have bestow'd
020 In purchasing the semblance of my soul
From out the state of hellish misery!
This comes too near the praising of myself;
Therefore no more of it: hear other things.
Lorenzo, I commit into your hands
025 The husbandry and manage of my house
Until my lord's return: for mine own part,
I have toward heaven breathed a secret vow
To live in prayer and contemplation,
Only attended by Nerissa here,
030 Until her husband and my lord's return:
There is a monastery two miles off;
And there will we abide. I do desire you
Not to deny this imposition;
The which my love and some necessity
Now lays upon you.
035 LOR. Madam, with all my heart;

I shall obey you in all fair commands.
Por. My people do already know my mind,
And will acknowledge you and Jessica
In place of Lord Bassanio and myself.
040 And so farewell, till we shall meet again.
Lor. Fair thoughts and happy hours attend on you!
Jes. I wish your ladyship all heart's content.
Por. I thank you for your wish, and am well pleased
To wish it back on you: fare you well, Jessica. [*Exeunt
Jessica and Lorenzo.*
045 Now, Balthasar,
As I have ever found thee honest-true,
So let me find thee still. Take this same letter,
And use thou all the endeavour of a man
In speed to Padua: see thou render this
050 Into my cousin's hand, Doctor Bellario;
And, look, what notes and garments he doth give
thee,
Bring them, I pray thee, with imagined speed
Unto the tranect, to the common ferry
Which trades to Venice. Waste no time in words,
055 But get thee gone: I shall be there before thee.
Balth. Madam, I go with all convenient speed. [*Exit.*
Por. Come on, Nerissa; I have work in hand
That you yet know not of: we'll see our husbands
Before they think of us.
Ner. Shall they see us?
060 *Por.* They shall, Nerissa; but in such a habit,
That they shall think we are accomplished
With that we lack. I'll hold thee any wager,
When we are both accoutred like young men,
I'll prove the prettier fellow of the two,
065 And wear my dagger with the braver grace,
And speak between the change of man and boy
With a reed voice, and turn two mincing steps
Into a manly stride, and speak of frays
Like a fine bragging youth; and tell quaint lies,
070 How honourable ladies sought my love,
Which I denying, they fell sick and died;
I could not do withal: then I'll repent,
And wish, for all that, that I had not kill'd them;
And twenty of these puny lies I'll tell,
075 That men shall swear I have discontinued school

Above a twelvemonth. I have within my mind
A thousand raw tricks of these bragging Jacks,
Which I will practise.
NER. Why, shall we turn to men?
POR. Fie, what a question's that,
080 If thou wert near a lewd interpreter!
But come, I'll tell thee all my whole device
When I am in my coach, which stays for us
At the park-gate; and therefore haste away,
For we must measure twenty miles to-day. [*Exeunt.*

SCENE V. THE SAME. A GARDEN.

ENTER LAUNCELOT AND JESSICA.

LAUN. Yes, truly; for, look you, the sins of the father
are to be laid upon the children: therefore, I
promise ye, I fear you. I was always plain with
you, and so now I speak my agitation of the matter: therefore be of good 005 cheer; for, truly, I think
you are damned. There is but one hope in it that
can do you any good; and that is but a kind of bastard hope neither.

JES. And what hope is that, I pray thee?

LAUN. Marry, you may partly hope that your father 010
got you not, that you are not the Jew's daughter.

JES. That were a kind of bastard hope, indeed: so the
sins of my mother should be visited upon me.

LAUN. Truly then I fear you are damned both by father and mother: thus when I shun Scylla, your father, I fall 015 into Charybdis, your mother: well,
you are gone both ways.

JES. I shall be saved by my husband; he hath made me
a Christian.

LAUN. Truly, the more to blame he: we were Christians enow before; e'en as many as could well live,
one by 020 another. This making of Christians will
raise the price of hogs: if we grow all to be pork-
eaters, we shall not shortly have a rasher on the
coals for money.

ENTER LORENZO.

Jes. I'll tell my husband, Launcelot, what you say:
here he comes.

025 *Lor.* I shall grow jealous of you shortly, Launcelot,
if you thus get my wife into corners.

Jes. Nay, you need not fear us, Lorenzo: Launcelot
and I are out. He tells me flatly, there is no mercy
for me in heaven, because I am a Jew's daughter:
and he says, 030 you are no good member of the
commonwealth; for, in converting Jews to Christians, you raise the price of pork.

Lor. I shall answer that better to the commonwealth
than you can the getting up of the negro's belly:
the Moor is with child by you, Launcelot.

035 *Laun.* It is much that the Moor should be more
than reason: but if she be less than an honest
woman, she is indeed more than I took her for.

Lor. How every fool can play upon the word! I think
the best grace of wit will shortly turn into silence;
and discourse 040 grow commendable in none only
but parrots. Go in, sirrah; bid them prepare for
dinner.

Laun. That is done, sir; they have all stomachs.

Lor. Goodly Lord, what a wit-snapper are you! then
bid them prepare dinner.

045 *Laun.* That is done too, sir; only 'cover' is the
word.

Lor. Will you cover, then, sir?

Laun. Not so, sir, neither; I know my duty.

Lor. Yet more quarrelling with occasion! Wilt thou
show the whole wealth of thy wit in an instant? I
pray 050 thee, understand a plain man in his plain
meaning: go to thy fellows; bid them cover the table, serve in the meat, and we will come in to
dinner.

Laun. For the table, sir, it shall be served in; for the
meat, sir, it shall be covered; for your coming in to
dinner, 055 sir, why, let it be as humours and conceits shall govern. [*Exit.*

Lor. O dear discretion, how his words are suited!
The fool hath planted in his memory
An army of good words; and I do know
A many fools, that stand in better place,
060 Garnish'd like him, that for a tricksy word

121

Defy the matter. How cheer'st thou, Jessica?
And now, good sweet, say thy opinion,
How dost thou like the Lord Bassanio's wife?
Jes. Past all expressing. It is very meet
065 The Lord Bassanio live an upright life;
For, having such a blessing in his lady,
He finds the joys of heaven here on earth;
And if on earth he do not mean it, then
In reason he should never come to heaven.
070 Why, if two gods should play some heavenly
    match
And on the wager lay two earthly women,
And Portia one, there must be something else
Pawn'd with the other; for the poor rude world
Hath not her fellow.
Lor. Even such a husband
075 Hast thou of me as she is for a wife.
Jes. Nay, but ask my opinion too of that.
Lor. I will anon: first, let us go to dinner.
Jes. Nay, let me praise you while I have a stomach.
Lor. No, pray thee, let it serve for table-talk;
080 Then, howsoe'er thou speak'st, 'mong other things
I shall digest it.
Jes. Well, I'll set you forth. [*Exeunt.*

ACT IV

SCENE I. VENICE. A COURT OF JUSTICE.

ENTER THE DUKE, *THE* MAGNIFICOES, ANTONIO, BASSANIO,
GRATIANO, SALERIO, *AND OTHERS*.

DUKE. What, is Antonio here?
ANT. Ready, so please your Grace.
DUKE. I am sorry for thee: thou art come to answer
A stony adversary, an inhuman wretch
005 Uncapable of pity, void and empty
From any dram of mercy.
ANT. I have heard
Your Grace hath ta'en great pains to qualify
His rigorous course; but since he stands obdurate,
And that no lawful means can carry me
010 Out of his envy's reach, I do oppose
My patience to his fury; and am arm'd
To suffer, with a quietness of spirit,
The very tyranny and rage of his.
DUKE. Go one, and call the Jew into the court.
015 *SALER.* He is ready at the door: he comes, my lord.

ENTER SHYLOCK.

DUKE. Make room, and let him stand before our face
Shylock, the world thinks, and I think so too,
That thou but lead'st this fashion of thy malice

To the last hour of act; and then 'tis thought
020 Thou'lt show thy mercy and remorse more strange
Than is thy strange apparent cruelty;
And where thou now exact'st the penalty,
Which is a pound of this poor merchant's flesh,
Thou wilt not only loose the forfeiture,
025 But, touch'd with human gentleness and love,
Forgive a moiety of the principal;
Glancing an eye of pity on his losses,
That have of late so huddled on his back,
Enow to press a royal merchant down,
030 And pluck commiseration of his state
From brassy bosoms and rough hearts of flint,
From stubborn Turks and Tartars, never train'd
To offices of tender courtesy.
We all expect a gentle answer, Jew.
035 *Shy.* I have possess'd your Grace of what I
    purpose;
And by our holy Sabbath have I sworn
To have the due and forfeit of my bond:
If you deny it, let the danger light
Upon your charter and your city's freedom.
040 You'll ask me, why I rather choose to have
A weight of carrion-flesh than to receive
Three thousand ducats: I'll not answer that:
But, say, it is my humour: is it answer'd?
What if my house be troubled with a rat,
045 And I be pleased to give ten thousand ducats
To have it baned? What, are you answer'd yet?
Some men there are love not a gaping pig;
Some, that are mad if they behold a cat;
And others, when the bagpipe sings i' the nose,
050 Cannot contain their urine: for affection,
Mistress of passion, sways it to the mood
Of what it likes or loathes. Now, for your answer:
As there is no firm reason to be render'd,
Why he cannot abide a gaping pig;
055 Why he, a harmless necessary cat;
Why he, a woollen bag-pipe; but of force
Must yield to such inevitable shame
As to offend, himself being offended;
So can I give no reason, nor I will not,
060 More than a lodged hate and a certain loathing

I bear Antonio, that I follow thus
A losing suit against him. Are you answer'd?
Bass. This is no answer, thou unfeeling man,
To excuse the current of thy cruelty.
065 *Shy.* I am not bound to please thee with my
   answers.
Bass. Do all men kill the things they do not love?
Shy. Hates any man the thing he would not kill?
Bass. Every offence is not a hate at first.
Shy. What, wouldst thou have a serpent sting thee
   twice?
070 *Ant.* I pray you, think you question with the Jew:
You may as well go stand upon the beach,
And bid the main flood bate his usual height;
You may as well use question with the wolf,
Why he hath made the ewe bleat for the lamb;
075 You may as well forbid the mountain pines
To wag their high tops, and to make no noise,
When they are fretten with the gusts of heaven;
You may as well do any thing most hard,
As seek to soften that—than which what's harder?—
080 His Jewish heart: therefore, I do beseech you,
Make no more offers, use no farther means,
But with all brief and plain conveniency
Let me have judgement and the Jew his will.
Bass. For thy three thousand ducats here is six.
085 *Shy.* If every ducat in six thousand ducats
Were in six parts and every part a ducat,
I would not draw them; I would have my bond.
Duke. How shalt thou hope for mercy, rendering
   none?
Shy. What judgement shall I dread, doing no wrong?
090 You have among you many a purchased slave,
Which, like your asses and your dogs and mules,
You use in abject and in slavish parts,
Because you bought them: shall I say to you,
Let them be free, marry them to your heirs?
095 Why sweat they under burthens? let their beds
Be made as soft as yours, and let their palates
Be season'd with such viands? You will answer
'The slaves are ours:' so do I answer you:
The pound of flesh, which I demand of him,
100 Is dearly bought; 'tis mine and I will have it.

If you deny me, fie upon your law!
There is no force in the decrees of Venice.
I stand for judgement: answer; shall I have it?
Duke. Upon my power I may dismiss this court,
105 Unless Bellario, a learned doctor,
Whom I have sent for to determine this,
Come here to-day.
Saler. My lord, here stays without
A messenger with letters from the doctor,
New come from Padua.
110 *Duke.* Bring us the letters; call the messenger.
Bass. Good cheer, Antonio! What, man, courage yet!
The Jew shall have my flesh, blood, bones, and all,
Ere thou shalt lose for me one drop of blood.
Ant. I am a tainted wether of the flock,
115 Meetest for death: the weakest kind of fruit
Drops earliest to the ground; and so let me:
You cannot better be employ'd, Bassanio,
Than to live still, and write mine epitaph.

Enter Nerissa, dressed like a lawyer's clerk.

Duke. Came you from Padua, from Bellario?
120 *Ner.* From both, my lord. Bellario greets your
      Grace. [*Presenting a letter.*
Bass. Why dost thou whet thy knife so earnestly?
Shy. To cut the forfeiture from that bankrupt there.
Gra. Not on thy sole, but on thy soul, harsh Jew,
Thou makest thy knife keen; but no metal can,
125 No, not the hangman's axe, bear half the keenness
Of thy sharp envy. Can no prayers pierce thee?
Shy. No, none that thou hast wit enough to make.
Gra. O, be thou damn'd, inexecrable dog!
And for thy life let justice be accused.
130 Thou almost makest me waver in my faith,
To hold opinion with Pythagoras,
That souls of animals infuse themselves
Into the trunks of men: thy currish spirit
Govern'd a wolf, who, hang'd for human slaughter,
135 Even from the gallows did his fell soul fleet,
And, whilst thou lay'st in thy unhallow'd dam,
Infused itself in thee; for thy desires
Are wolvish, bloody, starved and ravenous.

Shy. Till thou canst rail the seal from off my bond,
140 Thou but offend'st thy lungs to speak so loud:
Repair thy wit, good youth, or it will fall
To cureless ruin. I stand here for law.
Duke. This letter from Bellario doth commend
A young and learned doctor to our court.
Where is he?
145 *Ner.* He attendeth here hard by,
To know your answer, whether you'll admit him.
Duke. With all my heart. Some three or four of you
Go give him courteous conduct to this place.
Meantime the court shall hear Bellario's letter.
150 *Clerk.* [*reads*] Your Grace shall understand that at
the receipt of your letter I am very sick: but in the
instant that your messenger came, in loving visitation was with me a young doctor of Rome; his
name is Balthasar. I acquainted him with the cause
in controversy between the Jew and Antonio the
merchant: we turned o'er many 155 books together:
he is furnished with my opinion; which, bettered
with his own learning,—the greatness whereof I
cannot enough commend,—comes with him, at
my importunity, to fill up your Grace's request in
my stead. I beseech you, let his lack of years be no
impediment to let him lack a reverend estimation;
for I never knew so young a 160 body with so old a
head. I leave him to your gracious acceptance,
whose trial shall better publish his commendation.
Duke. You hear the learn'd Bellario, what he writes:
And here, I take it, is the doctor come.

Enter Portia *for* Balthasar.

Give me your hand. Come you from old Bellario?
Por. I did, my lord.
165 *Duke.* You are welcome: take your place.
Are you acquainted with the difference
That holds this present question in the court?
Por. I am informed throughly of the cause.
Which is the merchant here, and which the Jew?
170 *Duke.* Antonio and old Shylock, both stand forth.
Por. Is your name Shylock?
Shy. Shylock is my name.

Por. Of a strange nature is the suit you follow;
Yet in such rule that the Venetian law
Cannot impugn you as you do proceed.
175 You stand within his danger, do you not?
Ant. Ay, so he says.
Por. Do you confess the bond?
Ant. I do.
Por. Then must the Jew be merciful.
Shy. On what compulsion must I? tell me that.
Por. The quality of mercy is not strain'd,
180 It droppeth as the gentle rain from heaven
Upon the place beneath: it is twice blest;
It blesseth him that gives, and him that takes:
'Tis mightiest in the mightiest: it becomes
The thronèd monarch better than his crown;
185 His sceptre shows the force of temporal power,
The attribute to awe and majesty,
Wherein doth sit the dread and fear of kings;
But mercy is above this sceptred sway;
It is enthronèd in the hearts of kings,
190 It is an attribute to God himself;
And earthly power doth then show likest God's
When mercy seasons justice. Therefore, Jew,
Though justice be thy plea, consider this,
That, in the course of justice, none of us
195 Should see salvation: we do pray for mercy;
And that same prayer doth teach us all to render
The deeds of mercy. I have spoke thus much
To mitigate the justice of thy plea;
Which if thou follow, this strict court of Venice
200 Must needs give sentence 'gainst the merchant
   there.
Shy. My deeds upon my head! I crave the law,
The penalty and forfeit of my bond.
Por. Is he not able to discharge the money?
Bass. Yes, here I tender it for him in the court;
205 Yea, twice the sum: if that will not suffice,
I will be bound to pay it ten times o'er,
On forfeit of my hands, my head, my heart:
If this will not suffice, it must appear
That malice bears down truth. And I beseech you,
210 Wrest once the law to your authority:
To do a great right, do a little wrong,

And curb this cruel devil of his will.

Por. It must not be; there is no power in Venice
Can alter a decree established:
215 'Twill be recorded for a precedent,
And many an error, by the same example,
Will rush into the state: it cannot be.

Shy. A Daniel come to judgement! yea, a Daniel!
O wise young judge, how I do honour thee!
220 *Por.* I pray you, let me look upon the bond.

Shy. Here 'tis, most reverend doctor, here it is.

Por. Shylock, there's thrice thy money offer'd thee.

Shy. An oath, an oath, I have an oath in heaven:
Shall I lay perjury upon my soul?
225 No, not for Venice.

Por. Why, this bond is forfeit;
And lawfully by this the Jew may claim
A pound of flesh, to be by him cut off
Nearest the merchant's heart. Be merciful:
Take thrice thy money; bid me tear the bond.
230 *Shy.* When it is paid according to the tenour.
It doth appear you are a worthy judge;
You know the law, your exposition
Hath been most sound: I charge you by the law,
Whereof you are a well-deserving pillar,
235 Proceed to judgement: by my soul I swear
There is no power in the tongue of man
To alter me: I stay here on my bond.

Ant. Most heartily I do beseech the court
To give the judgement.

Por. Why then, thus it is:
240 You must prepare your bosom for his knife.

Shy. O noble judge! O excellent young man!

Por. For the intent and purpose of the law
Hath full relation to the penalty,
Which here appeareth due upon the bond.
245 *Shy.* 'Tis very true: O wise and upright judge!
How much more elder art thou than thy looks!

Por. Therefore lay bare your bosom.

Shy. Ay, his breast:
So says the bond:—doth it not, noble judge?—
'Nearest his heart:' those are the very words.
250 *Por.* It is so. Are there balance here to weigh
The flesh?

SHY. I have them ready.
POR. Have by some surgeon, Shylock, on your
    charge,
To stop his wounds, lest he do bleed to death.
SHY. Is it so nominated in the bond?
255 POR. It is not so express'd: but what of that?
'Twere good you do so much for charity.
SHY. I cannot find it; 'tis not in the bond.
POR. You, merchant, have you any thing to say?
ANT. But little: I am arm'd and well prepared.
260 Give me your hand, Bassanio: fare you well!
Grieve not that I am fallen to this for you;
For herein Fortune shows herself more kind
Than is her custom: it is still her use
To let the wretched man outlive his wealth,
265 To view with hollow eye and wrinkled brow
An age of poverty; from which lingering penance
Of such misery doth she cut me off.
Commend me to your honourable wife:
Tell her the process of Antonio's end;
270 Say how I loved you, speak me fair in death;
And, when the tale is told, bid her be judge
Whether Bassanio had not once a love.
Repent but you that you shall lose your friend,
And he repents not that he pays your debt;
275 For if the Jew do cut but deep enough,
I'll pay it presently with all my heart.
BASS. Antonio, I am married to a wife
Which is as dear to me as life itself;
But life itself, my wife, and all the world,
280 Are not with me esteem'd above thy life:
I would lose all, ay, sacrifice them all
Here to this devil, to deliver you.
POR. Your wife would give you little thanks for that,
If she were by, to hear you make the offer.
285 GRA. I have a wife, whom, I protest, I love:
I would she were in heaven, so she could
Entreat some power to change this currish Jew.
NER. 'Tis well you offer it behind her back;
The wish would make else an unquiet house.
290 SHY. These be the Christian husbands. I have a
    daughter;
Would any of the stock of Barrabas

Had been her husband rather than a Christian! [*Aside.*
We trifle time: I pray thee, pursue sentence.
Por. A pound of that same merchant's flesh is thine:
295 The court awards it, and the law doth give it.
Shy. Most rightful judge!
Por. And you must cut this flesh from off his breast:
The law allows it, and the court awards it.
Shy. Most learned judge! A sentence! Come, prepare!
300 *Por.* Tarry a little; there is something else.
This bond doth give thee here no jot of blood;
The words expressly are 'a pound of flesh:'
Take then thy bond, take thou thy pound of flesh;
But, in the cutting it, if thou dost shed
305 One drop of Christian blood, thy lands and goods
Are, by the laws of Venice, confiscate
Unto the state of Venice.
Gra. O upright judge! Mark, Jew: O learned judge!
Shy. Is that the law?
Por. Thyself shalt see the act:
310 For, as thou urgest justice, be assured
Thou shalt have justice, more than thou desirest.
Gra. O learned judge! Mark, Jew: a learned judge!
Shy. I take this offer, then; pay the bond thrice,
And let the Christian go.
Bass. Here is the money.
315 *Por.* Soft!
The Jew shall have all justice; soft! no haste:
He shall have nothing but the penalty.
Gra. O Jew! an upright judge, a learned judge!
Por. Therefore prepare thee to cut off the flesh.
320 Shed thou no blood; nor cut thou less nor more
But just a pound of flesh: if thou cut'st more
Or less than a just pound, be it but so much
As makes it light or heavy in the substance,
Or the division of the twentieth part
325 Of one poor scruple, nay, if the scale do turn
But in the estimation of a hair,
Thou diest and all thy goods are confiscate.
Gra. A second Daniel, a Daniel, Jew!
Now, infidel, I have you on the hip.
330 *Por.* Why doth the Jew pause? take thy forfeiture.
Shy. Give me my principal, and let me go.
Bass. I have it ready for thee; here it is.

Por. He hath refused it in the open court:
He shall have merely justice and his bond.
335 *Gra.* A Daniel, still say I, a second Daniel!
I thank thee, Jew, for teaching me that word.
Shy. Shall I not have barely my principal?
Por. Thou shalt have nothing but the forfeiture,
To be so taken at thy peril, Jew.
340 *Shy.* Why, then the devil give him good of it!
I'll stay no longer question.
Por. Tarry, Jew:
The law hath yet another hold on you.
It is enacted in the laws of Venice,
If it be proved against an alien
345 That by direct or indirect attempts
He seek the life of any citizen,
The party 'gainst the which he doth contrive
Shall seize one half his goods; the other half
Comes to the privy coffer of the state;
350 And the offender's life lies in the mercy
Of the Duke only, 'gainst all other voice.
In which predicament, I say, thou stand'st;
For it appears, by manifest proceeding,
That indirectly, and directly too,
355 Thou hast contrived against the very life
Of the defendant; and thou hast incurr'd
The danger formerly by me rehearsed.
Down, therefore, and beg mercy of the Duke.
Gra. Beg that thou mayst have leave to hang thyself:
360 And yet, thy wealth being forfeit to the state,
Thou hast not left the value of a cord;
Therefore thou must be hang'd at the state's charge.
Duke. That thou shalt see the difference of our spirits,
I pardon thee thy life before thou ask it:
365 For half thy wealth, it is Antonio's;
The other half comes to the general state,
Which humbleness may drive unto a fine.
Por. Ay, for the state, not for Antonio.
Shy. Nay, take my life and all; pardon not that:
370 You take my house, when you do take the
That doth sustain my house; you take my life,
When you do take the means whereby I live.
Por. What mercy can you render him, Antonio?
Gra. A halter gratis; nothing else, for God's sake.

375 *Ant.* So please my lord the Duke and all the court
To quit the fine for one half of his goods,
I am content; so he will let me have
The other half in use, to render it,
Upon his death, unto the gentleman
380 That lately stole his daughter:
Two things provided more, that, for this favour,
He presently become a Christian;
The other, that he do record a gift,
Here in the court, of all he dies possess'd,
385 Unto his son Lorenzo and his daughter.
Duke. He shall do this, or else I do recant
The pardon that I late pronounced here.
Por. Art thou contented, Jew? what dost thou say?
Shy. I am content.
Por. Clerk, draw a deed of gift.
390 *Shy.* I pray you, give me leave to go from hence;
I am not well: send the deed after me,
And I will sign it.
Duke. Get thee gone, but do it.
Gra. In christening shalt thou have two godfathers:
Had I been judge, thou shouldst have had ten more,
395 To bring thee to the gallows, not the font. [*Exit
     Shylock.*
Duke. Sir, I entreat you home with me to dinner.
Por. I humbly do desire your Grace of pardon:
I must away this night toward Padua,
And it is meet I presently set forth.
400 *Duke.* I am sorry that your leisure serves you not.
Antonio, gratify this gentleman,
For, in my mind, you are much bound to him. [*Exeunt
     Duke and his train.*
Bass. Most worthy gentleman, I and my friend
Have by your wisdom been this day acquitted
405 Of grievous penalties; in lieu whereof,
Three thousand ducats, due unto the Jew,
We freely cope your courteous pains withal.
Ant. And stand indebted, over and above,
In love and service to you evermore.
410 *Por.* He is well paid that is well satisfied;
And I, delivering you, am satisfied
And therein do account myself well paid:
My mind was never yet more mercenary.

I pray you, know me when we meet again:
415 I wish you well, and so I take my leave.
Bass. Dear sir, of force I must attempt you further:
Take some remembrance of us, as a tribute,
Not as a fee: grant me two things, I pray you,
Not to deny me, and to pardon me.
420 *Por.* You press me far, and therefore I will yield.
Give me your gloves, I'll wear them for your sake;
    [*To Ant.*
And, for your love, I'll take this ring from you [*To
    Bass.*]:
Do not draw back your hand; I'll take no more;
And you in love shall not deny me this.
425 *Bass.* This ring, good sir, alas, it is a trifle!
I will not shame myself to give you this.
Por. I will have nothing else but only this;
And now methinks I have a mind to it.
Bass. There's more depends on this than on the value.
430 The dearest ring in Venice will I give you,
And find it out by proclamation:
Only for this, I pray you, pardon me.
Por. I see, sir, you are liberal in offers:
You taught me first to beg; and now methinks
435 You teach me how a beggar should be answer'd.
Bass. Good sir, this ring was given me by my wife;
And when she put it on, she made me vow
That I should neither sell nor give nor lose it.
Por. That 'scuse serves many men to save their gifts.
440 An if your wife be not a mad-woman,
And know how well I have deserved the ring,
She would not hold out enemy for ever,
For giving it to me. Well, peace be with you! [*Exeunt
    Portia and Nerissa.*
Ant. My Lord Bassanio, let him have the ring:
445 Let his deservings and my love withal
Be valued 'gainst your wife's commandment.
Bass. Go, Gratiano, run and overtake him;
Give him the ring; and bring him, if thou canst,
Unto Antonio's house: away! make haste. [*Exit
    Gratiano.*
450 Come, you and I will thither presently;
And in the morning early will we both
Fly toward Belmont: come, Antonio. [*Exeunt.*

SCENE II. THE SAME. A STREET

ENTER PORTIA *AND* NERISSA.

POR. Inquire the Jew's house out, give him this deed
And let him sign it: we'll away to-night
And be a day before our husbands home:
This deed will be well welcome to Lorenzo.

ENTER GRATIANO.

005 GRA. Fair sir, you are well o'erta'en:
My Lord Bassanio upon more advice
Hath sent you here this ring, and doth entreat
Your company at dinner.
POR. That cannot be:
His ring I do accept most thankfully:
010 And so, I pray you, tell him: furthermore,
I pray you, show my youth old Shylock's house.
GRA. That will I do.
NER. Sir, I would speak with you.
I'll see if I can get my husband's ring, [*Aside to Portia.*
Which I did make him swear to keep for ever.
015 POR. [*Aside to Ner.*] Thou mayst, I warrant. We
    shall have old swearing
That they did give the rings away to men;
But we'll outface them, and outswear them too.
[*Aloud*] Away! make haste: thou know'st where I will
    tarry.
NER. Come, good sir, will you show me to this house?
    [*Exeunt.*

ACT V

SCENE I. BELMONT. AVENUE TO PORTIA'S HOUSE.

ENTER LORENZO *AND* JESSICA.

LOR. The moon shines bright: in such a night as this,
When the sweet wind did gently kiss the trees
And they did make no noise, in such a night
Troilus methinks mounted the Troyan walls,
005 And sigh'd his soul toward the Grecian tents,
Where Cressid lay that night.
JES. In such a night
Did Thisbe fearfully o'ertrip the dew,
And saw the lion's shadow ere himself.
And ran dismay'd away.
LOR. In such a night
010 Stood Dido with a willow in her hand
Upon the wild sea-banks, and waft her love
To come again to Carthage.
JES. In such a night
Medea gather'd the enchanted herbs
That did renew old Æson.
LOR. In such a night
015 Did Jessica steal from the wealthy Jew
And with an unthrift love did run from Venice
As far as Belmont.
JES. In such a night
Did young Lorenzo swear he loved her well,

137

Stealing her soul with many vows of faith
And ne'er a true one.

020 *LOR.* In such a night
Did pretty Jessica, like a little shrew,
Slander her love, and he forgave it her.

JES. I would out-night you, did no body come;
But, hark, I hear the footing of a man.

ENTER STEPHANO.

025 *LOR.* Who comes so fast in silence of the night?

STEPH. A friend.

LOR. A friend! what friend? your name, I pray you,
    friend?

STEPH. Stephano is my name; and I bring word
My mistress will before the break of day
030 Be here at Belmont: she doth stray about
By holy crosses, where she kneels and prays
For happy wedlock hours.

LOR. Who comes with her?

STEPH. None but a holy hermit and her maid.
I pray you, is my master yet return'd?

035 *LOR.* He is not, nor we have not heard from him.
But go we in, I pray thee, Jessica,
And ceremoniously let us prepare
Some welcome for the mistress of the house.

ENTER LAUNCELOT.

LAUN. Sola, sola! wo ha, ho! sola, sola!

040 *LOR.* Who calls?

LAUN. Sola! did you see Master Lorenzo? Master
    Lorenzo, sola, sola!

LOR. Leave hollaing, man: here.

LAUN. Sola! where? where?

045 *LOR.* Here.

LAUN. Tell him there's a post come from my master,
    with his horn full of good news: my master will be
    here ere morning. [*Exit.*

LOR. Sweet soul, let's in, and there expect their
    coming.

050 And yet no matter: why should we go in?
My friend Stephano, signify, I pray you,

Within the house, your mistress is at hand;
And bring your music forth into the air. [*Exit
    Stephano.*
How sweet the moonlight sleeps upon this bank!
055 Here will we sit, and let the sounds of music
Creep in our ears: soft stillness and the night
Become the touches of sweet harmony.
Sit, Jessica. Look how the floor of heaven
Is thick inlaid with patines of bright gold:
060 There's not the smallest orb which thou behold'st
But in his motion like an angel sings,
Still quiring to the young-eyed cherubins;
Such harmony is in immortal souls;
But whilst this muddy vesture of decay
065 Doth grossly close it in, we cannot hear it.

Enter Musicians.

Come, ho, and wake Diana with a hymn!
With sweetest touches pierce your mistress' ear,
And draw her home with music. [*Music.*
JES. I am never merry when I hear sweet music.
070 LOR. The reason is, your spirits are attentive:
For do but note a wild and wanton herd,
Or race of youthful and unhandled colts,
Fetching mad bounds, bellowing and neighing loud,
Which is the hot condition of their blood;
075 If they but hear perchance a trumpet sound,
Or any air of music touch their ears,
You shall perceive them make a mutual stand,
Their savage eyes turn'd to a modest gaze
By the sweet power of music: therefore the poet
080 Did feign that Orpheus drew trees, stones and
    floods;
Since nought so stockish, hard and full of rage,
But music for the time doth change his nature.
The man that hath no music in himself,
Nor is not moved with concord of sweet sounds,
085 Is fit for treasons, stratagems and spoils;
The motions of his spirit are dull as night,
And his affections dark as Erebus:
Let no such man be trusted. Mark the music.

ENTER PORTIA *AND* NERISSA.

POR. That light we see is burning in my hall.
090 How far that little candle throws his beams!
So shines a good deed in a naughty world.
NER. When the moon shone, we did not see the
  candle.
POR. So doth the greater glory dim the less:
A substitute shines brightly as a king,
095 Until a king be by; and then his state
Empties itself, as doth an inland brook
Into the main of waters. Music! hark!
NER. It is your music, madam, of the house.
POR. Nothing is good, I see, without respect:
100 Methinks it sounds much sweeter than by day.
NER. Silence bestows that virtue on it, madam.
POR. The crow doth sing as sweetly as the lark,
When neither is attended; and I think
The nightingale, if she should sing by day,
105 When every goose is cackling, would be thought
No better a musician than the wren.
How many things by season season'd are
To their right praise and true perfection!
Peace, ho! the moon sleeps with Endymion,
110 And would not be awaked. [*Music ceases.*
110 *LOR.* That is the voice,
Or I am much deceived, of Portia.
POR. He knows me as the blind man knows the
  cuckoo,
By the bad voice.
LOR. Dear lady, welcome home.
POR. We have been praying for our husbands'
  healths,
115 Which speed, we hope, the better for our words.
Are they return'd?
LOR. Madam, they are not yet;
But there is come a messenger before,
To signify their coming.
POR. Go in, Nerissa;
Give order to my servants that they take
120 No note at all of our being absent hence;
Nor you, Lorenzo; Jessica, nor you. [*A tucket sounds.*
LOR. Your husband is at hand; I hear his trumpet:

We are no tell-tales, madam; fear you not.
Por. This night methinks is but the daylight sick;
125 It looks a little paler: 'tis a day,
Such as the day is when the sun is hid.

Enter BASSANIO, ANTONIO, GRATIANO, and their followers.

Bass. We should hold day with the Antipodes,
If you would walk in absence of the sun.
Por. Let me give light, but let me not be light;
130 For a light wife doth make a heavy husband,
And never be Bassanio so for me:
But God sort all! You are welcome home, my lord.
Bass. I thank you, madam. Give welcome to my
    friend.
This is the man, this is Antonio,
135 To whom I am so infinitely bound.
Por. You should in all sense be much bound to him,
For, as I hear, he was much bound for you.
Ant. No more than I am well acquitted of.
Por. Sir, you are very welcome to our house:
140 It must appear in other ways than words,
Therefore I scant this breathing courtesy.
Gra. [*To Nerissa*] By yonder moon I swear you do me
    wrong;
In faith, I gave it to the judge's clerk:
Would he were gelt that had it, for my part,
145 Since you do take it, love, so much at heart.
Por. A quarrel, ho, already! what's the matter?
Gra. About a hoop of gold, a paltry ring
That she did give me, whose posy was
For all the world like cutler's poetry
150 Upon a knife, 'Love me, and leave me not.'
Ner. What talk you of the posy or the value?
You swore to me, when I did give it you,
That you would wear it till your hour of death,
And that it should lie with you in your grave:
155 Though not for me, yet for your vehement oaths,
You should have been respective, and have kept it.
Gave it a judge's clerk! no, God's my judge,
The clerk will ne'er wear hair on's face that had it.
Gra. He will, an if he live to be a man.
160 *Ner.* Ay, if a woman live to be a man.

GRA. Now, by this hand, I gave it to a youth,
A kind of boy, a little scrubbed boy,
No higher than thyself, the judge's clerk,
A prating boy, that begg'd it as a fee:
165 I could not for my heart deny him.
POR. You were to blame, I must be plain with you,
To part so slightly with your wife's first gift;
A thing stuck on with oaths upon your finger
And so riveted with faith unto your flesh.
170 I gave my love a ring, and made him swear
Never to part with it; and here he stands;
I dare be sworn for him he would not leave it
Nor pluck it from his finger, for the wealth
That the world masters. Now, in faith, Gratiano,
175 You give your wife too unkind a cause of grief:
An 'twere to me, I should be mad at it.
BASS. [*Aside*] Why, I were best to cut my left hand off,
And swear I lost the ring defending it.
GRA. My Lord Bassanio gave his ring away
180 Unto the judge that begg'd it and indeed
Deserved it too; and then the boy, his clerk,
That took some pains in writing, he begg'd mine;
And neither man nor master would take aught
But the two rings.
POR. What ring gave you, my lord?
185 Not that, I hope, which you received of me.
BASS. If I could add a lie unto a fault,
I would deny it; but you see my finger
Hath not the ring upon it, it is gone.
POR. Even so void is your false heart of truth.
190 By heaven, I will ne'er come in your bed
Until I see the ring.
NER. Nor I in yours
Till I again see mine.
BASS. Sweet Portia,
If you did know to whom I gave the ring,
If you did know for whom I gave the ring,
195 And would conceive for what I gave the ring,
And how unwillingly I left the ring,
When nought would be accepted but the ring,
You would abate the strength of your displeasure.
POR. If you had known the virtue of the ring,
200 Or half her worthiness that gave the ring,

Or your own honour to contain the ring,
You would not then have parted with the ring.
What man is there so much unreasonable,
If you had pleased to have defended it
205 With any terms of zeal, wanted the modesty
To urge the thing held as a ceremony?
Nerissa teaches me what to believe:
I'll die for't but some woman had the ring.
Bass. No, by my honour, madam, by my soul,
210 No woman had it, but a civil doctor,
Which did refuse three thousand ducats of me,
And begg'd the ring; the which I did deny him,
And suffered him to go displeased away;
Even he that did uphold the very life
215 Of my dear friend. What should I say, sweet lady;
I was enforced to send it after him;
I was beset with shame and courtesy;
My honour would not let ingratitude
So much besmear it. Pardon me, good lady;
220 For, by these blessed candles of the night,
Had you been there, I think you would have begg'd
The ring of me to give the worthy doctor.
Por. Let not that doctor e'er come near my house:
Since he hath got the jewel that I loved,
225 And that which you did swear to keep for me,
I will become as liberal as you;
I'll not deny him any thing I have,
No, not my body nor my husband's bed:
Know him I shall, I am well sure of it:
230 Lie not a night from home; watch me like Argus:
If you do not, if I be left alone,
Now, by mine honour, which is yet mine own,
I'll have that doctor for my bedfellow.
Ner. And I his clerk; therefore be well advised
235 How you do leave me to mine own protection.
Gra. Well, do you so: let not me take him, then;
For if I do, I'll mar the young clerk's pen.
Ant. I am the unhappy subject of these quarrels.
Por. Sir, grieve not you; you are welcome not-
        withstanding.
240 *Bass.* Portia, forgive me this enforced wrong;
And, in the hearing of these many friends,
I swear to thee, even by thine own fair eyes,

Wherein I see myself,—
Por. Mark you but that!
In both my eyes he doubly sees himself;
245 In each eye, one: swear by your double self,
And there's an oath of credit.
Bass. Nay, but hear me:
Pardon this fault, and by my soul I swear
I never more will break an oath with thee.
Ant. I once did lend my body for his wealth;
250 Which, but for him that had your husband's ring,
Had quite miscarried: I dare be bound again,
My soul upon the forfeit, that your lord
Will never more break faith advisedly.
Por. Then you shall be his surety. Give him this,
255 And bid him keep it better than the other.
Ant. Here, Lord Bassanio; swear to keep this ring.
Bass. By heaven, it is the same I gave the doctor!
Por. I had it of him: pardon me, Bassanio;
For, by this ring, the doctor lay with me.
260 *Ner.* And pardon me, my gentle Gratiano;
For that same scrubbed boy, the doctor's clerk,
In lieu of this last night did lie with me.
Gra. Why, this is like the mending of highways
In summer, where the ways are fair enough:
265 What, are we cuckolds ere we have deserved it?
Por. Speak not so grossly. You are all amazed:
Here is a letter; read it at your leisure;
It comes from Padua, from Bellario:
There you shall find that Portia was the doctor,
270 Nerissa there her clerk: Lorenzo here
Shall witness I set forth as soon as you,
And even but now return'd; I have not yet
Enter'd my house. Antonio, you are welcome;
And I have better news in store for you
275 Than you expect: unseal this letter soon;
There you shall find three of your argosies
Are richly come to harbour suddenly:
You shall not know by what strange accident
I chanced on this letter.
Ant. I am dumb.
280 *Bass.* Were you the doctor and I knew you not?
Gra. Were you the clerk that is to make me cuckold?
Ner. Ay, but the clerk that never means to do it,

Unless he live until he be a man.
Bass. Sweet doctor, you shall be my bedfellow:
285 When I am absent, then lie with my wife.
Ant. Sweet lady, you have given me life and living;
For here I read for certain that my ships
Are safely come to road.
Por. How now, Lorenzo!
My clerk hath some good comforts too for you.
290 *Ner.* Ay, and I'll give them him without a fee.
There do I give to you and Jessica,
From the rich Jew, a special deed of gift,
After his death, of all he dies possess'd of.
Lor. Fair ladies, you drop manna in the way
Of starved people.
295 *Por.* It is almost morning,
And yet I am sure you are not satisfied
Of these events at full. Let us go in;
And charge us there upon inter'gatories,
And we will answer all things faithfully.
300 *Gra.* Let it be so: the first inter'gatory
That my Nerissa shall be sworn on is,
Whether till the next night she had rather stay,
Or go to bed now, being two hours to day:
But were the day come, I should wish it dark,
305 That I were couching with the doctor's clerk.
Well, while I live I'll fear no other thing
So sore as keeping safe Nerissa's ring. [*Exeunt.*

MUCH ADO ABOUT
NOTHING

DRAMATIS PERSONÆ

Don Pedro, prince of Arragon.
Don John, his bastard brother.
Claudio, a young lord of Florence.
Benedick, a young lord of Padua.
Leonato, governor of Messina.
Antonio, his brother.
Balthasar, attendant on Don Pedro.
Conrade, follower of Don John.
Borachio,   "   "   "
Friar Francis.
Dogberry, a constable.
Verges, a headborough.
A Sexton.
A Boy.
Hero, daughter to Leonato.
Beatrice, niece to Leonato.
Margaret, gentlewoman attending on Hero.
Ursula,   "   "   "
Messengers, Watch, Attendants, &c.

Scene—*Messina.*

ACT I

SCENE I. BEFORE LEONATO'S HOUSE.

(Enter LEONATO, HERO, and BEATRICE, with a Messenger.)

LEON. I learn in this letter that Don Peter of Arragon
 comes this night to Messina.

MESS. He is very near by this: he was not three
 leagues off when I left him.

005 LEON. How many gentlemen have you lost in this
 action?

MESS. But few of any sort, and none of name.

LEON. A victory is twice itself when the achiever
 brings home full numbers. I find here that Don
 Peter hath bestowed much honour on a young
 Florentine called Claudio.

010 MESS. Much deserved on his part, and equally re-
 membered by Don Pedro: he hath borne himself
 beyond the promise of his age; doing, in the figure
 of a lamb, the feats of a lion: he hath indeed better
 bettered expectation than you must expect of me
 to tell you how.

015 LEON. He hath an uncle here in Messina will be
 very much glad of it.

MESS. I have already delivered him letters, and there
 appears much joy in him; even so much, that joy
 could not show itself modest enough without a
 badge of bitterness.

020 *Leon.* Did he break out into tears?

Mess. In great measure.

Leon. A kind overflow of kindness: there are no faces truer than those that are so washed. How much better is it to weep at joy than to joy at weeping!

025 *Beat.* I pray you, is Signior Mountanto returned from the wars or no?

Mess. I know none of that name, lady: there was none such in the army of any sort.

Leon. What is he that you ask for, niece?

030 *Hero.* My cousin means Signior Benedick of Padua.

Mess. O, he's returned; and as pleasant as ever he was.

Beat. He set up his bills here in Messina and challenged Cupid at the flight; and my uncle's fool, reading the challenge, subscribed for Cupid, and challenged him at the 035 bird-bolt. I pray you, how many hath he killed and eaten in these wars? But how many hath he killed? for, indeed, I promised to eat all of his killing.

Leon. Faith, niece, you tax Signior Benedick too much; but he'll be meet with you, I doubt it not.

040 *Mess.* He hath done good service, lady, in these wars.

Beat. You had musty victual, and he hath help to eat it: he is a very valiant trencher-man; he hath an excellent stomach.

Mess. And a good soldier too, lady.

045 *Beat.* And a good soldier to a lady: but what is he to a lord?

Mess. A lord to a lord, a man to a man; stuffed with all honourable virtues.

Beat. It is so, indeed; he is no less than a stuffed 050 man: but for the stuffing,—well, we are all mortal.

Leon. You must not, sir, mistake my niece. There is a kind of merry war betwixt Signior Benedick and her: they never meet but there's a skirmish of wit between them.

Beat. Alas, he gets nothing by that! In our last conflict 055 four of his five wits went halting off, and now is the whole man governed with one: so that if he have wit enough to keep himself warm, let him

bear it for a difference between himself and his
horse; for it is all the wealth that he hath left, to be
known a reasonable creature. Who is his companion $_{060}$ now? He hath every month a new
sworn brother.

Mess. Is't possible?

Beat. Very easily possible: he wears his faith but as
the fashion of his hat; it ever changes with the next
block.

Mess. I see, lady, the gentleman is not in your books.

$_{065}$ *Beat.* No; an he were, I would burn my study. But,
pray you, who is his companion? Is there no
young squarer now that will make a voyage with
him to the devil?

Mess. He is most in the company of the right noble
Claudio.

$_{070}$ *Beat.* O Lord, he will hang upon him like a disease: he is sooner caught than the pestilence, and
the taker runs presently mad. God help the noble
Claudio! if he have caught the Benedick, it will
cost him a thousand pound ere a' be cured.

$_{075}$ *Mess.* I will hold friends with you, lady.

Beat. Do, good friend.

Leon. You will never run mad, niece.

Beat. No, not till a hot January.

Mess. Don Pedro is approached.

(*Enter Don Pedro, Don John, Claudio, Benedick, and
Balthasar.*)

$_{080}$ *D. Pedro.* Good Signior Leonato, you are come to
meet your trouble: the fashion of the world is to
avoid cost, and you encounter it.

Leon. Never came trouble to my house in the likeness
of your Grace: for trouble being gone, comfort
should $_{085}$ remain; but when you depart from me,
sorrow abides, and happiness takes his leave.

D. Pedro. You embrace your charge too willingly. I
think this is your daughter.

Leon. Her mother hath many times told me so.

$_{090}$ *Bene.* Were you in doubt, sir, that you asked her?

Leon. Signior Benedick, no; for then were you a child.

D. Pedro. You have it full, Benedick: we may guess

by this what you are, being a man. Truly, the lady
fathers herself. Be happy, lady; for you are like an
honourable ₀₉₅ father.

BENE. If Signior Leonato be her father, she would not
have his head on her shoulders for all Messina, as
like him as she is.

BEAT. I wonder that you will still be talking, Signior
₁₀₀ Benedick: nobody marks you.

BENE. What, my dear Lady Disdain! are you yet
living?

BEAT. Is it possible disdain should die while she hath
such meet food to feed it, as Signior Benedick?
Courtesy itself must convert to disdain, if you
come in her presence.

₁₀₅ *BENE.* Then is courtesy a turncoat. But it is certain I
am loved of all ladies, only you excepted: and I
would I could find in my heart that I had not a
hard heart; for, truly, I love none.

BEAT. A dear happiness to women: they would else
have ₁₁₀ been troubled with a pernicious suitor. I
thank God and my cold blood, I am of your hu-
mour for that: I had rather hear my dog bark at a
crow than a man swear he loves me.

BENE. God keep your ladyship still in that mind! so
some gentleman or other shall 'scape a predesti-
nate scratched face.

₁₁₅ *BEAT.* Scratching could not make it worse, an
'twere such a face as yours were.

BENE. Well, you are a rare parrot-teacher.

BEAT. A bird of my tongue is better than a beast of
yours.

BENE. I would my horse had the speed of your
tongue, ₁₂₀ and so good a continuer. But keep your
way, i' God's name; I have done.

BEAT. You always end with a jade's trick: I know you
of old.

D. PEDRO. That is the sum of all, Leonato. Signior ₁₂₅
Claudio and Signior Benedick, my dear friend
Leonato hath invited you all. I tell him we shall
stay here at the least a month; and he heartily
prays some occasion may detain us longer. I dare
swear he is no hypocrite, but prays from his heart.

₁₃₀ *LEON.* If you swear, my lord, you shall not be for-

sworn. *(To Don John)* Let me bid you welcome, my lord: being reconciled to the prince your brother, I owe you all duty.

D. JOHN. I thank you: I am not of many words, but I thank you.

135 LEON. Please it your Grace lead on?

D. PEDRO. Your hand, Leonato; we will go together. *(Exeunt all except Benedick and Claudio.)*

CLAUD. Benedick, didst thou note the daughter of Signior Leonato?

BENE. I noted her not; but I looked on her.

140 CLAUD. Is she not a modest young lady?

BENE. Do you question me, as an honest man should do, for my simple true judgement; or would you have me speak after my custom, as being a professed tyrant to their sex?

CLAUD. No; I pray thee speak in sober judgement.

145 BENE. Why, i'faith, methinks she's too low for a high praise, too brown for a fair praise, and too little for a great praise: only this commendation I can afford her, that were she other than she is, she were unhandsome; and being no other but as she is, I do not like her.

150 CLAUD. Thou thinkest I am in sport: I pray thee tell me truly how thou likest her.

BENE. Would you buy her, that you inquire after her?

CLAUD. Can the world buy such a jewel?

BENE. Yea, and a case to put it into. But speak you this 155 with a sad brow? or do you play the flouting Jack, to tell us Cupid is a good hare-finder, and Vulcan a rare carpenter? Come, in what key shall a man take you, to go in the song?

CLAUD. In mine eye she is the sweetest lady that ever I looked on.

160 BENE. I can see yet without spectacles, and I see no such matter: there's her cousin, an she were not possessed with a fury, exceeds her as much in beauty as the first of May doth the last of December. But I hope you have no intent to turn husband, have you?

165 CLAUD. I would scarce trust myself, though I had sworn the contrary, if Hero would be my wife.

BENE. Is't come to this? In faith, hath not the world

one man but he will wear his cap with suspicion? Shall I never see a bachelor of threescore again? Go to, i'faith; 170 an thou wilt needs thrust thy neck into a yoke, wear the print of it, and sigh away Sundays. Look; Don Pedro is returned to seek you.

(RE-ENTER DON PEDRO.)

D. PEDRO. What secret hath held you here, that you followed not to Leonato's?

175 BENE. I would your Grace would constrain me to tell.

D. PEDRO. I charge thee on thy allegiance.

BENE. You hear, Count Claudio: I can be secret as a dumb man; I would have you think so; but, on my allegiance, mark you this, on my allegiance. He is in love. 180 With who? now that is your Grace's part. Mark how short his answer is;—With Hero, Leonato's short daughter.

CLAUD. If this were so, so were it uttered.

BENE. Like the old tale, my lord: 'it is not so, nor 'twas not so, but, indeed, God forbid it should be so.'

185 CLAUD. If my passion change not shortly, God forbid it should be otherwise.

D. PEDRO. Amen, if you love her; for the lady is very well worthy.

CLAUD. You speak this to fetch me in, my lord.

190 D. PEDRO. By my troth, I speak my thought.

CLAUD. And, in faith, my lord, I spoke mine.

BENE. And, by my two faiths and troths, my lord, I spoke mine.

CLAUD. That I love her, I feel.

195 D. PEDRO. That she is worthy, I know.

BENE. That I neither feel how she should be loved, nor know how she should be worthy, is the opinion that fire cannot melt out of me: I will die in it at the stake.

D. PEDRO. Thou wast ever an obstinate heretic in the 200 despite of beauty.

CLAUD. And never could maintain his part but in the force of his will.

Bene. That a woman conceived me, I thank her; that
she brought me up, I likewise give her most humble
thanks: 205 but that I will have a recheat winded in
my forehead, or hang my bugle in an invisible
baldrick, all women shall pardon me. Because I will
not do them the wrong to mistrust any, I will do
myself the right to trust none; and the fine is, for the
which I may go the finer, I will live a bachelor.

210 *D. Pedro.* I shall see thee, ere I die, look pale with
love.

Bene. With anger, with sickness, or with hunger, my
lord; not with love: prove that ever I lose more
blood with love than I will get again with drinking, pick out mine eyes with a ballad-maker's pen,
and hang me up at the door of 215 a brothel-house
for the sign of blind Cupid.

D. Pedro. Well, if ever thou dost fall from this faith,
thou wilt prove a notable argument.

Bene. If I do, hang me in a bottle like a cat, and shoot
at me; and he that hits me, let him be clapped on
the 220 shoulder, and called Adam.

D. Pedro. Well, as time shall try: 'In time the savage
bull doth bear the yoke.'

Bene. The savage bull may; but if ever the sensible
Benedick bear it, pluck off the bull's horns, and set
them 225 in my forehead: and let me be vilely
painted; and in such great letters as they write
'Here is good horse to hire,' let them signify under
my sign 'Here you may see Benedick the married
man.'

Claud. If this should ever happen, thou wouldst be
230 horn-mad.

D. Pedro. Nay, if Cupid have not spent all his quiver
in Venice, thou wilt quake for this shortly.

Bene. I look for an earthquake too, then.

D. Pedro. Well, you will temporize with the hours.
In 235 the meantime, good Signior Benedick, repair
to Leonato's: commend me to him, and tell him I
will not fail him at supper; for indeed he hath
made great preparation.

Bene. I have almost matter enough in me for such an
embassage; and so I commit you—

240 *CLAUD.* To the tuition of God: From my house, if I
    had it,—

D. PEDRO. The sixth of July: Your loving friend,
    Benedick.

BENE. Nay, mock not, mock not. The body of your dis-
    course 245 is sometime guarded with fragments,
    and the guards are but slightly basted on neither:
    ere you flout old ends any further, examine your
    conscience: and so I leave you. *(Exit.)*

CLAUD. My liege, your highness now may do me
    good.

D. PEDRO. My love is thine to teach: teach it but how,
250 And thou shalt see how apt it is to learn
Any hard lesson that may do thee good.

CLAUD. Hath Leonato any son, my lord?

D. PEDRO. No child but Hero; she's his only heir.
Dost thou affect her, Claudio?

CLAUD. O, my lord,
255 When you went onward on this ended action,
I look'd upon her with a soldier's eye,
That liked, but had a rougher task in hand
Than to drive liking to the name of love:
But now I am return'd and that war-thoughts
260 Have left their places vacant, in their rooms
Come thronging soft and delicate desires,
All prompting me how fair young Hero is,
Saying, I liked her ere I went to wars.

D. PEDRO. Thou wilt be like a lover presently,
265 And tire the hearer with a book of words.
If thou dost love fair Hero, cherish it;
And I will break with her and with her father,
And thou shalt have her. Was't not to this end
That thou began'st to twist so fine a story?

270 *CLAUD.* How sweetly you do minister to love,
That know love's grief by his complexion!
But lest my liking might too sudden seem,
I would have salved it with a longer treatise.

D. PEDRO. What need the bridge much broader than
    the flood?
275 The fairest grant is the necessity.
Look, what will serve is fit: 'tis once, thou lovest,
And I will fit thee with the remedy.
I know we shall have revelling to-night:

I will assume thy part in some disguise,
280 And tell fair Hero I am Claudio;
And in her bosom I'll unclasp my heart,
And take her hearing prisoner with the force
And strong encounter of my amorous tale:
Then after to her father will I break;
285 And the conclusion is, she shall be thine.
In practice let us put it presently. *(Exeunt.)*

SCENE II. A ROOM IN LEONATO'S HOUSE.

(Enter LEONATO and ANTONIO, meeting.)

LEON. How now, brother! Where is my cousin, your
son? hath he provided this music?

ANT. He is very busy about it. But, brother, I can tell
you strange news, that you yet dreamt not of.

005 LEON. Are they good?

ANT. As the event stamps them: but they have a good
cover; they show well outward. The prince and
Count Claudio, walking in a thick-pleached alley
in mine orchard, were thus much overheard by a
man of mine: the prince 010 discovered to Claudio
that he loved my niece your daughter, and meant
to acknowledge it this night in a dance; and if he
found her accordant, he meant to take the present
time by the top, and instantly break with you of it.

LEON. Hath the fellow any wit that told you this?

015 ANT. A good sharp fellow: I will send for him; and
question him yourself.

LEON. No, no; we will hold it as a dream till it appear
itself: but I will acquaint my daughter withal, that
she may be the better prepared for an answer, if
peradventure this be 020 true. Go you and tell her
of it. *(Enter attendants.)* Cousins, you know what
you have to do. O, I cry you mercy, friend; go you
with me, and I will use your skill. Good cousin,
have a care this busy time. *(Exeunt.)*

SCENE III. THE SAME.

(ENTER DON JOHN AND CONRADE.)

Con. What the good-year, my lord! why are you thus
out of measure sad?

D. John. There is no measure in the occasion that
breeds; therefore the sadness is without limit.

005 Con. You should hear reason.

D. John. And when I have heard it, what blessing
brings it?

Con. If not a present remedy, at least a patient sufferance.

D. John. I wonder that thou, being *(as thou sayest thou
010 art)* born under Saturn, goest about to apply a
moral medicine to a mortifying mischief. I cannot
hide what I am: I must be sad when I have cause,
and smile at no man's jests; eat when I have stomach, and wait for no man's leisure; sleep when I
am drowsy, and tend on no man's business; 015
laugh when I am merry, and claw no man in his
humour.

Con. Yea, but you must not make the full show of this
till you may do it without controlment. You have
of late stood out against your brother, and he hath
ta'en you newly into his grace; where it is impossible you should take true 020 root but by the fair
weather that you make yourself: it is needful that
you frame the season for your own harvest.

D. John. I had rather be a canker in a hedge than a
rose in his grace; and it better fits my blood to be
disdained of all than to fashion a carriage to rob
love from any: in this, 025 though I cannot be said
to be a flattering honest man, it must not be denied but I am a plain-dealing villain. I am trusted
with a muzzle, and enfranchised with a clog;
therefore I have decreed not to sing in my cage. If I
had my mouth, I would bite; if I had my liberty, I
would do my 030 liking: in the meantime let me be
that I am, and seek not to alter me.

Con. Can you make no use of your discontent?

D. John. I make all use of it, for I use it only. Who
comes here?

(Enter Borachio.)

035 What news, Borachio?

Bora. I came yonder from a great supper: the prince
 your brother is royally entertained by Leonato;
 and I can give you intelligence of an intended
 marriage.

D. John. Will it serve for any model to build mischief
 040 on? What is he for a fool that betroths himself
 to unquietness?

Bora. Marry, it is your brother's right hand.

D. John. Who? the most exquisite Claudio?

Bora. Even he.

045 *D. John.* A proper squire! And who, and who?
 which way looks he?

Bora. Marry, on Hero, the daughter and heir of
 Leonato.

D. John. A very forward March-chick! How came
 you to this?

050 *Bora.* Being entertained for a perfumer, as I was
 smoking a musty room, comes me the prince and
 Claudio, hand in hand, in sad conference: I whipt
 me behind the arras; and there heard it agreed
 upon, that the prince should woo Hero for himself, and having obtained her, give 055 her to Count
 Claudio.

D. John. Come, come, let us thither: this may prove
 food to my displeasure. That young start-up hath
 all the glory of my overthrow: if I can cross him
 any way, I bless myself every way. You are both
 sure, and will assist me?

060 *Con.* To the death, my lord.

D. John. Let us to the great supper: their cheer is the
 greater that I am subdued. Would the cook were of
 my mind! Shall we go prove what's to be done?

Bora. We'll wait upon your lordship. *(Exeunt.)*

ACT II

SCENE I. A HALL IN LEONATO'S HOUSE.

(ENTER LEONATO, ANTONIO, HERO, BEATRICE, AND OTHERS.)

LEON. Was not Count John here at supper?

ANT. I saw him not.

BEAT. How tartly that gentleman looks! I never can see him but I am heart-burned an hour after.

005 *HERO.* He is of a very melancholy disposition.

BEAT. He were an excellent man that were made just in the midway between him and Benedick: the one is too like an image and says nothing, and the other too like my lady's eldest son, evermore tattling.

010 *LEON.* Then half Signior Benedick's tongue in Count John's mouth, and half Count John's melancholy in Signior Benedick's face,—

BEAT. With a good leg and a good foot, uncle, and money enough in his purse, such a man would win any 015 woman in the world, if a' could get her good-will.

LEON. By my troth, niece, thou wilt never get thee a husband, if thou be so shrewd of thy tongue.

ANT. In faith, she's too curst.

BEAT. Too curst is more than curst: I shall lessen God's 020 sending that way; for it is said, 'God sends a

curst cow short horns;' but to a cow too curst he
sends none.

LEON. So, by being too curst, God will send you no
horns.

BEAT. Just, if he send me no husband; for the which
blessing I am at him upon my knees every
morning and $_{025}$ evening. Lord, I could not endure
a husband with a beard on his face: I had rather lie
in the woollen.

LEON. You may light on a husband that hath no beard.

BEAT. What should I do with him? dress him in my
apparel, and make him my waiting-gentlewoman?
He that $_{030}$ hath a beard is more than a youth; and
he that hath no beard is less than a man: and he
that is more than a youth is not for me; and he that
is less than a man, I am not for him: therefore I
will even take sixpence in earnest of the bear-
ward, and lead his apes into hell.

$_{035}$ LEON. Well, then, go you into hell?

BEAT. No, but to the gate; and there will the devil
meet me, like an old cuckold, with horns on his
head, and say 'Get you to heaven, Beatrice, get
you to heaven; here's no place for you maids:' so
deliver I up my apes, and away $_{040}$ to Saint Peter
for the heavens; he shows me where the bachelors
sit, and there live we as merry as the day is long.

ANT. *(To Hero)* Well, niece, I trust you will be ruled by
your father.

BEAT. Yes, faith; it is my cousin's duty to make courtesy, and say, 'Father, as it please you.' But yet for
all $_{045}$ that, cousin, let him be a handsome fellow,
or else make another courtesy, and say, 'Father, as
it please me.'

LEON. Well, niece, I hope to see you one day fitted
with a husband.

$_{050}$ BEAT. Not till God make men of some other metal
than earth. Would it not grieve a woman to be
overmastered with a piece of valiant dust? to
make an account of her life to a clod of wayward
marl? No, uncle, I'll none: Adam's sons are my
brethren; and, truly, I hold it a sin to match $_{055}$ in
my kindred.

Leon. Daughter, remember what I told you: if the
   prince do solicit you in that kind, you know your
   answer.

Beat. The fault will be in the music, cousin, if you be
   not wooed in good time: if the prince be too important, tell $_{060}$ him there is measure in every
   thing, and so dance out the answer. For, hear me,
   Hero: wooing, wedding, and repenting, is as a
   Scotch jig, a measure, and a cinque pace: the first
   suit is hot and hasty, like a Scotch jig, and full as
   fantastical; the wedding, mannerly-modest, as a
   measure, $_{065}$ full of state and ancientry; and then
   comes repentance, and, with his bad legs, falls into
   the cinque pace faster and faster, till he sink into
   his grave.

Leon. Cousin, you apprehend passing shrewdly.

Beat. I have a good eye, uncle; I can see a church by
   $_{070}$ daylight.

Leon. The revellers are entering, brother: make good
   room. *(All put on their masks.)*

*(Enter Don Pedro, Claudio, Benedick, Balthasar, Don
John, Borachio, Margaret, Ursula, and others, masked.)*

D. Pedro. Lady, will you walk about with your
   friend?

Hero. So you walk softly, and look sweetly, and say
   $_{075}$ nothing, I am yours for the walk; and especially when I walk away.

D. Pedro. With me in your company?

Hero. I may say so, when I please.

D. Pedro. And when please you to say so?

$_{080}$ *Hero.* When I like your favour; for God defend the
   lute should be like the case!

D. Pedro. My visor is Philemon's roof; within the
   house is Jove.

Hero. Why, then, your visor should be thatched.

$_{085}$ *D. Pedro.* Speak low, if you speak love. *(Drawing
   her aside.)*

Balth. Well, I would you did like me.

Marg. So would not I, for your own sake; for I have
   many ill qualities.

BALTH. Which is one?

090 *MARG.* I say my prayers aloud.

BALTH. I love you the better: the hearers may cry, Amen.

MARG. God match me with a good dancer!

BALTH. *Amen.*

MARG. And God keep him out of my sight when the
095 dance is done! Answer, clerk.

BALTH. No more words: the clerk is answered.

URS. I know you well enough; you are Signior Antonio.

ANT. At a word, I am not.

URS. I know you by the waggling of your head.

100 *ANT.* To tell you true, I counterfeit him.

URS. You could never do him so ill-well; unless you were the very man. Here's his dry hand up and down: you are he, you are he.

ANT. At a word, I am not.

105 *URS.* Come, come, do you think I do not know you by your excellent wit? can virtue hide itself? Go to, mum, you are he: graces will appear, and there's an end.

BEAT. Will you not tell me who told you so?

BENE. No, you shall pardon me.

110 *BEAT.* Nor will you not tell me who you are?

BENE. Not now.

BEAT. That I was disdainful, and that I had my good wit out of the 'Hundred Merry Tales':—well, this was Signior Benedick that said so.

115 *BENE.* What's he?

BEAT. I am sure you know him well enough.

BENE. Not I, believe me.

BEAT. Did he never make you laugh?

BENE. I pray you, what is he?

120 *BEAT.* Why, he is the prince's jester: a very dull fool; only his gift is in devising impossible slanders: none but libertines delight in him; and the commendation is not in his wit, but in his villany; for he both pleases men and angers them, and then they laugh at him and beat him. I 125 am sure he is in the fleet: I would he had boarded me.

BENE. When I know the gentleman, I'll tell him what you say.

Beat. Do, do: he'll but break a comparison or two on
   me; which, peradventure not marked or not
   laughed at, 130 strikes him into melancholy; and
   then there's a partridge wing saved, for the fool
   will eat no supper that night. *(Music.)* We must
   follow the leaders.

Bene. In every good thing.

Beat. Nay, if they lead to any ill, I will leave them at
   135 the next turning. *(Dance. Then exeunt all except
   Don John, Borachio, and Claudio.)*

D. John. Sure my brother is amorous on Hero, and
   hath withdrawn her father to break with him
   about it. The ladies follow her, and but one visor
   remains.

Bora. And that is Claudio: I know him by his
   bearing.

140 *D. John.* Are not you Signior Benedick?

Claud. You know me well; I am he.

D. John. Signior, you are very near my brother in his
   love: he is enamoured on Hero; I pray you, dis-
   suade him from her: she is no equal for his birth:
   you may do the 145 part of an honest man in it.

Claud. How know you he loves her?

D. John. I heard him swear his affection.

Bora. So did I too; and he swore he would marry her
   to-night.

150 *D. John.* Come, let us to the banquet. *(Exeunt Don
   John and Borachio.)*

Claud. Thus answer I in name of Benedick,
But hear these ill news with the ears of Claudio.
'Tis certain so; the prince wooes for himself.
Friendship is constant in all other things
155 Save in the office and affairs of love:
Therefore all hearts in love use their own tongues;
Let every eye negotiate for itself,
And trust no agent; for beauty is a witch,
Against whose charms faith melteth into blood.
160 This is an accident of hourly proof,
Which I mistrusted not. Farewell, therefore, Hero!

(Re-enter Benedick.)

Bene. Count Claudio?

Claud. Yea, the same.

Bene. Come, will you go with me?

165 *Claud.* Whither?

Bene. Even to the next willow, about your own business, county. What fashion will you wear the garland of? about your neck, like an usurer's chain? or under your arm, like a lieutenant's scarf? You must wear it one way, for the 170 prince hath got your *Hero.*

Claud. I wish him joy of her.

Bene. Why, that's spoken like an honest drovier: so they sell bullocks. But did you think the prince would have served you thus?

175 *Claud.* I pray you, leave me.

Bene. Ho! now you strike like the blind man: 'twas the boy that stole your meat, and you'll beat the post.

Claud. If it will not be, I'll leave you. *(Exit.)*

Bene. Alas, poor hurt fowl! now will he creep into 180 sedges. But, that my Lady Beatrice should know me, and not know me! The prince's fool! Ha? It may be I go under that title because I am merry. Yea, but so I am apt to do myself wrong; I am not so reputed: it is the base, though bitter, disposition of Beatrice that puts the world 185 into her person, and so gives me out. Well, I'll be revenged as I may.

(Re-enter Don Pedro.)

D. Pedro. Now, signior, where's the count? did you see him?

Bene. Troth, my lord, I have played the part of Lady 190 Fame. I found him here as melancholy as a lodge in a warren: I told him, and I think I told him true, that your grace had got the good will of this young lady; and I offered him my company to a willow-tree, either to make him a garland, as being forsaken, or to bind him up a rod, as being 195 worthy to be whipped.

D. Pedro. To be whipped! What's his fault?

Bene. The flat transgression of a school-boy, who,

being overjoyed with finding a birds' nest, shows it his companion, and he steals it.

200 *D. Pedro.* Wilt thou make a trust a transgression? The transgression is in the stealer.

Bene. Yet it had not been amiss the rod had been made, and the garland too; for the garland he might have worn himself, and the rod he might have bestowed on you, 205 who, as I take it, have stolen his birds' nest.

D. Pedro. I will but teach them to sing, and restore them to the owner.

Bene. If their singing answer your saying, by my faith, you say honestly.

210 *D. Pedro.* The Lady Beatrice hath a quarrel to you: the gentleman that danced with her told her she is much wronged by you.

Bene. O, she misused me past the endurance of a block! an oak but with one green leaf on it would have 215 answered her; my very visor began to assume life and scold with her. She told me, not thinking I had been myself, that I was the prince's jester, that I was duller than a great thaw; huddling jest upon jest, with such impossible conveyance, upon me, that I stood like a man at 220 a mark, with a whole army shooting at me. She speaks poniards, and every word stabs: if her breath were as terrible as her terminations, there were no living near her; she would infect to the north star. I would not marry her, though she were endowed with all that Adam had 225 left him before he transgressed: she would have made Hercules have turned spit, yea, and have cleft his club to make the fire too. Come, talk not of her: you shall find her the infernal Ate in good apparel. I would to God some scholar would conjure her; for certainly, while she is 230 here, a man may live as quiet in hell as in a sanctuary; and people sin upon purpose, because they would go thither; so, indeed, all disquiet, horror, and perturbation follows her.

D. Pedro. Look, here she comes.

(*Enter Claudio, Beatrice, Hero, and Leonato.*)

235 *Bene.* Will your grace command me any service to
the world's end? I will go on the slightest errand
now to the Antipodes that you can devise to send
me on; I will fetch you a toothpicker now from the
furthest inch of Asia; bring you the length of
Prester John's foot; fetch you a 240 hair off the great
Cham's beard; do you any embassage to the Pig-
mies; rather than hold three words' conference
with this harpy. You have no employment for me?

D. Pedro. None, but to desire your good company.

Bene. O God, sir, here's a dish I love not: I cannot 245
endure my Lady Tongue. (*Exit.*)

D. Pedro. Come, lady, come; you have lost the heart
of Signior Benedick.

Beat. Indeed, my lord, he lent it me awhile; and I
gave him use for it, a double heart for his single
one: 250 marry, once before he won it of me with
false dice, therefore your Grace may well say I
have lost it.

D. Pedro. You have put him down, lady, you have
put him down.

Beat. So I would not he should do me, my lord, lest I
255 should prove the mother of fools. I have
brought Count Claudio, whom you sent me to
seek.

D. Pedro. Why, how now, count! wherefore are
you sad?

Claud. Not sad, my lord.

260 *D. Pedro.* How then? sick?

Claud. Neither, my lord.

Beat. The count is neither sad, nor sick, nor merry,
nor well; but civil count, civil as an orange, and
something of that jealous complexion.

265 *D. Pedro.* I' faith, lady, I think your blazon to be
true; though, I'll be sworn, if he be so, his conceit
is false. Here, Claudio, I have wooed in thy name,
and fair Hero is won: I have broke with her father,
and his good will obtained: name the day of marriage, and God give thee 270 joy!

Leon. Count, take of me my daughter, and with her
my fortunes: his Grace hath made the match, and
all grace say Amen to it.

Beat. Speak, count, 'tis your cue.

₂₇₅ CLAUD. Silence is the perfectest herald of joy: I
were but little happy, if I could say how much.
Lady, as you are mine, I am yours: I give away
myself for you, and dote upon the exchange.

BEAT. Speak, cousin; or, if you cannot, stop his mouth
₂₈₀ with a kiss, and let not him speak neither.

D. PEDRO. In faith, lady, you have a merry heart.

BEAT. Yea, my lord; I thank it, poor fool, it keeps on
the windy side of care. My cousin tells him in his
ear that he is in her heart.

₂₈₅ CLAUD. And so she doth, cousin.

BEAT. Good Lord, for alliance! Thus goes every one to
the world but I, and I am sun-burnt; I may sit in a
corner, and cry heigh-ho for a husband!

D. PEDRO. Lady Beatrice, I will get you one.

₂₉₀ BEAT. I would rather have one of your father's get-
ting. Hath your Grace ne'er a brother like you?
Your father got excellent husbands, if a maid
could come by them.

D. PEDRO. Will you have me, lady?

BEAT. No, my lord, unless I might have another for
₂₉₅ working-days: your Grace is too costly to
wear every day. But, I beseech your Grace,
pardon me: I was born to speak all mirth and no
matter.

D. PEDRO. Your silence most offends me, and to be
merry best becomes you; for, out of question, you
were ₃₀₀ born in a merry hour.

BEAT. No, sure, my lord, my mother cried; but then
there was a star danced, and under that was I
born. Cousins, God give you joy!

LEON. Niece, will you look to those things I told ₃₀₅
you of?

BEAT. I cry you mercy, uncle. By your Grace's pardon.
(Exit.)

D. PEDRO. By my troth, a pleasant-spirited lady.

LEON. There's little of the melancholy element in her,
₃₁₀ my lord: she is never sad but when she sleeps;
and not ever sad then; for I have heard my
daughter say, she hath often dreamed of unhappi-
ness, and waked herself with laughing.

D. PEDRO. She cannot endure to hear tell of a
husband.

315 *Leon.* O, by no means: she mocks all her wooers out of suit.

D. Pedro. She were an excellent wife for Benedick.

Leon. O Lord, my lord, if they were but a week married, they would talk themselves mad.

320 *D. Pedro.* County Claudio, when mean you to go to church?

Claud. To-morrow, my lord: time goes on crutches till love have all his rites.

Leon. Not till Monday, my dear son, which is hence a 325 just seven-night; and a time too brief, too, to have all things answer my mind.

D. Pedro. Come, you shake the head at so long a breathing: but, I warrant thee, Claudio, the time shall not go dully by us. I will, in the interim, undertake one of 330 Hercules' labours; which is, to bring Signior Benedick and the Lady Beatrice into a mountain of affection the one with the other. I would fain have it a match; and I doubt not but to fashion it, if you three will but minister such assistance as I shall give you direction.

335 *Leon.* My lord, I am for you, though it cost me ten nights' watchings.

Claud. And I, my lord.

D. Pedro. And you too, gentle Hero?

Hero. I will do any modest office, my lord, to help 340 my cousin to a good husband.

D. Pedro. And Benedick is not the unhopefullest husband that I know. Thus far can I praise him; he is of a noble strain, of approved valour, and confirmed honesty. I will teach you how to humour your cousin, that she shall 345 fall in love with Benedick; and I, with your two helps, will so practise on Benedick, that, in despite of his quick wit and his queasy stomach, he shall fall in love with Beatrice. If we can do this, Cupid is no longer an archer: his glory shall be ours, for we are the only love-gods. Go 350 in with me, and I will tell you my drift. *(Exeunt.)*

SCENE II. THE SAME.

(Enter Don John and Borachio.)

D. John. It is so; the Count Claudio shall marry the daughter of Leonato.

Bora. Yea, my lord; but I can cross it.

D. John. Any bar, any cross, any impediment will be medicinable to me: I am sick in displeasure to him; and whatsoever comes athwart his affection ranges evenly with mine. How canst thou cross this marriage?

Bora. Not honestly, my lord; but so covertly that no dishonesty shall appear in me.

D. John. Show me briefly how.

Bora. I think I told your lordship, a year since, how much I am in the favour of Margaret, the waiting gentlewoman to *Hero.*

D. John. I remember.

Bora. I can, at any unseasonable instant of the night, appoint her to look out at her lady's chamber window.

D. John. What life is in that, to be the death of this marriage?

Bora. The poison of that lies in you to temper. Go you to the prince your brother; spare not to tell him that he hath wronged his honour in marrying the renowned Claudio—whose estimation do you mightily hold up—to a contaminated stale, such a one as *Hero.*

D. John. What proof shall I make of that?

Bora. Proof enough to misuse the prince, to vex Claudio, to undo Hero, and kill Leonato. Look you for any other issue?

D. John. Only to despite them, I will endeavour any thing.

Bora. Go, then; find me a meet hour to draw Don Pedro and the Count Claudio alone: tell them that you know that Hero loves me; intend a kind of zeal both to the prince and Claudio, as,—in love of your brother's honour, who hath made this match, and his friend's reputation, who is thus like to be cozened with the semblance of a maid,—that you have discovered thus. They will scarcely believe this without trial: offer them instances; which shall bear no less likelihood than to see me at her chamber-window; hear me call Margaret, Hero; hear Margaret term me Claudio; and 040 bring them to see this the very night before the intended wedding,—for in the meantime I will so fashion the matter that Hero shall be absent,—and there shall appear such seeming truth of Hero's disloyalty, that jealousy shall be called assurance and all the preparation overthrown.

045 *D. JOHN.* Grow this to what adverse issue it can, I will put it in practice. Be cunning in the working this, and thy fee is a thousand ducats.

BORA. Be you constant in the accusation, and my cunning shall not shame me.

050 *D. JOHN.* I will presently go learn their day of marriage. *(Exeunt.)*

SCENE III. LEONATO'S ORCHARD.

(Enter BENEDICK.)

BENE. Boy!

(Enter Boy.)

BOY. Signior?

BENE. In my chamber-window lies a book: bring it hither to me in the orchard.

005 *BOY.* I am here already, sir.

BENE. I know that; but I would have thee hence, and here again. *(Exit Boy.)* I do much wonder that one man, seeing how much another man is a fool when he dedicates his behaviours to love, will, after he hath laughed at such 010 shallow follies in others, become the argument of his own scorn by falling in love: and such a man is Claudio. I have known when there was no music with him but the drum and the fife; and now had he rather hear the tabor and the pipe: I have known when he would

have walked ten mile a-foot $_{015}$ to see a good ar-
mour; and now will he lie ten nights awake,
carving the fashion of a new doublet. He was
wont to speak plain and to the purpose, like an
honest man and a soldier; and now is he turned
orthography; his words are a very fantastical banquet,—just so many strange dishes. May I $_{020}$ be so
converted, and see with these eyes? I cannot tell; I
think not: I will not be sworn but love may trans-
form me to an oyster; but I'll take my oath on it,
till he have made an oyster of me, he shall never
make me such a fool. One woman is fair, yet I am
well; another is wise, yet I am $_{025}$ well; another virtuous, yet I am well: but till all graces be in one
woman, one woman shall not come in my grace.
Rich she shall be, that's certain; wise, or I'll none;
virtuous, or I'll never cheapen her; fair, or I'll
never look on her; mild, or come not near me; noble, or not I for an $_{030}$ angel; of good discourse, an
excellent musician, and her hair shall be of what
colour it please God. Ha! the prince and Monsieur
Love! I will hide me in the arbour. *(Withdraws.)*

(ENTER DON PEDRO, CLAUDIO, AND LEONATO.)

D. PEDRO. Come, shall we hear this music?
CLAUD. Yea, my good lord. How still the evening is,
$_{035}$ As hush'd on purpose to grace harmony!
D. PEDRO. See you where Benedick hath hid himself?
CLAUD. O, very well, my lord: the music ended,
We'll fit the kid-fox with a pennyworth.

(Enter BALTHASAR with Music.)

D. PEDRO. Come, Balthasar, we'll hear that song
   again.
$_{040}$ **BALTH.** O, good my lord, tax not so bad a voice
To slander music any more than once.
D. PEDRO. It is the witness still of excellency
To put a strange face on his own perfection.
I pray thee, sing, and let me woo no more.
$_{045}$ **BALTH.** Because you talk of wooing, I will sing;
Since many a wooer doth commence his suit

To her he thinks not worthy, yet he wooes,
Yet will he swear he loves.

D. PEDRO.
Nay, pray thee, come;
Or, if thou wilt hold longer argument,
Do it in notes.

BALTH.
050 Note this before my notes;
There's not a note of mine that's worth the noting.

D. PEDRO. Why, these are very crotchets that he
speaks;
Note, notes, forsooth, and nothing. *(Air.)*

BENE. Now, divine air! now is his soul ravished! Is it
055 not strange that sheeps' guts should hale souls
out of men's bodies? Well, a horn for my money,
when all's done.

(The Song.)

BALTH. Sigh no more, ladies, sigh no more,
Men were deceivers ever,
One foot in sea and one on shore,
060 To one thing constant never:
Then sigh not so, but let them go,
And be you blithe and bonny,
Converting all your sounds of woe
Into Hey nonny, nonny.
065 Sing no more ditties, sing no moe,
Of dumps so dull and heavy;
The fraud of men was ever so,
Since summer first was leavy:
Then sigh not so, &c.

070 *D. PEDRO.* By my troth, a good song.

BALTH. And an ill singer, my lord.

D. PEDRO. Ha, no, no, faith; thou singest well enough
for a shift.

BENE. An he had been a dog that should have howled
075 thus, they would have hanged him: and I pray
God his bad voice bode no mischief. I had as lief
have heard the night-raven, come what plague
could have come after it.

D. PEDRO. Yea, marry, dost thou hear, Balthasar? I
pray thee, get us some excellent music; for to-

morrow night $_{080}$ we would have it at the Lady
Hero's chamber-window.

BALTH. The best I can, my lord.

D. PEDRO. Do so: farewell. *(Exit Balthasar.)* Come
hither, Leonato. What was it you told me of to-day,
that your niece Beatrice was in love with Signior
$_{085}$ Benedick?

CLAUD. O, ay: stalk on, stalk on; the fowl sits. I did
never think that lady would have loved any man.

LEON. No, nor I neither; but most wonderful that she
should so dote on Signior Benedick, whom she
hath in all $_{090}$ outward behaviours seemed ever to
abhor.

BENE. Is't possible? Sits the wind in that corner?

LEON. By my troth, my lord, I cannot tell what to
think of it, but that she loves him with an enraged
affection; it is past the infinite of thought.

$_{095}$ *D. PEDRO.* May be she doth but counterfeit.

CLAUD. Faith, like enough.

LEON. O God, counterfeit! There was never counterfeit of passion came so near the life of passion as
she discovers it.

D. PEDRO. Why, what effects of passion shows she?

$_{100}$ *CLAUD.* Bait the hook well; this fish will bite.

LEON. What effects, my lord? She will sit you, you
heard my daughter tell you how.

CLAUD. She did, indeed.

D. PEDRO. How, how, I pray you? You amaze me: I $_{105}$
would have thought her spirit had been invincible
against all assaults of affection.

LEON. I would have sworn it had, my lord; especially
against Benedick.

BENE. I should think this a gull, but that the white-
bearded $_{110}$ fellow speaks it: knavery cannot, sure,
hide himself in such reverence.

CLAUD. He hath ta'en the infection: hold it up.

D. PEDRO. Hath she made her affection known to
Benedick?

$_{115}$ *LEON.* No; and swears she never will: that's her
torment.

CLAUD. 'Tis true, indeed; so your daughter says: 'Shall
I,' says she, 'that have so oft encountered him with
scorn, $_{120}$ write to him that I love him?'

LEON. This says she now when she is beginning to write to him; for she'll be up twenty times a night; and there will she sit in her smock till she have writ a sheet of paper: my daughter tells us all.

125 CLAUD. Now you talk of a sheet of paper, I remember a pretty jest your daughter told us of.

LEON. O, when she had writ it, and was reading it over, she found Benedick and Beatrice between the sheet?

CLAUD. That.

130 LEON. O, she tore the letter into a thousand half-pence; railed at herself, that she should be so immodest to write to one that she knew would flout her; 'I measure him,' says she, 'by my own spirit; for I should flout him, if he writ to me; yea, though I love him, I should.'

135 CLAUD. Then down upon her knees she falls, weeps, sobs, beats her heart, tears her hair, prays, curses; 'O sweet Benedick! God give me patience!'

LEON. She doth indeed; my daughter says so: and the ecstasy hath so much overborne her, that my daughter is 140 sometime afeard she will do a desperate outrage to herself: it is very true.

D. PEDRO. It were good that Benedick knew of it by some other, if she will not discover it.

CLAUD. To what end? He would make but a sport of 145 it, and torment the poor lady worse.

D. PEDRO. An he should, it were an alms to hang him. She's an excellent sweet lady; and, out of all suspicion, she is virtuous.

CLAUD. And she is exceeding wise.

150 D. PEDRO. In every thing but in loving Benedick.

LEON. O, my lord, wisdom and blood combating in so tender a body, we have ten proofs to one that blood hath the victory. I am sorry for her, as I have just cause, being her uncle and her guardian.

155 D. PEDRO. I would she had bestowed this dotage on me: I would have daffed all other respects, and made her half myself. I pray you, tell Benedick of it, and hear what a' will say.

LEON. Were it good, think you?

160 *CLAUD.* Hero thinks surely she will die; for she says she will die, if he love her not; and she will die, ere she make her love known; and she will die, if he woo her, rather than she will bate one breath of her accustomed crossness.

D. PEDRO. She doth well: if she should make tender of 165 her love, 'tis very possible he'll scorn it; for the man, as you know all, hath a contemptible spirit.

CLAUD. He is a very proper man.

D. PEDRO. He hath indeed a good outward happiness.

CLAUD. Before God! and in my mind, very wise.

170 *D. PEDRO.* He doth indeed show some sparks that are like wit.

CLAUD. And I take him to be valiANT.

D. PEDRO. As Hector, I assure you: and in the managing of quarrels you may say he is wise; for either he avoids 175 them with great discretion, or undertakes them with a most Christian-like fear.

LEON. If he do fear God, a' must necessarily keep peace: if he break the peace, he ought to enter into a quarrel with fear and trembling.

180 *D. PEDRO.* And so will he do; for the man doth fear God, howsoever it seems not in him by some large jests he will make. Well, I am sorry for your niece. Shall we go seek Benedick, and tell him of her love?

CLAUD. Never tell him, my lord: let her wear it out 185 with good counsel.

LEON. Nay, that's impossible: she may wear her heart out first.

D. PEDRO. Well, we will hear further of it by your daughter: let it cool the while. I love Benedick well; and 190 I could wish he would modestly examine himself, to see how much he is unworthy so good a lady.

LEON. My lord, will you walk? dinner is ready.

CLAUD. If he do not dote on her upon this, I will never trust my expectation.

195 *D. PEDRO.* Let there be the same net spread for her; and that must your daughter and her gentlewomen carry. The sport will be, when they hold

one an opinion of another's dotage, and no such
matter: that's the scene that I would see, which
will be merely a dumb-show. Let us send $_{200}$ her to
call him in to dinner. *(Exeunt Don Pedro, Claudio,
and Leonato.)*

BENE. *(Coming forward)* This can be no trick: the conference was sadly borne. They have the truth of
this from Hero. They seem to pity the lady: it
seems her affections have their full bent. Love me!
why, it must be requited. $_{205}$ I hear how I am cen-
sured: they say I will bear myself proudly, if I perceive the love come from her; they say too that she
will rather die than give any sign of affection. I did
never think to marry: I must not seem proud:
happy are they that hear their detractions, and can
put them to $_{210}$ mending. They say the lady is fair,
—'tis a truth, I can bear them witness; and virtuous,—'tis so, I cannot reprove it; and wise, but for
loving me,—by my troth, it is no addition to her
wit, nor no great argument of her folly, for I will
be horribly in love with her. I may chance have
some $_{215}$ odd quirks and remnants of wit broken
on me, because I have railed so long against marriage: but doth not the appetite alter? a man loves
the meat in his youth that he cannot endure in his
age. Shall quips and sentences and these paper
bullets of the brain awe a man from the career $_{220}$
of his humour? No, the world must be peopled.
When I said I would die a bachelor, I did not think
I should live till I were married. Here comes Beatrice. By this day! she's a fair lady: I do spy some
marks of love in her.

(ENTER BEATRICE.)

BEAT. Against my will I am sent to bid you come in to
$_{225}$ dinner.

BENE. Fair Beatrice, I thank you for your pains.

BEAT. I took no more pains for those thanks than you
take pains to thank me: if it had been painful, I
would not have come.

$_{230}$ BENE. You take pleasure, then, in the message?

BEAT. Yea, just so much as you may take upon a

knife's point, and choke a daw withal. You have
no stomach, signior: fare you well. *(Exit.)*

BENE. Ha! 'Against my will I am sent to bid you come
235 in to dinner;' there's a double meaning in that.
'I took no more pains for those thanks than you
took pains to thank me;' that's as much as to say,
Any pains that I take for you is as easy as thanks.
If I do not take pity of her, I am a villain; if I do not
love her, I am a Jew. I will go get 240 her picture.
(Exit.)

ACT III

SCENE I. LEONATO'S GARDEN.

(ENTER HERO, MARGARET, AND URSULA.)

HERO. Good Margaret, run thee to the parlour;
There shalt thou find my cousin Beatrice
Proposing with the prince and Claudio:
Whisper her ear, and tell her, I and Ursula
005 Walk in the orchard, and our whole discourse
Is all of her; say that thou overheard'st us;
And bid her steal into the pleached bower,
Where honeysuckles, ripen'd by the sun,
Forbid the sun to enter; like favourites,
010 Made proud by princes, that advance their pride
Against that power that bred it: there will she
    hide her,
To listen our propose. This is thy office;
Bear thee well in it, and leave us alone.
MARG. I'll make her come, I warrant you, presently.
    (Exit.)
015 *HERO.* Now, Ursula, when Beatrice doth come,
As we do trace this alley up and down,
Our talk must only be of Benedick.
When I do name him, let it be thy part
To praise him more than ever man did merit:
020 My talk to thee must be, how Benedick
Is sick in love with Beatrice. Of this matter

Is little Cupid's crafty arrow made,
That only wounds by hearsay.

(Enter BEATRICE, behind.)

Now begin;
For look where Beatrice, like a lapwing, runs
025 Close by the ground, to hear our conference.
URS. The pleasant'st angling is to see the fish
Cut with her golden oars the silver stream,
And greedily devour the treacherous bait:
So angle we for Beatrice; who even now
030 Is couched in the woodbine coverture.
Fear you not my part of the dialogue.
HERO. Then go we near her, that her ear lose nothing
Of the false sweet bait that we lay for it. *(Approaching
    the bower.)*
No, truly, Ursula, she is too disdainful;
035 I know her spirits are as coy and wild
As haggerds of the rock.
URS. But are you sure
That Benedick loves Beatrice so entirely?
HERO. So says the prince and my new-trothed lord.
URS. And did they bid you tell her of it, madam?
040 *HERO.* They did entreat me to acquaint her of it;
But I persuaded them, if they loved Benedick,
To wish him wrestle with affection,
And never to let Beatrice know of it.
URS. Why did you so? Doth not the gentleman
045 Deserve as full as fortunate a bed
As ever Beatrice shall couch upon?
HERO. O god of love! I know he doth deserve
As much as may be yielded to a man:
But Nature never framed a woman's heart
050 Of prouder stuff than that of Beatrice;
Disdain and scorn ride sparkling in her eyes,
Misprising what they look on; and her wit
Values itself so highly, that to her
All matter else seems weak: she cannot love,
055 Nor take no shape nor project of affection,
She is so self-endeared.
URS. Sure, I think so;
And therefore certainly it were not good

She knew his love, lest she make sport at it.
Hero. Why, you speak truth. I never yet saw man,
060 How wise, how noble, young, how rarely featured,
But she would spell him backward: if fair-faced,
She would swear the gentleman should be her sister;
If black, why, Nature, drawing of an antique,
Made a foul blot; if tall, a lance ill-headed;
065 If low, an agate very vilely cut;
If speaking, why, a vane blown with all winds;
If silent, why, a block moved with none.
So turns she every man the wrong side out;
And never gives to truth and virtue that
070 Which simpleness and merit purchaseth.
Urs. Sure, sure, such carping is not commendable.
Hero. No, not to be so odd, and from all fashions,
As Beatrice is, cannot be commendable:
But who dare tell her so? If I should speak,
075 She would mock me into air; O, she would
    laugh me
Out of myself, press me to death with wit!
Therefore let Benedick, like cover'd fire,
Consume away in sighs, waste inwardly:
It were a better death than die with mocks,
080 Which is as bad as die with tickling.
Urs. Yet tell her of it: hear what she will say.
Hero. No; rather I will go to Benedick,
And counsel him to fight against his passion.
And, truly, I'll devise some honest slanders
085 To stain my cousin with: one doth not know
How much an ill word may empoison liking.
Urs. O, do not do your cousin such a wrong!
She cannot be so much without true judgement,—
Having so swift and excellent a wit
090 As she is prized to have,—as to refuse
So rare a gentleman as Signior Benedick.
Hero. He is the only man of Italy,
Always excepted my dear Claudio.
Urs. I pray you, be not angry with me, madam,
095 Speaking my fancy: Signior Benedick,
For shape, for bearing, argument and valour,
Goes foremost in report through Italy.
Hero. Indeed, he hath an excellent good name.
Urs. His excellence did earn it, ere he had it.

100 When are you married, madam?

Hero. Why, every day, to-morrow. Come, go in:
I'll show thee some attires; and have thy counsel
Which is the best to furnish me to-morrow.

Urs. She's limed, I warrant you: we have caught her,
madam.

105 *Hero.* If it prove so, then loving goes by haps:
Some Cupid kills with arrows, some with traps.
(Exeunt Hero and Ursula.)

Beat. *(Coming forward)* What fire is in mine ears? Can
this be true?

Stand I condemn'd for pride and scorn so much?
Contempt, farewell! and maiden pride, adieu!
110 No glory lives behind the back of such.
And, Benedick, love on; I will requite thee,
Taming my wild heart to thy loving hand:
If thou dost love, my kindness shall incite thee
To bind our loves up in a holy band;
115 For others say thou dost deserve, and I
Believe it better than reportingly. *(Exit.)*

SCENE II. A ROOM IN LEONATO'S HOUSE

(Enter Don Pedro, Claudio, Benedick, and Leonato.)

D. Pedro. I do but stay till your marriage be consum-
mate, and then go I toward Arragon.

Claud. I'll bring you thither, my lord, if you'll vouchsafe me.

005 *D. Pedro.* Nay, that would be as great a soil in the
new gloss of your marriage, as to show a child his
new coat and forbid him to wear it. I will only be
bold with Benedick for his company; for, from the
crown of his head to the sole of his foot, he is all
mirth: he hath twice or thrice cut 010 Cupid's bow-
string, and the little hangman dare not shoot at
him; he hath a heart as sound as a bell, and his
tongue is the clapper, for what his heart thinks his
tongue speaks.

Bene. Gallants, I am not as I have been.

Leon. So say I: methinks you are sadder.

015 *Claud.* I hope he be in love.

D. Pedro. Hang him, truant! there's no true drop of blood in him, to be truly touched with love: if he be sad, he wants money.

Bene. I have the toothache.

020 *D. Pedro.* Draw it.

Bene. Hang it!

Claud. You must hang it first, and draw it afterwards.

D. Pedro. What! sigh for the toothache?

Leon. Where is but a humour or a worm.

025 *Bene.* Well, every one can master a grief but he that has it.

Claud. Yet say I, he is in love.

D. Pedro. There is no appearance of fancy in him, unless it be a fancy that he hath to strange disguises; as, to 030 be a Dutchman to-day, a Frenchman to-morrow; or in the shape of two countries at once, as, a German from the waist downward, all slops, and a Spaniard from the hip upward, no doublet. Unless he have a fancy to this foolery, as it appears he hath, he is no fool for fancy, as you would have 035 it appear he is.

Claud. If he be not in love with some woman, there is no believing old signs: a' brushes his hat o' mornings; what should that bode?

D. Pedro. Hath any man seen him at the barber's?

040 *Claud.* No, but the barber's man hath been seen with him; and the old ornament of his cheek hath already stuffed tennis-balls.

Leon. Indeed, he looks younger than he did, by the loss of a beard.

045 *D. Pedro.* Nay, a' rubs himself with civet: can you smell him out by that?

Claud. That's as much as to say, the sweet youth's in love.

D. Pedro. The greatest note of it is his melancholy.

Claud. And when was he wont to wash his face?

050 *D. Pedro.* Yea, or to paint himself? for the which, I hear what they say of him.

Claud. Nay, but his jesting spirit; which is now crept into a lute-string, and now governed by stops.

D. Pedro. Indeed, that tells a heavy tale for him: conclude, 055 conclude he is in love.

Claud. Nay, but I know who loves him.

D. PEDRO. That would I know too: I warrant, one that knows him not.

CLAUD. Yes, and his ill conditions; and, in despite of 060 all, dies for him.

D. PEDRO. She shall be buried with her face upwards.

BENE. Yet is this no charm for the toothache. Old signior, walk aside with me: I have studied eight or nine wise words to speak to you, which these hobby-horses must not 065 hear. *(Exeunt Benedick and Leonato.)*

D. PEDRO. For my life, to break with him about Beatrice.

CLAUD. 'Tis even so. Hero and Margaret have by this played their parts with Beatrice; and then the two bears will not bite one another when they meet.

(ENTER DON JOHN.)

070 D. JOHN. My lord and brother, God save you!

D. PEDRO. Good den, brother.

D. JOHN. If your leisure served, I would speak with you.

D. PEDRO. In private?

D. JOHN. If it please you: yet Count Claudio may 075 hear; for what I would speak of concerns him.

D. PEDRO. What's the matter?

D. JOHN. *(To Claudio)* Means your lordship to be married to-morrow?

D. PEDRO. You know he does.

080 D. JOHN. I know not that, when he knows what I know.

CLAUD. If there be any impediment, I pray you discover it.

D. JOHN. You may think I love you not: let that appear hereafter, and aim better at me by that I now will 085 manifest. For my brother, I think he holds you well, and in dearness of heart hath holp to effect your ensuing marriage,—surely suit ill spent and labour ill bestowed.

D. PEDRO. Why, what's the matter?

D. JOHN. I came hither to tell you; and, circumstances 090 shortened, for she has been too long a talking of, the lady is disloyal.

CLAUD. Who, Hero?

D. JOHN. Even she; Leonato's Hero, your Hero, every man's *HERO.*

095 *CLAUD.* Disloyal?

D. JOHN. The word is too good to paint out her wickedness; I could say she were worse: think you of a worse title, and I will fit her to it. Wonder not till further warrant: go but with me to-night, you shall see her chamber-window 100 entered, even the night before her wedding-day: if you love her then, to-morrow wed her; but it would better fit your honour to change your mind.

CLAUD. May this be so?

D. PEDRO. I will not think it.

105 *D. JOHN.* If you dare not trust that you see, confess not that you know: if you will follow me, I will show you enough; and when you have seen more, and heard more, proceed accordingly.

CLAUD. If I see any thing to-night why I should not 110 marry her to-morrow, in the congregation, where I should wed, there will I shame her.

D. PEDRO. And, as I wooed for thee to obtain her, I will join with thee to disgrace her.

D. JOHN. I will disparage her no farther till you are my 115 witnesses: bear it coldly but till midnight, and let the issue show itself.

D. PEDRO. O day untowardly turned!

CLAUD. O mischief strangely thwarting!

D. JOHN. O plague right well prevented! so will you 120 say when you have seen the sequel. *(Exeunt.)*

SCENE III. A STREET.

(Enter DOGBERRY and VERGES with the Watch.)

DOG. Are you good men and true?

VERG. Yea, or else it were pity but they should suffer salvation, body and soul.

DOG. Nay, that were a punishment too good for them, 005 if they should have any allegiance in them, being chosen for the prince's watch.

Verg. Well, give them their charge, neighbour
Dogberry.

Dog. First, who think you the most desartless man to
be constable?

010 *First Watch.* Hugh Otecake, sir, or George Seacole; for they can write and read.

Dog. Come hither, neighbour Seacole. God hath
blessed you with a good name: to be a well-
favoured man is the gift of fortune; but to write
and read comes by nature.

015 *Sec. Watch.* Both which, master constable,—

Dog. You have: I knew it would be your answer.
Well, for your favour, sir, why, give God thanks,
and make no boast of it; and for your writing and
reading, let that appear when there is no need of
such vanity. You are thought 020 here to be the
most senseless and fit man for the constable of the
watch; therefore bear you the lantern. This is your
charge: you shall comprehend all vagrom men;
you are to bid any man stand, in the prince's
name.

Sec. Watch. How if a' will not stand?

025 *Dog.* Why, then, take no note of him, but let him
go; and presently call the rest of the watch together, and thank God you are rid of a knave.

Verg. If he will not stand when he is bidden, he is
none of the prince's subjects.

030 *Dog.* True, and they are to meddle with none but
the prince's subjects. You shall also make no noise
in the streets; for for the watch to babble and to
talk is most tolerable and not to be endured.

Watch. We will rather sleep than talk: we know what
035 belongs to a watch.

Dog. Why, you speak like an ancient and most quiet
watchman; for I cannot see how sleeping should
offend: only, have a care that your bills be not
stolen. Well, you are to call at all the ale-houses,
and bid those that are 040 drunk get them to bed.

Watch. How if they will not?

Dog. Why, then, let them alone till they are sober: if
they make you not then the better answer, you
may say they are not the men you took them for.

045 *Watch.* Well, sir.

DoG. If you meet a thief, you may suspect him, by
   virtue of your office, to be no true man; and, for
   such kind of men, the less you meddle or make
   with them, why, the more is for your honesty.

050 WATCH. If we know him to be a thief, shall we not
   lay hands on him?

DoG. Truly, by your office, you may; but I think they
   that touch pitch will be defiled: the most peaceable
   way for you, if you do take a thief, is to let him
   show himself 055 what he is, and steal out of your
   company.

VERG. You have been always called a merciful man,
   partner.

DoG. Truly, I would not hang a dog by my will, much
   more a man who hath any honesty in him.

060 VERG. If you hear a child cry in the night, you
   must call to the nurse and bid her still it.

WATCH. How if the nurse be asleep and will not
   hear us?

DoG. Why, then, depart in peace, and let the child
   wake 065 her with crying; for the ewe that will not
   hear her lamb when it baes will never answer a
   calf when he bleats.

VERG. 'Tis very true.

DoG. This is the end of the charge:—you, constable,
   are to present the prince's own person: if you meet
   the 070 prince in the night, you may stay him.

VERG. Nay, by'r lady, that I think a' cannot.

DoG. Five shillings to one on't, with any man that
   knows the statues, he may stay him: marry, not
   without the prince be willing; for, indeed, the
   watch ought to offend no 075 man; and it is an offence to stay a man against his will.

VERG. By'r lady, I think it be so.

DoG. Ha, ah, ha! Well, masters, good night: an there
   be any matter of weight chances, call up me: keep
   your fellows' counsels and your own; and good
   night. Come, 080 neighbour.

WATCH. Well, masters, we hear our charge: let us go
   sit here upon the church-bench till two, and then
   all to bed.

DoG. One word more, honest neighbours. I pray you,
   085 watch about Signior Leonato's door; for the

wedding being there to-morrow, there is a great
coil to-night. Adieu: be vigitant, I beseech you.
(Exeunt Dogberry and Verges.)

(ENTER BORACHIO AND CONRADE.)

BORA. What, Conrade!

WATCH. *(Aside)* Peace! stir not.

090 *BORA.* Conrade, I say!

CON. Here, man; I am at thy elbow.

BORA. Mass, and my elbow itched; I thought there
would a scab follow.

CON. I will owe thee an answer for that: and now forward 095 with thy tale.

BORA. Stand thee close, then, under this pent-house,
for it drizzles rain; and I will, like a true drunkard,
utter all to thee.

WATCH. *(Aside)* Some treason, masters: yet stand close.

100 *BORA.* Therefore know I have earned of Don John
a thousand ducats.

CON. Is it possible that any villany should be so dear?

BORA. Thou shouldst rather ask, if it were possible
any villany should be so rich; for when rich villains have need 105 of poor ones, poor ones may
make what price they will.

CON. I wonder at it.

BORA. That shows thou art unconfirmed. Thou
knowest that the fashion of a doublet, or a hat, or
a cloak, is nothing to a man.

110 *CON.* Yes, it is apparel.

BORA. I mean, the fashion.

CON. Yes, the fashion is the fashion.

BORA. Tush! I may as well say the fool's the fool. But
seest thou not what a deformed thief this
fashion is?

115 *WATCH.* *(Aside)* I know that Deformed; a' has been
a vile thief this seven year; a' goes up and down
like a gentleman: I remember his name.

BORA. Didst thou not hear somebody?

CON. No; 'twas the vane on the house.

120 *BORA.* Seest thou not, I say, what a deformed thief
this fashion is? how giddily a' turns about all the
hot bloods between fourteen and five-and-thirty?

sometimes fashioning them like Pharaoh's soldiers in the reeky painting, sometime like god Bel's priests in the old church-window, sometime 125 like the shaven Hercules in the smirched worm-eaten tapestry, where his codpiece seems as massy as his club?

CON. All this I see; and I see that the fashion wears out more apparel than the man. But art not thou thyself giddy with the fashion too, that thou hast shifted out of 130 thy tale into telling me of the fashion?

BORA. Not so, neither: but know that I have to-night wooed Margaret, the Lady Hero's gentlewoman, by the name of Hero: she leans me out at her mistress' chamber-window, bids me a thousand times good night,—I tell this 135 tale vilely:—I should first tell thee how the prince, Claudio and my master, planted and placed and possessed by my master Don John, saw afar off in the orchard this amiable encounter.

CON. And thought they Margaret was Hero?

140 BORA. Two of them did, the prince and Claudio; but the devil my master knew she was Margaret; and partly by his oaths, which first possessed them, partly by the dark night, which did deceive them, but chiefly by my villany, which did confirm any slander that Don John had made, 145 away went Claudio enraged; swore he would meet her, as he was appointed, next morning at the temple, and there, before the whole congregation, shame her with what he saw o'er night, and send her home again without a husband.

FIRST WATCH. We charge you, in the prince's name, 150 stand!

SEC. WATCH. Call up the right master constable. We have here recovered the most dangerous piece of lechery that ever was known in the commonwealth.

FIRST WATCH. And one Deformed is one of them: I 155 know him; a' wears a lock.

CON. Masters, masters,—

SEC. WATCH. You'll be made bring Deformed forth, I warrant you.

Con. Masters,—?

160 *First Watch.* Never speak: we charge you let us obey you to go with us.

Bora. We are like to prove a goodly commodity, being taken up of these men's bills.

Con. A commodity in question, I warrant you. Come, 165 we'll obey you. *(Exeunt.)*

SCENE IV. HERO'S APARTMENT.

(Enter Hero, Margaret, and Ursula.)

Hero. Good Ursula, wake my cousin Beatrice, and desire her to rise.

Urs. I will, lady.

Hero. And bid her come hither.

005 *Urs.* Well. *(Exit.)*

Marg. Troth, I think your other rabato were better.

Hero. No, pray thee, good Meg, I'll wear this.

Marg. By my troth's not so good; and I warrant your cousin will say so.

010 *Hero.* My cousin's a fool, and thou art another: I'll wear none but this.

Marg. I like the new tire within excellently, if the hair were a thought browner; and your gown's a most rare fashion, i' faith. I saw the Duchess of Milan's gown that 015 they praise so.

Hero. O, that exceeds, they say.

Marg. By my troth's but a night-gown in respect of yours,—cloth o' gold, and cuts, and laced with silver, set with pearls, down sleeves, side sleeves, and skirts, round 020 underborne with a bluish tinsel: but for a fine, quaint, graceful and excellent fashion, yours is worth ten on't.

Hero. God give me joy to wear it! for my heart is exceeding heavy.

Marg. 'Twill be heavier soon by the weight of a man.

025 *Hero.* Fie upon thee! art not ashamed?

Marg. Of what, lady? of speaking honourably? Is not marriage honourable in a beggar? Is not your lord honourable without marriage? I think you would have me say, 'saving your reverence, a husband:'

an bad thinking do 030 not wrest true speaking, I'll offend nobody: is there any harm in 'the heavier for a husband'? None, I think, an it be the right husband and the right wife; otherwise 'tis light, and not heavy: ask my Lady Beatrice else; here she comes.

(ENTER BEATRICE.)

HERO. Good morrow, coz.

035 BEAT. Good morrow, sweet HERO.

HERO. Why, how now? do you speak in the sick tune?

BEAT. I am out of all other tune, methinks.

MARG. Clap's into 'Light o' love;' that goes without a burden: do you sing it, and I'll dance it.

040 BEAT. Ye light o' love, with your heels! then, if your husband have stables enough, you'll see he shall lack no barns.

MARG. O illegitimate construction! I scorn that with my heels.

045 BEAT. 'Tis almost five o'clock, cousin; 'tis time you were ready. By my troth, I am exceeding ill: heigh-ho!

MARG. For a hawk, a horse, or a husband?

BEAT. For the letter that begins them all, H.

MARG. Well, an you be not turned Turk, there's no 050 more sailing by the star.

BEAT. What means the fool, trow?

MARG. Nothing I; but God send every one their heart's desire!

HERO. These gloves the count sent me; they are an 055 excellent perfume.

BEAT. I am stuffed, cousin; I cannot smell.

MARG. A maid, and stuffed! there's goodly catching of cold.

BEAT. O, God help me! God help me! how long have 060 you professed apprehension?

MARG. Even since you left it. Doth not my wit become me rarely?

BEAT. It is not seen enough, you should wear it in your cap. By my troth, I am sick.

065 MARG. Get you some of this distilled Carduus

Benedictus, and lay it to your heart: it is the only
thing for a qualm.

Hero. There thou prickest her with a thistle.

Beat. Benedictus! why Benedictus? you have some 070
moral in this Benedictus.

Marg. Moral! no, by my troth, I have no moral meaning; I meant, plain holy-thistle. You may think perchance that I think you are in love: nay, by'r lady, I
am not such a fool to think what I list; nor I list not
to think what I 075 can; nor, indeed, I cannot think,
if I would think my heart out of thinking, that you
are in love, or that you will be in love, or that you
can be in love. Yet Benedick was such another, and
now is he become a man: he swore he would
never marry; and yet now, in despite of his heart,
he eats 080 his meat without grudging: and how
you may be converted, I know not; but methinks
you look with your eyes as other women do.

Beat. What pace is this that thy tongue keeps?

Marg. Not a false gallop.

(Re-enter Ursula.)

085 *Urs.* Madam, withdraw: the prince, the count,
Signior Benedick, Don John, and all the gallants of
the town, are come to fetch you to church.

Hero. Help to dress me, good coz, good Meg, good
Ursula. *(Exeunt.)*

SCENE V. ANOTHER ROOM IN LEONATO'S HOUSE.

(Enter Leonato, with Dogberry and Verges.)

Leon. What would you with me, honest neighbour?

Dog. Marry, sir, I would have some confidence with
you that decerns you nearly.

Leon. Brief, I pray you; for you see it is a busy time
005 with me.

Dog. Marry, this it is, sir.

Verg. Yes, in truth it is, sir.

Leon. What is it, my good friends?

Dog. Goodman Verges, sir, speaks a little off the mat-

ter: $_{010}$ an old man, sir, and his wits are not so
blunt as, God help, I would desire they were; but,
in faith, honest as the skin between his brows.

VERG. Yes, I thank God I am as honest as any man
living that is an old man and no honester than I.

$_{015}$ DOG. Comparisons are odorous: palabras, neighbour Verges.

LEON. Neighbours, you are tedious.

DOG. It pleases your worship to say so, but we are the
poor duke's officers; but truly, for mine own part,
if I were $_{020}$ as tedious as a king, I could find in my
heart to bestow it all of your worship.

LEON. All thy tediousness on me, ah?

DOG. Yea, an 'twere a thousand pound more than 'tis;
for I hear as good exclamation on your worship as
of any $_{025}$ man in the city; and though I be but a
poor man, I am glad to hear it.

VERG. And so am I.

LEON. I would fain know what you have to say.

VERG. Marry, sir, our watch to-night, excepting your
$_{030}$ worship's presence, ha' ta'en a couple of as arrant knaves as any in Messina.

DOG. A good old man, sir; he will be talking: as they
say, When the age is in, the wit is out: God help
us! it is a world to see. Well said, i' faith, neighbour Verges: well, $_{035}$ God's a good man; an two
men ride of a horse, one must ride behind. An
honest soul, i' faith, sir; by my troth he is, as ever
broke bread; but God is to be worshipped; all men
are not alike; alas, good neighbour!

LEON. Indeed, neighbour, he comes too short of you.

$_{040}$ DOG. Gifts that God gives.

LEON. I must leave you.

DOG. One word, sir: our watch, sir, have indeed com-
prehended two aspicious persons, and we would
have them this morning examined before your
worship.

$_{045}$ LEON. Take their examination yourself, and bring it
me: I am now in great haste, as it may appear
unto you.

DOG. It shall be suffigance.

LEON. Drink some wine ere you go: fare you well.

(Enter a Messenger.)

Mess. My lord, they stay for you to give your
daughter $_{050}$ to her husband.

Leon. I'll wait upon them: I am ready. *(Exeunt Leonato
and Messenger.)*

Dog. Go, good partner, go, get you to Francis Seacole;
bid him bring his pen and inkhorn to the gaol: we
are now to examination these men.

$_{055}$ *Verg.* And we must do it wisely.

Dog. We will spare for no wit, I warrant you; here's
that shall drive some of them to a noncome: only
get the learned writer to set down our excommu-
nication, and meet me at the gaol. *(Exeunt.)*

ACT IV

SCENE I. A CHURCH.

(Enter Don Pedro, Don John, Leonato, Friar Francis, Claudio, Benedick, Hero, Beatrice, and attendants.)

Leon. Come, Friar Francis, be brief; only to the plain
form of marriage, and you shall recount their particular duties afterwards.

Friar. You come hither, my lord, to marry this lady.

005 *Claud.* No.

Leon. To be married to her: friar, you come to
marry her.

Friar. Lady, you come hither to be married to this
count.

010 *Hero.* I do.

Friar. If either of you know any inward impediment
why you should not be conjoined, I charge you, on
your souls, to utter it.

Claud. Know you any, Hero?

015 *Hero.* None, my lord.

Friar. Know you any, count?

Leon. I dare make his answer, none.

Claud. O, what men dare do! what men may do!
what men daily do, not knowing what they do!

020 *Bene.* How now! interjections? Why, then, some be
of laughing, as, ah, ha, he!

Claud. Stand thee by, Friar. Father, by your leave:

Will you with free and unconstrained soul
Give me this maid, your daughter?
025 *Leon.* As freely, son, as God did give her me.
Claud. And what have I to give you back, whose worth
May counterpoise this rich and precious gift?
D. Pedro. Nothing, unless you render her again.
Claud. Sweet prince, you learn me noble thankfulness.
030 There, Leonato, take her back again:
Give not this rotten orange to your friend;
She's but the sign and semblance of her honour.
Behold how like a maid she blushes here!
O, what authority and show of truth
035 Can cunning sin cover itself withal!
Comes not that blood as modest evidence
To witness simple virtue? Would you not swear,
All you that see her, that she were a maid,
By these exterior shows? But she is none:
040 She knows the heat of a luxurious bed;
Her blush is guiltiness, not modesty.
Leon. What do you mean, my lord?
Claud. Not to be married,
Not to knit my soul to an approved wanton.
Leon. Dear my lord, if you, in your own proof,
045 Have vanquish'd the resistance of her youth,
And made defeat of her virginity,—
Claud. I know what you would say: if I have known her,
You will say she did embrace me as a husband,
And so extenuate the 'forehand sin:
050 No, Leonato,
I never tempted her with word too large;
But, as a brother to his sister, show'd
Bashful sincerity and comely love.
Hero. And seem'd I ever otherwise to you?
055 *Claud.* Out on thee! Seeming! I will write against it:
You seem to me as Dian in her orb,
As chaste as is the bud ere it be blown;
But you are more intemperate in your blood
Than Venus, or those pamper'd animals
060 That rage in savage sensuality.

HERO. Is my lord well, that he doth speak so wide?
LEON. Sweet prince, why speak not you?
D. PEDRO.
What should I speak?
I stand dishonour'd, that have gone about
To link my dear friend to a common stale.
065 *LEON.* Are these things spoken, or do I but dream?
D. JOHN. Sir, they are spoken, and these things are
    true.
BENE. This looks not like a nuptial.
HERO. True! O God!
CLAUD. Leonato, stand I here?
Is this the prince? is this the prince's brother?
070 Is this face Hero's? are our eyes our own?
LEON. All this is so: but what of this, my lord?
CLAUD. Let me but move one question to your
    daughter;
And, by that fatherly and kindly power
That you have in her, bid her answer truly.
075 *LEON.* I charge thee do so, as thou art my child.
HERO. O, God defend me! how am I beset!
What kind of catechising call you this?
CLAUD. To make you answer truly to your name.
HERO. Is it not Hero? Who can blot that name
With any just reproach?
080 *CLAUD.* Marry, that can Hero;
Hero itself can blot out Hero's virtue.
What man was he talk'd with you yesternight
Out at your window betwixt twelve and one?
Now, if you are a maid, answer to this.
085 *HERO.* I talk'd with no man at that hour, my lord.
D. PEDRO. Why, then are you no maiden. Leonato,
I am sorry you must hear: upon mine honour,
Myself, my brother, and this grieved count
Did see her, hear her, at that hour last night
090 Talk with a ruffian at her chamber-window;
Who hath indeed, most like a liberal villain,
Confess'd the vile encounters they have had
A thousand times in secret.
D. JOHN. Fie, fie! they are not to be named, my lord,
095 Not to be spoke of;
There is not chastity enough in language,
Without offence to utter them. Thus, pretty lady,

I am sorry for thy much misgovernment.

CLAUD. O Hero, what a Hero hadst thou been,
100 If half thy outward graces had been placed
About thy thoughts and counsels of thy heart!
But fare thee well, most foul, most fair! farewell,
Thou pure impiety and impious purity!
For thee I'll lock up all the gates of love,
105 And on my eyelids shall conjecture hang,
To turn all beauty into thoughts of harm,
And never shall it more be gracious.

LEON. Hath no man's dagger here a point for me?
(Hero swoons.)

BEAT. Why, how now, cousin! wherefore sink you
down?

D. JOHN. Come, let us go. These things, come thus to
110 light,

*Smother her spirits up. (Exeunt Don Pedro, Don John, and
Claudio.)*

BENE. How doth the lady?

BEAT. Dead, I think. Help, uncle!
Hero! why, Hero! Uncle! Signior Benedick! Friar!

LEON. O Fate! take not away thy heavy hand.
115 Death is the fairest cover for her shame
That may be wish'd for.

BEAT. How now, cousin Hero!

FRIAR. Have comfort, lady.

LEON. Dost thou look up?

FRIAR. Yea, wherefore should she not?
120 *LEON.* Wherefore! Why, doth not every earthly
thing
Cry shame upon her? Could she here deny
The story that is printed in her blood?
Do not live, Hero; do not ope thine eyes:
For, did I think thou wouldst not quickly die,
125 Thought I thy spirits were stronger than thy
shames,
Myself would, on the rearward of reproaches,
Strike at thy life. Grieved I, I had but one?
Chid I for that at frugal nature's frame?
O, one too much by thee! Why had I one?
130 Why ever wast thou lovely in my eyes?
Why had I not with charitable hand
Took up a beggar's issue at my gates,

Who smirched thus and mired with infamy,
I might have said, 'No part of it is mine;
135 This shame derives itself from unknown loins'?
But mine, and mine I loved, and mine I praised,
And mine that I was proud on, mine so much
That I myself was to myself not mine,
Valuing of her,—why, she, O, she is fallen
140 Into a pit of ink, that the wide sea
Hath drops too few to wash her clean again,
And salt too little which may season give
To her foul-tainted flesh!
Bene. Sir, sir, be patient.
For my part, I am so attired in wonder,
145 I know not what to say.
Beat. O, on my soul, my cousin is belied!
Bene. Lady, were you her bedfellow last night?
Beat. No, truly, not; although, until last night,
I have this twelvemonth been her bedfellow.
150 *Leon.* Confirm'd, confirm'd! O, that is stronger made
Which was before barr'd up with ribs of iron!
Would the two princes lie, and Claudio lie,
Who loved her so, that, speaking of her foulness,
Wash'd it with tears? Hence from her! let her die.
155 *Friar.* Hear me a little;
For I have only been silent so long,
And given way unto this course of fortune,
By noting of the lady: I have mark'd
A thousand blushing apparitions
160 To start into her face; a thousand innocent shames
In angel whiteness beat away those blushes;
And in her eye there hath appear'd a fire,
To burn the errors that these princes hold
Against her maiden truth. Call me a fool;
165 Trust not my reading nor my observations,
Which with experimental seal doth warrant
The tenour of my book; trust not my age,
My reverence, calling, nor divinity,
If this sweet lady lie not guiltless here
Under some biting error.
170 *Leon.* Friar, it cannot be.
Thou seest that all the grace that she hath left
Is that she will not add to her damnation

A sin of perjury; she not denies it:
Why seek'st thou, then, to cover with excuse
175 That which appears in proper nakedness?
FRIAR. Lady, what man is he you are accused of?
HERO. They know that do accuse me; I know none:
If I know more of any man alive
Than that which maiden modesty doth warrant,
180 Let all my sins lack mercy! O my father,
Prove you that any man with me conversed
At hours unmeet, or that I yesternight
Maintain'd the change of words with any creature,
Refuse me, hate me, torture me to death!
185 *FRIAR.* There is some strange misprision in the
     princes.
BENE. Two of them have the very bent of honour;
And if their wisdoms be misled in this,
The practice of it lives in John the bastard,
Whose spirits toil in frame of villanies.
190 *LEON.* I know not. If they speak but truth of her,
These hands shall tear her; if they wrong her honour,
The proudest of them shall well hear of it.
Time hath not yet so dried this blood of mine,
Nor age so eat up my invention,
195 Nor fortune made such havoc of my means,
Nor my bad life reft me so much of friends,
But they shall find, awaked in such a kind,
Both strength of limb and policy of mind,
Ability in means and choice of friends,
To quit me of them throughly.
200 *FRIAR.* Pause awhile,
And let my counsel sway you in this case.
Your daughter here the princes left for dead:
Let her awhile be secretly kept in,
And publish it that she is dead indeed;
205 Maintain a mourning ostentation,
And on your family's old monument
Hang mournful epitaphs, and do all rites
That appertain unto a burial.
LEON. What shall become of this? what will this do?
210 *FRIAR.* Marry, this, well carried, shall on her behalf
Change slander to remorse; that is some good:
But not for that dream I on this strange course,
But on this travail look for greater birth.

She dying, as it must be so maintain'd,
₂₁₅ Upon the instant that she was accused,
Shall be lamented, pitied, and excused
Of every hearer: for it so falls out,
That what we have we prize not to the worth
Whiles we enjoy it; but being lack'd and lost,
₂₂₀ Why, then we rack the value, then we find
The virtue that possession would not show us
Whiles it was OURS. So will it fare with Claudio:
When he shall hear she died upon his words,
The idea of her life shall sweetly creep
₂₂₅ Into his study of imagination;
And every lovely organ of her life
Shall come apparell'd in more precious habit,
More moving-delicate and full of life,
Into the eye and prospect of his soul,
₂₃₀ Than when she lived indeed; then shall he
      mourn,
If ever love had interest in his liver,
And wish he had not so accused her,
No, though he thought his accusation true.
Let this be so, and doubt not but success
₂₃₅ Will fashion the event in better shape
Than I can lay it down in likelihood.
But if all aim but this be levell'd false,
The supposition of the lady's death
Will quench the wonder of her infamy:
₂₄₀ And if it sort not well, you may conceal her,
As best befits her wounded reputation,
In some reclusive and religious life,
Out of all eyes, tongues, minds, and injuries.
BENE. Signior Leonato, let the Friar advise you:
₂₄₅ And though you know my inwardness and love
Is very much unto the prince and Claudio,
Yet, by mine honour, I will deal in this
As secretly and justly as your soul
Should with your body.
LEON.
Being that I flow in grief,
₂₅₀ The smallest twine may lead me.
FRIAR. 'Tis well consented: presently away;
For to strange sores strangely they strain the cure.
Come, lady, die to live: this wedding-day

Perhaps is but prolong'd: have patience and endure.
   (*Exeunt all but Benedick and Beatrice.*)
255 *Bene.* Lady Beatrice, have you wept all this while?
Beat. Yea, and I will weep a while longer.
Bene. I will not desire that.
Beat. You have no reason; I do it freely.
Bene. Surely I do believe your fair cousin is wronged.
260 *Beat.* Ah, how much might the man deserve of me
   that would right her!
Bene. Is there any way to show such friendship?
Beat. A very even way, but no such friend.
Bene. May a man do it?
265 *Beat.* It is a man's office, but not yours.
Bene. I do love nothing in the world so well as you: is
   not that strange?
Beat. As strange as the thing I know not. It were as
   possible for me to say I loved nothing so well as
   you: but 270 believe me not; and yet I lie not; I con-
   fess nothing, nor I deny nothing. I am sorry for my
   cousin.
Bene. By my sword, Beatrice, thou lovest me.
Beat. Do not swear, and eat it.
Bene. I will swear by it that you love me; and I will
   275 make him eat it that says I love not you.
Beat. Will you not eat your word?
Bene. With no sauce that can be devised to it. I protest
   I love thee.
Beat. Why, then, God forgive me!
280 *Bene.* What offence, sweet Beatrice?
Beat. You have stayed me in a happy hour: I was
   about to protest I loved you.
Bene. And do it with all thy heart.
Beat. I love you with so much of my heart, that none
   285 is left to protest.
Bene. Come, bid me do any thing for thee.
Beat. Kill Claudio.
Bene. Ha! not for the wide world.
Beat. You kill me to deny it. Farewell.
290 *Bene.* Tarry, sweet Beatrice.
Beat. I am gone, though I am here: there is no love in
   you: nay, I pray you, let me go.
Bene. Beatrice,—
Beat. In faith, I will go.

₂₉₅ *Bene.* We'll be friends first.

Beat. You dare easier be friends with me than fight with mine enemy.

Bene. Is Claudio thine enemy?

Beat. Is he not approved in the height a villain, that ₃₀₀ hath slandered, scorned, dishonoured my kinswoman? O that I were a man! What, bear her in hand until they come to take hands; and then, with public accusation, uncovered slander, unmitigated rancour,—O God, that I were a man! I would eat his heart in the market-place.

₃₀₅ *Bene.* Hear me, Beatrice,—

Beat. Talk with a man out at a window! A proper saying!

Bene. Nay, but, Beatrice,—

Beat. Sweet Hero! She is wronged, she is slandered, ₃₁₀ she is undone.

Bene. Beat—

Beat. Princes and counties! Surely, a princely testimony, a goodly count, Count Comfect; a sweet gallant, surely! O that I were a man for his sake! or that I had ₃₁₅ any friend would be a man for my sake! But manhood is melted into courtesies, valour into compliment, and men are only turned into tongue, and trim ones too: he is now as valiant as Hercules that only tells a lie, and swears it. I cannot be a man with wishing, therefore I will die a ₃₂₀ woman with grieving.

Bene. Tarry, good Beatrice. By this hand, I love thee.

Beat. Use it for my love some other way than swearing by it.

Bene. Think you in your soul the Count Claudio hath ₃₂₅ wronged Hero?

Beat. Yea, as sure as I have a thought or a soul.

Bene. Enough, I am engaged; I will challenge him. I will kiss your hand, and so I leave you. By this hand, Claudio shall render me a dear account. As you hear of ₃₃₀ me, so think of me. Go, comfort your cousin: I must say she is dead: and so, farewell. *(Exeunt.)*

SCENE II. A PRISON.

(Enter DOGBERRY, VERGES, *and Sexton, in gowns; and the Watch, with* CONRADE *and* BORACHIO.)

DOG. Is our whole dissembly appeared?

VERG. O, a stool and a cushion for the sexton.

SEX. Which be the malefactors?

DOG. Marry, that am I and my partner.

005 VERG. Nay, that's certain; we have the exhibition to examine.

SEX. But which are the offenders that are to be examined? let them come before master constable.

DOG. Yea, marry, let them come before me. What is 010 your name, friend?

BORA. Borachio.

DOG. Pray, write down, Borachio. Yours, sirrah?

CON. I am a gentleman, sir, and my name is Conrade.

DOG. Write down, master gentleman Conrade. Masters, 015 do you serve God?

CON. }

BORA. } Yea, sir, we hope.

DOG. Write down, that they hope they serve God: and write God first; for God defend but God should go before such villains! Masters, it is proved already that you 020 are little better than false knaves; and it will go near to be thought so shortly. How answer you for yourselves?

CON. Marry, sir, we say we are none.

DOG. A marvellous witty fellow, I assure you; but I will go about with him. Come you hither, sirrah; a word 025 in your ear: sir, I say to you, it is thought you are false knaves.

BORA. Sir, I say to you we are none.

DOG. Well, stand aside. 'Fore God, they are both in a tale. Have you writ down, that they are none?

030 SEX. Master constable, you go not the way to examine: you must call forth the watch that are their accusers.

DOG. Yea, marry, that's the eftest way. Let the watch come forth. Masters, I charge you, in the prince's name, accuse these men.

_035_ FIRST WATCH. This man said, sir, that Don John,
the prince's brother, was a villain.

DOG. Write down, Prince John a villain. Why, this is
flat perjury, to call a prince's brother villain.

BORA. Master constable,—

_040_ DOG. Pray thee, fellow, peace: I do not like thy
look, I promise thee.

SEX. What heard you him say else?

SEC. WATCH. Marry, that he had received a thousand
ducats of Don John for accusing the Lady Hero _045_
wrongfully.

DOG. Flat burglary as ever was committed.

VERG. Yea, by mass, that it is.

SEX. What else, fellow?

FIRST WATCH. And that Count Claudio did mean,
upon _050_ his words, to disgrace Hero before the
whole assembly, and not marry her.

DOG. O villain! thou wilt be condemned into ever-
lasting redemption for this.

SEX. What else?

_055_ WATCH. This is all.

SEX. And this is more, masters, than you can deny.
Prince John is this morning secretly stolen away;
Hero was in this manner accused, in this very
manner refused, and upon the grief of this suddenly died. Master Constable, let _060_ these men be
bound, and brought to Leonato's: I will go before
and show him their examination. _(Exit.)_

DOG. Come, let them be opinioned.

VERG. Let them be in the hands—

CON. Off, coxcomb!

_065_ DOG. God's my life, where's the sexton? let him
write down, the prince's officer, coxcomb. Come,
bind them. Thou naughty varlet!

CON. Away! you are an ass, you are an ass.

DOG. Dost thou not suspect my place? dost thou not
_070_ suspect my years? O that he were here to write
me down an ass! But, masters, remember that I am
an ass; though it be not written down, yet forget
not that I am an ass. No, thou villain, thou art full
of piety, as shall be proved upon thee by good witness. I am a wise fellow; and, which _075_ is more, an
officer; and, which is more, a householder; and,

which is more, as pretty a piece of flesh as any is
in Messina; and one that knows the law, go to; and
a rich fellow enough, go to; and a fellow that hath
had losses; and one that hath two gowns, and
every thing handsome about him. Bring $_{080}$ him
away. O that I had been writ down an ass!
(Exeunt.)

ACT V

SCENE I. BEFORE LEONATO'S HOUSE.

(Enter Leonato and Antonio.)

Ant. If you go on thus, you will kill yourself;
And 'tis not wisdom thus to second grief
Against yourself.
Leon. I pray thee, cease thy counsel,
Which falls into mine ears as profitless
005 As water in a sieve: give not me counsel;
Nor let no comforter delight mine ear
But such a one whose wrongs do suit with mine.
Bring me a father that so loved his child,
Whose joy of her is overwhelm'd like mine,
010 And bid him speak of patience;
Measure his woe the length and breadth of mine,
And let it answer every strain for strain,
As thus for thus, and such a grief for such,
In every lineament, branch, shape, and form:
015 If such a one will smile, and stroke his beard,
Bid sorrow wag, cry 'hem!' when he should groan,
Patch grief with proverbs, make misfortune drunk
With candle-wasters; bring him yet to me,
And I of him will gather patience.
020 But there is no such man: for, brother, men
Can counsel and speak comfort to that grief
Which they themselves not feel; but, tasting it,

Their counsel turns to passion, which before
Would give preceptial medicine to rage,
025 Fetter strong madness in a silken thread,
Charm ache with air, and agony with words:
No, no; 'tis all men's office to speak patience
To those that wring under the load of sorrow,
But no man's virtue nor sufficiency,
030 To be so moral when he shall endure
The like himself. Therefore give me no counsel:
My griefs cry louder than advertisement.
ANT. Therein do men from children nothing differ.
LEON. I pray thee, peace. I will be flesh and blood;
035 For there was never yet philosopher
That could endure the toothache patiently,
However they have writ the style of gods,
And made a push at chance and sufferance.
ANT. Yet bend not all the harm upon yourself;
040 Make those that do offend you suffer too.
LEON. There thou speak'st reason: nay, I will do so.
My soul doth tell me Hero is belied;
And that shall Claudio know; so shall the prince,
And all of them that thus dishonour her.
045 *ANT.* Here comes the prince and Claudio hastily.

(*ENTER DON PEDRO AND CLAUDIO.*)

D. PEDRO. Good den, good den.
CLAUD. Good day to both of you.
LEON. Hear you, my lords,—
D. PEDRO. We have some haste, Leonato.
LEON. Some haste, my lord! well, fare you well, my
    lord:
Are you so hasty now? well, all is one.
050 *D. PEDRO.* Nay, do not quarrel with us, good
    old man.
ANT. If he could right himself with quarrelling,
Some of us would lie low.
CLAUD. Who wrongs him?
LEON. Marry, thou dost wrong me; thou dissembler,
    thou:—
Nay, never lay thy hand upon thy sword:
I fear thee not.
055 *CLAUD.* Marry, beshrew my hand,

If it should give your age such cause of fear:
In faith, my hand meant nothing to my sword.
Leon. Tush, tush, man; never fleer and jest at me:
I speak not like a dotard nor a fool,
060 As, under privilege of age, to brag
What I have done being young, or what would do,
Were I not old. Know, Claudio, to thy head,
Thou hast so wrong'd mine innocent child and me,
That I am forced to lay my reverence by,
065 And, with grey hairs and bruise of many days,
Do challenge thee to trial of a man.
I say thou hast belied mine innocent child;
Thy slander hath gone through and through her
    heart,
And she lies buried with her ancestors;
070 O, in a tomb where never scandal slept,
Save this of hers, framed by thy villany!
Claud. My villany?
Leon. Thine, Claudio; thine, I say.
D. Pedro. You say not right, old man.
Leon. My lord, my lord,
I'll prove it on his body, if he dare,
075 Despite his nice fence and his active practice,
His May of youth and bloom of lustihood.
Claud. Away! I will not have to do with you.
Leon. Canst thou so daff me? Thou hast kill'd my
    child:
If thou kill'st me, boy, thou shalt kill a man.
080 *Ant.* He shall kill two of us, and men indeed:
But that's no matter; let him kill one first;
Win me and wear me; let him answer me.
Come, follow me, boy; come, sir boy, come,
    follow me:
Sir boy, I'll whip you from your foining fence;
085 Nay, as I am a gentleman, I will.
Leon. Brother,—
Ant. Content yourself. God knows I loved my niece;
And she is dead, slander'd to death by villains,
That dare as well answer a man indeed
090 As I dare take a serpent by the tongue:
Boys, apes, braggarts, Jacks, milksops!
Leon. Brother Antony,—
Ant. Hold you content. What, man! I know them, yea,

213

And what they weigh, even to the utmost scruple,—
Scambling, out-facing, fashion-monging boys,
095 That lie, and cog, and flout, deprave, and slander,
Go antiquely, and show outward hideousness,
And speak off half a dozen dangerous words,
How they might hurt their enemies, if they durst;
And this is all.

Leon. But, brother Antony,—

100 *Ant.* Come, 'tis no matter:
Do not you meddle; let me deal in this.

D. Pedro. Gentlemen both, we will not wake your
patience.
My heart is sorry for your daughter's death:
But, on my honour, she was charged with nothing
105 But what was true, and very full of proof.

Leon. My lord, my lord,—

D. Pedro. I will not hear you.

Leon. No? Come, brother; away! I will be heard.

Ant. And shall, or some of us will smart for it.

(*Exeunt Leonato and Antonio.*)

110 *D. Pedro.* See, see; here comes the man we went
to seek.

(*Enter Benedick.*)

Claud. Now, signior, what news?

Bene. Good day, my lord.

D. Pedro. Welcome, signior: you are almost come to
part almost a fray.

115 *Claud.* We had like to have had our two noses
snapped off with two old men without teeth.

D. Pedro. Leonato and his brother. What thinkest
thou? Had we fought, I doubt we should have
been too young for them.

120 *Bene.* In a false quarrel there is no true valour. I
came to seek you both.

Claud. We have been up and down to seek thee; for
we are high-proof melancholy, and would fain
have it beaten away. Wilt thou use thy wit?

125 *Bene.* It is in my scabbard: shall I draw it?

D. Pedro. Dost thou wear thy wit by thy side?

Claud. Never any did so, though very many have

been beside their wit. I will bid thee draw, as we do the minstrels; draw, to pleasure us.

130 *D. PEDRO.* As I am an honest man, he looks pale. Art thou sick, or angry?

CLAUD. What, courage, man! What though care killed a cat, thou hast mettle enough in thee to kill care.

BENE. Sir, I shall meet your wit in the career, an you 135 charge it against me. I pray you choose another subject.

CLAUD. Nay, then, give him another staff: this last was broke cross.

D. PEDRO. By this light, he changes more and more: I think he be angry indeed.

140 *CLAUD.* If he be, he knows how to turn his girdle.

BENE. Shall I speak a word in your ear?

CLAUD. God bless me from a challenge!

BENE. (Aside to Claudio) You are a villain; I jest not: I will make it good how you dare, with what you dare, and 145 when you dare. Do me right, or I will protest your cowardice. You have killed a sweet lady, and her death shall fall heavy on you. Let me hear from you.

CLAUD. Well, I will meet you, so I may have good cheer.

D. PEDRO. What, a feast, a feast?

150 *CLAUD.* I' faith, I thank him; he hath bid me to a calf's-head and a capon; the which if I do not carve most curiously, say my knife's naught. Shall I not find a woodcock too?

BENE. Sir, your wit ambles well; it goes easily.

155 *D. PEDRO.* I'll tell thee how Beatrice praised thy wit the other day. I said, thou hadst a fine wit: 'True,' said she, 'a fine little one.' 'No,' said I, 'a great wit:' 'Right,' says she, 'a great gross one.' 'Nay,' said I, 'a good wit:' 'Just,' said she, 'it hurts nobody.' 'Nay,' said I, 'the 160 gentleman is wise:' 'Certain,' said she, 'a wise gentleman.' 'Nay,' said I, 'he hath the tongues:' 'That I believe,' said she, 'for he swore a thing to me on Monday night, which he forswore on Tuesday morning; there's a double tongue; there's two tongues.' Thus did she, an hour 165 together, trans-shape thy particular

virtues: yet at last she concluded with a sigh, thou
wast the properest man in Italy.

Claud. For the which she wept heartily, and said she
cared not.

D. Pedro. Yea, that she did; but yet, for all that, an 170
if she did not hate him deadly, she would love him
dearly: the old man's daughter told us all.

Claud. All, all; and, moreover, God saw him when he
was hid in the garden.

D. Pedro. But when shall we set the savage bull's 175
horns on the sensible Benedick's head?

Claud. Yea, and text underneath, 'Here dwells
Benedick the married man'?

Bene. Fare you well, boy: you know my mind. I will
leave you now to your gossip-like humour: you
break 180 jests as braggarts do their blades, which,
God be thanked, hurt not. My lord, for your many
courtesies I thank you: I must discontinue your
company: your brother the bastard is fled from
Messina: you have among you killed a sweet and
innocent lady. For my Lord Lackbeard there, he
and 185 I shall meet: and till then peace be with
him. *(Exit.)*

D. Pedro. He is in earnest.

Claud. In most profound earnest; and, I'll warrant
you, for the love of Beatrice.

D. Pedro. And hath challenged thee.

190 *Claud.* Most sincerely.

D. Pedro. What a pretty thing man is when he goes
in his doublet and hose, and leaves off his wit!

Claud. He is then a giant to an ape: but then is an ape
a doctor to such a man.

195 *D. Pedro.* But, soft you, let me be: pluck up, my
heart, and be sad. Did he not say, my brother was
fled?

(Enter Dogberry, Verges, and the Watch, with Conrade and Borachio.)

Dog. Come, you, sir: if justice cannot tame you, she
shall ne'er weigh more reasons in her balance: nay,
an you be a cursing hypocrite once, you must be
looked to.

200 *D. Pedro.* How now? two of my brother's men bound! Borachio one!

Claud. Hearken after their offence, my lord.

D. Pedro. Officers, what offence have these men done?

Dog. Marry, sir, they have committed false report; 205 moreover, they have spoken untruths; secondarily, they are slanders; sixth and lastly, they have belied a lady; thirdly, they have verified unjust things; and, to conclude, they are lying knaves.

D. Pedro. First, I ask thee what they have done; thirdly, 210 I ask thee what's their offence; sixth and lastly, why they are committed; and, to conclude, what you lay to their charge.

Claud. Rightly reasoned, and in his own division; and, by my troth, there's one meaning well suited.

215 *D. Pedro.* Who have you offended, masters, that you are thus bound to your answer? this learned constable is too cunning to be understood: what's your offence?

Bora. Sweet prince, let me go no farther to mine answer: do you hear me, and let this count kill me. I have 220 deceived even your very eyes: what your wisdoms could not discover, these shallow fools have brought to light; who, in the night, overheard me confessing to this man, how Don John your brother incensed me to slander the Lady Hero; how you were brought into the orchard, and 225 saw me court Margaret in Hero's garments: how you disgraced her, when you should marry her: my villany they have upon record; which I had rather seal with my death than repeat over to my shame. The lady is dead upon mine and my master's false accusation; and, briefly, I desire 230 nothing but the reward of a villain.

D. Pedro. Runs not this speech like iron through your blood?

Claud. I have drunk poison whiles he utter'd it.

D. Pedro. But did my brother set thee on to this?

Bora. Yea, and paid me richly for the practice of it.

235 *D. Pedro.* He is composed and framed of treachery: And fled he is upon this villany.

CLAUD. Sweet Hero! now thy image doth appear In
  the rare semblance that I loved it first.
DOG. Come, bring away the plaintiffs: by this time
  our 240 sexton hath reformed Signior Leonato of
  the matter: and, masters, do not forget to specify,
  when time and place shall serve, that I am an ass.
VERG. Here, here comes master Signior Leonato, and
  the sexton too.

(Re-enter LEONATO and ANTONIO, with the Sexton.)

245 LEON. Which is the villain? let me see his eyes,
That, when I note another man like him,
I may avoid him: which of these is he?
BORA. If you would know your wronger, look on me.
LEON. Art thou the slave that with thy breath hast
  kill'd
Mine innocent child?
250 BORA. Yea, even I alone.
LEON. No, not so, villain; thou beliest thyself:
Here stand a pair of honourable men;
A third is fled, that had a hand in it.
I thank you, princes, for my daughter's death:
255 Record it with your high and worthy deeds:
'Twas bravely done, if you bethink you of it.
CLAUD. I know not how to pray your patience;
Yet I must speak. Choose your revenge yourself;
Impose me to what penance your invention
260 Can lay upon my sin: yet sinn'd I not
But in mistaking.
D. PEDRO. By my soul, nor I:
And yet, to satisfy this good old man,
I would bend under any heavy weight
That he'll enjoin me to.
265 LEON. I cannot bid you bid my daughter live;
That were impossible: but, I pray you both,
Possess the people in Messina here
How innocent she died; and if your love
Can labour ought in sad invention,
270 Hang her an epitaph upon her tomb,
And sing it to her bones, sing it to-night:
To-morrow morning come you to my house;
And since you could not be my son-in-law,

Be yet my nephew: my brother hath a daughter,
275 Almost the copy of my child that's dead,
And she alone is heir to both of us:
Give her the right you should have given her cousin,
And so dies my revenge.

Claud. O noble sir,
Your over-kindness doth wring tears from me!
280 I do embrace your offer; and dispose
For henceforth of poor Claudio.

Leon. To-morrow, then, I will expect your coming;
To-night I take my leave. This naughty man
Shall face to face be brought to Margaret,
285 Who I believe was pack'd in all this wrong,
Hired to it by your brother.

Bora. No, by my soul, she was not;
Nor knew not what she did when she spoke to me;
But always hath been just and virtuous
In any thing that I do know by her.

290 *Dog.* Moreover, sir, which indeed is not under
white and black, this plaintiff here, the offender,
did call me ass: I beseech you, let it be remem-
bered in his punishment. And also, the watch
heard them talk of one Deformed: they say he
wears a key in his ear, and a lock 295 hanging by it;
and borrows money in God's name, the which he
hath used so long and never paid, that now men
grow hard-hearted, and will lend nothing for
God's sake: pray you, examine him upon that
point.

Leon. I thank thee for thy care and honest pains.

300 *Dog.* Your worship speaks like a most thankful
and reverend youth; and I praise God for you.

Leon. There's for thy pains.

Dog. God save the foundation!

Leon. Go, I discharge thee of thy prisoner, and I
thank 305 thee.

Dog. I leave an arrant knave with your worship;
which I beseech your worship to correct yourself,
for the example of others. God keep your worship!
I wish your worship well; God restore you to
health! I humbly give you leave 310 to depart; and
if a merry meeting may be wished, God prohibit
it! Come, neighbour. (*Exeunt Dogberry and Verges.*)

Leon. Until to-morrow morning, lords, farewell.

Ant. Farewell, my lords: we look for you to-morrow.

D. Pedro. We will not fail.

Claud. To-night I'll mourn with *Hero.*

Leon. (To the Watch) Bring you these fellows on.
315 We'll talk with Margaret,
How her acquaintance grew with this lewd fellow.
(Exeunt, severally.)

SCENE II. LEONATO'S GARDEN

(Enter Benedick and Margaret, meeting.)

Bene. Pray thee, sweet Mistress Margaret, deserve
well at my hands by helping me to the speech of
Beatrice.

Marg. Will you, then, write me a sonnet in praise of
my beauty?

005 *Bene.* In so high a style, Margaret, that no man
living shall come over it; for, in most comely truth,
thou deservest it.

Marg. To have no man come over me! why, shall I always keep below stairs?

010 *Bene.* Thy wit is as quick as the greyhound's
mouth; it catches.

Marg. And yours as blunt as the fencer's foils, which
hit, but hurt not.

Bene. A most manly wit, Margaret; it will not hurt a
015 woman: and so, I pray thee, call Beatrice: I give
thee the bucklers.

Marg. Give us the swords; we have bucklers of
our own.

Bene. If you use them, Margaret, you must put in the
pikes with a vice; and they are dangerous
weapons for maids.

020 *Marg.* Well, I will call Beatrice to you, who I think
hath legs.

Bene. And therefore will come. *(Exit Margaret.)*
(Singing) The god of love,
That sits above,
025 And knows me, and knows me,
How pitiful I deserve,—

I mean in singing; but in loving, Leander the good
swimmer, Troilus the first employer of panders,
and a whole bookful of these quondam carpet-
mongers, whose names $_{030}$ yet run smoothly in the
even road of a blank verse, why, they were never
so truly turned over and over as my poor self in
love. Marry, I cannot show it in rhyme; I have
tried: I can find out no rhyme to 'lady' but 'baby,'
an innocent rhyme; for 'scorn,' 'horn,' a hard
rhyme; for $_{035}$ 'school,' 'fool,' a babbling rhyme;
very ominous endings: no, I was not born under a
rhyming planet, nor I cannot woo in festival
terms.

(ENTER BEATRICE.)

Sweet Beatrice, wouldst thou come when I called
thee?

BEAT. Yea, signior, and depart when you bid me.

$_{040}$ *BENE.* O, stay but till then!

BEAT. 'Then' is spoken; fare you well now: and yet,
ere I go, let me go with that I came; which is, with
knowing what hath passed between you and
Claudio.

BENE. Only foul words; and thereupon I will kiss thee.

$_{045}$ *BEAT.* Foul words is but foul wind, and foul wind
is but foul breath, and foul breath is noisome;
therefore I will depart unkissed.

BENE. Thou hast frighted the word out of his right
sense, so forcible is thy wit. But I must tell thee
plainly, $_{050}$ Claudio undergoes my challenge; and
either I must shortly hear from him, or I will subscribe him a coward. And, I pray thee now, tell me
for which of my bad parts didst thou first fall in
love with me?

BEAT. For them all together; which maintained so
politic $_{055}$ a state of evil, that they will not admit
any good part to intermingle with them. But for
which of my good parts did you first suffer love
for me?

BENE. Suffer love,—a good epithet! I do suffer love indeed, for I love thee against my will.

$_{060}$ *BEAT.* In spite of your heart, I think; alas, poor heart! If you spite it for my sake, I will spite it for yours; for I will never love that which my friend hates.

Bene. Thou and I are too wise to woo peaceably.

Beat. It appears not in this confession: there's not one $_{065}$ wise man among twenty that will praise himself.

Bene. An old, an old instance, Beatrice, that lived in the time of good neighbours. If a man do not erect in this age his own tomb ere he dies, he shall live no longer in monument than the bell rings and the widow weeps.

$_{070}$ *Beat.* And how long is that, think you?

Bene. Question: why, an hour in clamour, and a quarter in rheum: therefore is it most expedient for the wise, if Don Worm, his conscience, find no impediment to the contrary, to be the trumpet of his own virtues, as I am to myself. So $_{075}$ much for praising myself, who, I myself will bear witness, is praiseworthy: and now tell me, how doth your cousin?

Beat. Very ill.

Bene. And how do you?

Beat. Very ill too.

$_{080}$ *Bene.* Serve God, love me, and mend. There will I leave you too, for here comes one in haste.

(Enter Ursula.)

Urs. Madam, you must come to your uncle. Yonder's old coil at home: it is proved my Lady Hero hath been falsely accused, the prince and Claudio mightily abused; $_{085}$ and Don John is the author of all, who is fled and gone. Will you come presently?

Beat. Will you go hear this news, signior?

Bene. I will live in thy heart, die in thy lap, and be buried in thy eyes; and moreover I will go with thee to $_{090}$ thy uncle's. *(Exeunt.)*

SCENE III. A CHURCH.

(Enter DON PEDRO, CLAUDIO, and three or four with tapers.)

CLAUD. Is this the monument of Leonato?
A LORD. It is, my lord.
CLAUD.*(Reading out of a scroll)*
Done to death by slanderous tongues
Was the Hero that here lies:
005 Death, in guerdon of her wrongs,
Gives her fame which never dies.
So the life that died with shame
Lives in death with glorious fame.
Hang thou there upon the tomb,
010 Praising her when I am dumb.
Now, music, sound, and sing your solemn hymn.

(SONG.)

Pardon, goddess of the night,
Those that slew thy virgin knight;
For the which, with songs of woe,
015 Round about her tomb they go.
Midnight, assist our moan;
Help us to sigh and groan,
Heavily, heavily:
Graves, yawn, and yield your dead,
020 Till death be uttered,
Heavily, heavily.
CLAUD. Now, unto thy bones good night!
Yearly will I do this rite.
D. PEDRO. Good morrow, masters; put your torches
out:
025 The wolves have prey'd; and look, the gentle day,
Before the wheels of Phœbus, round about
Dapples the drowsy east with spots of grey.
Thanks to you all, and leave us: fare you well.
CLAUD. Good morrow, masters: each his several way.
030 D. PEDRO. Come, let us hence, and put on other
weeds;
And then to Leonato's we will go.
CLAUD. And Hymen now with luckier issue speed's
Than this for whom we render'd up this woe.
    (Exeunt.)

SCENE IV. A ROOM IN LEONATO'S HOUSE.

(Enter Leonato, Antonio, Benedick, Beatrice, Margaret, Ursula, Friar Francis, and Hero.)

FRIAR. Did I not tell you she was innocent?
LEON. So are the prince and Claudio, who accused her
Upon the error that you heard debated:
But Margaret was in some fault for this,
005 Although against her will, as it appears
In the true course of all the question.
ANT. Well, I am glad that all things sort so well.
BENE. And so am I, being else by faith enforced
To call young Claudio to a reckoning for it.
010 LEON. Well, daughter, and you gentlewomen all,
Withdraw into a chamber by yourselves,
And when I send for you, come hither mask'd.
    (Exeunt Ladies.)
The prince and Claudio promised by this hour
To visit me. You know your office, brother:
015 You must be father to your brother's daughter,
And give her to young Claudio.
ANT. Which I will do with confirm'd countenance.
BENE. Friar, I must entreat your pains, I think.
FRIAR. To do what, signior?
020 BENE. To bind me, or undo me; one of them.
Signior Leonato, truth it is, good signior,
Your niece regards me with an eye of favour.
LEON. That eye my daughter lent her: 'tis most true.
BENE. And I do with an eye of love requite her.
025 LEON. The sight whereof I think you had from me,
From Claudio, and the prince: but what's your will?
BENE. Your answer, sir, is enigmatical:
But, for my will, my will is, your good will
May stand with ours, this day to be conjoin'd
030 In the state of honourable marriage:
In which, good friar, I shall desire your help.
LEON. My heart is with your liking.
FRIAR. And my help.
Here comes the prince and Claudio.

(Enter Don Pedro and Claudio, and two or three others.)

D. Pedro. Good morrow to this fair assembly.

035 *Leon.* Good morrow, prince; good morrow,
    Claudio:
We here attend you. Are you yet determin'd
To-day to marry with my brother's daughter?

Claud. I'll hold my mind, were she an Ethiope.

Leon. Call her forth, brother; here's the friar ready.
    (Exit Antonio.)

D. Pedro. Good morrow, Benedick. Why, what's the
    040 matter,
That you have such a February face,
So full of frost, of storm, and cloudiness?

Claud. I think he thinks upon the savage bull.
Tush, fear not, man; we'll tip thy horns with gold,
045 And all Europa shall rejoice at thee;
As once Europa did at lusty Jove,
When he would play the noble beast in love.

Bene. Bull Jove, sir, had an amiable low;
And some such strange bull leap'd your father's cow,
050 And got a calf in that same noble feat
Much like to you, for you have just his bleat.

Claud. For this I owe you: here comes other
    reckonings.

    (Re-enter Antonio, with the Ladies masked.)

Which is the lady I must seize upon?

Ant. This same is she, and I do give you her.

Claud. Why, then she's mine. Sweet, let me see your
    055 face.

Leon. No, that you shall not, till you take her hand
Before this friar, and swear to marry her.

Claud. Give me your hand: before this holy friar,
I am your husband, if you like of me.

060 *Hero.* And when I lived, I was your other wife:
    (Unmasking.)
And when you loved, you were my other husband.

Claud. Another Hero!

Hero. Nothing certainer:
One Hero died defiled; but I do live,
And surely as I live, I am a maid.

065 *D. Pedro.* The former Hero! Hero that is dead!

Leon. She died, my lord, but whiles her slander lived.

Friar. All this amazement can I qualify;
When after that the holy rites are ended,
I'll tell you largely of fair Hero's death:
070 Meantime let wonder seem familiar,
And to the chapel let us presently.

Bene. Soft and fair, friar. Which is Beatrice?

Beat. (*Unmasking*) I answer to that name. What is
your will?

Bene. Do not you love me?

Beat. Why, no; no more than reason.

075 *Bene.* Why, then your uncle, and the prince, and
Claudio
Have been deceived; they swore you did.

Beat. Do not you love me?

Bene. Troth, no; no more than reason.

Beat. Why, then my cousin, Margaret, and Ursula
Are much deceived; for they did swear you did.

080 *Bene.* They swore that you were almost sick
for me.

Beat. They swore that you were well-nigh dead
for me.

Bene. 'Tis no such matter. Then you do not love me?

Beat. No, truly, but in friendly recompense.

Leon. Come, cousin, I am sure you love the
gentleman.

085 *Claud.* And I'll be sworn upon't that he loves her;
For here's a paper, written in his hand,
A halting sonnet of his own pure brain,
Fashion'd to Beatrice.

Hero. And here's another,
Writ in my cousin's hand, stolen from her pocket,
090 Containing her affection unto Benedick.

Bene. A miracle! here's our own hands against our
hearts. Come, I will have thee; but, by this light, I
take thee for pity.

Beat. I would not deny you; but, by this good day, I
095 yield upon great persuasion; and partly to save
your life, for I was told you were in a con-
sumption.

Bene. Peace! I will stop your mouth. (*Kissing her.*)

D. Pedro. How dost thou, Benedick, the married
man?

Bene. I'll tell thee what, prince; a college of wit-

crackers $_{100}$ cannot flout me out of my humour.
Dost thou think I care for a satire or an epigram?
No: if a man will be beaten with brains, a' shall
wear nothing handsome about him. In brief, since
I do purpose to marry, I will think nothing to any
purpose that the world can say against it; and
therefore $_{105}$ never flout at me for what I have said
against it; for man is a giddy thing, and this is my
conclusion. For thy part, Claudio, I did think to
have beaten thee; but in that thou art like to be my
kinsman, live unbruised, and love my cousin.

CLAUD. I had well hoped thou wouldst have denied
Beatrice, $_{110}$ that I might have cudgelled thee out
of thy single life, to make thee a double-dealer;
which, out of question, thou wilt be, if my cousin
do not look exceeding narrowly to thee.

BENE. Come, come, we are friends: let's have a dance
ere we are married, that we may lighten our own
hearts, $_{115}$ and our wives' heels.

LEON. We'll have dancing afterward.

BENE. First, of my word; therefore play, music. Prince,
thou art sad; get thee a wife, get thee a wife: there
is no staff more reverend than one tipped with
horn.

(Enter a Messenger.)

$_{120}$ MESS. My lord, your brother John is ta'en in flight,
And brought with armed men back to Messina.

BENE. Think not on him till to-morrow: I'll devise thee
brave punishments for him. Strike up, pipers.
(Dance.) (Exeunt.)

THE TAMING OF THE SHREW

DRAMATIS PERSONÆ

A LORD.
CHRISTOPHER SLY, a tinker.
HOSTESS, PAGE, PLAYERS, HUNTSMEN, and SERVANTS.
BAPTISTA, a rich Gentleman of Padua.
VINCENTIO, an old Gentleman of Pisa.
LUCENTIO, son to Vincentio; in love with Bianca.
PETRUCHIO, a Gentleman of Verona; Suitor to
    Katharina.
GREMIO, HORTENSIO, Suitors to Bianca.
TRANIO, Biondello, Servants to Lucentio.
GRUMIO, Curtis, Servants to Petruchio.
PEDANT, set up to personate Vincentio.
KATHARINA, the Shrew, BIANCA, Daughters to Baptista.
WIDOW.
TAILOR, HABERDASHER, and SERVANTS attending on
    Baptista and Petruchio.

SCENE: Padua, and Petruchio's country house.

INDUCTION

SCENE I. BEFORE AN ALEHOUSE ON A HEATH.

Enter Hostess *and* Sly.

Sly. I'll pheeze you, in faith.
Host. A pair of stocks, you rogue!
Sly. Y'are a baggage: the Slys are no rogues; look in
the chronicles; we came in with Richard Conqueror.
    Therefore
5 paucas pallabris; let the world slide: sessa!
Host. You will not pay for the glasses you have
    burst?
Sly. No, not a denier. Go by, Jeronimy: go to thy
cold bed, and warm thee.
10 Host. I know my remedy; I must go fetch the third-
    borough.

[Exit.

Sly. Third, or fourth, or fifth borough, I'll answer him
by law: I'll not budge an inch, boy: let him come, and
kindly. [Falls asleep.

Horns winded. Enter a Lord from hunting, with his train.

Lord. Huntsman, I charge thee, tender well my
    hounds:

₁₅ Brach Merriman, the poor cur is emboss'd;
And couple Clowder with the deep-mouth'd brach.
Saw'st thou not, boy, how Silver made it good
At the hedge-corner, in the coldest fault?
I would not lose the dog for twenty pound.
₂₀ *First Hun.* Why, Belman is as good as he, my lord;
He cried upon it at the merest loss
And twice to-day pick'd out the dullest scent:
Trust me, I take him for the better dog.
Lord. Thou art a fool: if Echo were as fleet,
₂₅ I would esteem him worth a dozen such.
But sup them well and look unto them all:
To-morrow I intend to hunt again.
First Hun. I will, my lord.
Lord. What's here? one dead, or drunk? See, doth he
      breathe?
₃₀ *Sec. Hun.* He breathes, my lord. Were he not
      warm'd with ale,
This were a bed but cold to sleep so soundly.
Lord. O monstrous beast! how like a swine he lies!
Grim death, how foul and loathsome is thine image!
Sirs, I will practise on this drunken man.
₃₅ What think you, if he were convey'd to bed,
Wrapp'd in sweet clothes, rings put upon his fingers,
A most delicious banquet by his bed,
And brave attendants near him when he wakes,
Would not the beggar then forget himself?
₄₀ *First Hun.* Believe me, lord, I think he cannot
      choose.
Sec. Hun. It would seem strange unto him when he
      waked.
Lord. Even as a flattering dream or worthless fancy.
Then take him up and manage well the jest:
Carry him gently to my fairest chamber
₄₅ And hang it round with all my wanton pictures:
Balm his foul head in warm distilled waters
And burn sweet wood to make the lodging sweet:
Procure me music ready when he wakes,
To make a dulcet and a heavenly sound;
₅₀ And if he chance to speak, be ready straight
And with a low submissive reverence
Say 'What is it your honour will command?'
Let one attend him with a silver basin

Full of rose-water and bestrew'd with flowers;
55 Another bear the ewer, the third a diaper,
And say 'Will't please your lordship cool your
    hands?'
Some one be ready with a costly suit
And ask him what apparel he will wear;
Another tell him of his hounds and horse,
60 And that his lady mourns at his disease:
Persuade him that he hath been lunatic;
And when he says he is, say that he dreams,
For he is nothing but a mighty lord.
This do and do it kindly, gentle sirs:
65 It will be pastime passing excellent,
If it be husbanded with modesty.
First Hun. My lord, I warrant you we will play our
    part,
As he shall think by our true diligence
He is no less than what we say he is.
70 *Lord.* Take him up gently and to bed with him;
And each one to his office when he wakes.

[Some bear out Sly. A trumpet sounds.

Sirrah, go see what trumpet 'tis that sounds: [*Exit
    Servingman.*
Belike, some noble gentleman that means,
Travelling some journey, to repose him here.

Re-enter Servingman.

How now! who is it?
75 *Serv.* An't please your honour, players
That offer service to your lordship.
Lord. Bid them come near.

Enter Players.

Now, fellows, you are welcome.
Players. We thank your honour.
Lord. Do you intend to stay with me to-night?
80 *A Player.* So please your lordship to accept our
    duty.
Lord. With all my heart. This fellow I remember,

Since once he play'd a farmer's eldest son:
'Twas where you woo'd the gentlewoman so well:
I have forgot your name; but, sure, that part
85 Was aptly fitted and naturally perform'd.
A PLAYER. I think 'twas Soto that your honour means.
LORD. Tis very true: thou didst it excellent.
Well, you are come to me in happy time;
The rather for I have some sport in hand
90 Wherein your cunning can assist me much.
There is a lord will hear you play to-night:
But I am doubtful of your modesties;
Lest over-eyeing of his odd behaviour,—
For yet his honour never heard a play,—
95 You break into some merry passion
And so offend him; for I tell you, sirs,
If you should smile he grows impatient.
A PLAYER. Fear not, my lord: we can contain
  ourselves,
Were he the veriest antic in the world.
100 *LORD.* Go, sirrah, take them to the buttery,
And give them friendly welcome every one:
Let them want nothing that my house affords.

[Exit one with the Players.

Sirrah, go you to Barthol'mew my page,
And see him dress'd in all suits like a lady:
105 That done, conduct him to the drunkard's
  chamber;
And call him 'madam,' do him obeisance.
Tell him from me, as he will win my love,
He bear himself with honourable action,
Such as he hath observed in noble ladies
110 Unto their lords, by them accomplished:
Such duty to the drunkard let him do
With soft low tongue and lowly courtesy,
And say, 'What is't your honour will command,
Wherein your lady and your humble wife
115 May show her duty and make known her love?'
And then with kind embracements, tempting kisses,
And with declining head into his bosom,
Bid him shed tears, as being overjoy'd
To see her noble lord restored to health,

120 Who for this seven years hath esteemed him
No better than a poor and loathsome beggar:
And if the boy have not a woman's gift
To rain a shower of commanded tears,
An onion will do well for such a shift,
125 Which in a napkin being close convey'd
Shall in despite enforce a watery eye.
See this dispatch'd with all the haste thou canst:
Anon I'll give thee more instructions. [*Exit a
    Servingman.*
I know the boy will well usurp the grace,
130 Voice, gait and action of a gentlewoman:
I long to hear him call the drunkard husband,
And how my men will stay themselves from laughter
When they do homage to this simple peasant.
I'll in to counsel them; haply my presence
135 May well abate the over-merry spleen
Which otherwise would grow into extremes. [*Exeunt.*

SCENE II. A BEDCHAMBER IN THE LORD'S HOUSE.

Enter aloft SLY, *with Attendants; some with apparel, others with
    basin and ewer and other appurtenances, and Lord.*

SLY. For God's sake, a pot of small ale.
FIRST SERV. Will't please your lordship drink a cup of
sack?
SEC. SERV. Will't please your honour taste of these
conserves?
THIRD SERV. What raiment will your honour wear
    to-day?
5 SLY. I am Christophero Sly; call not me 'honour' nor
'lordship:' I ne'er drank sack in my life; and if you
    give me
any conserves, give me conserves of beef: ne'er
    ask me
what raiment I'll wear; for I have no more doublets
    than
backs, no more stockings than legs, nor no more
    shoes than
10 feet; nay, sometime more feet than shoes, or such
    shoes as

my toes look through the overleather.

LORD. Heaven cease this idle humour in your honour!
O, that a mighty man of such descent,
Of such possessions and so high esteem,
₁₅ Should be infused with so foul a spirit!

SLY. What, would you make me mad? Am not I
Christopher Sly, old Sly's son of Burton-heath, by
    birth a
pedlar, by education a card-maker, by transmutation a
bear-herd, and now by present profession a
    tinker? Ask
₂₀ Marian Hacket, the fat ale-wife of Wincot, if she
    know me
not: if she say I am not fourteen pence on the score for
sheer ale, score me up for the lyingest knave in
    Christendom.
What! I am not bestraught: here's—

THIRD SERV. O, this it is that makes your lady mourn!
₂₅ *SEC. SERV.* O, this is it that makes your servants
    droop!

LORD. Hence comes it that your kindred shuns your
    house,
As beaten hence by your strange lunacy.
O noble lord, bethink thee of thy birth,
Call home thy ancient thoughts from banishment
₃₀ And banish hence these abject lowly dreams.
Look how thy servants do attend on thee,
Each in his office ready at thy beck.
Wilt thou have music? hark! Apollo plays, [*Music.*
And twenty caged nightingales do sing:
₃₅ Or wilt thou sleep? we'll have thee to a couch
Softer and sweeter than the lustful bed
On purpose trimm'd up for Semiramis.
Say thou wilt walk; we will bestrew the ground:
Or wilt thou ride? thy horses shall be trapp'd,
₄₀ Their harness studded all with gold and pearl.
Dost thou love hawking? thou hast hawks will soar
Above the morning lark: or wilt thou hunt?
Thy hounds shall make the welkin answer them,
And fetch shrill echoes from the hollow earth.
₄₅ *FIRST SERV.* Say thou wilt course; thy greyhounds
    are as swift
As breathed stags, ay, fleeter than the roe.

SEC. SERV. Dost thou love pictures? we will fetch thee
    straight
Adonis painted by a running brook
And Cytherea all in sedges hid
50 Which seem to move and wanton with her breath,
Even as the waving sedges play with wind.
LORD. We'll show thee Io as she was a maid
And how she was beguiled and surprised,
As lively painted as the deed was done.
55 THIRD SERV. Or Daphne roaming through a thorny
    wood,
Scratching her legs that one shall swear she bleeds,
And at that sight shall sad Apollo weep,
So workmanly the blood and tears are drawn.
LORD. Thou art a lord and nothing but a lord:
60 Thou hast a lady far more beautiful
Than any woman in this waning age.
FIRST SERV. And till the tears that she hath shed
    for thee
Like envious floods o'er-run her lovely face,
She was the fairest creature in the world;
65 And yet she is inferior to none.
SLY. Am I a lord? and have I such a lady?
Or do I dream? or have I dream'd till now?
I do not sleep: I see, I hear, I speak;
I smell sweet savours and I feel soft things:
70 Upon my life, I am a lord indeed
And not a tinker nor Christophero Sly.
Well, bring our lady hither to our sight;
And once again, a pot o' the smallest ale.
SEC. SERV. Will't please your mightiness to wash your
    hands?
75 O, how we joy to see your wit restored!
O, that once more you knew but what you are!
These fifteen years you have been in a dream;
Or when you waked, so waked as if you slept.
SLY. These fifteen years! by my fay, a goodly nap.
80 But did I never speak of all that time?
FIRST SERV. O, yes, my lord, but very idle words:
For though you lay here in this goodly chamber,
Yet would you say ye were beaten out of door;
And rail upon the hostess of the house;
85 And say you would present her at the leet,

Because she brought stone jugs and no seal'd quarts:
Sometimes you would call out for Cicely Hacket.
Sly. Ay, the woman's maid of the house.
Third Serv. Why, sir, you know no house nor no such
    maid,
90 Nor no such men as you have reckon'd up,
As Stephen Sly and old John Naps of Greece
And Peter Turph and Henry Pimpernell
And twenty more such names and men as these
Which never were nor no man ever saw.
95 *Sly.* Now Lord be thanked for my good amends!
All. Amen.
Sly. I thank thee: thou shalt not lose by it.

Enter the Page as a lady, attended.

Page. How fares my noble lord?
Sly. Marry, I fare well; for here is cheer enough.
100 Where is my wife?
Page. Here, noble lord: what is thy will with her?
Sly. Are you my wife and will not call me husband?
My men should call me 'lord:' I am your good-man.
Page. My husband and my lord, my lord and
    husband;
105 I am your wife in all obedience.
Sly. I know it well. What must I call her?
Lord. Madam.
Sly. Al'ce madam, or Joan madam?
Lord. 'Madam,' and nothing else: so lords call ladies.
110 *Sly.* Madam wife, they say that I have dream'd
And slept above some fifteen year or more.
Page. Ay, and the time seems thirty unto me,
Being all this time abandon'd from your bed.
Sly. 'Tis much. Servants, leave me and her alone.
115 Madam, undress you and come now to bed.
Page. Thrice-noble lord, let me entreat of you
To pardon me yet for a night or two;
Or, if not so, until the sun be set:
For your physicians have expressly charged,
120 In peril to incur your former malady,
That I should yet absent me from your bed:
I hope this reason stands for my excuse.
Sly. Ay, it stands so that I may hardly tarry so long.

But I would be loath to fall into my dreams again:
    I will
125 therefore tarry in despite of the flesh and the
    blood.

Enter a Messenger.

MESS. Your honour's players, hearing your
    amendment,
Are come to play a pleasant comedy;
For so your doctors hold it very meet,
Seeing too much sadness hath congeal'd your blood,
130 And melancholy is the nurse of frenzy:
Therefore they thought it good you hear a play
And frame your mind to mirth and merriment.
Which bars a thousand harms and lengthens life.
SLY. Marry, I will, let them play it. Is not a comonty
135 a Christmas gambold or a tumbling-trick?
PAGE. No, my good lord; it is more pleasing stuff.
SLY. What, household stuff?
PAGE. It is a kind of history.
SLY. Well, we'll see't. Come, madam wife, sit by my
140 side and let the world slip: we shall ne'er be
    younger.

Flourish.

ACT I

SCENE I: PADUA. A PUBLIC PLACE.

Enter LUCENTIO and his man TRANIO.

Luc. Tranio, since for the great desire I had
To see fair Padua, nursery of arts,
I am arrived for fruitful Lombardy,
The pleasant garden of great Italy;
5 And by my father's love and leave am arm'd
With his good will and thy good company,
My trusty servant, well approved in all,
Here let us breathe and haply institute
A course of learning and ingenious studies.
10 Pisa renowned for grave citizens
Gave me my being and my father first,
A merchant of great traffic through the world,
Vincentio, come of the Bentivolii.
Vincentio's son brought up in Florence
15 It shall become to serve all hopes conceived,
To deck his fortune with his virtuous deeds:
And therefore, Tranio, for the time I study,
Virtue and that part of philosophy
Will I apply that treats of happiness
20 By virtue specially to be achieved.
Tell me thy mind; for I have Pisa left
And am to Padua come, as he that leaves
A shallow plash to plunge him in the deep

And with satiety seeks to quench his thirst.
25 *Tra.* *Mi perdonato*, gentle master mine,
I am in all affected as yourself;
Glad that you thus continue your resolve
To suck the sweets of sweet philosophy.
Only, good master, while we do admire
30 This virtue and this moral discipline,
Let's be no stoics nor no stocks, I pray;
Or so devote to Aristotle's checks
As Ovid be an outcast quite abjured:
Balk logic with acquaintance that you have
35 And practise rhetoric in your common talk;
Music and poesy use to quicken you;
The mathematics and the metaphysics,
Fall to them as you find your stomach serves you;
No profit grows where is no pleasure ta'en:
40 In brief, sir, study what you most affect.
Luc. Gramercies, Tranio, well dost thou advise.
If, Biondello, thou wert come ashore,
We could at once put us in readiness,
And take a lodging fit to entertain
45 Such friends as time in Padua shall beget.
But stay a while: what company is this?
Tra. Master, some show to welcome us to town.

Enter Baptista, Katharina, Bianca, Gremio, *and*
Hortensio. Lucentio *and* Tranio *stand by.*

Bap. Gentlemen, importune me no farther,
For how I firmly am resolved you know;
50 That is, not to bestow my youngest daughter
Before I have a husband for the elder:
If either of you both love Katharina,
Because I know you well and love you well,
Leave shall you have to court her at your pleasure.
55 *Gre.* [*Aside*] To cart her rather: she's too rough
      for me.
There, there, Hortensio, will you any wife?
Kath. I pray you, sir, is it your will
To make a stale of me amongst these mates?
Hor. Mates, maid! how mean you that? no mates
      for you,
60 Unless you were of gentler, milder mould.

244

KATH. I'faith, sir, you shall never need to fear:
I wis it is not half way to her heart;
But if it were, doubt not her care should be
To comb your noddle with a three-legg'd stool
65 And paint your face and use you like a fool.
HOR. From all such devils, good Lord deliver us!
GRE. And me too, good Lord!
TRA. Husht, master! here's some good pastime
      toward:
That wench is stark mad or wonderful froward.
70 *LUC.* But in the other's silence do I see
Maid's mild behaviour and sobriety.
Peace, Tranio!
TRA. Well said, master; mum! and gaze your fill.
BAP. Gentlemen, that I may soon make good
75 What I have said, Bianca, get you in:
And let it not displease thee, good Bianca,
For I will love thee ne'er the less, my girl.
KATH. A pretty peat! it is best
Put finger in the eye, an she knew why.
80 *BIAN.* Sister, content you in my discontent.
Sir, to your pleasure humbly I subscribe:
My books and instruments shall be my company,
On them to look and practise by myself.
LUC. Hark, Tranio! thou may'st hear Minerva speak.
85 *HOR.* Signior Baptista, will you be so strange?
Sorry am I that our good will effects
Bianca's grief.
GRE. Why will you mew her up,
Signior Baptista, for this fiend of hell,
And make her bear the penance of her tongue?
90 *BAP.* Gentlemen, content ye; I am resolved:
Go in, Bianca: [*Exit Bianca.*
And for I know she taketh most delight
In music, instruments and poetry,
Schoolmasters will I keep within my house,
95 Fit to instruct her youth. If you, Hortensio,
Or Signior Gremio, you, know any such,
Prefer them hither; for to cunning men
I will be very kind, and liberal
To mine own children in good bringing-up:
100 And so farewell. Katharina, you may stay;
For I have more to commune with Bianca. [*Exit.*

KATH. Why, and I trust I may go too, may I not?
What, shall I be appointed hours; as though, belike,
I knew not what to take, and what to leave, ha? [*Exit.*
105 *GRE.* You may go to the devil's dam: your gifts are so
good, here's none will hold you. Their love is not so great,
Hortensio, but we may blow our nails together, and fast it
fairly out: our cake's dough on both sides. Farewell:
yet, for the love I bear my sweet Bianca, if I can by any
110 means light on a fit man to teach her that wherein she
delights, I will wish him to her father.
HOR. So will I, Signior Gremio: but a word, I pray.
Though the nature of our quarrel yet never brooked parle,
know now, upon advice, it toucheth us both, that we may
115 yet again have access to our fair mistress, and be happy rivals
in Bianca's love, to labour and effect one thing specially.
GRE. What's that, I pray?
HOR. Marry, sir, to get a husband for her sister.
GRE. A husband! a devil.
120 *HOR.* I say, a husband.
GRE. I say, a devil. Thinkest thou, Hortensio, though
her father be very rich, any man is so very a fool to be
married to hell?
HOR. Tush, Gremio, though it pass your patience and
125 mine to endure her loud alarums, why, man, there be good
fellows in the world, an a man could light on them, would
take her with all faults, and money enough.
GRE. I cannot tell; but I had as lief take her dowry with
this condition, to be whipped at the high-cross every morning.
130 *HOR.* Faith, as you say, there's small choice in rotten

apples. But come; since this bar in law makes us
    friends,
it shall be so far forth friendly maintained till by
    helping
Baptista's eldest daughter to a husband we set his
    youngest
free for a husband, and then have to't afresh. Sweet
    Bianca!
135 Happy man be his dole! He that runs fastest gets
the ring. How say you, Signior Gremio?
GRE. I am agreed; and would I had given him the best
horse in Padua to begin his wooing that would
    thoroughly
woo her, wed her and bed her and rid the house
    of her!
140 Come on. [*Exeunt Gremio and Hortensio.*
TRA. I pray, sir, tell me, is it possible
That love should of a sudden take such hold?
LUC. O Tranio, till I found it to be true,
I never thought it possible or likely;
145 But see, while idly I stood looking on,
I found the effect of love in idleness:
And now in plainness do confess to thee,
That art to me as secret and as dear
As Anna to the Queen of Carthage was,
150 Tranio, I burn, I pine, I perish, Tranio,
If I achieve not this young modest girl.
Counsel me, Tranio, for I know thou canst;
Assist me, Tranio, for I know thou wilt.
TRA. Master, it is no time to chide you now;
155 Affection is not rated from the heart:
If love have touch'd you, nought remains but so,
'Redime te captum quam queas minimo.'
LUC. Gramercies, lad, go forward; this contents:
The rest will comfort, for thy counsel's sound.
160 TRA. Master, you look'd so longly on the maid,
Perhaps you mark'd not what's the pith of all.
LUC. O yes, I saw sweet beauty in her face,
Such as the daughter of Agenor had,
That made great Jove to humble him to her hand,
165 When with his knees he kiss'd the Cretan strond.
TRA. Saw you no more? mark'd you not how her
    sister

Began to scold and raise up such a storm
That mortal ears might hardly endure the din?
Luc. Tranio, I saw her coral lips to move
₁₇₀ And with her breath she did perfume the air:
Sacred and sweet was all I saw in her.
Tra. Nay, then, 'tis time to stir him from his trance.
I pray, awake, sir: if you love the maid,
Bend thoughts and wits to achieve her. Thus it stands:
₁₇₅ Her eldest sister is so curst and shrewd
That till the father rid his hands of her,
Master, your love must live a maid at home;
And therefore has he closely mew'd her up,
Because she will not be annoy'd with suitors.
₁₈₀ *Luc.* Ah, Tranio, what a cruel father's he!
But art thou not advised, he took some care
To get her cunning schoolmasters to instruct her?
Tra. Ay, marry, am I, sir; and now 'tis plotted.
Luc. I have it, Tranio.
Tra. Master, for my hand,
₁₈₅ Both our inventions meet and jump in one.
Luc. Tell me thine first.
Tra. You will be schoolmaster
And undertake the teaching of the maid:
That's your device.
Luc. It is: may it be done?
Tra. Not possible; for who shall bear your part,
₁₉₀ And be in Padua here Vincentio's son;
Keep house and ply his book, welcome his friends,
Visit his countrymen and banquet them?
Luc. Basta; content thee, for I have it full.
We have not yet been seen in any house,
₁₉₅ Nor can we be distinguish'd by our faces
For man or master; then it follows thus;
Thou shalt be master, Tranio, in my stead,
Keep house and port and servants, as I should:
I will some other be; some Florentine,
₂₀₀ Some Neapolitan, or meaner man of Pisa.
'Tis hatch'd and shall be so: Tranio, at once
Uncase thee; take my colour'd hat and cloak:
When Biondello comes, he waits on thee;
But I will charm him first to keep his tongue.
₂₀₅ *Tra.* So had you need.
In brief, sir, sith it your pleasure is,

And I am tied to be obedient;
For so your father charged me at our parting,
'Be serviceable to my son,' quoth he,
₂₁₀ Although I think 'twas in another sense;
I am content to be Lucentio,
Because so well I love Lucentio.
Luc. Tranio, be so, because Lucentio loves:
And let me be a slave, to achieve that maid
₂₁₅ Whose sudden sight hath thrall'd my wounded
    eye.
Here comes the rogue.

ENTER BIONDELLO.

Sirrah, where have you been?
BION. Where have I been! Nay, how now! where are
you? Master, has my fellow Tranio stolen your
    clothes?
Or you stolen his? or both? pray, what's the news?
₂₂₀ *Luc.* Sirrah, come hither: 'tis no time to jest,
And therefore frame your manners to the time.
Your fellow Tranio here, to save my life,
Puts my apparel and my countenance on,
And I for my escape have put on his;
₂₂₅ For in a quarrel since I came ashore
I kill'd a man and fear I was descried:
Wait you on him, I charge you, as becomes,
While I make way from hence to save my life:
You understand me?
BION. I, sir! ne'er a whit.
₂₃₀ *Luc.* And not a jot of Tranio in your mouth:
Tranio is changed into Lucentio.
BION. The better for him: would I were so too!
TRA. So could I, faith, boy, to have the next wish after,
That Lucentio indeed had Baptista's youngest
    daughter.
₂₃₅ But, sirrah, not for my sake, but your master's, I
    advise
You use your manners discreetly in all kind of
    companies:
When I am alone, why, then I am Tranio;
But in all places else your master Lucentio.
Luc. Tranio, let's go: one thing more rests, that thyself

~240~ execute, to make one among these wooers: if
    thou ask
me why, sufficeth, my reasons are both good and
    weighty. [*Exeunt.*

The presenters above speak.

FIRST SERV. My lord, you nod; you do not mind the
    play.
SLY. Yes, by Saint Anne, do I. A good matter, surely:
comes there any more of it?
~245~ PAGE. My lord, 'tis but begun.
SLY. 'Tis a very excellent piece of work, madam lady:
would 'twere done! [They sit and mark.

SCENE II

PADUA. BEFORE HORTENSIO'S HOUSE.
Enter PETRUCHIO *and his man* GRUMIO.

PET. Verona, for a while I take my leave,
To see my friends in Padua, but of all
My best beloved and approved friend,
Hortensio; and I trow this is his house.
~5~ Here, sirrah Grumio; knock, I say.
GRU. Knock, sir! whom should I knock? is there any
man has rebused your worship?
PET. Villain, I say, knock me here soundly.
GRU. Knock you here, sir! why, sir, what am I, sir,
~10~ that I should knock you here, sir?
PET. Villain, I say, knock me at this gate
And rap me well, or I'll knock your knave's pate.
GRU. My master is grown quarrelsome. I should
    knock you first,
And then I know after who comes by the worst.
~15~ PET. Will it not be?
Faith, sirrah, an you'll not knock, I'll ring it;
I'll try how you can *sol, fa,* and sing it. [*He wrings him
    by the ears.*
GRU. Help, masters, help! my master is mad.
PET. Now, knock when I bid you, sirrah villain!

Enter Hortensio.

Hor. ₂₀ How now! what's the matter? My old friend
    Grumio!
and my good friend Petruchio! How do you all at
Verona?
Pet. Signior Hortensio, come you to part the fray?
'Con tutto il core ben trovato,' may I say.
₂₅ *Hor.* 'Alla nostra casa ben venuto, molto honorato
signor mio Petrucio.'
Rise, Grumio, rise: we will compound this quarrel.
Gru. Nay, 'tis no matter, sir, what he 'leges in Latin. If
this be not a lawful cause for me to leave his service,
    look
₃₀ you, sir, he bid me knock him and rap him soundly,
    sir:
well, was it fit for a servant to use his master so, being
    perhaps,
for aught I see, two-and-thirty, a pip out?
Whom would to God I had well knock'd at first,
Then had not Grumio come by the worst.
₃₅ *Pet.* A senseless villain! Good Hortensio,
I bade the rascal knock upon your gate
And could not get him for my heart to do it.
Gru. Knock at the gate! O heavens! Spake you not
these words plain, 'Sirrah, knock me here, rap me
    here,
₄₀ knock me well, and knock me soundly'? And
    come you
now with, 'knocking at the gate'?
Pet. Sirrah, be gone, or talk not, I advise you.
Hor. Petruchio, patience; I am Grumio's pledge:
Why, this's a heavy chance 'twixt him and you,
₄₅ Your ancient, trusty, pleasant servant Grumio.
And tell me now, sweet friend, what happy gale
Blows you to Padua here from old Verona?
Pet. Such wind as scatters young men through the
    world
To seek their fortunes farther than at home
₅₀ Where small experience grows. But in a few,
Signior Hortensio, thus it stands with me:
Antonio, my father, is deceased;
And I have thrust myself into this maze,

Haply to wive and thrive as best I may:
₅₅ Crowns in my purse I have and goods at home
And so am come abroad to see the world.
Hor. Petruchio, shall I then come roundly to thee
And wish thee to a shrewd ill-favour'd wife?
Thou'ldst thank me but a little for my counsel:
₆₀ And yet I'll promise thee she shall be rich
And very rich: but thou'rt too much my friend,
And I'll not wish thee to her.
Pet. Signior Hortensio, 'twixt such friends as we
Few words suffice; and therefore, if thou know
₆₅ One rich enough to be Petruchio's wife,
As wealth is burden of my wooing dance,
Be she as foul as was Florentius' love,
As old as Sibyl, and as curst and shrewd
As Socrates' Xanthippe, or a worse,
₇₀ She moves me not, or not removes, at least,
Affection's edge in me, were she as rough
As are the swelling Adriatic seas:
I come to wive it wealthily in Padua;
If wealthily, then happily in Padua.
₇₅ *Gru.* Nay, look you, sir, he tells you flatly what
his mind
is: why, give him gold enough and marry him to a
puppet
or an aglet-baby; or an old trot with ne'er a tooth
in her
head, though she have as many diseases as two and
fifty
horses: why, nothing comes amiss, so money comes
withal.
₈₀ *Hor.* Petruchio, since we are stepp'd thus far in,
I will continue that I broach'd in jest.
I can, Petruchio, help thee to a wife
With wealth enough and young and beauteous,
Brought up as best becomes a gentlewoman:
₈₅ Her only fault, and that is faults enough,
Is that she is intolerable curst
And shrewd and froward, so beyond all measure,
That, were my state far worser than it is,
I would not wed her for a mine of gold.
₉₀ *Pet.* Hortensio, peace! thou know'st not gold's
effect:

Tell me her father's name and 'tis enough;
For I will board her, though she chide as loud
As thunder when the clouds in autumn crack.
95 *Hor.* Her father is Baptista Minola,
An affable and courteous gentleman:
Her name is Katharina Minola,
Renown'd in Padua for her scolding tongue.
Pet. I know her father, though I know not her;
And he knew my deceased father well.
100 I will not sleep, Hortensio, till I see her;
And therefore let me be thus bold with you
To give you over at this first encounter,
Unless you will accompany me thither.
Gru. I pray you, sir, let him go while the humour
    lasts.
105 O' my word, an she knew him as well as I do, she
    would think
scolding would do little good upon him: she may
    perhaps
call him half a score knaves or so: why, that's
    nothing; an
he begin once, he'll rail in his rope-tricks. I'll tell you
    what,
sir, an she stand him but a little, he will throw a
    figure in
110 her face and so disfigure her with it that she shall
    have no
more eyes to see withal than a cat. You know him
    not, sir.
Hor. Tarry, Petruchio, I must go with thee;
For in Baptista's keep my treasure is:
He hath the jewel of my life in hold,
115 His youngest daughter, beautiful Bianca;
And her withholds from me and other more,
Suitors to her and rivals in my love;
Supposing it a thing impossible,
For those defects I have before rehearsed,
120 That ever Katharina will be woo'd;
Therefore this order hath Baptista ta'en,
That none shall have access unto Bianca
Till Katharine the curst have got a husband.
Gru. Katharine the curst!
125 A title for a maid of all titles the worst.

Hor. Now shall my friend Petruchio do me grace;
And offer me disguised in sober robes
To old Baptista as a schoolmaster
Well seen in music, to instruct Bianca;
130 That so I may, by this device, at least
Have leave and leisure to make love to her
And unsuspected court her by herself.
Gru. Here's no knavery! See, to beguile the old
folks, how the young folks lay their heads together!

ENTER GREMIO, AND LUCENTIO DISGUISED.

135 Master, master, look about you: who goes
there, ha?
Hor. Peace, Grumio! it is the rival of my love.
Petruchio, stand by a while.
Gru. A proper stripling and an amorous!
Gre. O, very well; I have perused the note.
140 Hark you, sir; I'll have them very fairly bound:
All books of love, see that at any hand;
And see you read no other lectures to her:
You understand me: over and beside
Signior Baptista's liberality,
145 I'll mend it with a largess. Take your paper too,
And let me have them very well perfumed:
For she is sweeter than perfume itself
To whom they go to. What will you read to her?
Luc. Whate'er I read to her, I'll plead for you
150 As for my patron, stand you so assured,
As firmly as yourself were still in place:
Yea, and perhaps with more successful words
Than you, unless you were a scholar, sir.
Gre. O this learning, what a thing it is!
155 *Gru.* O this woodcock, what an ass it is!
Pet. Peace, sirrah!
Hor. Grumio, mum! God save you, Signior Gremio.
Gre. And you are well met, Signior Hortensio.
Trow you whither I am going? To Baptista Minola.
160 I promised to inquire carefully
About a schoolmaster for the fair Bianca:
And by good fortune I have lighted well
On this young man, for learning and behaviour
Fit for her turn, well read in poetry

₁₆₅ And other books, good ones, I warrant ye.
Hor. 'Tis well; and I have met a gentleman
Hath promised me to help me to another,
A fine musician to instruct our mistress;
So shall I no whit be behind in duty
₁₇₀ To fair Bianca, so beloved of me.
Gre. Beloved of me; and that my deeds shall prove.
Gru. And that his bags shall prove.
Hor. Gremio, 'tis now no time to vent our love:
Listen to me, and if you speak me fair,
₁₇₅ I'll tell you news indifferent good for either.
Here is a gentleman whom by chance I met,
Upon agreement from us to his liking,
Will undertake to woo curst Katharine,
Yea, and to marry her, if her dowry please.
₁₈₀ *Gre.* So said, so done, is well.
Hortensio, have you told him all her faults?
Pet. I know she is an irksome brawling scold:
If that be all, masters, I hear no harm.
Gre. No, say'st me so, friend? What countryman?
₁₈₅ *Pet.* Born in Verona, old Antonio's son:
My father dead, my fortune lives for me;
And I do hope good days and long to see.
Gre. O sir, such a life, with such a wife, were strange!
But if you have a stomach, to't i' God's name:
₁₉₀ You shall have me assisting you in all.
But will you woo this wild-cat?
Pet. Will I live?
Gru. Will he woo her? ay, or I'll hang her.
Pet. Why came I hither but to that intent?
Think you a little din can daunt mine ears?
₁₉₅ Have I not in my time heard lions roar?
Have I not heard the sea puff'd up with winds
Rage like an angry boar chafed with sweat?
Have I not heard great ordnance in the field,
And heaven's artillery thunder in the skies?
₂₀₀ Have I not in a pitched battle heard
Loud 'larums, neighing steeds, and trumpets' clang?
And do you tell me of a woman's tongue,
That gives not half so great a blow to hear
As will a chestnut in a farmer's fire?
Tush, tush! fear boys with bugs.
₂₀₅ *Gru.* For he fears none.

Gre. Hortensio, hark:
This gentleman is happily arrived,
My mind presumes, for his own good and ours.
Hor. I promised we would be contributors
210 And bear his charge of wooing, whatsoe'er.
Gre. And so we will, provided that he win her.
Gru. I would I were as sure of a good dinner.

ENTER TRANIO *BRAVE, AND* BIONDELLO.

Tra. Gentlemen, God save you. If I may be bold,
Tell me, I beseech you, which is the readiest way
215 To the house of Signior Baptista Minola?
Bion. He that has the two fair daughters: is't he you
mean?
Tra. Even he, Biondello.
Gre. Hark you, sir; you mean not her to—
220 *Tra.* Perhaps, him and her, sir: what have you
to do?
Pet. Not her that chides, sir, at any hand, I pray.
Tra. I love no chiders, sir. Biondello, let's away.
Luc. Well begun, Tranio.
Hor. Sir, a word ere you go;
225 Are you a suitor to the maid you talk of, yea or no?
Tra. And if I be, sir, is it any offence?
Gre. No; if without more words you will get you
hence.
Tra. Why, sir, I pray, are not the streets as free
For me as for you?
Gre. But so is not she.
230 *Tra.* For what reason, I beseech you?
Gre. For this reason, if you'll know,
That she's the choice love of Signior Gremio.
Hor. That she's the chosen of Signior Hortensio.
Tra. Softly, my masters! if you be gentlemen,
Do me this right; hear me with patience.
235 Baptista is a noble gentleman,
To whom my father is not all unknown;
And were his daughter fairer than she is,
She may more suitors have and me for one.
240 Fair Leda's daughter had a thousand wooers;
Then well one more may fair Bianca have:
And so she shall; Lucentio shall make one,

Though Paris came in hope to speed alone.
Gre. What, this gentleman will out-talk us all!
245 *Luc.* Sir, give him head: I know he'll prove a jade.
Pet. Hortensio, to what end are all these words?
Hor. Sir, let me be so bold as ask you,
Did you yet ever see Baptista's daughter?
Tra. No, sir; but hear I do that he hath two,
250 The one as famous for a scolding tongue
As is the other for beauteous modesty.
Pet. Sir, sir, the first's for me; let her go by.
Gre. Yea, leave that labour to great Hercules;
And let it be more than Alcides' twelve.
255 *Pet.* Sir, understand you this of me in sooth:
The youngest daughter whom you hearken for
Her father keeps from all access of suitors;
And will not promise her to any man
Until the elder sister first be wed:
260 The younger then is free and not before.
Tra. If it be so, sir, that you are the man
Must stead us all and me amongst the rest;
And if you break the ice and do this feat,
Achieve the elder, set the younger free
265 For our access, whose hap shall be to have her
Will not so graceless be to be ingrate.
Hor. Sir, you say well and well you do conceive;
And since you do profess to be a suitor,
You must, as we do, gratify this gentleman,
270 To whom we all rest generally beholding.
Tra. Sir, I shall not be slack: in sign whereof,
Please ye we may contrive this afternoon,
And quaff carouses to our mistress' health,
And do as adversaries do in law,
275 Strive mightily, but eat and drink as friends.
Gru. & Bion. O excellent motion! Fellows, let's be
   gone.
Hor. The motion's good indeed and be it so,
Petruchio, I shall be your ben venuto. [*Exeunt.*

ACT II

SCENE I: PADUA. A ROOM IN BAPTISTA'S HOUSE.

ENTER KATHARINA *AND* BIANCA.

BIAN. Good sister, wrong me not, nor wrong yourself,
To make a bondmaid and a slave of me;
That I disdain: but for these other gawds,
Unbind my hands, I 'll pull them off myself,
5 Yea, all my raiment, to my petticoat;
Or what you will command me will I do,
So well I know my duty to my elders.
KATH. Of all thy suitors, here I charge thee, tell
Whom thou lovest best: see thou dissemble not.
10 *BIAN.* Believe me, sister, of all the men alive
I never yet beheld that special face
Which I could fancy more than any other.
KATH. Minion, thou liest. Is't not Hortensio?
BIAN. If you affect him, sister, here I swear
15 I'll plead for you myself, but you shall have him.
KATH. O then, belike, you fancy riches more:
You will have Gremio to keep you fair.
BIAN. Is it for him you do envy me so?
Nay then you jest, and now I well perceive
20 You have but jested with me all this while:
I prithee, sister Kate, untie my hands.
KATH. If that be jest, then all the rest was so. [*Strikes
    her.*

ENTER BAPTISTA.

BAP. Why, how now, dame! whence grows this in-
   solence?
Bianca, stand aside. Poor girl! she weeps.
25 Go ply thy needle; meddle not with her.
For shame, thou hilding of a devilish spirit,
Why dost thou wrong her that did ne'er wrong thee?
When did she cross thee with a bitter word?
KATH. Her silence flouts me, and I'll be revenged.
[Flies after Bianca.
30 *BAP.* What, in my sight? Bianca, get thee in.
[Exit Bianca.
KATH. What, will you not suffer me? Nay, now I see
She is your treasure, she must have a husband;
I must dance bare-foot on her wedding day
And for your love to her lead apes in hell.
35 Talk not to me: I will go sit and weep
Till I can find occasion of revenge. *[Exit.*
BAP. Was ever gentleman thus grieved as I?
But who comes here?

Enter GREMIO, LUCENTIO *in the habit of a mean man;* PETRUCHIO,
with HORTENSIO *as a musician; and* TRANIO, *with* BIONDELLO
bearing a lute and books.

GRE. Good morrow, neighbour Baptista.
40 *BAP.* Good morrow, neighbour Gremio. God
   save you,
gentlemen!
PET. And you, good sir! Pray, have you not a
   daughter
Call'd Katharina, fair and virtuous?
BAP. I have a daughter, sir, called Katharina.
45 *GRE.* You are too blunt: go to it orderly.
PET. You wrong me, Signior Gremio: give me leave.
I am a gentleman of Verona, sir,
That, hearing of her beauty and her wit,
Her affability and bashful modesty,
50 Her wondrous qualities and mild behaviour,
Am bold to show myself a forward guest
Within your house, to make mine eye the witness
Of that report which I so oft have heard.

And, for an entrance to my entertainment,
₅₅ I do present you with a man of mine, [*Presenting Hortensio.*
Cunning in music and the mathematics,
To instruct her fully in those sciences,
Whereof I know she is not ignorant:
Accept of him, or else you do me wrong:
₆₀ His name is Licio, born in Mantua.
BAP. You're welcome, sir; and he, for your good sake.
But for my daughter Katharine, this I know,
She is not for your turn, the more my grief.
PET. I see you do not mean to part with her,
₆₅ Or else you like not of my company.
BAP. Mistake me not; I speak but as I find.
Whence are you, sir? what may I call your name?
PET. Petruchio is my name; Antonio's son,
A man well known throughout all Italy.
₇₀ *BAP.* I know him well: you are welcome for his sake.
GRE. Saving your tale, Petruchio, I pray,
Let us, that are poor petitioners, speak too:
Baccare! you are marvellous forward.
PET. O, pardon me, Signior Gremio; I would fain be doing.
₇₅ *GRE.* I doubt it not, sir; but you will curse your wooing.
Neighbour, this is a gift very grateful, I am sure of it. To
express the like kindness, myself, that have been more
kindly beholding to you than any, freely give unto you
this young scholar [*presenting Lucentio*], that hath been
₈₀ long studying at Rheims; as cunning in Greek, Latin, and
other languages, as the other in music and mathematics:
his name is Cambio; pray, accept his service.
BAP. A thousand thanks, Signior Gremio. Welcome,
good Cambio. But, gentle sir [*to Tranio*], methinks you
₈₅ walk like a stranger: may I be so bold to know the cause
of your coming?

TRA. Pardon me, sir, the boldness is mine own;
That, being a stranger in this city here,
Do make myself a suitor to your daughter,
90 Unto Bianca, fair and virtuous.
Nor is your firm resolve unknown to me,
In the preferment of the eldest sister.
This liberty is all that I request,
That, upon knowledge of my parentage,
95 I may have welcome 'mongst the rest that woo
And free access and favour as the rest:
And, toward the education of your daughters,
I here bestow a simple instrument,
And this small packet of Greek and Latin books:
100 If you accept them, then their worth is great.
BAP. Lucentio is your name; of whence, I pray?
TRA. Of Pisa, sir; son to Vincentio.
BAP. A mighty man of Pisa; by report
I know him well: you are very welcome, sir.
105 Take you the lute, and you the set of books;
You shall go see your pupils presently.
Holla, within!

Enter a Servant.

Sirrah, lead these gentlemen
To my daughters; and tell them both,
These are their tutors: bid them use them well.
[Exit Servant, with Luc. and Hor., Bio. following.
110 We will go walk a little in the orchard,
And then to dinner. You are passing welcome,
And so I pray you all to think yourselves.
PET. Signior Baptista, my business asketh haste,
And every day I cannot come to woo.
115 You knew my father well, and in him me,
Left solely heir to all his lands and goods,
Which I have better'd rather than decreased:
Then tell me, if I get your daughter's love,
What dowry shall I have with her to wife?
120 *BAP.* After my death the one half of my lands,
And in possession twenty thousand crowns.
PET. And, for that dowry, I 'll assure her of
Her widowhood, be it that she survive me,
In all my lands and leases whatsoever:

125 Let specialties be therefore drawn between us,
That covenants may be kept on either hand.
Bap. Ay, when the special thing is well obtain'd,
That is, her love; for that is all in all.
Pet. Why, that is nothing; for I tell you, father,
130 I am as peremptory as she proud-minded;
And where two raging fires meet together
They do consume the thing that feeds their fury:
Though little fire grows great with little wind,
Yet extreme gusts will blow out fire and all:
135 So I to her and so she yields to me;
For I am rough and woo not like a babe.
Bap. Well mayst thou woo, and happy be thy speed!
But be thou arm'd for some unhappy words.
Pet. Ay, to the proof; as mountains are for winds,
140 That shake not, though they blow perpetually.

Re-enter HORTENSIO, *with his head broke.*

Bap. How now, my friend! why dost thou look so
  pale?
Hor. For fear, I promise you, if I look pale.
Bap. What, will my daughter prove a good musician?
Hor. I think she'll sooner prove a soldier:
145 Iron may hold with her, but never lutes.
Bap. Why, then thou canst not break her to the lute?
Hor. Why, no; for she hath broke the lute to me.
I did but tell her she mistook her frets,
And bow'd her hand to teach her fingering;
150 When, with a most impatient devilish spirit,
'Frets, call you these?' quoth she; 'I'll fume with
  them:'
And, with that word, she struck me on the head,
And through the instrument my pate made way;
And there I stood amazed for a while,
155 As on a pillory, looking through the lute;
While she did call me rascal fiddler
And twangling Jack; with twenty such vile terms,
As had she studied to misuse me so.
Pet. Now, by the world, it is a lusty wench;
160 I love her ten times more than e'er I did:
O, how I long to have some chat with her!
Bap. Well, go with me and be not so discomfited:

Proceed in practice with my younger daughter;
She's apt to learn and thankful for good turns.
165 Signior Petruchio, will you go with us,
Or shall I send my daughter Kate to you?
PET. I pray you do; I will attend her here,

[Exeunt Baptista, Gremio, Tranio, and Hortensio.

And woo her with some spirit when she comes.
Say that she rail; why then I'll tell her plain
170 She sings as sweetly as a nightingale:
Say that she frown; I'll say she looks as clear
As morning roses newly wash'd with dew:
Say she be mute and will not speak a word;
Then I'll commend her volubility,
175 And say she uttereth piercing eloquence:
If she do bid me pack, I'll give her thanks,
As though she bid me stay by her a week:
If she deny to wed, I'll crave the day
When I shall ask the banns, and when be married.
180 But here she comes; and now, Petruchio, speak.

ENTER KATHARINA.

Good morrow, Kate; for that's your name, I hear.
KATH. Well have you heard, but something hard of
        hearing:
They call me Katharine that do talk of me.
PET. You lie, in faith; for you are call'd plain Kate,
185 And bonny Kate, and sometimes Kate the curst;
But Kate, the prettiest Kate in Christendom,
Kate of Kate-Hall, my super-dainty Kate,
For dainties are all Kates, and therefore, Kate,
Take this of me, Kate of my consolation;
190 Hearing thy mildness praised in every town,
Thy virtues spoke of, and thy beauty sounded,
Yet not so deeply as to thee belongs,
Myself am moved to woo thee for my wife.
KATH. Moved! in good time: let him that moved you
        hither
195 Remove you hence: I knew you at the first
You were a moveable.
PET. Why, what's a moveable?

KATH. A join'd-stool.

PET. Thou hast hit it: come, sit on me.

KATH. Asses are made to bear, and so are you.

PET. Women are made to bear, and so are you.

200 *KATH.* No such jade as you, if me you mean.

PET. Alas, good Kate, I will not burden thee!

For, knowing thee to be but young and light,—

KATH. Too light for such a swain as you to catch;

And yet as heavy as my weight should be.

PET. Should be! should—buzz!

205 *KATH.* Well ta'en, and like a buzzard.

PET. O slow-wing'd turtle! shall a buzzard take thee?

KATH. Ay, for a turtle, as he takes a buzzard.

PET. Come, come, you wasp; i' faith, you are too

angry.

KATH. If I be waspish, best beware my sting.

210 *PET.* My remedy is then, to pluck it out.

KATH. Ay, if the fool could find it where it lies.

PET. Who knows not where a wasp does wear his

sting?

In his tail.

KATH. In his tongue.

PET. Whose tongue?

KATH. Yours, if you talk of tails: and so farewell.

215 *PET.* What, with my tongue in your tail? nay, come

again,

Good Kate; I am a gentleman.

KATH. *That I'll try. [She strikes him.*

PET. I swear I'll cuff you, if you strike again.

KATH. So may you lose your arms:

If you strike me, you are no gentleman;

220 And if no gentleman, why then no arms.

PET. A herald, Kate? O, put me in thy books!

KATH. What is your crest? a coxcomb?

PET. A combless cock, so Kate will be my hen.

KATH. No cock of mine; you crow too like a craven.

225 *PET.* Nay, come, Kate, come; you must not look so

sour.

KATH. It is my fashion, when I see a crab.

PET. Why, here's no crab; and therefore look not sour.

KATH. There is, there is.

PET. Then show it me.

KATH. Had I a glass, I would.

PET. What, you mean my face?

230 *KATH.* Well aim'd of such a young one.

PET. Now, by Saint George, I am too young for you.

KATH. Yet you are wither'd.

PET. 'Tis with cares.

KATH. I care not.

PET. Nay, hear you, Kate: in sooth you scape not so.

KATH. I chafe you, if I tarry: let me go.

235 *PET.* No, not a whit: I find you passing gentle.
'Twas told me you were rough and coy and sullen,
And now I find report a very liar;
For thou art pleasant, gamesome, passing courteous,
But slow in speech, yet sweet as spring-time flowers:
240 Thou canst not frown, thou canst not look askance,
Nor bite the lip, as angry wenches will,
Nor hast thou pleasure to be cross in talk,
But thou with mildness entertain'st thy wooers,
With gentle conference, soft and affable.
245 Why does the world report that Kate doth limp?
O slanderous world! Kate like the hazel-twig
Is straight and slender and as brown in hue
As hazel-nuts and sweeter than the kernels.
O, let me see thee walk: thou dost not halt.

250 *KATH.* Go, fool, and whom thou keep'st command.

PET. Did ever Dian so become a grove
As Kate this chamber with her princely gait?
O, be thou Dian, and let her be Kate;
And then let Kate be chaste and Dian sportful!

255 *KATH.* Where did you study all this goodly speech?

PET. It is extempore, from my mother-wit.

KATH. A witty mother! witless else her son.

PET. Am I not wise?

KATH. Yes; keep you warm.

PET. Marry, so I mean, sweet Katharine, in thy bed:
260 And therefore, setting all this chat aside,
Thus in plain terms: your father hath consented
That you shall be my wife; your dowry 'greed on;
And, will you, nill you, I will marry you.
Now, Kate, I am a husband for your turn;
265 For, by this light, whereby I see thy beauty,
Thy beauty, that doth make me like thee well,
Thou must be married to no man but me;
For I am he am born to tame you Kate,

And bring you from a wild Kate to a Kate
₂₇₀ Conformable as other household Kates.
Here comes your father: never make denial;
I must and will have Katharine to my wife.

RE-ENTER BAPTISTA, GREMIO, *AND* TRANIO.

BAP. Now, Signior Petruchio, how speed you with my
  daughter?
PET. How but well, sir? how but well?
₂₇₅ It were impossible I should speed amiss.
BAP. Why, how now, daughter Katharine! in your
  dumps?
KATH. Call you me daughter? now, I promise you
You have show'd a tender fatherly regard,
To wish me wed to one half lunatic;
₂₈₀ A mad-cap ruffian and a swearing Jack,
That thinks with oaths to face the matter out.
PET. Father, 'tis thus: yourself and all the world,
That talk'd of her, have talk'd amiss of her:
If she be curst, it is for policy,
₂₈₅ For she's not froward, but modest as the dove;
She is not hot, but temperate as the morn;
For patience she will prove a second Grissel,
And Roman Lucrece for her chastity:
And to conclude, we have 'greed so well together,
₂₉₀ That upon Sunday is the wedding-day.
KATH. I'll see thee hang'd on Sunday first.
GRE. Hark, Petruchio; she says she'll see thee hang'd
  first.
TRA. Is this your speeding? nay, then, good night our
  part!
PET. Be patient, gentlemen; I choose her for myself:
₂₉₅ If she and I be pleased, what's that to you?
'Tis bargain'd 'twixt us twain, being alone,
That she shall still be curst in company.
I tell you, 'tis incredible to believe
How much she loves me: O, the kindest Kate!
₃₀₀ She hung about my neck; and kiss on kiss
She vied so fast, protesting oath on oath,
That in a twink she won me to her love.
O, you are novices! 'tis a world to see,
How tame, when men and women are alone,

₃₀₅ A meacock wretch can make the curstest shrew.
Give me thy hand, Kate: I will unto Venice,
To buy apparel 'gainst the wedding-day.
Provide the feast, father, and bid the guests;
I will be sure my Katharine shall be fine.
₃₁₀ *BAP.* I know not what to say: but give me your
hands;
God send you joy, Petruchio! 'tis a match.
GRE. TRA. Amen, say we: we will be witnesses.
PET. Father, and wife, and gentlemen, adieu;
I will to Venice; Sunday comes apace:
₃₁₅ We will have rings, and things, and fine array;
And, kiss me, Kate, we will be married o' Sunday.
[*Exeunt Petruchio and Katharina severally.*
GRE. Was ever match clapp'd up so suddenly?
BAP. Faith, gentlemen, now I play a merchant's part,
And venture madly on a desperate mart.
₃₂₀ *TRA.* 'Twas a commodity lay fretting by you:
'Twill bring you gain, or perish on the seas.
BAP. The gain I seek is, quiet in the match.
GRE. No doubt but he hath got a quiet catch.
But now, Baptista, to your younger daughter:
₃₂₅ Now is the day we long have looked for:
I am your neighbour, and was suitor first.
TRA. And I am one that love Bianca more
Than words can witness, or your thoughts can guess.
GRE. Youngling, thou canst not love so dear as I.
TRA. Greybeard, thy love doth freeze.
₃₃₀ *GRE.* But thine doth fry.
Skipper, stand back: 'tis age that nourisheth.
TRA. But youth in ladies' eyes that flourisheth.
BAP. Content you, gentlemen: I will compound this
strife:
'Tis deeds must win the prize; and he, of both,
₃₃₅ That can assure my daughter greatest dower
Shall have my Bianca's love.
Say, Signior Gremio, what can you assure her?
GRE. First, as you know, my house within the city
Is richly furnished with plate and gold;
₃₄₀ Basins and ewers to lave her dainty hands;
My hangings all of Tyrian tapestry;
In ivory coffers I have stuff'd my crowns;
In cypress chests my arras counterpoints,

Costly apparel, tents, and canopies,
345 Fine linen, Turkey cushions boss'd with pearl,
Valance of Venice gold in needlework,
Pewter and brass and all things that belong
To house or housekeeping: then, at my farm
I have a hundred milch-kine to the pail,
350 Sixscore fat oxen standing in my stalls,
And all things answerable to this portion.
Myself am struck in years, I must confess;
And if I die to-morrow, this is hers,
If whilst I live she will be only mine.
355 *TRA.* That 'only' came well in. Sir, list to me:
I am my father's heir and only son:
If I may have your daughter to my wife,
I'll leave her houses three or four as good,
Within rich Pisa walls, as any one
360 Old Signior Gremio has in Padua;
Besides two thousand ducats by the year
Of fruitful land, all which shall be her jointure.
What, have I pinch'd you, Signior Gremio?
GRE. Two thousand ducats by the year of land!
365 My land amounts not to so much in all:
That she shall have; besides an argosy
That now is lying in Marseilles' road.
What, have I choked you with an argosy?
TRA. Gremio, 'tis known my father hath no less
370 Than three great argosies; besides two galliasses,
And twelve tight galleys: these I will assure her,
And twice as much, whate'er thou offer'st next.
GRE. Nay, I have offer'd all, I have no more;
And she can have no more than all I have:
375 If you like me, she shall have me and mine.
TRA. Why, then the maid is mine from all the world,
By your firm promise: Gremio is out-vied.
BAP. I must confess your offer is the best;
And, let your father make her the assurance,
380 She is your own; else, you must pardon me,
If you should die before him, where's her dower?
TRA. That's but a cavil: he is old, I young.
GRE. And may not young men die, as well as old?
BAP. Well, gentlemen,
385 I am thus resolved: on Sunday next you know
My daughter Katharine is to be married:

Now, on the Sunday following, shall Bianca
Be bride to you, if you make this assurance;
If not, to Signior Gremio:
390 And so, I take my leave, and thank you both.
GRE. Adieu, good neighbour. [*Exit Baptista.*
Now I fear thee not:
Sirrah young gamester, your father were a fool
To give thee all, and in his waning age
Set foot under thy table: tut, a toy!
395 An old Italian fox is not so kind, my boy. [*Exit.*
TRA. A vengeance on your crafty wither'd hide!
Yet I have faced it with a card of ten.
'Tis in my head to do my master good:
I see no reason but supposed Lucentio
400 Must get a father, call'd—supposed Vincentio;
And that's a wonder: fathers commonly
Do get their children; but in this case of wooing,
A child shall get a sire, if I fail not of my cunning.
    [*Exit.*

ACT III

SCENE I. PADUA. BAPTISTA'S HOUSE

ENTER LUCENTIO, HORTENSIO, *AND* BIANCA.

Luc. Fiddler, forbear; you grow too forward, sir:
Have you so soon forgot the entertainment
Her sister Katharine welcomed you withal?
Hor. But, wrangling pedant, this is
₅ The patroness of heavenly harmony:
Then give me leave to have prerogative;
And when in music we have spent an hour,
Your lecture shall have leisure for as much.
Luc. Preposterous ass, that never read so far
₁₀ To know the cause why music was ordain'd!
Was it not to refresh the mind of man
After his studies or his usual pain?
Then give me leave to read philosophy,
And while I pause, serve in your harmony.
₁₅ *Hor.* Sirrah, I will not bear these braves of thine.
Bian. Why, gentlemen, you do me double wrong,
To strive for that which resteth in my choice:
I am no breeching scholar in the schools;
I'll not be tied to hours nor 'pointed times,
₂₀ But learn my lessons as I please myself.
And, to cut off all strife, here sit we down:
Take you your instrument, play you the whiles;

His lecture will be done ere you have tuned.
Hor. You'll leave his lecture when I am in tune?
25 *Luc.* That will be never: tune your instrument.
Bian. Where left we last?
Luc. Here, madam:
'Hic ibat Simois; hic est Sigeia tellus;
Hic steterat Priami regia celsa senis.'
30 *Bian.* Construe them.
Luc. 'Hic ibat,' as I told you before,—'Simois,' I am
Lucentio,—'hic est,' son unto Vincentio of Pisa,—
'Sigeia
tellus,' disguised thus to get your love;—' Hic steterat,' and
that Lucentio that comes a-wooing,—'Priami,' is
my man
35 Tranio,—'regia,' bearing my port,—'celsa senis,'
that we
might beguile the old pantaloon.
Hor. Madam, my instrument's in tune.
Bian. Let's hear. O fie! the treble jars.
Luc. Spit in the hole, man, and tune again.
40 *Bian.* Now let me see if I can construe it:
'Hic ibat Simois,' I know you not,—'hic est Sigeia
tellus,'
I trust you not;—'Hic steterat Priami,' take heed he
hear us not,—'regia,' presume not,—'celsa senis,'
despair not.
Hor. Madam, 'tis now in tune.
Luc. All but the base.
45 *Hor.* The base is right; 'tis the base knave that jars.
[*Aside*] How fiery and forward our pedant is!
Now, for my life, the knave doth court my love:
Pedascule, I'll watch you better yet.
Bian. In time I may believe, yet I mistrust.
50 *Luc.* Mistrust it not; for, sure, Æacides
Was Ajax, call'd so from his grandfather.
Bian. I must believe my master; else, I promise you,
I should be arguing still upon that doubt:
But let it rest. Now, Licio, to you:
55 Good masters, take it not unkindly, pray,
That I have been thus pleasant with you both.
Hor. You may go walk, and give me leave a while:
My lessons make no music in three parts.

Luc. Are you so formal, sir? well, I must wait,
60 [*Aside*] And watch withal; for, but I be deceived,
Our fine musician groweth amorous.
Hor. Madam, before you touch the instrument,
To learn the order of my fingering,
I must begin with rudiments of art;
65 To teach you gamut in a briefer sort,
More pleasant, pithy, and effectual,
Than hath been taught by any of my trade:
And there it is in writing, fairly drawn.
Bian. Why, I am past my gamut long ago.
70 *Hor.* Yet read the gamut of Hortensio.
Bian. [*reads*] "'Gamut' I am, the ground of all accord,
'A re,' to plead Hortensio's passion;
'B mi,' Bianca, take him for thy lord,
'C fa ut,' that loves with all affection:
75 'D sol re,' one clef, two notes have I:
'E la mi,' show pity, or I die."
Call you this gamut? tut, I like it not:
Old fashions please me best; I am not so nice,
To change true rules for old inventions.

Enter a Servant.

80 *Serv.* Mistress, your father prays you leave your
    books,
And help to dress your sister's chamber up:
You know to morrow is the wedding-day.
Bian. Farewell, sweet masters both; I must be gone.
[*Exeunt Bianca and Servant.*
Luc. Faith, mistress, then I have no cause to stay.
    [*Exit.*
85 *Hor.* But I have cause to pry into this pedant:
Methinks he looks as though he were in love:
Yet if thy thoughts, Bianca, be so humble,
To cast thy wandering eyes on every stale,
Seize thee that list: if once I find thee ranging,
90 Hortensio will be quit with thee by changing.
    [*Exit.*

SCENE II. PADUA. BEFORE BAPTISTA'S HOUSE

ENTER Baptista, Gremio, Tranio, Katharina, Bianca,
Lucentio, *AND* OTHERS, ATTENDANTS.

Bap. Signior Lucentio [*to Tranio*], this is the 'pointed
   day.
That Katharine and Petruchio should be married,
And yet we hear not of our son-in-law.
What will be said? what mockery will it be,
5 To want the bridegroom when the priest attends
To speak the ceremonial rites of marriage!
What says Lucentio to this shame of ours?
Kath. No shame but mine: I must, forsooth, be forced
To give my hand, opposed against my heart,
10 Unto a mad-brain rudesby, full of spleen;
Who woo'd in haste, and means to wed at leisure.
I told you, I, he was a frantic fool,
Hiding his bitter jests in blunt behaviour:
And, to be noted for a merry man.
15 He'll woo a thousand, 'point the day of marriage,
Make friends, invite, and proclaim the banns;
Yet never means to wed where he hath woo'd.
Now must the world point at poor Katharine,
And say, 'Lo, there is mad Petruchio's wife,
20 If it would please him come and marry her!'
Tra. Patience, good Katharine, and Baptista too.
Upon my life, Petruchio means but well,
Whatever fortune stays him from his word:
Though he be blunt, I know him passing wise;
25 Though he be merry, yet withal he's honest.
Kath. Would Katharine had never seen him though!
[*Exit weeping, followed by Bianca and others.*
Bap. Go, girl; I cannot blame thee now to weep;
For such an injury would vex a very saint,
Much more a shrew of thy impatient humour.

ENTER Biondello.

30 *Bion.* Master, master! news, old news, and
   such news
as you never heard of!

Bap. Is it new and old too? how may that be?
Bion. Why, is it not news, to hear of Petruchio's
     coming?
Bap. Is he come?
35 *Bion.* Why, no, sir.
Bap. What then?
Bion. He is coming.
Bap. When will he be here?
Bion. When he stands where I am and sees you there.
40 *Tra.* But say, what to thine old news?
Bion. Why, Petruchio is coming in a new hat and
     an old
jerkin, a pair of old breeches thrice turned, a pair of
     boots
that have been candle-cases, one buckled, another
     laced, an
old rusty sword ta'en out of the town-armoury, with a
45 broken hilt, and chapeless; with two broken
     points: his
horse hipped with an old mothy saddle and stirrups
     of no
kindred; besides, possessed with the glanders and
     like to
mose in the chine; troubled with the lampass, infected
     with
the fashions, full of windgalls, sped with spavins,
     rayed with
50 the yellows, past cure of the fives, stark spoiled
     with the
staggers, begnawn with the bots, swayed in the
     back and
shoulder-shotten; near-legged before and with a half-
     checked
bit and a head-stall of sheep's leather which, being
restrained to keep him from stumbling, hath been
     often
55 burst and now repaired with knots; one girth six
     times
pieced and a woman's crupper of velure, which
     hath two
letters for her name fairly set down in studs, and
     here and
there pieced with packthread.

BAP. Who comes with him?

60 *BION.* O, sir, his lackey, for all the world caparisoned

like the horse; with a linen stock on one leg, and a kersey

boot-hose on the other, gartered with a red and blue list;

an old hat, and 'the humour of forty fancies' pricked in't

for a feather: a monster, a very monster in apparel, and

65 not like a Christian footboy or a gentleman's lackey.

TRA. 'Tis some odd humour pricks him to this fashion;

Yet oftentimes he goes but mean-apparell'd.

BAP. I am glad he's come, howsoe'er he comes.

BION. Why, sir, he comes not.

70 *BAP.* Didst thou not say he comes?

BION. Who? that Petruchio came?

BAP. Ay, that Petruchio came.

BION. No, sir; I say his horse comes, with him on his back.

75 *BAP.* Why, that's all one.

BION. Nay, by Saint Jamy,

I hold you a penny,

A horse and a man

Is more than one,

80 And yet not many.

ENTER PETRUCHIO *AND* GRUMIO.

PET. Come, where be these gallants? who's at home?

BAP. You are welcome, sir.

PET. And yet I come not well.

BAP. And yet you halt not.

TRA. Not so well apparell'd

As I wish you were.

85 *PET.* Were it better, I should rush in thus.

But where is Kate? where is my lovely bride?

How does my father? Gentles, methinks you frown:

And wherefore gaze this goodly company,

As if they saw some wondrous monument,

90 Some comet or unusual prodigy?

Bap. Why, sir, you know this is your wedding-day:
First were we sad, fearing you would not come;
Now sadder, that you come so unprovided.
Fie, doff this habit, shame to your estate,
₉₅ An eye-sore to our solemn festival!
Tra. And tell us, what occasion of import
Hath all so long detain'd you from your wife,
And sent you hither so unlike yourself?
Pet. Tedious it were to tell, and harsh to hear:
₁₀₀ Sufficeth, I am come to keep my word,
Though in some part enforced to digress;
Which, at more leisure, I will so excuse
As you shall well be satisfied withal.
But where is Kate? I stay too long from her:
₁₀₅ The morning wears, 'tis time we were at church.
Tra. See not your bride in these unreverent robes:
Go to my chamber; put on clothes of mine.
Pet. Not I, believe me: thus I'll visit her.
Bap. But thus, I trust, you will not marry her.
₁₁₀ *Pet.* Good sooth, even thus; therefore ha' done
  with words:
To me she's married, not unto my clothes:
Could I repair what she will wear in me,
As I can change these poor accoutrements,
'Twere well for Kate and better for myself.
₁₁₅ But what a fool am I to chat with you,
When I should bid good morrow to my bride,
And seal the title with a lovely kiss!
[Exeunt Petruchio and Gremio.
Tra. He hath some meaning in his mad attire:
We will persuade him, be it possible,
₁₂₀ To put on better ere he go to church.
Bap. I'll after him, and see the event of this.
[Exeunt Baptista, Gremio, and attendants.
Tra. But to her love concerneth us to add
Her father's liking: which to bring to pass,
As I before imparted to your worship,
₁₂₅ I am to get a man,—whate'er he be,
It skills not much, we'll fit him to our turn,—
And he shall be Vincentio of Pisa;
And make assurance here in Padua
Of greater sums than I have promised.
₁₃₀ So shall you quietly enjoy your hope,

And marry sweet Bianca with consent.
Luc. Were it not that my fellow-schoolmaster
Doth watch Bianca's steps so narrowly,
'Twere good, methinks, to steal our marriage;
135 Which once perform'd, let all the world say no,
I'll keep mine own, despite of all the world.
Tra. That by degrees we mean to look into,
And watch our vantage in this business:
We'll over-reach the greybeard, Gremio,
140 The narrow-prying father, Minola,
The quaint musician, amorous Licio;
All for my master's sake, Lucentio.

Re-enter Gremio.

Signior Gremio, came you from the church?
Gre. As willingly as e'er I came from school.
145 *Tra.* And is the bride and bridegroom coming
home?
Gre. A bridegroom say you? 'tis a groom indeed,
A grumbling groom, and that the girl shall find.
Tra. Curster than she? why, 'tis impossible.
Gre. Why, he's a devil, a devil, a very fiend.
150 *Tra.* Why, she's a devil, a devil, the devil's dam.
Gre. Tut, she's a lamb, a dove, a fool to him!
I'll tell you, Sir Lucentio: when the priest
Should ask, if Katharine should be his wife,
'Ay, by gogs-wouns,' quoth he; and swore so loud,
155 That, all amazed, the priest let fall the book;
And, as he stoop'd again to take it up,
The mad-brain'd bridegroom took him such a cuff,
That down fell priest and book, and book and priest:
'Now take them up,' quoth he, 'if any list.'
160 *Tra.* What said the wench when he rose again?
Gre. Trembled and shook; for why he stamp'd and
swore,
As if the vicar meant to cozen him.
But after many ceremonies done,
He calls for wine: 'A health!' quoth he; as if
165 He had been aboard, carousing to his mates
After a storm: quaff'd off the muscadel,
And threw the sops all in the sexton's face;
Having no other reason

But that his beard grew thin and hungerly
$_{170}$ And seem'd to ask him sops as he was drinking.
This done, he took the bride about the neck
And kiss'd her lips with such a clamorous smack
That at the parting all the church did echo:
And I seeing this came thence for very shame;
$_{175}$ And after me, I know, the rout is coming.
Such a mad marriage never was before:
Hark, hark! I hear the minstrels play. [*Music.*

RE-ENTER *Petruchio, Katharina, Bianca, Baptista, Hortensio,*
GRUMIO, and Train.

PET. Gentlemen and friends, I thank you for your
    pains:
I know you think to dine with me to-day,
$_{180}$ And have prepared great store of wedding cheer;
But so it is, my haste doth call me hence,
And therefore here I mean to take my leave.
BAP. Is't possible you will away to-night?
PET. I must away to-day, before night come:
$_{185}$ Make it no wonder; if you knew my business,
You would entreat me rather go than stay.
And, honest company, I thank you all,
That have beheld me give away myself
To this most patient, sweet, and virtuous wife:
$_{190}$ Dine with my father, drink a health to me;
For I must hence; and farewell to you all.
TRA. Let us entreat you stay till after dinner.
PET. It may not be.
GRU. Let me entreat you.
PET. It cannot be.
KATH. Let me entreat you.
PET. I am content.
$_{195}$ KATH. Are you content to stay?
PET. I am content you shall entreat me stay;
But yet not stay, entreat me how you can.
KATH. Now, if you love me, stay.
PET. Grumio, my horse.
GRU. Ay, sir, they be ready: the oats have eaten the
$_{200}$ horses.
KATH. Nay, then,
Do what thou canst, I will not go to-day;

No, nor to-morrow, not till I please myself.
The door is open, sir; there lies your way;
205 You may be jogging whiles your boots are green;
For me, I'll not be gone till I please myself:
'Tis like you'll prove a jolly surly groom,
That take it on you at the first so roundly.
PET. O Kate, content thee; prithee, be not angry.
210 *KATH.* I will be angry: what hast thou to do?
Father, be quiet: he shall stay my leisure.
GRE. Ay, marry, sir, now it begins to work.
KATH. Gentlemen, forward to the bridal dinner:
I see a woman may be made a fool,
215 If she had not a spirit to resist.
PET. They shall go forward, Kate, at thy command.
Obey the bride, you that attend on her;
Go to the feast, revel and domineer,
Carouse full measure to her maidenhead,
220 Be mad and merry, or go hang yourselves:
But for my bonny Kate, she must with me.
Nay, look not big, nor stamp, nor stare, nor fret;
I will be master of what is mine own:
She is my goods, my chattels; she is my house,
225 My household stuff, my field, my barn,
My horse, my ox, my ass, my any thing;
And here she stands, touch her whoever dare;
I'll bring mine action on the proudest he
That stops my way in Padua. Grumio,
230 Draw forth thy weapon, we are beset with thieves;
Rescue thy mistress, if thou be a man.
Fear not, sweet wench, they shall not touch thee,
    Kate:
I'll buckler thee against a million.

[Exeunt Petruchio, Katharina, and Grumio.

BAP. Nay, let them go, a couple of quiet ones.
235 *GRE.* Went they not quickly, I should die with
    laughing.
TRA. Of all mad matches never was the like.
LUC. Mistress, what's your opinion of your sister?
BIAN. That, being mad herself, she's madly mated.
GRE. I warrant him, Petruchio is Kated.
240 *BAP.* Neighbours and friends, though bride and

    bridegroom wants
For to supply the places at the table,
You know there wants no junkets at the feast.
Lucentio, you shall supply the bridegroom's place;
And let Bianca take her sister's room.
245 *TRA.* Shall sweet Bianca practise how to bride it?
BAP. She shall, Lucentio. Come, gentlemen, let's go.
    [*Exeunt.*

ACT IV

SCENE I. PETRUCHIO'S COUNTRY HOUSE

Enter GRUMIO.

GRU. Fie, fie on all tired jades, on all mad masters,
and all foul ways! Was ever man so beaten? was ever
man so rayed? was ever man so weary? I am sent
    before
to make a fire, and they are coming after to warm
    them.
5 Now, were not I a little pot, and soon hot, my
    very lips
might freeze to my teeth, my tongue to the roof of my
mouth, my heart in my belly, ere I should come by
    a fire
to thaw me: but I, with blowing the fire, shall warm
    myself;
for, considering the weather, a taller man than I will
10 take cold. Holla, ho! Curtis!

Enter CURTIS.

CURT. Who is that calls so coldly?
GRU. A piece of ice: if thou doubt it, thou mayst slide
from my shoulder to my heel with no greater a run
    but my
head and my neck. A fire, good Curtis.

15 *Curt.* Is my master and his wife coming, Grumio?
Gru. O, ay, Curtis, ay: and therefore fire, fire; cast on
no water.
Curt. Is she so hot a shrew as she's reported?
Gru. She was, good Curtis, before this frost: but, thou
20 knowest, winter tames man, woman, and beast; for
it hath
tamed my old master, and my new mistress, and
myself,
fellow Curtis.
Curt. Away, you three-inch fool! I am no beast.
Gru. Am I but three inches? why, thy horn is a foot;
25 and so long am I at the least. But wilt thou make a
fire,
or shall I complain on thee to our mistress, whose
hand,
she being now at hand, thou shalt soon feel, to
thy cold
comfort, for being slow in thy hot office?
30 *Curt.* I prithee, good Grumio, tell me, how goes the
world?
Gru. A cold world, Curtis, in every office but thine;
and therefore fire: do thy duty, and have thy duty; for
my master and mistress are almost frozen to death.
Curt. There's fire ready; and therefore, good Grumio,
35 the news.
Gru. Why, 'Jack, boy! ho! boy!' and as much news
as thou wilt.
Curt. Come, you are so full of cony-catching!
Gru. Why, therefore fire; for I have caught extreme
40 cold. Where's the cook? is supper ready, the house
trimmed,
rushes strewed, cobwebs swept; the serving-men in
their new fustian, their white stockings, and every
officer
his wedding-garment on? Be the jacks fair within, the
jills
fair without, the carpets laid, and every thing in
order?
45 *Curt.* All ready; and therefore, I pray thee, news.
Gru. First, know, my horse is tired; my master and
mistress fallen out.
Curt. How?

Gru. Out of their saddles into the dirt; and thereby
50 hangs a tale.

Curt. Let's ha't, good Grumio.

Gru. Lend thine ear.

Curt. Here.

Gru. There. [Strikes him.

55 *Curt.* This is to feel a tale, not to hear a tale.

Gru. And therefore 'tis called a sensible tale: and this
cuff was but to knock at your ear, and beseech
    listening.

Now I begin: *Imprimis,* we came down a foul hill, my
    master

riding behind my mistress,—

60 *Curt.* Both of one horse?

Gru. What's that to thee?

Curt. Why, a horse.

Gru. Tell thou the tale: but hadst thou not crossed
me, thou shouldst have heard how her horse fell
    and she
65 under her horse; thou shouldst have heard in how
    miry a
place, how she was bemoiled, how he left her with
    the horse
upon her, how he beat me because her horse
    stumbled,
how she waded through the dirt to pluck him off
    me, how
he swore, how she prayed, that never prayed before,
    how I
70 cried, how the horses ran away, how her bridle was
    burst,
how I lost my crupper, with many things of worthy
    memory,
which now shall die in oblivion and thou return un-
    experienced
to thy grave.

Curt. By this reckoning he is more shrew than she.

75 *Gru.* Ay; and that thou and the proudest of you all
shall find when he comes home. But what talk I of
    this?

Call forth Nathaniel, Joseph, Nicholas, Philip, Walter,
    Sugarsop

and the rest: let their heads be sleekly combed,

their blue coats brushed and their garters of an indifferent
80 knit: let them curtsy with their left legs and not
presume
to touch a hair of my master's horse-tail till they kiss
their
hands. Are they all ready?

Curt. They are.

Gru. Call them forth.

85 *Curt.* Do you hear, ho? you must meet my
master to
countenance my mistress!

Gru. Why, she hath a face of her own.

Curt. Who knows not that?

Gru. Thou, it seems, that calls for company to countenance
90 her.

Curt. I call them forth to credit her.

Gru. Why, she comes to borrow nothing of them.

Enter four or five serving-men.

Nath. Welcome home, Grumio!

Phil. How now, Grumio!

95 *Jos.* What, Grumio!

Nich. Fellow Grumio!

Nath. How now, old lad?

Gru. Welcome, you;—how now, you;—what, you;
—fellow,
you;—and thus much for greeting. Now, my spruce
100 companions, is all ready, and all things neat?

Nath. All things is ready. How near is our master?

Gru. E'en at hand, alighted by this; and therefore be
not—Cock's passion, silence! I hear my master.

Enter Petruchio and Katharina.

Pet. Where be these knaves? What, no man at door
105 To hold my stirrup nor to take my horse!
Where is Nathaniel, Gregory, Philip?

All Serv. Here, here, sir; here, sir.

Pet. Here, sir! here, sir! here, sir! here, sir!
You logger-headed and unpolish'd grooms!

286

₁₁₀ What, no attendance? no regard? no duty?
Where is the foolish knave I sent before?
GRU. Here, sir; as foolish as I was before.
PET. You peasant swain! you whoreson malt-horse
    drudge!
Did I not bid thee meet me in the park,
₁₁₅ And bring along these rascal knaves with thee?
GRU. Nathaniel's coat, sir, was not fully made,
And Gabriel's pumps were all unpink'd i' the heel;
There was no link to colour Peter's hat,
And Walter's dagger was not come from sheathing:
₁₂₀ There were none fine but Adam, Ralph, and
    Gregory;
The rest were ragged, old, and beggarly;
Yet, as they are, here are they come to meet you.
PET. Go, rascals, go, and fetch my supper in. [*Exeunt
    Servants.*
[*Singing*] Where is the life that late I led—
₁₂₅ Where are those—Sit down, Kate, and welcome.—
Soud, soud, soud, soud!

Re-enter Servants with supper.

Why, when, I say? Nay, good sweet Kate, be merry.
Off with my boots, you rogues! you villains, when?
    [*Sings.*
It was the friar of orders grey,
₁₃₀ As he forth walked on his way:—
Out, you rogue! you pluck my foot awry:
Take that, and mend the plucking off the other.
    [*Strikes him.*
Be merry, Kate. Some water, here; what, ho!
Where's my spaniel Troilus? Sirrah, get you hence,
₁₃₅ And bid my cousin Ferdinand come hither:
One, Kate, that you must kiss, and be acquainted
    with.
Where are my slippers? Shall I have some water?

Enter one with water.

Come, Kate, and wash, and welcome heartily.
You whoreson villain! will you let it fall? [*Strikes him.*
₁₄₀ *KATH.* Patience, I pray you; 'twas a fault unwilling.

287

Pet. A whoreson beetle-headed, flap-ear'd knave!
Come, Kate, sit down; I know you have a stomach.
Will you give thanks, sweet Kate; or else shall I?
What's this? mutton?
First Serv. Ay.
Pet. Who brought it?
Peter. I.
145 *Pet.* 'Tis burnt; and so is all the meat.
What dogs are these! Where is the rascal cook?
How durst you, villains, bring it from the dresser,
And serve it thus to me that love it not?
There, take it to you, trenchers, cups, and all:
[Throws the meat, &c. about the stage.
150 You heedless joltheads and unmanner'd slaves!
What, do you grumble? I'll be with you straight.
Kath. I pray you, husband, be not so disquiet:
The meat was well, if you were so contented.
Pet. I tell thee, Kate, 'twas burnt and dried away;
155 And I expressly am forbid to touch it,
For it engenders choler, planteth anger;
And better 'twere that both of us did fast,
Since, of ourselves, ourselves are choleric,
Than feed it with such over-roasted flesh.
160 Be patient; to-morrow't shall be mended,
And, for this night, we'll fast for company:
Come, I will bring thee to thy bridal chamber. *[Exeunt.*

Re-enter Servants severally.

Nath. Peter, didst ever see the like?
Peter. He kills her in her own humour.

Re-enter Curtis.

165 *Gru.* Where is he?
Curt. In her chamber, making a sermon of continency
to her;
And rails, and swears, and rates, that she, poor soul,
Knows not which way to stand, to look, to speak,
170 And sits as one new-risen from a dream.
Away, away! for he is coming hither. *[Exeunt.*

Re-enter Petruchio.

Pet. Thus have I politicly begun my reign,
And 'tis my hope to end successfully.
My falcon now is sharp and passing empty;
175 And till she stoop she must not be full-gorged,
For then she never looks upon her lure.
Another way I have to man my haggard,
To make her come and know her keeper's call,
That is, to watch her, as we watch these kites
180 That bate and beat and will not be obedient.
She eat no meat to-day, nor none shall eat;
Last night she slept not, nor to-night she shall not;
As with the meat, some undeserved fault
I'll find about the making of the bed;
185 And here I'll fling the pillow, there the bolster,
This way the coverlet, another way the sheets:
Ay, and amid this hurly I intend
That all is done in reverend care of her;
And in conclusion she shall watch all night:
190 And if she chance to nod I'll rail and brawl
And with the clamour keep her still awake.
This is a way to kill a wife with kindness;
And thus I'll curb her mad and headstrong humour.
He that knows better how to tame a shrew,
195 Now let him speak: 'tis charity to show. [*Exit.*

SCENE II. PADUA. BEFORE BAPTISTA'S HOUSE

Enter TRANIO *and* HORTENSIO.

Tra. Is't possible, friend Licio, that Mistress Bianca
Doth fancy any other but Lucentio?
I tell you, sir, she bears me fair in hand.
Hor. Sir, to satisfy you in what I have said,
5 Stand by and mark the manner of his teaching.

Enter BIANCA *and* LUCENTIO.

Luc. Now, mistress, profit you in what you read?
Bian. What, master, read you? first resolve me
    that.
Luc. I read that I profess, the Art to Love.
Bian. And may you prove, sir, master of your art!

₁₀ *Luc.* While you, sweet dear, prove mistress of my
    heart!

Hor. Quick proceeders, marry! Now, tell me, I pray,
You that durst swear that your mistress Bianca
Loved none in the world so well as Lucentio.

Tra. O despiteful love! unconstant womankind!
₁₅ I tell thee, Licio, this is wonderful.

Hor. Mistake no more: I am not Licio,
Nor a musician, as I seem to be;
But one that scorn to live in this disguise,
For such a one as leaves a gentleman,
₂₀ And makes a god of such a cullion:
Know, sir, that I am call'd Hortensio.

Tra. Signior Hortensio, I have often heard
Of your entire affection to Bianca;
And since mine eyes are witness of her lightness,
₂₅ I will with you, if you be so contented,
Forswear Bianca and her love for ever.

Hor. See, how they kiss and court! Signior Lucentio,
Here is my hand, and here I firmly vow
Never to woo her more, but do forswear her,
₃₀ As one unworthy all the former favours
That I have fondly flatter'd her withal.

Tra. And here I take the like unfeigned oath,
Never to marry with her though she would entreat:
Fie on her! see, how beastly she doth court him!

₃₅ *Hor.* Would all the world but he had quite
    forsworn!
For me, that I may surely keep mine oath,
I will be married to a wealthy widow,
Ere three days pass, which hath as long loved me
As I have loved this proud disdainful haggard.
₄₀ And so farewell, Signior Lucentio.
Kindness in women, not their beauteous looks,
Shall win my love: and so I take my leave,
In resolution as I swore before. [*Exit.*

Tra. Mistress Bianca, bless you with such grace
₄₅ As 'longeth to a lover's blessed case!
Nay, I have ta'en you napping, gentle love,
And have forsworn you with Hortensio.

Bian. Tranio, you jest: but have you both forsworn
    me?

Tra. Mistress, we have.

Luc. Then we are rid of Licio.

₅₀ *Tra.* I'faith, he'll have a lusty widow now,
That shall be woo'd and wedded in a day.

Bian. God give him joy!

Tra. Ay, and he'll tame her.

Bian. He says so, Tranio.

Tra. Faith, he is gone unto the taming-school.

₅₅ *Bian.* The taming-school! what, is there such a
place?

Tra. Ay, mistress, and Petruchio is the master;
That teacheth tricks eleven and twenty long,
To tame a shrew and charm her chattering tongue.

Enter Biondello.

Bion. O master, master, I have watch'd so long

₆₀ That I am dog-weary! but at last I spied
An ancient angel coming down the hill,
Will serve the turn.

Tra. What is he, Biondello?

Bion. Master, a mercatantè, or a pedant,
I know not what; but formal in apparel,

₆₅ In gait and countenance surely like a father.

Luc. And what of him, Tranio?

Tra. If he be credulous and trust my tale,
I'll make him glad to seem Vincentio,
And give assurance to Baptista Minola,

₇₀ As if he were the right Vincentio.
Take in your love, and then let me alone.
[Exeunt Lucentio and Bianca.
Enter a Pedant.

Ped. God save you, sir!

Tra. And you, sir! you are welcome.
Travel you far on, or are you at the farthest?

Ped. Sir, at the farthest for a week or two:

₇₅ But then up farther, and as far as Rome;
And so to Tripoli, if God lend me life.

Tra. What countryman, I pray?

Ped. Of Mantua.

Tra. Of Mantua, sir? marry, God forbid!
And come to Padua, careless of your life?

₈₀ *Ped.* My life, sir! how, I pray? for that goes hard.

Tra. 'Tis death for any one in Mantua

To come to Padua. Know you not the cause?
Your ships are stay'd at Venice; and the Duke,
For private quarrel 'twixt your duke and him,
₈₅ Hath publish'd and proclaim'd it openly:
'Tis marvel, but that you are but newly come,
You might have heard it else proclaim'd about.
PED. Alas, sir, it is worse for me than so!
For I have bills for money by exchange
₉₀ From Florence, and must here deliver them.
TRA. Well, sir, to do you courtesy,
This will I do, and this I will advise you:
First, tell me, have you ever been at Pisa?
PED. Ay, sir, in Pisa have I often been;
₉₅ Pisa renowned for grave citizens.
TRA. Among them know you one Vincentio?
PED. I know him not, but I have heard of him;
A merchant of incomparable wealth.
TRA. He is my father, sir; and, sooth to say,
₁₀₀ In countenance somewhat doth resemble you.
BION. As much as an apple doth an oyster, and all
  one. [*Aside.*
TRA. To save your life in this extremity,
This favour will I do you for his sake;
And think it not the worst of all your fortunes
₁₀₅ That you are [like to Sir Vincentio.
His name and credit shall you undertake,
And in my house you shall be friendly lodged:
Look that you take upon you as you should;
You understand me, sir: so shall you stay
₁₁₀ Till you have done your business in the city:
If this be courtesy, sir, accept of it.
PED. O sir, I do; and will repute you ever
The patron of my life and liberty.
TRA. Then go with me to make the matter good.
₁₁₅ This, by the way, I let you understand;
My father is here look'd for every day,
To pass assurance of a dower in marriage
'Twixt me and one Baptista's daughter here:
In all these circumstances I'll instruct you:
₁₂₀ Go with me to clothe you as becomes you. [*Exeunt.*

SCENE III. A ROOM IN PETRUCHIO'S HOUSE

ENTER KATHARINA *AND* GRUMIO.

GRU. No, no, forsooth; I dare not for my life.
KATH. The more my wrong, the more his spite
    appears:
What, did he marry me to famish me?
Beggars, that come unto my father's door,
5 Upon entreaty have a present alms;
If not, elsewhere they meet with charity:
But I, who never knew how to entreat,
Nor never needed that I should entreat,
Am starved for meat, giddy for lack of sleep;
10 With oaths kept waking, and with brawling fed:
And that which spites me more than all these wants,
He does it under name of perfect love;
As who should say, if I should sleep or eat,
'Twere deadly sickness or else present death.
15 I prithee go and get me some repast;
I care not what, so it be wholesome food.
GRU. What say you to a neat's foot?
KATH. 'Tis passing good: I prithee let me have it.
GRU. I fear it is too choleric a meat.
20 How say you to a fat tripe finely broil'd?
KATH. I like it well: good Grumio, fetch it me.
GRU. I cannot tell; I fear 'tis choleric.
What say you to a piece of beef and mustard?
KATH. A dish that I do love to feed upon.
25 GRU. Ay, but the mustard is too hot a little.
KATH. Why then, the beef, and let the mustard rest.
GRU. Nay then, I will not: you shall have the mustard,
Or else you get no beef of Grumio.
KATH. Then both, or one, or any thing thou wilt.
30 GRU. Why then, the mustard without the beef.
KATH. Go, get thee gone, thou false deluding slave,
    [*Beats him.*
That feed'st me with the very name of meat:
Sorrow on thee and all the pack of you
That triumph thus upon my misery!
35 Go, get thee gone, I say.

ENTER PETRUCHIO *AND* HORTENSIO *WITH MEAT.*

PET. How fares my Kate? What, sweeting, all amort?
HOR. Mistress, what cheer?
KATH. Faith, as cold as can be.
PET. Pluck up thy spirits; look cheerfully upon me.
Here, love; thou see'st how diligent I am
40 To dress thy meat myself and bring it thee:
I am sure, sweet Kate, this kindness merits thanks.
What, not a word? Nay, then thou lovest it not;
And all my pains is sorted to no proof.
Here, take away this dish.
KATH. I pray you, let it stand.
45 *PET.* The poorest service is repaid with thanks;
And so shall mine, before you touch the meat.
KATH. I thank you, sir.
HOR. Signior Petruchio, fie! you are to blame.
Come, Mistress Kate, I'll bear you company.
50 *PET.* Eat it up all, Hortensio, if thou lovest me.
    [*Aside.*
Much good do it unto thy gentle heart!
Kate, eat apace: and now, my honey love,
Will we return unto thy father's house,
And revel it as bravely as the best,
55 With silken coats and caps and golden rings,
With ruffs and cuffs and fardingales and things;
With scarfs and fans and double change of bravery,
With amber bracelets, beads and all this knavery.
What, hast thou dined? The tailor stays thy leisure,
60 To deck thy body with his ruffling treasure.

Enter Tailor.

Come, tailor, let us see these ornaments;
Lay forth the gown.

Enter Haberdasher.

What news with you, sir?
HAB. Here is the cap your worship did bespeak.
PET. Why, this was moulded on a porringer;
65 A velvet dish: fie, fie! 'tis lewd and filthy:
Why, 'tis a cockle or a walnut-shell,

A knack, a toy, a trick, a baby's cap:
Away with it! come, let me have a bigger.
Kath. I'll have no bigger: this doth fit the time
70 And gentlewomen wear such caps as these.
Pet. When you are gentle, you shall have one too,
And not till then.
Hor. That will not be in haste. [*Aside.*
Kath. Why, sir, I trust I may have leave to speak;
And speak I will; I am no child, no babe:
75 Your betters have endured me say my mind,
And if you cannot, best you stop your ears.
My tongue will tell the anger of my heart,
Or else my heart concealing it will break;
And rather than it shall, I will be free
80 Even to the uttermost, as I please, in words.
Pet. Why, thou say'st true; it is a paltry cap,
A custard-coffin, a bauble, a silken pie:
I love thee well, in that thou likest it not.
Kath. Love me or love me not, I like the cap;
85 And it I will have, or I will have none. [*Exit Hab-
erdasher.*
Pet. Thy gown? why, ay: come, tailor, let us see't.
O mercy, God! what masquing stuff is here?
What's this? a sleeve? 'tis like a demi-cannon:
What, up and down, carved like an apple-tart?
90 Here's snip and nip and cut and slish and slash,
Like to a censer in a barber's shop:
Why, what, i' devil's name, tailor, call'st thou this?
Hor. I see she's like to have neither cap nor gown.
[*Aside.*
Tai. You bid me make it orderly and well,
95 According to the fashion and the time.
Pet. Marry, and did; but if you be remember'd,
I did not bid you mar it to the time.
Go, hop me over every kennel home,
For you shall hop without my custom, sir:
100 I'll none of it: hence! make your best of it.
Kath. I never saw a better-fashion'd gown,
More quaint, more pleasing, nor more commendable:
Belike you mean to make a puppet of me.
Pet. Why, true; he means to make a puppet of thee.
105 *Tai.* She says your worship means to make a
puppet of her.

Pet. O monstrous arrogance! Thou liest, thou thread, thou thimble,
Thou yard, three-quarters, half-yard, quarter, nail!
Thou flea, thou nit, thou winter-cricket thou!
110 Braved in mine own house with a skein of thread?
Away, thou rag, thou quantity, thou remnant;
Or I shall so be-mete thee with thy yard,
As thou shalt think on prating whilst thou livest!
I tell thee, I, that thou hast marr'd her gown.
115 *Tai.* Your worship is deceived; the gown is made
Just as my master had direction:
Grumio gave order how it should be done.
Gru. I gave him no order; I gave him the stuff.
Tai. But how did you desire it should be made?
120 *Gru.* Marry, sir, with needle and thread.
Tai. But did you not request to have it cut?
Gru. Thou hast faced many things.
Tai. I have.
Gru. Face not me: thou hast braved many men; brave
125 not me; I will neither be faced nor braved. I say unto
thee, I bid thy master cut out the gown; but I did not bid
him cut it to pieces: ergo, thou liest.
Tai. Why, here is the note of the fashion to testify.
Pet. Read it.
130 *Gru.* The note lies in's throat, if he say I said so.
Tai. [*reads*] 'Imprimis, a loose-bodied gown:'
Gru. Master, if ever I said loose-bodied gown, sew me
in the skirts of it, and beat me to death with a bottom of
brown thread: I said a gown.
135 *Pet.* Proceed.
Tai. [*reads*] 'With a small compassed cape:'
Gru. I confess the cape.
Tai. [*reads*] 'With a trunk sleeve:'
Gru. I confess two sleeves.
140 *Tai.* [*reads*] 'The sleeves curiously cut.'
Pet. Ay, there's the villany.
Gru. Error i' the bill, sir; error i' the bill. I commanded
the sleeves should be cut out, and sewed up again;

and that I'll prove upon thee, though thy little
  finger be
₁₄₅ armed in a thimble.
Tai. This is true that I say: an I had thee in place
where, thou shouldst know it.
Gru. I am for thee straight: take thou the bill, give
me thy mete-yard, and spare not me.
₁₅₀ *Hor.* God-a-mercy, Grumio! then he shall have no
  odds.
Pet. Well, sir, in brief, the gown is not for me.
Gru. You are i' the right, sir: 'tis for my mistress.
Pet. Go, take it up unto thy master's use.
Gru. Villain, not for thy life: take up my mistress'
₁₅₅ gown for thy master's use!
Pet. Why, sir, what's your conceit in that?
Gru. O, sir, the conceit is deeper than you think for:
Take up my mistress' gown to his master's use!
O, fie, fie, fie!
₁₆₀ *Pet.* Hortensio, say thou wilt see the tailor paid.
  [*Aside.*
Go take it hence; be gone, and say no more.
Hor. Tailor, I'll pay thee for thy gown to-morrow:
Take no unkindness of his hasty words:
Away! I say; commend me to thy master. [*Exit Tailor.*
₁₆₅ *Pet.* Well, come, my Kate; we will unto your
  father's
Even in these honest mean habiliments:
Our purses shall be proud, our garments poor;
For 'tis the mind that makes the body rich;
And as the sun breaks through the darkest clouds,
₁₇₀ So honour peereth in the meanest habit.
What is the jay more precious than the lark,
Because his feathers are more beautiful?
Or is the adder better than the eel,
Because his painted skin contents the eye?
₁₇₅ O, no, good Kate; neither art thou the worse
For this poor furniture and mean array.
If thou account'st it shame, lay it on me;
And therefore frolic: we will hence forthwith,
To feast and sport us at thy father's house.
₁₈₀ Go, call my men, and let us straight to him;
And bring our horses unto Long-lane end;
There will we mount, and thither walk on foot.

Let's see; I think 'tis now some seven o'clock,
And well we may come there by dinner-time.
185 *KATH.* I dare assure you, sir, 'tis almost two;
And 'twill be supper-time ere you come there.
PET. It shall be seven ere I go to horse:
Look, what I speak, or do, or think to do,
You are still crossing it. Sirs, let't alone:
190 I will not go to-day; and ere I do,
It shall be what o'clock I say it is.
HOR. Why, so this gallant will command the sun.
   [*Exeunt.*

SCENE IV. PADUA. BEFORE BAPTISTA'S HOUSE

Enter TRANIO, and the Pedant dressed like VINCENTIO.

TRA. Sir, this is the house: please it you that I call?
PED. Ay, what else? and but I be deceived
Signior Baptista may remember me,
Near twenty years ago, in Genoa,
5 Where we were lodgers at the Pegasus.
TRA. 'Tis well; and hold your own, in any case,
With such austerity as 'longeth to a father.
PED. I warrant you.

ENTER BIONDELLO.

But, sir, here comes your boy;
'Twere good he were school'd.
10 *TRA.* Fear you not him. Sirrah Biondello,
Now do your duty throughly, I advise you:
Imagine 'twere the right Vincentio.
BION. Tut, fear not me.
TRA. But hast thou done thy errand to Baptista?
15 *BION.* I told him that your father was at Venice;
And that you look'd for him this day in Padua.
TRA. Thou'rt a tall fellow: hold thee that to drink.
Here comes Baptista: set your countenance, sir.

ENTER BAPTISTA AND LUCENTIO.

Signior Baptista, you are happily met.

20 [*To the Pedant*] Sir, this is the gentleman I told
  you of:
I pray you, stand good father to me now,
Give me Bianca for my patrimony.
PED. Soft, son!
Sir, by your leave: having come to Padua
25 To gather in some debts, my son Lucentio
Made me acquainted with a weighty cause
Of love between your daughter and himself:
And, for the good report I hear of you,
And for the love he beareth to your daughter,
30 And she to him, to stay him not too long,
I am content, in a good father's care,
To have him match'd; and, if you please to like
No worse than I, upon some agreement
Me shall you find ready and willing
35 With one consent to have her so bestow'd;
For curious I cannot be with you,
Signior Baptista, of whom I hear so well.
BAP. Sir, pardon me in what I have to say:
Your plainness and your shortness please me well.
40 Right true it is, your son Lucentio here
Doth love my daughter, and she loveth him,
Or both dissemble deeply their affections:
And therefore, if you say no more than this.
That like a father you will deal with him,
45 And pass my daughter a sufficient dower,
The match is made, and all is done:
Your son shall have my daughter with consent.
TRA. I thank you, sir. Where then do you know best
We be affied and such assurance ta'en
50 As shall with either part's agreement stand?
BAP. Not in my house, Lucentio; for, you know,
Pitchers have ears, and I have many servants:
Besides, old Gremio is hearkening still;
And happily we might be interrupted.
55 *TRA.* Then at my lodging, an it like you:
There doth my father lie; and there, this night,
We'll pass the business privately and well.
Send for your daughter by your servant here;
My boy shall fetch the scrivener presently.
60 The worst is this, that, at so slender warning,
You are like to have a thin and slender pittance.

Bap. It likes me well. Cambio, his you home,
And bid Bianca make her ready straight;
And, if you will, tell what hath happened,
65 Lucentio's father is arrived in Padua,
And how she's like to be Lucentio's wife.
Bion. I pray the gods she may with all my heart!
Tra. Dally not with the gods, but get thee gone.
      [*Exit Bion*
Signior Baptista, shall I lead the way?
70 Welcome! one mess is like to be your cheer:
Come, sir; we will better it in Pisa.
Bap. I follow you.

[*Exeunt Tranio, Pedant, and Baptista. Re-enter* Biondello.

Bion. Cambio.
Luc. What sayest thou, Biondello?
75 *Bion.* You saw my master wink and laugh
      upon you?
Luc. Biondello, what of that?
Bion. Faith, nothing; but has left me here behind, to
expound the meaning or moral of his signs and
      tokens.
Luc. I pray thee, moralize them.
80 *Bion.* Then thus. Baptista is safe, talking with the
deceiving father of a deceitful son.
Luc. And what of him?
Bion. His daughter is to be brought by you to the
      supper.
Luc. And then?
85 *Bion.* The old priest at Saint Luke's church is
      at your
command at all hours.
Luc. And what of all this?
Bion. I cannot tell; expect they are busied about a
counterfeit assurance: take you assurance of her, 'cum
      privilegio
90 ad imprimendum solum:' to the church; take the
priest, clerk, and some sufficient honest witnesses:
If this be not that you look for, I have no more to say,
But bid Bianca farewell for ever and a day.
Luc. Hearest thou, Biondello?
95 *Bion.* I cannot tarry: I knew a wench married in an

afternoon as she went to the garden for parsley to
  stuff a
rabbit; and so may you, sir: and so, adieu, sir. My
  master
hath appointed me to go to Saint Luke's, to bid the
  priest be
ready to come against you come with your appendix.
  [*Exit.*
100 *Luc.* I may, and will, if she be so contented:
She will be pleased; then wherefore should I doubt?
Hap what hap may, I'll roundly go about her:
It shall go hard if Cambio go without her. [*Exit.*

SCENE V. A PUBLIC ROAD

ENTER PETRUCHIO, KATHARINA, HORTENSIO, *AND* SERVANTS.

PET. Come on, i' God's name; once more toward our
  father's.
Good Lord, how bright and goodly shines the moon!
KATH. The moon! the sun: it is not moonlight now.
PET. I say it is the moon that shines so bright.
5 *KATH.* I know it is the sun that shines so bright.
PET. Now, by my mother's son, and that's myself,
It shall be moon, or star, or what I list,
Or ere I journey to your father's house.
Go on, and fetch our horses back again.
10 Evermore cross'd and cross'd; nothing but cross'd!
HOR. Say as he says, or we shall never go.
KATH. Forward, I pray, since we have come so far,
And be it moon, or sun, or what you please:
An if you please to call it a rush-candle,
15 Henceforth I vow it shall be so for me.
PET. I say it is the moon.
KATH. I know it is the moon.
PET. Nay, then you lie: it is the blessed sun.
KATH. Then, God be bless'd, it is the blessed sun:
But sun it is not, when you say it is not;
20 And the moon changes even as your mind.
What you will have it named, even that it is;
And so it shall be so for Katharine.
HOR. Petruchio, go thy ways; the field is won.

Pet. Well, forward, forward! thus the bowl
    should run,
₂₅ And not unluckily against the bias.
But, soft! company is coming here.

Enter Vincentio.

[*To Vincentio*] Good morrow, gentle mistress: where
    away?
Tell me, sweet Kate, and tell me truly too,
Hast thou beheld a fresher gentlewoman?
₃₀ Such war of white and red within her cheeks!
What stars do spangle heaven with such beauty,
As those two eyes become that heavenly face?
Fair lovely maid, once more good day to thee.
Sweet Kate, embrace her for her beauty's sake.
₃₅ *Hor.* A' will make the man mad, to make a woman
    of him.
Kath. Young budding virgin, fair and fresh and
    sweet,
Whither away, or where is thy abode?
Happy the parents of so fair a child;
Happier the man, whom favourable stars
₄₀ Allot thee for his lovely bed-fellow!
Pet. Why, how now, Kate! I hope thou art not mad:
This is a man, old, wrinkled, faded, wither'd;
And not a maiden, as thou say'st he is.
Kath. Pardon, old father, my mistaking eyes,
₄₅ That have been so bedazzled with the sun,
That every thing I look on seemeth green:
Now I perceive thou art a reverend father;
Pardon, I pray thee, for my mad mistaking.
Pet. Do, good old grandsire; and withal make known
₅₀ Which way thou travellest: if along with us,
We shall be joyful of thy company.
Vin. Fair sir, and you my merry mistress,
That with your strange encounter much amazed me,
My name is call'd Vincentio; my dwelling Pisa;
₅₅ And bound I am to Padua; there to visit
A son of mine, which long I have not seen.
Pet. What is his name?
Vin. Lucentio, gentle sir.
Pet. Happily met; the happier for thy son.

And now by law, as well as reverend age,
60 I may entitle thee my loving father:
The sister to my wife, this gentlewoman,
Thy son by this hath married. Wonder not,
Nor be not grieved: she is of good esteem,
Her dowry wealthy, and of worthy birth;
65 Beside, so qualified as may beseem
The spouse of any noble gentleman.
Let me embrace with old Vincentio,
And wander we to see thy honest son,
Who will of thy arrival be full joyous.
70 *Vin.* But is this true? or is it else your pleasure,
Like pleasant travellers, to break a jest
Upon the company you overtake?
Hor. I do assure thee, father, so it is.
Pet. Come, go along, and see the truth hereof;
75 For our first merriment hath made thee jealous.
    [*Exeunt all but Hortensio.*
Hor. Well, Petruchio, this has put me in heart.
Have to my widow! and if she be froward,
Then hast thou taught Hortensio to be untoward.
    [*Exit.*

ACT V

SCENE I. PADUA. BEFORE LUCENTIO'S HOUSE

GREMIO *DISCOVERED. ENTER BEHIND* BIONDELLO, LUCENTIO,
AND BIANCA.

BION. Softly and swiftly, sir; for the priest is ready.
Luc. I fly, Biondello: but they may chance to need
thee at home; therefore leave us.
BION. Nay, faith, I'll see the church o' your back; and
5 then come back to my master's as soon as I can.

[Exeunt Lucentio, Bianca, and Biondello.

GRE. I marvel Cambio comes not all this while.

ENTER PETRUCHIO, KATHARINA, VINCENTIO, GRUMIO, *WITH*
ATTENDANTS.

PET. Sir, here's the door, this is Lucentio's house:
My father's bears more toward the market-place;
Thither must I, and here I leave you, sir.
10 *VIN.* You shall not choose but drink before you go:
I think I shall command your welcome here,
And, by all likelihood, some cheer is toward. *[Knocks.*
GRE. They're busy within; you were best knock
louder.
Pedant looks out of the window.

305

PED. What's he that knocks as he would beat down
₁₅ the gate?

VIN. Is Signior Lucentio within, sir?

PED. He's within, sir, but not to be spoken withal.

VIN. What if a man bring him a hundred pound or
two, to make merry withal?

₂₀ *PED.* Keep your hundred pounds to yourself: he shall

need none, so long as I live.

PET. Nay, I told you your son was well beloved in
Padua. Do you hear, sir?—to leave frivolous circumstances,—I

pray you, tell Signior Lucentio, that his father is
₂₅ come from Pisa, and is here at the door to speak
with him.

PED. Thou liest: his father is come from Padua, and
here looking out at the window.

VIN. Art thou his father?

PED. Ay, sir; so his mother says, if I may believe her.

₃₀ *PET.* [*To Vincentio*] Why, how now, gentleman! why,
this is flat knavery, to take upon you another man's
name.

PED. Lay hands on the villain: I believe a' means to
cozen somebody in this city under my countenance.

RE-ENTER BIONDELLO.

BION. I have seen them in the church together: God
₃₅ send 'em good shipping! But who is here? mine old
master Vincentio! now we are undone, and brought to
nothing.

VIN. [*Seeing Biondello*] Come hither, crack-hemp.

BION. I hope I may choose, sir.

₄₀ *VIN.* Come hither, you rogue. What, have you forgot

me?

BION. Forgot you! no, sir: I could not forget you, for
I never saw you before in all my life.

VIN. What, you notorious villain, didst thou never see
₄₅ thy master's father, Vincentio?

BION. What, my old worshipful old master? yes,
marry,

sir: see where he looks out of the window.

Vin. Is't so, indeed? [*Beats Biondello.*
50 *Bion.* Help, help, help! here's a madman will
murder me. [*Exit.*
Ped. Help, son! help, Signior Baptista! [*Exit from
above.*
Pet. Prithee, Kate, let's stand aside, and see the end
of this
controversy. [*They retire.*

Re-enter Pedant *below;* Tranio, Baptista, *and* Servants.

Tra. Sir, what are you, that offer to beat my servant?
55 *Vin.* What am I, sir! nay, what are you, sir? O
immortal
gods! O fine villain! A silken doublet! a velvet
hose! a scarlet cloak! and a copatain hat! O, I am
undone!
I am undone! while I play the good husband at
home, my son and my servant spend all at the uni-
versity.
60 *Tra.* How now! what's the matter?
Bap. What, is the man lunatic?
Tra. Sir, you seem a sober ancient gentleman by your
habit, but your words show you a madman. Why, sir,
what 'cerns it you if I wear pearl and gold? I
thank my
65 good father, I am able to maintain it.
Vin. Thy father! O villain! he is a sail-maker in
Bergamo.
Bap. You mistake, sir, you mistake, sir. Pray, what
do you think is his name?
70 *Vin.* His name! as if I knew not his name: I have
brought him up ever since he was three years old,
and his
name is Tranio.
Ped. Away, away, mad ass! his name is Lucentio;
and he is mine only son, and heir to the lands of me,
Signior
75 Vincentio.
Vin. Lucentio! O, he hath murdered his master!
Lay hold on him, I charge you, in the Duke's name. O,
my son, my son! Tell me, thou villain, where is
my son

307

Lucentio?
80 *TRA.* Call forth an officer.

Enter one with an Officer.

Carry this mad knave to the gaol. Father Baptista, I
charge you see that he be forthcoming.
VIN. Carry me to the gaol!
GRE. Stay, officer: he shall not go to prison.
85 *BAP.* Talk not, Signior Gremio: I say he shall go to
prison.
GRE. Take heed, Signior Baptista, lest you be cony-
catched
in this business: I dare swear this is the right
Vincentio.
90 *PED.* Swear, if thou darest.
GRE. Nay, I dare not swear it.
TRA. Then thou wert best say that I am not Lucentio.
GRE. Yes, I know thee to be Signior Lucentio.
BAP. Away with the dotard! to the gaol with him!
95 *VIN.* Thus strangers may be haled and abused:
O monstrous villain!

RE-ENTER BIONDELLO, *WITH* LUCENTIO *AND* BIANCA.

BION. O, we are spoiled! and—yonder he is:
deny him,
forswear him, or else we are all undone.
LUC. Pardon, sweet father. [*Kneeling.*
VIN. Lives my sweet son?

[*Exeunt Biondello, Tranio, and Pedant, as fast as may be.*

BIAN. Pardon, dear father.
100 *BAP.* How hast thou offended?
Where is Lucentio?
LUC. Here's Lucentio,
Right son to the right Vincentio;
That have by marriage made thy daughter mine,
While counterfeit supposes blear'd thine eyne.
105 *GRE.* Here's packing, with a witness, to deceive
us all!
VIN. Where is that damned villain Tranio,

That faced and braved me in this matter so?
Bap. Why, tell me, is not this my Cambio?
Bian. Cambio is changed into Lucentio.
110 *Luc.* Love wrought these miracles. Bianca's love
Made me exchange my state with Tranio,
While he did bear my countenance in the town
And happily I have arrived at the last
Unto the wished haven of my bliss.
115 What Tranio did, myself enforced him to;
Then pardon him, sweet father, for my sake.
Vin. I'll slit the villain's nose, that would have sent
me to the gaol.
Bap. But do you hear, sir? have you married my
120 daughter without asking my good will?
Vin. Fear not, Baptista; we will content you, go to:
but I will in, to be revenged for this villany. [*Exit.*
Bap. And I, to sound the depth of this knavery. [*Exit.*
Luc. Look not pale, Bianca; thy father will not frown.

[*Exeunt Lucentio and Bianca.*

125 *Gre.* My cake is dough: but I'll in among the rest;
Out of hope of all, but my share of the feast. [*Exit.*
Kath. Husband, let's follow, to see the end of
this ado.
Pet. First kiss me, Kate, and we will.
Kath. What, in the midst of the street?
130 *Pet.* What, art thou ashamed of me?
Kath. No, sir, God forbid; but ashamed to kiss.
Pet. Why, then let's home again. Come, sirrah, let's
away.
Kath. Nay, I will give thee a kiss: now pray thee, love,
stay.
Pet. Is not this well? Come, my sweet Kate:
135 Better once than never, for never too late. [*Exeunt.*

SCENE II. PADUA. LUCENTIO'S HOUSE

Enter Baptista, Vincentio, Gremio, *the* Pedant, Lucentio,
Bianca, Petruchio, Katharina, Hortensio, *and* Widow,
Tranio, Biondello, *and* Grumio: *the Serving-men with
Tranio bringing in a banquet.*

Luc. At last, though long, our jarring notes agree:
And time it is, when raging war is done,
To smile at scapes and perils overblown.
My fair Bianca, bid my father welcome,
5 While I with self-same kindness welcome thine.
Brother Petruchio, sister Katharina,
And thou, Hortensio, with thy loving widow,
Feast with the best, and welcome to my house:
My banquet is to close our stomachs up,
10 After our great good cheer. Pray you, sit down;
For now we sit to chat, as well as eat.
Pet. Nothing but sit and sit, and eat and eat!
Bap. Padua affords this kindness, son Petruchio.
Pet. Padua affords nothing but what is kind.
15 *Hor.* For both our sakes, I would that word were
    true.
Pet. Now, for my life, Hortensio fears his widow.
Wid. Then never trust me, if I be afeard.
Pet. You are very sensible, and yet you miss my
    sense:
I mean, Hortensio is afeard of you.
20 *Wid.* He that is giddy thinks the world turns round.
Pet. Roundly replied.
Kath. Mistress, how mean you that?
Wid. Thus I conceive by him.
Pet. Conceives by me! How likes Hortensio that?
Hor. My widow says, thus she conceives her tale.
25 *Pet.* Very well mended. Kiss him for that, good
    widow.
Kath. 'He that is giddy thinks the world turns
    round:'
I pray you, tell me what you meant by that.
Wid. Your husband, being troubled with a shrew,
Measures my husband's sorrow by his woe:
30 And now you know my meaning.
Kath. A very mean meaning.
Wid. Right, I mean you.
Kath. And I am mean, indeed, respecting you.
Pet. To her, Kate!
Hor. To her, widow!
35 *Pet.* A hundred marks, my Kate does put her
    down.
Hor. That's my office.

Pet. Spoke like an officer: ha' to thee, lad.

[Drinks to Hortensio.

Bap. How likes Gremio these quick-witted folks?
Gre. Believe me, sir, they butt together well.
₄₀ *Bian.* Head, and butt! an hasty-witted body
Would say your head and butt were head and horn.
Vin. Ay, mistress bride, hath that awaken'd you?
Bian. Ay, but not frighted me; therefore I'll sleep
  again.
Pet. Nay, that you shall not: since you have begun,
₄₅ Have at you for a bitter jest or two!
Bian. Am I your bird? I mean to shift my bush;
And then pursue me as you draw your bow.
You are welcome all.

[Exeunt Bianca, Katharina, and Widow.

Pet. She hath prevented me. Here, Signior Tranio,
₅₀ This bird you aim'd at, though you hit her not;
Therefore a health to all that shot and miss'd.
Tra. O, sir, Lucentio slipp'd me like his greyhound,
Which runs himself, and catches for his master.
Pet. A good swift simile, but something currish.
₅₅ *Tra.* 'Tis well, sir, that you hunted for yourself:
'Tis thought your deer does hold you at a bay.
Bap. O ho, Petruchio! Tranio hits you now.
Luc. I thank thee for that gird, good Tranio.
Hor. Confess, confess, hath he not hit you here?
₆₀ *Pet.* A' has a little gall'd me, I confess;
And, as the jest did glance away from me,
'Tis ten to one it maim'd you two outright.
Bap. Now, in good sadness, son Petruchio,
I think thou hast the veriest shrew of all.
₆₅ *Pet.* Well, I say no: and therefore for assurance
Let's each one send unto his wife;
And he whose wife is most obedient
To come at first when he doth send for her,
Shall win the wager which we will propose.
Hor. Content. What is the wager?
₇₀ *Luc.* Twenty crowns.
Pet. Twenty crowns!

I'll venture so much of my hawk or hound,
But twenty times so much upon my wife.
Luc. A hundred then.
Hor. Content.
Pet. A match! 'tis done.
Hor. Who shall begin?
₇₅ *Luc.* That will I.
Go, Biondello, bid your mistress come to me.
Bion. I go. [*Exit.*
Bap. Son, I'll be your half, Bianca comes.
Luc. I'll have no halves; I'll bear it all myself.

Re-enter BIONDELLO.

How now! what news?
₈₀ *Bion.* Sir, my mistress sends you word
That she is busy, and she cannot come.
Pet. How! she is busy, and she cannot come!
Is that an answer?
Gre. Ay, and a kind one too:
Pray God, sir, your wife send you not a worse.
₈₅ *Pet.* I hope, better.
Hor. Sirrah Biondello, go and entreat my wife
To come to me forthwith. [*Exit Biondello.*
Pet. O, ho! entreat her!
Nay, then she must needs come.
Hor. I am afraid, sir,
Do what you can, yours will not be entreated.

Re-enter BIONDELLO.

₉₀ Now, where's my wife?
Bion. She says you have some goodly jest in hand:
She will not come; she bids you come to her.
Pet. Worse and worse; she will not come! O vile,
Intolerable, not to be endured!
₉₅ Sirrah Grumio, go to your mistress;
Say, I command her come to me. [*Exit Grumio.*
Hor. I know her answer.
Pet. What?
Hor. She will not.
Pet. The fouler fortune mine, and there an end.
Bap. Now, by my holidame, here comes Katharina!

RE-ENTER KATHARINA.

₁₀₀ *KATH.* What is your will, sir, that you send for me?
PET. Where is your sister, and Hortensio's wife?
KATH. They sit conferring by the parlour fire.
PET. Go, fetch them hither: if they deny to come,
Swinge me them soundly forth unto their husbands:
₁₀₅ Away, I say, and bring them hither straight. [*Exit
Katharina.*
LUC. Here is a wonder, if you talk of a wonder.
HOR. And so it is: I wonder what it bodes.
PET. Marry, peace it bodes, and love, and quiet life,
An awful rule, and right supremacy;
₁₁₀ And, to be short, what not, that's sweet and
happy?
BAP. Now, fair befal thee, good Petruchio!
The wager thou hast won; and I will add
Unto their losses twenty thousand crowns;
Another dowry to another daughter,
₁₁₅ For she is changed, as she had never been.
PET. Nay, I will win my wager better yet,
And show more sign of her obedience,
Her new-built virtue and obedience.
See where she comes and brings your froward wives
₁₂₀ As prisoners to her womanly persuasion.

RE-ENTER KATHARINA, *WITH* BIANCA *AND* WIDOW.

Katharine, that cap of yours becomes you not:
Off with that bauble, throw it under-foot.
Wid. Lord, let me never have a cause to sigh,
Till I be brought to such a silly pass!
₁₂₅ *BIAN.* Fie, what a foolish duty call you this?
LUC. I would your duty were as foolish too:
The wisdom of your duty, fair Bianca,
Hath cost me an hundred crowns since supper-time.
BIAN. The more fool you, for laying on my duty.
₁₃₀ *PET.* Katharine, I charge thee, tell these headstrong
women
What duty they do owe their lords and husbands.
Wid. Come, come, you're mocking: we will have no
telling.
PET. Come on, I say; and first begin with her.

Wid. She shall not.

135 *PET.* I say she shall: and first begin with her.

KATH. Fie, fie! unknit that threatening unkind brow;
And dart not scornful glances from those eyes,
To wound thy lord, thy king, thy governor:
It blots thy beauty as frosts do bite the meads,
140 Confounds thy fame as whirlwinds shake fair
    buds,
And in no sense is meet or amiable.
A woman moved is like a fountain troubled,
Muddy, ill-seeming, thick, bereft of beauty;
And while it is so, none so dry or thirsty
145 Will deign to sip or touch one drop of it.
Thy husband is thy lord, thy life, thy keeper,
Thy head, thy sovereign; one that cares for thee,
And for thy maintenance commits his body
To painful labour both by sea and land,
150 To watch the night in storms, the day in cold,
Whilst thou liest warm at home, secure and safe;
And craves no other tribute at thy hands
But love, fair looks and true obedience;
Too little payment for so great a debt.
155 Such duty as the subject owes the prince
Even such a woman oweth to her husband;
And when she is froward, peevish, sullen, sour,
And not obedient to his honest will,
What is she but a foul contending rebel,
160 And graceless traitor to her loving lord?
I am ashamed that women are so simple
To offer war where they should kneel for peace;
Or seek for rule, supremacy and sway,
When they are bound to serve, love and obey.
165 Why are our bodies soft and weak and smooth,
Unapt to toil and trouble in the world,
But that our soft conditions and our hearts
Should well agree with our external parts?
Come, come, you froward and unable worms!
170 My mind hath been as big as one of yours,
My heart as great, my reason haply more,
To bandy word for word and frown for frown;
But now I see our lances are but straws,
Our strength as weak, our weakness past compare,

175 That seeming to be most which we indeed
    least are.
Then vail your stomachs, for it is no boot,
And place your hands below your husband's foot:
In token of which duty, if he please,
My hand is ready, may it do him ease.
180 *PET.* Why, there's a wench! Come on, and kiss me,
    Kate.
Luc. Well, go thy ways, old lad; for thou shalt ha't.
VIN. 'Tis a good hearing, when children are toward.
Luc. But a harsh hearing, when women are froward.
PET. Come, Kate, we'll to bed.
185 We three are married, but you two are sped.
'Twas I won the wager, though you hit the white; [*To
    Lucentio.*
And, being a winner, God give you good night!

[*Exeunt Petruchio and Katharina.*

HOR. Now, go thy ways; thou hast tamed a curst
    shrew.
Luc. 'Tis a wonder, by your leave, she will be tamed
    so. [*Exeunt.*

THE TEMPEST

DRAMATIS PERSONÆ

ALONSO, King of Naples.
SEBASTIAN, his brother.
PROSPERO, the right Duke of Milan.
ANTONIO, his brother, the usurping Duke of Milan.
FERDINAND, son to the King of Naples.
GONZALO, an honest old Counsellor.
ADRIAN, Lords.
FRANCISCO, ""
CALIBAN, a savage and deformed Slave.
TRINCULO, a Jester.
STEPHANO, a drunken Butler.
MASTER OF A SHIP.
BOATSWAIN.
MARINERS.
MIRANDA, daughter to Prospero.
ARIEL, an airy Spirit.
IRIS, CERES, JUNO, NYMPHS, REAPERS, presented by
    Spirits.
Other Spirits attending on Prospero.

SCENE—A ship at sea: an uninhabited island.

ACT I

SCENE I. ON A SHIP AT SEA: A TEMPESTUOUS NOISE
OF THUNDER AND LIGHTNING HEARD.

Enter a Ship-Master *and* a Boatswain.

Mast. Boatswain!
Boats. Here, master: what cheer?
Mast. Good, speak to the mariners: fall to't, yarely, or
    we run ourselves aground: bestir, bestir. *Exit.*

Enter Mariners.

5 *Boats.* Heigh, my hearts! cheerly, cheerly, my
    hearts! yare, yare! Take in the topsail. Tend to the
    master's whistle. Blow, till thou burst thy wind, if
    room enough!

Enter Alonso, Sebastian, Antonio, Ferdinand, Gonzalo,
and others.

Alon. Good boatswain, have care. Where's the mas-
    ter? Play the men.
10 *Boats.* I pray now, keep below.
Ant. Where is the master, boatswain?
Boats. Do you not hear him? You mar our labour:
    keep your cabins: you do assist the storm.
Gon. Nay, good, be patient.

15 *Boats.* When the sea is. Hence! What cares these
roarers for the name of king? To cabin: silence!
trouble us not.

Gon. Good, yet remember whom thou hast aboard.

Boats. None that I more love than myself. You are a
20 Counsellor; if you can command these elements
to silence, and work the peace of the present, we
will not hand a rope more; use your authority: if
you cannot, give thanks you have lived so long,
and make yourself ready in your cabin for the
mischance of the hour, if it so hap. Cheerly, good
25 hearts! Out of our way, I say. *Exit.*

Gon. I have great comfort from this fellow: methinks
he hath no drowning mark upon him; his complexion is perfect gallows. Stand fast, good Fate, to
his hanging: make the rope of his destiny our ca-
ble, for our own doth 30 little advantage. If he be
not born to be hanged, our case is miserable.
Exeunt.

Re-enter Boatswain.

Boats. Down with the topmast! yare! lower, lower!
Bring her to try with main-course. [*A cry within.*] A
plague upon this howling! they are louder than
the weather 35 or our office.

RE-*ENTER* Sebastian, Antonio, *and* Gonzalo.

Yet again! what do you here? Shall we give o'er, and
drown? Have you a mind to sink?

Seb. A pox o' your throat, you bawling, blasphemous,
incharitable dog!

40 *Boats.* Work you, then.

Ant. Hang, cur! hang, you whoreson, insolent noise-
maker. We are less afraid to be drowned than
thou art.

Gon. I'll warrant him for drowning; though the ship
were no stronger than a nutshell, and as leaky as
an unstanched 45 wench.

Boats. Lay her a-hold, a-hold! set her two courses off
to sea again; lay her off.

Enter Mariners wet.

MARINERS. All lost! to prayers, to prayers! all lost!

BOATS. What, must our mouths be cold?

50 GON. The king and prince at prayers! let's assist them,

For our case is as theirs.

SEB. I'm out of patience.

ANT. We are merely cheated of our lives by drunkards:

This wide-chapp'd rascal,—would thou mightst lie drowning

The washing of ten tides!

GON. He'll be hang'd yet,

55 Though every drop of water swear against it,

And gape at widest to glut him.

A confused noise within: "Mercy on us!"—"We split, we split!"—"Farewell my wife and children!"— "Farewell, brother!"—"We split, we split, we split!"

60 ANT. Let's all sink with the king.

SEB. Let's take leave of him. *Exeunt* ANT. *and* SEB.

GON. Now would I give a thousand furlongs of sea for an acre of barren ground, long heath, brown furze, any thing. The wills above be done! but I would fain die a 65 dry death. *Exeunt.*

SCENE II. THE ISLAND. BEFORE PROSPERO'S CELL.

ENTER PROSPERO *AND* MIRANDA.

MIR. If by your art, my dearest father, you have

Put the wild waters in this roar, allay them.

The sky, it seems, would pour down stinking pitch,

But that the sea, mounting to the welkin's cheek,

5 Dashes the fire out. O, I have suffer'd

With those that I saw suffer! a brave vessel,

Who had, no doubt, some noble creature in her,

Dash'd all to pieces. O, the cry did knock

Against my very heart! Poor souls, they perish'd!

10 Had I been any god of power, I would

Have sunk the sea within the earth, or ere

It should the good ship so have swallow'd and
The fraughting souls within her.
Pros. Be collected:
No more amazement: tell your piteous heart
There's no harm done.
Mir. O, woe the day!
Pros. ₁₅ No harm.
I have done nothing but in care of thee,
Of thee, my dear one, thee, my daughter, who
Art ignorant of what thou art, nought knowing
Of whence I am, nor that I am more better
₂₀ Than Prospero, master of a full poor cell,
And thy no greater father.
Mir. More to know
Did never meddle with my thoughts.
Pros. 'Tis time
I should inform thee farther. Lend thy hand,
And pluck my magic garment from me.—So: *Lays
down his mantle.*
₂₅ Lie there, my art. Wipe thou thine eyes; have
comfort.
The direful spectacle of the wreck, which touch'd
The very virtue of compassion in thee,
I have with such provision in mine art
So safely order'd, that there is no soul,
₃₀ No, not so much perdition as an hair
Betid to any creature in the vessel
Which thou heard'st cry, which thou saw'st sink. Sit
down;
For thou must now know farther.
Mir. You have often
Begun to tell me what I am; but stopp'd,
₃₅ And left me to a bootless inquisition,
Concluding "Stay: not yet."
Pros. The hour's now come;
The very minute bids thee ope thine ear;
Obey, and be attentive. Canst thou remember
A time before we came unto this cell?
₄₀ I do not think thou canst, for then thou wast not
Out three years old.
Mir. Certainly, sir, I can.
Pros. By what? by any other house or person?
Of any thing the image tell me that

Hath kept with thy remembrance.

Mir. 'Tis far off,

45 And rather like a dream than an assurance
That my remembrance warrants. Had I not
Four or five women once that tended me?

Pros. Thou hadst, and more, Miranda. But how is it
That this lives in thy mind? What seest thou else
50 In the dark backward and abysm of time?
If thou remember'st ought ere thou camest here,
How thou camest here thou mayst.

Mir. But that I do not.

Pros. Twelve year since, Miranda, twelve year since,
Thy father was the Duke of Milan, and
A prince of power.

Mir. 55 Sir, are not you my father?

Pros. Thy mother was a piece of virtue, and
She said thou wast my daughter; and thy father
Was Duke of Milan; and his only heir
And princess, no worse issued.

Mir. O the heavens!

60 What foul play had we, that we came from thence?
Or blessed was't we did?

Pros. Both, both, my girl:
By foul play, as thou say'st, were we heaved thence;
But blessedly holp hither.

Mir. O, my heart bleeds
To think o' the teen that I have turn'd you to.
65 Which is from my remembrance! Please you,
     farther.

Pros. My brother, and thy uncle, call'd Antonio,—
I pray thee, mark me,—that a brother should
Be so perfidious!—he whom, next thyself,
Of all the world I loved, and to him put
70 The manage of my state; as, at that time,
Through all the signories it was the first,
And Prospero the prime duke, being so reputed
In dignity, and for the liberal arts
Without a parallel; those being all my study,
75 The government I cast upon my brother,
And to my state grew stranger, being transported
And rapt in secret studies. Thy false uncle—
Dost thou attend me?

Mir. Sir, most heedfully.

Pros. Being once perfected how to grant suits,
80 How to deny them, whom to advance, and whom
To trash for over-topping, new created
The creatures that were mine, I say, or changed 'em,
Or else new form'd 'em; having both the key
Of officer and office, set all hearts i' the state
85 To what tune pleased his ear; that now he was
The ivy which had hid my princely trunk,
And suck'd my verdure out on't. Thou attend'st not.
Mir. O, good sir, I do.
Pros. I pray thee, mark me.
I, thus neglecting worldly ends, all dedicated
90 To closeness and the bettering of my mind
With that which, but by being so retired,
O'er-prized all popular rate, in my false brother
Awaked an evil nature; and my trust,
Like a good parent, did beget of him
95 A falsehood in its contrary, as great
As my trust was; which had indeed no limit,
A confidence sans bound. He being thus lorded,
Not only with what my revenue yielded,
But what my power might else exact, like one
100 Who having into truth, by telling of it,
Made such a sinner of his memory,
To credit his own lie, he did believe
He was indeed the duke; out o' the substitution,
And executing the outward face of royalty,
105 With all prerogative:—hence his ambition
    growing,—
Dost thou hear?
Mir. Your tale, sir, would cure deafness.
Pros. To have no screen between this part he play'd
And him he play'd it for, he needs will be
Absolute Milan. Me, poor man, my library
110 Was dukedom large enough: of temporal royalties
He thinks me now incapable; confederates,
So dry he was for sway, wi' the King of Naples
To give him annual tribute, do him homage,
Subject his coronet to his crown, and bend
115 The dukedom, yet unbow'd,—alas, poor Milan!—
To most ignoble stooping.
Mir. O the heavens!
Pros. Mark his condition, and th' event; then tell me

If this might be a brother.
Mir. I should sin
To think but nobly of my grandmother:
Good wombs have borne bad sons.
Pros. 120 Now the condition.
This King of Naples, being an enemy
To me inveterate, hearkens my brother's suit;
Which was, that he, in lieu o' the premises,
Of homage and I know not how much tribute,
125 Should presently extirpate me and mine
Out of the dukedom, and confer fair Milan,
With all the honours, on my brother: whereon,
A treacherous army levied, one midnight
Fated to the purpose, did Antonio open
130 The gates of Milan; and, i' the dead of darkness,
The ministers for the purpose hurried thence
Me and thy crying self.
Mir. Alack, for pity!
I, not remembering how I cried out then,
Will cry it o'er again: it is a hint
That wrings mine eyes to't.
Pros. 135 Hear a little further,
And then I'll bring thee to the present business
Which now's upon 's; without the which, this story
Were most impertinent.
Mir. Wherefore did they not
That hour destroy us?
Pros. Well demanded, wench:
140 My tale provokes that question. Dear, they
        durst not,
So dear the love my people bore me; nor set
A mark so bloody on the business; but
With colours fairer painted their foul ends.
In few, they hurried us aboard a bark,
145 Bore us some leagues to sea; where they prepared
A rotten carcass of a boat, not rigg'd,
Nor tackle, sail, nor mast; the very rats
Instinctively have quit it: there they hoist us,
To cry to the sea that roar'd to us; to sigh
150 To the winds, whose pity, sighing back again,
Did us but loving wrong.
Mir. Alack, what trouble
Was I then to you!

Pros. O, a cherubin
Thou wast that did preserve me. Thou didst smile,
Infused with a fortitude from heaven,
155 When I have deck'd the sea with drops full salt,
Under my burthen groan'd; which raised in me
An undergoing stomach, to bear up
Against what should ensue.
Mir. How came we ashore?
Pros. By Providence divine.
160 Some food we had, and some fresh water, that
A noble Neapolitan, Gonzalo,
Out of his charity, who being then appointed
Master of this design, did give us, with
Rich garments, linens, stuffs and necessaries,
165 Which since have steaded much; so, of his gen-
tleness,
Knowing I loved my books, he furnish'd me
From mine own library with volumes that
I prize above my dukedom.
Mir. Would I might
But ever see that man!
Pros. Now I arise: *Resumes his mantle.*
170 Sit still, and hear the last of our sea-sorrow.
Here in this island we arrived; and here
Have I, thy schoolmaster, made thee more profit
Than other princesses can, that have more time
For vainer hours, and tutors not so careful.
175 *Mir.* Heavens thank you for't! And now, I pray
you, sir,
For still 'tis beating in my mind, your reason
For raising this sea-storm?
Pros. Know thus far forth.
By accident most strange, bountiful Fortune,
Now my dear lady, hath mine enemies
180 Brought to this shore; and by my prescience
I find my zenith doth depend upon
A most auspicious star, whose influence
If now I court not, but omit, my fortunes
Will ever after droop. Here cease more questions:
185 Thou art inclined to sleep; 'tis a good dulness,
And give it way: I know thou canst not choose. *Mi-
randa sleeps.*
Come away, servant, come. I am ready now.

Approach, my Ariel, come.

Enter ARIEL.

ARI. All hail, great master! grave sir, hail! I come
₁₉₀ To answer thy best pleasure; be't to fly,
To swim, to dive into the fire, to ride
On the curl'd clouds, to thy strong bidding task
Ariel and all his quality.
PROS.   Hast thou, spirit,
Perform'd to point the tempest that I bade thee?
₁₉₅ ARI. To every article.
I boarded the king's ship; now on the beak,
Now in the waist, the deck, in every cabin,
I flamed amazement: sometime I'ld divide,
And burn in many places; on the topmast,
₂₀₀ The yards and bowsprit, would I flame distinctly,
Then meet and join. Jove's lightnings, the precursors
O' the dreadful thunder-claps, more momentary
And sight-outrunning were not: the fire and cracks
Of sulphurous roaring the most mighty Neptune
₂₀₅ Seem to besiege, and make his bold waves
    tremble,
Yea, his dread trident shake.
PROS.   My brave spirit!
Who was so firm, so constant, that this coil
Would not infect his reason?
ARI.   Not a soul
But felt a fever of the mad, and play'd
₂₁₀ Some tricks of desperation. All but mariners
Plunged in the foaming brine, and quit the vessel,
Then all afire with me: the king's son, Ferdinand,
With hair up-staring,—then like reeds, not hair,—
Was the first man that leap'd; cried, "Hell is empty,
And all the devils are here."
PROS. ₂₁₅ Why, that's my spirit!
But was not this nigh shore?
ARI.   Close by, my master.
PROS. But are they, Ariel, safe?
ARI.   Not a hair perish'd;
On their sustaining garments not a blemish,
But fresher than before: and, as thou badest me,
₂₂₀ In troops I have dispersed them 'bout the isle.

The king's son have I landed by himself;
Whom I left cooling of the air with sighs
In an odd angle of the isle, and sitting,
His arms in this sad knot.
Pros. Of the king's ship
225 The mariners, say how thou hast disposed,
And all the rest o' the fleet.
Ari. Safely in harbour
Is the king's ship; in the deep nook, where once
Thou call'dst me up at midnight to fetch dew
From the still-vex'd Bermoothes, there she's hid:
230 The mariners all under hatches stow'd;
Who, with a charm join'd to their suffer'd labour,
I have left asleep: and for the rest o' the fleet,
Which I dispersed, they all have met again,
And are upon the Mediterranean flote,
235 Bound sadly home for Naples;
Supposing that they saw the king's ship wreck'd,
And his great person perish.
Pros. Ariel, thy charge
Exactly is perform'd: but there's more work.
What is the time o' the day?
Ari. Past the mid season.
240 *Pros.* At least two glasses. The time 'twixt six
    and now
Must by us both be spent most preciously.
Ari. Is there more toil? Since thou dost give me pains,
Let me remember thee what thou hast promised,
Which is not yet perform'd me.
Pros. How now? moody?
What is't thou canst demand?
Ari. 245 My liberty.
Pros. Before the time be out? no more!
Ari. I prithee,
Remember I have done thee worthy service;
Told thee no lies, made thee no mistakings, served
Without or grudge or grumblings: thou didst promise
To bate me a full year.
Pros. 250 Dost thou forget
From what a torment I did free thee?
Ari. No.
Pros. Thou dost; and think'st it much to tread
    the ooze

Of the salt deep,
To run upon the sharp wind of the north,
₂₅₅ To do me business in the veins o' the earth
When it is baked with frost.

ARI. I do not, sir.

PROS. Thou liest, malignant thing! Hast thou forgot
The foul witch Sycorax, who with age and envy
Was grown into a hoop? hast thou forgot her?

ARI. No, sir.

PROS. ₂₆₀ Thou hast. Where was she born? speak;
tell me.

ARI. Sir, in Argier.

PROS. O, was she so? I must
Once in a month recount what thou hast been,
Which thou forget'st. This damn'd witch Sycorax,
For mischiefs manifold, and sorceries terrible
₂₆₅ To enter human hearing, from Argier,
Thou know'st, was banish'd: for one thing she did
They would not take her life. Is not this true?

ARI. Ay, sir.

PROS. This blue-eyed hag was hither brought with
child,
₂₇₀ And here was left by the sailors. Thou, my slave,
As thou report'st thyself, wast then her servant;
And, for thou wast a spirit too delicate
To act her earthy and abhorr'd commands,
Refusing her grand hests, she did confine thee,
₂₇₅ By help of her more potent ministers,
And in her most unmitigable rage,
Into a cloven pine; within which rift
Imprison'd thou didst painfully remain
A dozen years; within which space she died,
₂₈₀ And left thee there; where thou didst vent thy
groans
As fast as mill-wheels strike. Then was this island—
Save for the son that she did litter here,
A freckled whelp hag-born—not honour'd with
A human shape.

ARI. Yes, Caliban her son.

₂₈₅ *PROS.* Dull thing, I say so; he, that Caliban,
Whom now I keep in service. Thou best know'st
What torment I did find thee in; thy groans
Did make wolves howl, and penetrate the breasts

Of ever-angry bears: it was a torment
₂₉₀ To lay upon the damn'd, which Sycorax
Could not again undo: it was mine art,
When I arrived and heard thee, that made gape
The pine, and let thee out.
ARI. I thank thee, master.
PROS. If thou more murmur'st, I will rend an oak,
₂₉₅ And peg thee in his knotty entrails, till
Thou hast howl'd away twelve winters.
ARI. Pardon, master:
I will be correspondent to command,
And do my spiriting gently.
PROS. Do so; and after two days
I will discharge thee.
ARI. That's my noble master!
₃₀₀ What shall I do? say what; what shall I do?
PROS. Go make thyself like a nymph o' the sea:
Be subject to no sight but thine and mine; invisible
To every eyeball else. Go take this shape,
And hither come in't: go, hence with diligence! *Exit
Ariel.*
₃₀₅ Awake, dear heart, awake! thou hast slept well;
Awake!
MIR. The strangeness of your story put
Heaviness in me.
PROS. Shake it off. Come on;
We'll visit Caliban my slave, who never
Yields us kind answer.
MIR. 'Tis a villain, sir,
I do not love to look on.
PROS. ₃₁₀ But, as 'tis,
We cannot miss him: he does make our fire,
Fetch in our wood, and serves in offices
That profit us. What, ho! slave! Caliban!
Thou earth, thou! speak.
CAL. [*within*] There's wood enough within.
₃₁₅ *PROS.* Come forth, I say! there's other business for
thee:
Come, thou tortoise! when?

Re-enter ARIEL like a water-nymph.

Fine apparition! My quaint Ariel,

Hark in thine ear.
Ari. My lord, it shall be done. *Exit.*
Pros. Thou poisonous slave, got by the devil himself
320 Upon thy wicked dam, come forth!

Enter CALIBAN.

Cal. As wicked dew as e'er my mother brush'd
With raven's feather from unwholesome fen
Drop on you both! a south-west blow on ye
And blister you all o'er!
325 *Pros.* For this, be sure, to-night thou shalt have cramps,
Side-stitches that shall pen thy breath up; urchins
Shall, for that vast of night that they may work,
All exercise on thee; thou shalt be pinch'd
As thick as honeycomb, each pinch more stinging
Than bees that made 'em.
Cal. 330 I must eat my dinner.
This island's mine, by Sycorax my mother,
Which thou takest from me. When thou camest first,
Thou strokedst me, and madest much of me; wouldst give me
Water with berries in't; and teach me how
335 To name the bigger light, and how the less,
That burn by day and night: and then I loved thee,
And show'd thee all the qualities o' th' isle,
The fresh springs, brine-pits, barren place and fertile:
Curs'd be I that did so! All the charms
340 Of Sycorax, toads, beetles, bats, light on you!
For I am all the subjects that you have,
Which first was mine own king: and here you sty me
In this hard rock, whiles you do keep from me
The rest o' th' island.
Pros. Thou most lying slave,
345 Whom stripes may move, not kindness! I have used thee,
Filth as thou art, with human care; and lodged thee
In mine own cell, till thou didst seek to violate
The honour of my child.
Cal. O ho, O ho! would 't had been done!
350 Thou didst prevent me; I had peopled else
This isle with Calibans.

Pros. Abhorred slave,
Which any print of goodness wilt not take,
Being capable of all ill! I pitied thee,
Took pains to make thee speak, taught thee each hour
355 One thing or other: when thou didst not, savage,
Know thine own meaning, but wouldst gabble like
A thing most brutish, I endow'd thy purposes
With words that made them known. But thy vile race,
Though thou didst learn, had that in't which good
   natures
360 Could not abide to be with; therefore wast thou
Deservedly confined into this rock,
Who hadst deserved more than a prison.
Cal. You taught me language; and my profit on't
Is, I know how to curse. The red plague rid you
For learning me your language!
Pros. 365 Hag-seed, hence!
Fetch us in fuel; and be quick, thou'rt best,
To answer other business. Shrug'st thou, malice?
If thou neglect'st, or dost unwillingly
What I command, I'll rack thee with old cramps,
370 Fill all thy bones with aches, make thee roar,
That beasts shall tremble at thy din.
Cal. No, pray thee.
[*Aside*] I must obey: his art is of such power,
It would control my dam's god, Setebos,
And make a vassal of him.
Pros. So, slave; hence! *Exit Caliban.*

Re-enter ARIEL, *invisible, playing and singing;* FERDINAND
following.

ARIEL'S SONG.

375 Come unto these yellow sands,
And then take hands:
Courtsied when you have and kiss'd
The wild waves whist:
Foot it featly here and there;
380 And, sweet sprites, the burthen bear.
Burthen [dispersedly]. Hark, hark!
Bow-wow.
The watch-dogs bark:

Bow-wow.

ARI. Hark, hark! I hear
385 The strain of strutting chanticleer
Cry, Cock-a-diddle-dow.

FER. Where should this music be? i' th' air or th'
earth?
It sounds no more: and, sure, it waits upon
Some god o' th' island. Sitting on a bank,
390 Weeping again the king my father's wreck,
This music crept by me upon the waters,
Allaying both their fury and my passion
With its sweet air: thence I have follow'd it.
Or it hath drawn me rather. But 'tis gone.
395 No, it begins again.

ARIEL sings.

Full fathom five thy father lies;
Of his bones are coral made;
Those are pearls that were his eyes:
Nothing of him that doth fade,
400 But doth suffer a sea-change
Into something rich and strange.
Sea-nymphs hourly ring his knell:
Burthen: Ding-dong.

ARI. Hark! now I hear them,—Ding-dong, bell.
405 *FER.* The ditty does remember my drown'd father.
This is no mortal business, nor no sound
That the earth owes:—I hear it now above me.

PROS. The fringed curtains of thine eye advance,
And say what thou seest yond.

MIR. What is't? a spirit?
410 Lord, how it looks about! Believe me, sir,
It carries a brave form. But 'tis a spirit.

PROS. No, wench; it eats and sleeps and hath such
senses
As we have, such. This gallant which thou seest
Was in the wreck; and, but he's something stain'd
415 With grief, that's beauty's canker, thou mightst
call him
A goodly person: he hath lost his fellows,
And strays about to find 'em.

MIR. I might call him

335

A thing divine; for nothing natural
I ever saw so noble.

Pros. [*Aside*]
It goes on, I see,
420 As my soul prompts it. Spirit, fine spirit! I'll
   free thee
Within two days for this.

Fer. Most sure, the goddess
On whom these airs attend! Vouchsafe my prayer
May know if you remain upon this island;
And that you will some good instruction give
425 How I may bear me here: my prime request,
Which I do last pronounce, is, O you wonder!
If you be maid or no?

Mir. No wonder, sir;
But certainly a maid.

Fer. My language! heavens!
I am the best of them that speak this speech,
Were I but where 'tis spoken.

Pros. 430 How? the best?
What wert thou, if the King of Naples heard thee?

Fer. A single thing, as I am now, that wonders
To hear thee speak of Naples. He does hear me;
And that he does I weep: myself am Naples,
435 Who with mine eyes, never since at ebb, beheld
The king my father wreck'd.

Mir. Alack, for mercy!

Fer. Yes, faith, and all his lords; the Duke of Milan
And his brave son being twain.

Pros. [*Aside*] The Duke of Milan
And his more braver daughter could control thee,
440 If now 'twere fit to do't. At the first sight
They have changed eyes. Delicate Ariel,
I'll set thee free for this. [*To Fer.*] A word, good sir;
I fear you have done yourself some wrong: a word.

Mir. Why speaks my father so ungently? This
445 Is the third man that e'er I saw; the first
That e'er I sigh'd for: pity move my father
To be inclined my way!

Fer. O, if a virgin,
And your affection not gone forth, I'll make you
The queen of Naples.

Pros. Soft, sir! one word more.

450 [*Aside*] They are both in either's powers: but this
    swift business
I must uneasy make, lest too light winning
Make the prize light. [*To* FER.] One word more; I
    charge thee
That thou attend me: thou dost here usurp
The name thou owest not; and hast put thyself
455 Upon this island as a spy, to win it
From me, the lord on't.
FER. No, as I am a man.
MIR. There's nothing ill can dwell in such a temple:
If the ill spirit have so fair a house,
Good things will strive to dwell with't.
PROS. Follow me.
460 Speak not you for him; he's a traitor. Come;
I'll manacle thy neck and feet together:
Sea-water shalt thou drink; thy food shall be
The fresh-brook muscles, wither'd roots, and husks
Wherein the acorn cradled. Follow.
FER. No;
465 I will resist such entertainment till
Mine enemy has more power. Draws, and is charmed from
    moving.
MIR. O dear father,
Make not too rash a trial of him, for
He's gentle, and not fearful.
PROS. What! I say,
My foot my tutor? Put thy sword up, traitor;
470 Who makest a show, but darest not strike, thy con-
    science
Is so possess'd with guilt: come from thy ward;
For I can here disarm thee with this stick
And make thy weapon drop.
MIR. Beseech you, father.
PROS. Hence! hang not on my garments.
MIR. Sir, have pity;
I'll be his surety.
PROS. 475 Silence! one word more
Shall make me chide thee, if not hate thee. What!
An advocate for an impostor! hush!
Thou think'st there is no more such shapes as he,
Having seen but him and Caliban: foolish wench!
480 To the most of men this is a Caliban,

And they to him are angels.
MIR. My affections
Are, then, most humble; I have no ambition
To see a goodlier man.
PROS. Come on; obey:
Thy nerves are in their infancy again,
And have no vigour in them.
FER. ₄₈₅ So they are:
My spirits, as in a dream, are all bound up.
My father's loss, the weakness which I feel,
The wreck of all my friends, nor this man's threats,
To whom I am subdued, are but light to me,
₄₉₀ Might I but through my prison once a day
Behold this maid: all corners else o' th' earth
Let liberty make use of; space enough
Have I in such a prison.
PROS. [*Aside*] It works. [*To FER.*] Come on.
Thou hast done well, fine Ariel! [*To FER.*] Follow me.
[*To ARI.*] Hark what thou else shalt do me.
MIR. ₄₉₅ Be of comfort;
My father's of a better nature, sir,
Than he appears by speech: this is unwonted
Which now came from him.
PROS. Thou shalt be as free
As mountain winds: but then exactly do
All points of my command.
ARI. ₅₀₀ To the syllable.
PROS. Come, follow. Speak not for him. *Exeunt.*

ACT II

SCENE I. ANOTHER PART OF THE ISLAND.

Enter ALONSO, SEBASTIAN, ANTONIO, GONZALO, ADRIAN,
FRANCISCO, *AND OTHERS.*

Gon. Beseech you, sir, be merry; you have cause,
So have we all, of joy; for our escape
Is much beyond our loss. Our hint of woe
Is common; every day, some sailor's wife,
₅ The masters of some merchant, and the merchant,
Have just our theme of woe; but for the miracle,
I mean our preservation, few in millions
Can speak like us: then wisely, good sir, weigh
Our sorrow with our comfort.
Alon. Prithee, peace.
₁₀ *Seb.* He receives comfort like cold porridge.
Ant. The visitor will not give him o'er so.
Seb. Look, he's winding up the watch of his wit; by
and by it will strike.
Gon. Sir,—
₁₅ *Seb.* One: tell.
Gon. When every grief is entertain'd that's offer'd,
Comes to the entertainer—
Seb. A dollar.
Gon. Dolour comes to him, indeed: you have spoken
₂₀ truer than you purposed.

Seb. You have taken it wiselier than I meant you
    should.

Gon. Therefore, my lord,—

Ant. Fie, what a spendthrift is he of his tongue!

Alon. I prithee, spare.

25 *Gon.* Well, I have done: but yet,—

Seb. He will be talking.

Ant. Which, of he or Adrian, for a good wager, first
    begins to crow?

Seb. The old cock.

30 *Ant.* The cockerel.

Seb. Done. The wager?

Ant. A laughter.

Seb. A match!

Adr. Though this island seem to be desert,—

35 *Seb.* Ha, ha, ha!—So, you're paid.

Adr. Uninhabitable, and almost inaccessible,—

Seb. Yet,—

Adr. Yet,—

Ant. He could not miss't.

40 *Adr.* It must needs be of subtle, tender and delicate
    temperance.

Ant. Temperance was a delicate wench.

Seb. Ay, and a subtle; as he most learnedly delivered.

Adr. The air breathes upon us here most sweetly.

45 *Seb.* As if it had lungs, and rotten ones.

Ant. Or as 'twere perfumed by a fen.

Gon. Here is every thing advantageous to life.

Ant. True; save means to live.

Seb. Of that there's none, or little.

50 *Gon.* How lush and lusty the grass looks! how
    green!

Ant. The ground, indeed, is tawny.

Seb. With an eye of green in't.

Ant. He misses not much.

Seb. No; he doth but mistake the truth totally.

55 *Gon.* But the rarity of it is,—which is indeed almost
    beyond credit,—

Seb. As many vouched rarities are.

Gon. That our garments, being, as they were,
    drenched in the sea, hold, notwithstanding, their
    freshness and glosses, 60 being rather new-dyed
    than stained with salt water.

Ant. If but one of his pockets could speak, would it
not say he lies?

Seb. Ay, or very falsely pocket up his report.

Gon. Methinks our garments are now as fresh as
when ₆₅ we put them on first in Afric, at the marriage of the king's fair daughter Claribel to the
King of Tunis.

Seb. 'Twas a sweet marriage, and we prosper well in
our return.

Adr. Tunis was never graced before with such a
paragon ₇₀ to their queen.

Gon. Not since widow Dido's time.

Ant. Widow! a pox o' that! How came that widow in?
widow Dido!

Seb. What if he had said 'widower Æneas' too? Good
₇₅ Lord, how you take it!

Adr. 'Widow Dido' said you? you make me study of
that: she was of Carthage, not of Tunis.

Gon. This Tunis, sir, was Carthage.

Adr. Carthage?

₈₀ *Gon.* I assure you, Carthage.

Seb. His word is more than the miraculous harp; he
hath raised the wall, and houses too.

Ant. What impossible matter will he make easy next?

Seb. I think he will carry this island home in his ₈₅
pocket, and give it his son for an apple.

Ant. And, sowing the kernels of it in the sea, bring
forth more islands.

Gon. Ay.

Ant. Why, in good time.

₉₀ *Gon.* Sir, we were talking that our garments seem
now as fresh as when we were at Tunis at the marriage of your daughter, who is now queen.

Ant. And the rarest that e'er came there.

Seb. Bate, I beseech you, widow Dido.

₉₅ *Ant.* O, widow Dido! ay, widow Dido.

Gon. Is not, sir, my doublet as fresh as the first day I
wore it? I mean, in a sort.

Ant. That sort was well fished for.

Gon. When I wore it at your daughter's marriage?

₁₀₀ *Alon.* You cram these words into mine ears
against
The stomach of my sense. Would I had never

Married my daughter there! for, coming thence,
My son is lost, and, in my rate, she too.
Who is so far from Italy removed
₁₀₅ I ne'er again shall see her. O thou mine heir
Of Naples and of Milan, what strange fish
Hath made his meal on thee?
FRAN. Sir, he may live:
I saw him beat the surges under him,
And ride upon their backs; he trod the water.
₁₁₀ Whose enmity he flung aside, and breasted
The surge most swoln that met him; his bold head
'Bove the contentious waves he kept, and oar'd
Himself with his good arms in lusty stroke
To the shore, that o'er his wave-worn basis bow'd,
₁₁₅ As stooping to relieve him: I not doubt
He came alive to land.
ALON. No, no, he's gone.
SEB. Sir, you may thank yourself for this great loss,
That would not bless our Europe with your daughter,
But rather lose her to an African;
₁₂₀ Where she, at least, is banish'd from your eye,
Who hath cause to wet the grief on't.
ALON. Prithee, peace.
SEB. You were kneel'd to, and importuned otherwise,
By all of us; and the fair soul herself
Weigh'd between loathness and obedience, at
₁₂₅ Which end o' the beam should bow. We have lost
your son,
I fear, for ever: Milan and Naples have
More widows in them of this business' making
Than we bring men to comfort them:
The fault's your own.
ALON. So is the dear'st o' the loss.
₁₃₀ *GON.* My lord Sebastian,
The truth you speak doth lack some gentleness,
And time to speak it in: you rub the sore,
When you should bring the plaster.
SEB. Very well.
ANT. And most chirurgeonly.
₁₃₅ *GON.* It is foul weather in us all, good sir,
When you are cloudy.
SEB. Foul weather?
ANT. Very foul.

Gon. Had I plantation of this isle, my lord,—
Ant. He'ld sow't with nettle-seed.
Seb. Or docks, or mallows.
Gon. And were the king on't, what would I do?
140 *Seb.* 'Scape being drunk for want of wine.
Gon. I' the commonwealth I would by contraries
Execute all things; for no kind of traffic
Would I admit; no name of magistrate;
Letters should not be known; riches, poverty,
145 And use of service, none; contract, succession,
Bourn, bound of land, tilth, vineyard, none;
No use of metal, corn, or wine, or oil;
No occupation; all men idle, all;
And women too, but innocent and pure;
150 No sovereignty;—
Seb. Yet he would be king on't.
Ant. The latter end of his commonwealth forgets the
beginning.
Gon. All things in common nature should produce
Without sweat or endeavour: treason, felony,
155 Sword, pike, knife, gun, or need of any engine,
Would I not have; but nature should bring forth,
Of its own kind, all foison, all abundance,
To feed my innocent people.
Seb. No marrying 'mong his subjects?
160 *Ant.* None, man; all idle; whores and knaves.
Gon. I would with such perfection govern, sir,
To excel the golden age.
Seb. 'Save his majesty!
Ant. Long live Gonzalo!
Gon. And,—do you mark me, sir?
Alon. Prithee, no more: thou dost talk nothing to me.
165 *Gon.* I do well believe your highness; and did it to
minister occasion to these gentlemen, who are of
such sensible and nimble lungs that they always
use to laugh at nothing.
Ant. 'Twas you we laughed at.
Gon. Who in this kind of merry fooling am nothing to
170 you: so you may continue, and laugh at
nothing still.
Ant. What a blow was there given!
Seb. An it had not fallen flat-long.
Gon. You are gentlemen of brave mettle; you would

lift the moon out of her sphere, if she would continue in it ₁₇₅ five weeks without changing.

Enter ARIEL (invisible) playing solemn music.

SEB. We would so, and then go a bat-fowling.
ANT. Nay, good my lord, be not angry.
GON. No, I warrant you; I will not adventure my dis-
cretion so weakly. Will you laugh me asleep, for I
am very ₁₈₀ heavy?
ANT. Go sleep, and hear us.

All sleep except ALON., SEB., and ANT.

ALON. What, all so soon asleep! I wish mine eyes
Would, with themselves, shut up my thoughts: I find
They are inclined to do so.
SEB. Please you, sir,
₁₈₅ Do not omit the heavy offer of it:
It seldom visits sorrow; when it doth,
It is a comforter.
ANT. We two, my lord,
Will guard your person while you take your rest,
And watch your safety.
ALON. Thank you.—Wondrous heavy.

Alonso sleeps. Exit Ariel.

₁₉₀ SEB. What a strange drowsiness possesses them!
ANT. It is the quality o' the climate.
SEB. Why
Doth it not then our eyelids sink? I find not
Myself disposed to sleep.
ANT. Nor I; my spirits are nimble.
They fell together all, as by consent;
₁₉₅ They dropp'd, as by a thunder-stroke. What might,
Worthy Sebastian?—O, what might?—No more:—
And yet methinks I see it in thy face,
What thou shouldst be: the occasion speaks thee; and
My strong imagination sees a crown
Dropping upon thy head.
SEB. ₂₀₀ What, art thou waking?
ANT. Do you not hear me speak?

Seb. I do; and surely
It is a sleepy language, and thou speak'st
Out of thy sleep. What is it thou didst say?
This is a strange repose, to be asleep
205 With eyes wide open; standing, speaking, moving,
And yet so fast asleep.
Ant. Noble Sebastian,
Thou let'st thy fortune sleep—die, rather; wink'st
Whiles thou art waking.
Seb. Thou dost snore distinctly;
There's meaning in thy snores.
210 *Ant.* I am more serious than my custom: you
Must be so too, if heed me; which to do
Trebles thee o'er.
Seb. Well, I am standing water.
Ant. I'll teach you how to flow.
Seb. Do so: to ebb
Hereditary sloth instructs me.
Ant. O,
215 If you but knew how you the purpose cherish
Whiles thus you mock it! how, in stripping it,
You more invest it! Ebbing men, indeed,
Most often do so near the bottom run
By their own fear or sloth.
Seb. Prithee, say on:
220 The setting of thine eye and cheek proclaim
A matter from thee; and a birth, indeed,
Which throes thee much to yield.
Ant. Thus, sir:
Although this lord of weak remembrance, this,
Who shall be of as little memory
225 When he is earth'd, hath here almost persuaded,—
For he's a spirit of persuasion, only
Professes to persuade,—the king his son's alive,
'Tis as impossible that he's undrown'd
As he that sleeps here swims.
Seb. I have no hope
That he's undrown'd.
Ant. 230 O, out of that 'no hope'
What great hope have you! no hope that way is
Another way so high a hope that even
Ambition cannot pierce a wink beyond,
But doubt discovery there. Will you grant with me

That Ferdinand is drown'd?
SEB. He's gone.
ANT. 235 Then, tell me,
Who's the next heir of Naples?
SEB. Claribel.
ANT. She that is queen of Tunis; she that dwells
Ten leagues beyond man's life; she that from Naples
Can have no note, unless the sun were post,—
240 The man i' the moon's too slow,—till new-born
     chins
Be rough and razorable; she that from whom
We all were sea-swallow'd, though some cast again,
And by that destiny, to perform an act
Whereof what's past is prologue; what to come,
In yours and my discharge.
SEB. 245 What stuff is this! How say you?
'Tis true, my brother's daughter's queen of Tunis;
So is she heir of Naples; 'twixt which regions
There is some space.
ANT. A space whose every cubit
Seems to cry out, "How shall that Claribel
250 Measure us back to Naples? Keep in Tunis,
And let Sebastian wake." Say, this were death
That now hath seized them; why, they were no worse
Than now they are. There be that can rule Naples
As well as he that sleeps; lords that can prate
255 As amply and unnecessarily
As this Gonzalo; I myself could make
A chough of as deep chat. O, that you bore
The mind that I do! what a sleep were this
For your advancement! Do you understand me?
SEB. Methinks I do.
ANT. 260 And how does your content
Tender your own good fortune?
SEB. I remember
You did supplant your brother Prospero.
ANT. True:
And look how well my garments sit upon me;
Much feater than before: my brother's servants
265 Were then my fellows; now they are my men.
SEB. But for your conscience.
ANT. Ay, sir; where lies that? if 'twere a kibe,
'Twould put me to my slipper: but I feel not

This deity in my bosom: twenty consciences,
₂₇₀ That stand 'twixt me and Milan, candied be they,
And melt, ere they molest! Here lies your brother,
No better than the earth he lies upon,
If he were that which now he's like, that's dead;
Whom I, with this obedient steel, three inches of it,
₂₇₅ Can lay to bed for ever; whiles you, doing thus,
To the perpetual wink for aye might put
This ancient morsel, this Sir Prudence, who
Should not upbraid our course. For all the rest,
They'll take suggestion as a cat laps milk;
₂₈₀ They'll tell the clock to any business that
We say befits the hour.

Seb. Thy case, dear friend,
Shall be my precedent; as thou got'st Milan,
I'll come by Naples. Draw thy sword: one stroke
Shall free thee from the tribute which thou payest;
And I the king shall love thee.

Ant. ₂₈₅ Draw together;
And when I rear my hand, do you the like,
To fall it on Gonzalo.

Seb. O, but one word. *They talk apart.*

Re-enter ARIEL *invisible.*

Ari. My master through his art foresees the danger
That you, his friend, are in; and sends me forth,—
₂₉₀ For else his project dies,—to keep them living.

Sings in Gonzalo's ear.

While you here do snoring lie,
Open-eyed conspiracy
His time doth take.
If of life you keep a care,
₂₉₅ Shake off slumber, and beware:
Awake, awake!

Ant. Then let us both be sudden.

Gon. Now, good angels
Preserve the king! *They wake.*

Alon. Why, how now? ho, awake!—Why are you
        drawn?
Wherefore this ghastly looking?

347

GON. 300 What's the matter?
SEB. Whiles we stood here securing your repose,
Even now, we heard a hollow burst of bellowing
Like bulls, or rather lions: did't not wake you?
It struck mine ear most terribly.
ALON. I heard nothing.
305 *ANT.* O, 'twas a din to fright a monster's ear,
To make an earthquake! sure, it was the roar
Of a whole herd of lions.
ALON. Heard you this, Gonzalo?
GON. Upon mine honour, sir, I heard a humming,
And that a strange one too, which did awake me:
310 I shaked you, sir, and cried: as mine eyes open'd,
I saw their weapons drawn:—there was a noise,
That's verily. 'Tis best we stand upon our guard,
Or that we quit this place: let's draw our weapons.
ALON. Lead off this ground; and let's make further
        search
For my poor son.
GON. 315 Heavens keep him from these beasts!
For he is, sure, i' th' island.
ALON. Lead away.
ARI. Prospero my lord shall know what I have done:
So, king, go safely on to seek thy son. *Exeunt.*

SCENE II. ANOTHER PART OF THE ISLAND.

Enter CALIBAN with a burden of wood. A noise of thunder heard.

CAL. All the infections that the sun sucks up
From bogs, fens, flats, on Prosper fall, and make him
By inch-meal a disease! His spirits hear me,
And yet I needs must curse. But they'll nor pinch,
5 Fright me with urchin-shows, pitch me i' the mire,
Nor lead me, like a firebrand, in the dark
Out of my way, unless he bid 'em: but
For every trifle are they set upon me;
Sometime like apes, that mow and chatter at me,
10 And after bite me; then like hedgehogs, which
Lie tumbling in my barefoot way, and mount
Their pricks at my footfall; sometime am I
All wound with adders, who with cloven tongues

Do hiss me into madness.

ENTER TRINCULO.

Lo, now, lo!
15 Here comes a spirit of his, and to torment me
For bringing wood in slowly. I'll fall flat;
Perchance he will not mind me.

TRIN. Here's neither bush nor shrub, to bear off any
weather at all, and another storm brewing; I hear
it sing i' 20 the wind: yond same black cloud, yond
huge one, looks like a foul bombard that would
shed his liquor. If it should thunder as it did before, I know not where to hide my head: yond
same cloud cannot choose but fall by pailfuls.
What have we here? a man or a fish? dead or
alive? A fish: he 25 smells like a fish; a very ancient
and fish-like smell; a kind of not of the newest
Poor-John. A strange fish! Were I in England now,
as once I was, and had but this fish painted, not a
holiday fool there but would give a piece of silver:
there would this monster make a man; any strange
30 beast there makes a man: when they will not
give a doit to relieve a lame beggar, they will lay
out ten to see a dead Indian. Legged like a man!
and his fins like arms! Warm o' my troth! I do now
let loose my opinion; hold it no longer: this is no
fish, but an islander, that hath lately suffered 35 by
a thunderbolt. [*Thunder.*] Alas, the storm is come
again! my best way is to creep under his gaberdine; there is no other shelter hereabout: misery
acquaints a man with strange bed-fellows. I will
here shroud till the dregs of the storm be past.

Enter STEPHANO, *singing: a bottle in his hand.*

40 STE. I shall no more to sea, to sea,
Here shall I die a-shore,—
This is a very scurvy tune to sing at a man's funeral:
well, here's my comfort. *Drinks.*
Sings. The master, the swabber, the boatswain, and I,
45 The gunner, and his mate,
Loved Mall, Meg, and Marian, and Margery,

But none of us cared for Kate;
For she had a tongue with a tang,
Would cry to a sailor, Go hang!
₅₀ She loved not the savour of tar nor of pitch;
Yet a tailor might scratch her where'er she did itch.
Then, to sea, boys, and let her go hang!
This is a scurvy tune too: but here's my comfort.
    Drinks.

CAL. Do not torment me:—O!

₅₅ *STE.* What's the matter? Have we devils here? Do
    you put tricks upon 's with savages and men of
    Ind, ha? I have not scaped drowning, to be afeard
    now of your four legs; for it hath been said, As
    proper a man as ever went on four legs cannot
    make him give ground; and it shall be ₆₀ said so
    again, while Stephano breathes at's nostrils.

CAL. The spirit torments me:—O!

STE. This is some monster of the isle with four legs,
    who hath got, as I take it, an ague. Where the devil
    should he learn our language? I will give him
    some relief, if it be ₆₅ but for that. If I can recover
    him, and keep him tame, and get to Naples with
    him, he's a present for any emperor that ever trod
    on neat's-leather.

CAL. Do not torment me, prithee; I'll bring my wood
    home faster.

₇₀ *STE.* He's in his fit now, and does not talk after the
    wisest. He shall taste of my bottle: if he have never
    drunk wine afore, it will go near to remove his fit.
    If I can recover him, and keep him tame, I will not
    take too much for him; he shall pay for him that
    hath him, and that soundly.

₇₅ *CAL.* Thou dost me yet but little hurt; thou wilt
    anon, I know it by thy trembling: now Prosper
    works upon thee.

STE. Come on your ways; open your mouth; here is
    that which will give language to you, cat: open
    your mouth; this will shake your shaking, I can
    tell you, and that soundly: ₈₀ you cannot tell who's
    your friend: open your chaps again.

TRIN. I should know that voice: it should be—but he
    is drowned; and these are devils:—O defend me!

STE. Four legs and two voices,—a most delicate monster! His forward voice, now, is to speak well of his friend; 85 his backward voice is to utter foul speeches and to detract. If all the wine in my bottle will recover him, I will help his ague. Come: —Amen! I will pour some in thy other mouth.

TRIN. Stephano!

90 *STE.* Doth thy other mouth call me? Mercy, mercy! This is a devil, and no monster: I will leave him; I have no long spoon.

TRIN. Stephano! If thou beest Stephano, touch me, and speak to me; for I am Trinculo,—be not afeard, —thy 95 good friend Trinculo.

STE. If thou beest Trinculo, come forth: I'll pull thee by the lesser legs: if any be Trinculo's legs, these are they. Thou art very Trinculo indeed! How earnest thou to be the siege of this moon-calf? can he vent Trinculos?

100 *TRIN.* I took him to be killed with a thunder-stroke. But art thou not drowned, Stephano? I hope, now, thou art not drowned. Is the storm overblown? I hid me under the dead moon-calf's gaberdine for fear of the storm. And art thou living, Stephano? O Stephano, two Neapolitans 105 scaped!

STE. Prithee, do not turn me about; my stomach is not constant.

CAL. [*aside*] These be fine things, an if they be not sprites. That's a brave god, and bears celestial liquor: 110 I will kneel to him.

STE. How didst thou 'scape? How camest thou hither? swear, by this bottle, how thou camest hither. I escaped upon a butt of sack, which the sailors heaved o'erboard, by this bottle! which I made of the bark of a tree with mine 115 own hands, since I was cast ashore.

CAL. I'll swear, upon that bottle, to be thy true subject; for the liquor is not earthly.

STE. Here; swear, then, how thou escapedst.

TRIN. Swum ashore, man, like a duck: I can swim 120 like a duck, I'll be sworn.

STE. Here, kiss the book. Though thou canst swim like a duck, thou art made like a goose.

TRIN. O Stephano, hast any more of this?

STE. The whole butt, man: my cellar is in a rock by 125
the sea-side, where my wine is hid. How now,
moon-calf! how does thine ague?

CAL. Hast thou not dropp'd from heaven?

STE. Out o' the moon, I do assure thee: I was the man
i' the moon when time was.

130 CAL. I have seen thee in her, and I do adore thee:
My mistress show'd me thee, and thy dog, and thy
bush.

STE. Come, swear to that; kiss the book: I will furnish
it anon with new contents: swear.

TRIN. By this good light, this is a very shallow monster! 135 I afeard of him! A very weak monster! The
man i' the moon! A most poor credulous monster!
Well drawn, monster, in good sooth!

CAL. I'll show thee every fertile inch o' th' island;
And I will kiss thy foot: I prithee, be my god.

140 TRIN. By this light, a most perfidious and drunken
monster! when 's god's asleep, he'll rob his bottle.

CAL. I'll kiss thy foot; I'll swear myself thy subject.

STE. Come on, then; down, and swear.

TRIN. I shall laugh myself to death at this puppy-
headed monster. A most scurvy monster! I could
find in 145 my heart to beat him,—

STE. Come, kiss.

TRIN. But that the poor monster's in drink: an abom-
inable monster!

150 CAL. I'll show thee the best springs; I'll pluck thee
berries;
I'll fish for thee, and get thee wood enough.
A plague upon the tyrant that I serve!
I'll bear him no more sticks, but follow thee,
Thou wondrous man.

TRIN. A most ridiculous monster, to make a wonder
155 of a poor drunkard!

CAL. I prithee, let me bring thee where crabs grow;
And I with my long nails will dig thee pig-nuts;
Show thee a jay's nest, and instruct thee how
160 To snare the nimble marmoset; I'll bring thee
To clustering filberts, and sometimes I'll get thee
Young scamels from the rock. Wilt thou go with me?

STE. I prithee now, lead the way, without any more
talking. Trinculo, the king and all our company

else being drowned, ₁₆₅ we will inherit here: here;
bear my bottle: fellow Trinculo, we'll fill him by
and by again.

CAL. sings drunkenly.] Farewell, master; farewell,
farewell!

TRIN. A howling monster; a drunken monster!

CAL. No more dams I'll make for fish;

₁₇₀ Nor fetch in firing

At requiring;

Nor scrape trencher, nor wash dish:

'Ban, 'Ban, Cacaliban

Has a new master:—get a new man.

₁₇₅ Freedom, hey-day! hey-day, freedom! freedom,
hey-day, freedom!

STE. O brave monster! Lead the way. *Exeunt.*

ACT III

SCENE I. BEFORE PROSPERO'S CELL.

Enter FERDINAND, bearing a log.

FER. There be some sports are painful, and their labour
Delight in them sets off: some kinds of baseness
Are nobly undergone, and most poor matters
Point to rich ends. This my mean task
5 Would be as heavy to me as odious, but
The mistress which I serve quickens what's dead,
And makes my labours pleasures: O, she is
Ten times more gentle than her father's crabbed.
And he's composed of harshness. I must remove
10 Some thousands of these logs, and pile them up,
Upon a sore injunction: my sweet mistress
Weeps when she sees me work, and says, such baseness
Had never like executor. I forget:
But these sweet thoughts do even refresh my labours,
Most busy lest, when I do it.

Enter MIRANDA; and PROSPERO at a distance, unseen.

MIR. 15 Alas, now, pray you,
Work not so hard: I would the lightning had
Burnt up those logs that you are enjoin'd to pile!

355

Pray, set it down, and rest you: when this burns,
'Twill weep for having wearied you. My father
₂₀ Is hard at study; pray, now, rest yourself;
He's safe for these three hours.

Fer. O most dear mistress,
The sun will set before I shall discharge
What I must strive to do.

Mir. If you'll sit down,
I'll bear your logs the while: pray, give me that;
I'll carry it to the pile.

Fer. ₂₅ No, precious creature;
I had rather crack my sinews, break my back,
Than you should such dishonour undergo,
While I sit lazy by.

Mir. It would become me
As well as it does you: and I should do it
₃₀ With much more ease; for my good will is to it,
And yours it is against.

Pros. Poor worm, thou art infected!
This visitation shows it.

Mir. You look wearily.

Fer. No, noble mistress; 'tis fresh morning with me
When you are by at night. I do beseech you,—
₃₅ Chiefly that I might set it in my prayers,—
What is your name?

Mir. Miranda.—O my father,
I have broke your hest to say so!

Fer. Admired Miranda!
Indeed the top of admiration! worth
What's dearest to the world! Full many a lady
₄₀ I have eyed with best regard, and many a time
The harmony of their tongues hath into bondage
Brought my too diligent ear: for several virtues
Have I liked several women; never any
With so full soul, but some defect in her
₄₅ Did quarrel with the noblest grace she owed,
And put it to the foil: but you, O you,
So perfect and so peerless, are created
Of every creature's best!

Mir. I do not know
One of my sex; no woman's face remember,
₅₀ Save, from my glass, mine own; nor have I seen
More that I may call men than you, good friend,

And my dear father: how features are abroad,
I am skilless of; but, by my modesty,
The jewel in my dower, I would not wish
55 Any companion in the world but you;
Nor can imagination form a shape,
Besides yourself, to like of. But I prattle
Something too wildly, and my father's precepts
I therein do forget.

Fer. I am, in my condition,
60 A prince, Miranda; I do think, a king;
I would, not so!—and would no more endure
This wooden slavery than to suffer
The flesh-fly blow my mouth. Hear my soul speak:
The very instant that I saw you, did
65 My heart fly to your service; there resides,
To make me slave to it; and for your sake
Am I this patient log-man.

Mir. Do you love me?

Fer. O heaven, O earth, bear witness to this sound,
And crown what I profess with kind event,
70 If I speak true! if hollowly, invert
What best is boded me to mischief! I,
Beyond all limit of what else i' the world,
Do love, prize, honour you.

Mir. I am a fool
To weep at what I am glad of.

Pros. Fair encounter
75 Of two most rare affections! Heavens rain grace
On that which breeds between 'em!

Fer. Wherefore weep you?

Mir. At mine unworthiness, that dare not offer
What I desire to give; and much less take
What I shall die to want. But this is trifling;
80 And all the more it seeks to hide itself,
The bigger bulk it shows. Hence, bashful cunning!
And prompt me, plain and holy innocence!
I am your wife, if you will marry me;
If not, I'll die your maid: to be your fellow
85 You may deny me; but I'll be your servant,
Whether you will or no.

Fer. My mistress, dearest;
And I thus humble ever.

Mir. My husband, then?

Fer. Ay, with a heart as willing
As bondage e'er of freedom: here's my hand.
90 *Mir.* And mine, with my heart in't: and now
farewell
Till half an hour hence.
Fer. A thousand thousand!

Exeunt FER. *and* MIR. *severally.*

Pros. So glad of this as they I cannot be,
Who are surprised withal; but my rejoicing
At nothing can be more. I'll to my book;
95 For yet, ere supper-time, must I perform
Much business appertaining. *Exit.*

SCENE II. ANOTHER PART OF THE ISLAND.

Enter CALIBAN, STEPHANO, *AND* TRINCULO.

Ste. Tell not me;—when the butt is out, we will drink
water; not a drop before: therefore bear up, and
board 'em. Servant-monster, drink to me.
Trin. Servant-monster! the folly of this island! They 5
say there's but five upon this isle: we are three of
them; if th' other two be brained like us, the state
totters.
Ste. Drink, servant-monster, when I bid thee: thy eyes
are almost set in thy head.
Trin. Where should they be set else? he were a
brave 10 monster indeed, if they were set in his
tail.
Ste. My man-monster hath drowned his tongue in
sack: for my part, the sea cannot drown me; I
swam, ere I could recover the shore, five-and-
thirty leagues off and on. By this light, thou shalt
be my lieutenant, monster, or my 15 standard.
Trin. Your lieutenant, if you list; he's no standard.
Ste. We'll not run, Monsieur Monster.
Trin. Nor go neither; but you'll lie, like dogs, and yet
say nothing neither.
20 *Ste.* Moon-calf, speak once in thy life, if thou beest
a good moon-calf.

CAL. How does thy honour? Let me lick thy shoe. I'll
not serve him, he is not valiant.
TRIN. Thou liest, most ignorant monster: I am in case
25 to justle a constable. Why, thou debauched fish,
thou, was there ever man a coward that hath
drunk so much sack as I to-day? Wilt thou tell a
monstrous lie, being but half a fish and half a
monster?
CAL. Lo, how he mocks me! wilt thou let him, my
lord?
30 TRIN. 'Lord,' quoth he! That a monster should be
such a natural!
CAL. Lo, lo, again! bite him to death, I prithee.
STE. Trinculo, keep a good tongue in your head: if you
prove a mutineer,—the next tree! The poor monster's my 35 subject, and he shall not suffer in-
dignity.
CAL. I thank my noble lord. Wilt thou be pleased to
hearken once again to the suit I made to thee?
STE. Marry, will I: kneel and repeat it; I will stand, and
so shall Trinculo.

Enter ARIEL, invisible.

40 CAL. As I told thee before, I am subject to a tyrant, a
sorcerer, that by his cunning hath cheated me of
the island.
ARI. Thou liest.
CAL. Thou liest, thou jesting monkey, thou:
I would my valiant master would destroy thee!
I do not lie.
45 STE. Trinculo, if you trouble him any more in's tale,
by this hand, I will supplant some of your teeth.
TRIN. Why, I said nothing.
STE. Mum, then, and no more. Proceed.
CAL. I say, by sorcery he got this isle;
50 From me he got it. If thy greatness will
Revenge it on him,—for I know thou darest,
But this thing dare not,—
STE. That's most certain.
CAL. Thou shalt be lord of it, and I'll serve thee.
55 STE. How now shall this be compassed? Canst thou
bring me to the party?

Cal. Yea, yea, my lord: I'll yield him thee asleep,
Where thou mayst knock a nail into his head.
Ari. Thou liest; thou canst not.
60 *Cal.* What a pied ninny's this! Thou scurvy patch!
I do beseech thy Greatness, give him blows,
And take his bottle from him: when that's gone,
He shall drink nought but brine; for I'll not show him
Where the quick freshes are.
65 *Ste.* Trinculo, run into no further danger: interrupt
the monster one word further, and, by this hand,
I'll turn my mercy out o' doors, and make a stock-
fish of thee.
Trin. Why, what did I? I did nothing. I'll go farther
off.
70 *Ste.* Didst thou not say he lied?
Ari. Thou liest.
Ste. Do I so? take thou that. [*Beats him.*] As you like
this, give me the lie another time.
Trin. I did not give the lie. Out o' your wits, and 75
hearing too? A pox o' your bottle! this can sack
and drinking do. A murrain on your monster, and
the devil take your fingers!
Cal. Ha, ha, ha!
Ste. Now, forward with your tale.—Prithee, stand far-
ther 80 off.
Cal. Beat him enough: after a little time, I'll beat
him too.
Ste. Stand farther. Come, proceed.
Cal. Why, as I told thee, 'tis a custom with him
I' th' afternoon to sleep: there thou mayst brain him,
85 Having first seized his books; or with a log
Batter his skull, or paunch him with a stake,
Or cut his wezand with thy knife. Remember
First to possess his books; for without them
He's but a sot, as I am, nor hath not
90 One spirit to command: they all do hate him
As rootedly as I. Burn but his books.
He has brave utensils,—for so he calls them,—
Which, when he has a house, he'll deck withal.
And that most deeply to consider is
95 The beauty of his daughter; he himself
Calls her a nonpareil: I never saw a woman,
But only Sycorax my dam and she;

But she as far surpasseth Sycorax
As great'st does least.

Ste. Is it so brave a lass?

100 *Cal.* Ay, lord; she will become thy bed, I warrant,
And bring thee forth brave brood.

Ste. Monster, I will kill this man: his daughter and I
will be king and queen,—save our Graces!—and
Trinculo and thyself shall be viceroys. Dost thou
like the plot, 105 Trinculo?

Trin. Excellent.

Ste. Give me thy hand: I am sorry I beat thee; but,
while thou livest, keep a good tongue in thy head.

Cal. Within this half hour will he be asleep:
Wilt thou destroy him then?

Ste. 110 Ay, on mine honour.

Ari. This will I tell my master.

Cal. Thou makest me merry; I am full of pleasure:
Let us be jocund: will you troll the catch
You taught me but while-ere?

115 *Ste.* At thy request, monster, I will do reason, any
reason. —Come on. Trinculo, let us sing. *Sings.*

Flout 'em and scout 'em, and scout 'em and flout 'em;
Thought is free.

Cal. That's not the tune.

Ariel plays the tune on a tabor and pipe.

120 *Ste.* What is this same?

Trin. This is the tune of our catch, played by the picture of Nobody.

Ste. If thou beest a man, show thyself in thy likeness:
if thou beest a devil, take't as thou list.

125 *Trin.* O, forgive me my sins!

Ste. He that dies pays all debts: I defy thee. Mercy
upon us!

Cal. Art thou afeard?

Ste. No, monster, not I.

130 *Cal.* Be not afeard; the isle is full of noises,
Sounds and sweet airs, that give delight, and
hurt not.
Sometimes a thousand twangling instruments
Will hum about mine ears; and sometime voices,
That, if I then had waked after long sleep,

135 Will make me sleep again: and then, in dreaming,
The clouds methought would open, and show riches
Ready to drop upon me; that, when I waked,
I cried to dream again.
Ste. This will prove a brave kingdom to me, where I
140 shall have my music for nothing.
Cal. When Prospero is destroyed.
Ste. That shall be by and by: I remember the story.
Trin. The sound is going away; let's follow it, and
after do our work.
145 *Ste.* Lead, monster; we'll follow. I would I could
see this taborer; he lays it on.
Trin. Wilt come? I'll follow, Stephano. *Exeunt.*

SCENE III. ANOTHER PART OF THE ISLAND.

Enter Alonso, Sebastian, Antonio, Gonzalo, Adrian,
Francisco, *and others.*

Gon. By'r lakin, I can go no further, sir;
My old bones ache: here's a maze trod, indeed,
Through forth-rights and meanders! By your patience,
I needs must rest me.
Alon. Old lord, I cannot blame thee,
5 Who am myself attach'd with weariness,
To the dulling of my spirits: sit down, and rest.
Even here I will put off my hope, and keep it
No longer for my flatterer: he is drown'd
Whom thus we stray to find; and the sea mocks
10 Our frustrate search on land. Well, let him go.
Ant. [*Aside to Seb.*] I am right glad that he's so out of
hope.
Do not, for one repulse, forego the purpose
That you resolved to effect.
Seb. [*Aside to Ant.*]
The next advantage
Will we take throughly.
Ant. [*Aside to Seb.*]
Let it be to-night;
15 For, now they are oppress'd with travel, they
Will not, nor cannot, use such vigilance

As when they are fresh.
SEB. [*Aside to Ant.*]
I say, to-night: no more.

Solemn and strange music.

ALON. What harmony is this?—My good friends,
    hark!
GON. Marvellous sweet music!
Enter PROSPERO *above, invisible. Enter several strange*
    Shapes, bringing in a banquet: they dance about it with
    gentle actions of salutation; and, inviting the King, &c.
    to eat, they depart.
20 *ALON.* Give us kind keepers, heavens!—What were
    these?
SEB. A living drollery. Now I will believe
That there are unicorns; that in Arabia
There is one tree, the phœnix' throne; one phœnix
At this hour reigning there.
ANT. I'll believe both;
25 And what does else want credit, come to me,
And I'll be sworn 'tis true: travellers ne'er did lie,
Though fools at home condemn 'em.
GON. If in Naples
I should report this now, would they believe me?
If I should say, I saw such islanders,—
30 For, certes, these are people of the island,—
Who, though they are of monstrous shape, yet, note,
Their manners are more gentle-kind than of
Our human generation you shall find
Many, nay, almost any.
PROS. [*Aside*] Honest lord,
35 Thou hast said well; for some of you there present
Are worse than devils.
ALON. I cannot too much muse
Such shapes, such gesture, and such sound, ex-
    pressing—
Although they want the use of tongue—a kind
Of excellent dumb discourse.
PROS. [*Aside*] Praise in departing.
FRAN. They vanish'd strangely.
SEB. 40 No matter, since

They have left their viands behind; for we have
    stomachs.—
Will't please you taste of what is here?
Alon. Not I.
Gon. Faith, sir, you need not fear. When we were
    boys,
Who would believe that there were mountaineers
45 Dew-lapp'd like bulls, whose throats had hanging
    at 'em
Wallets of flesh? or that there were such men
Whose heads stood in their breasts? which now
    we find
Each putter-out of five for one will bring us
Good warrant of.
Alon. I will stand to, and feed,
50 Although my last: no matter, since I feel
The best is past. Brother, my lord the duke,
Stand to, and do as we.

*Thunder and lightning. Enter ARIEL, like a harpy; claps his wings
upon the table; and, with a quaint device, the banquet vanishes.*

Ari. You are three men of sin, whom Destiny,—
That hath to instrument this lower world
55 And what is in't,—the never-surfeited sea
Hath caused to belch up you; and on this island,
Where man doth not inhabit,—you 'mongst men
Being most unfit to live. I have made you mad;
And even with such-like valour men hang and drown
Their proper selves. *ALON., SEB. &c. draw their swords.*
60 You fools! I and my fellows
Are ministers of Fate: the elements,
Of whom your swords are temper'd, may as well
Wound the loud winds, or with bemock'd-at stabs
Kill the still-closing waters, as diminish
65 One dowle that's in my plume: my fellow-ministers
Are like invulnerable. If you could hurt,
Your swords are now too massy for your strengths,
And will not be uplifted. But remember,—
For that's my business to you,—that you three
70 From Milan did supplant good Prospero;
Exposed unto the sea, which hath requit it,
Him and his innocent child: for which foul deed

The powers, delaying, not forgetting, have
Incensed the seas and shores, yea, all the creatures,
₇₅ Against your peace. Thee of thy son, Alonso,
They have bereft; and do pronounce by me:
Lingering perdition—worse than any death
Can be at once—shall step by step attend
You and your ways; whose wraths to guard you from,
—
₈₀ Which here, in this most desolate isle, else falls
Upon your heads,—is nothing but heart-sorrow
And a clear life ensuing.

*He vanishes in thunder; then, to soft music, enter the Shapes
again, and dance, with mocks and mows, and carrying out the
table.*

PROS. Bravely the figure of this harpy hast thou
Perform'd, my Ariel; a grace it had, devouring:
₈₅ Of my instruction hast thou nothing bated
In what thou hadst to say: so, with good life
And observation strange, my meaner ministers
Their several kinds have done. My high charms work,
And these mine enemies are all knit up
₉₀ In their distractions: they now are in my power;
And in these fits I leave them, while I visit
Young Ferdinand,—whom they suppose is drown'd,
—
And his and mine loved darling. *Exit above.*
GON. I' the name of something holy, sir, why
    stand you
In this strange stare?
ALON. ₉₅ O, it is monstrous, monstrous!
Methought the billows spoke, and told me of it;
The winds did sing it to me; and the thunder,
That deep and dreadful organ-pipe, pronounced
The name of Prosper: it did bass my trespass.
₁₀₀ Therefore my son i' th' ooze is bedded; and
I'll seek him deeper than e'er plummet sounded,
And with him there lie mudded. *Exit.*
SEB. But one fiend at a time,
I'll fight their legions o'er.
ANT. I'll be thy second.

Exeunt SEB. *and* ANT.

GON. All three of them are desperate: their great guilt,
105 Like poison given to work a great time after,
Now 'gins to bite the spirits. I do beseech you,
That are of suppler joints, follow them swiftly,
And hinder them from what this ecstasy
May now provoke them to.
ADR. Follow, I pray you. *Exeunt.*

ACT IV

SCENE I. BEFORE PROSPERO'S CELL.

ENTER PROSPERO, FERDINAND, *AND* MIRANDA.

PROS. If I have too austerely punish'd you,
Your compensation makes amends; for I
Have given you here a third of mine own life,
Or that for which I live; who once again
5 I tender to thy hand: all thy vexations
Were but my trials of thy love, and thou
Hast strangely stood the test: here, afore Heaven,
I ratify this my rich gift. O Ferdinand,
Do not smile at me that I boast her off,
10 For thou shalt find she will outstrip all praise,
And make it halt behind her.
FER. I do believe it
Against an oracle.
PROS. Then, as my gift, and thine own acquisition
Worthily purchased, take my daughter: but
15 If thou dost break her virgin-knot before
All sanctimonious ceremonies may
With full and holy rite be minister'd,
No sweet aspersion shall the heavens let fall
To make this contract grow; but barren hate,
20 Sour-eyed disdain and discord shall bestrew
The union of your bed with weeds so loathly
That you shall hate it both: therefore take heed,

As Hymen's lamps shall light you.

FER. As I hope
For quiet days, fair issue and long life,
25 With such love as 'tis now, the murkiest den,
The most opportune place, the strong'st suggestion
Our worser Genius can, shall never melt
Mine honour into lust, to take away
The edge of that day's celebration
30 When I shall think, or Phœbus' steeds are
    founder'd,
Or Night kept chain'd below.

PROS. Fairly spoke.
Sit, then, and talk with her; she is thine own.
What, Ariel! my industrious servant, Ariel!

Enter ARIEL.

ARI. What would my potent master? here I am.
35 *PROS.* Thou and thy meaner fellows your last
    service
Did worthily perform; and I must use you
In such another trick. Go bring the rabble,
O'er whom I give thee power, here to this place:
Incite them to quick motion; for I must
40 Bestow upon the eyes of this young couple
Some vanity of mine art: it is my promise,
And they expect it from me.

ARI. Presently?

PROS. Ay, with a twink.

ARI. Before you can say, 'come,' and 'go,'
45 And breathe twice, and cry, 'so, so,'
Each one, tripping on his toe,
Will be here with mop and mow.
Do you love me, master? no?

PROS. Dearly, my delicate Ariel. Do not approach
Till thou dost hear me call.

ARI. 50 Well, I conceive. *Exit.*

PROS. Look thou be true; do not give dalliance
Too much the rein: the strongest oaths are straw
To the fire i' the blood: be more abstemious,
Or else, good night your vow!

FER. I warrant you, sir;
55 The white cold virgin snow upon my heart

Abates the ardour of my liver.
Pros. Well.
Now come, my Ariel! bring a corollary,
Rather than want a spirit: appear, and pertly!
No tongue! all eyes! be silent. *Soft music.*

Enter IRIS.

60 *IRIS.* Ceres, most bounteous lady, thy rich leas
Of wheat, rye, barley, vetches, oats, and pease;
Thy turfy mountains, where live nibbling sheep,
And flat meads thatch'd with stover, them to keep;
Thy banks with pioned and twilled brims,
65 Which spongy April at thy best betrims,
To make cold nymphs chaste crowns; and thy broom-
groves,
Whose shadow the dismissed bachelor loves,
Being lass-lorn; thy pole-clipt vineyard;
And thy sea-marge, sterile and rocky-hard,
70 Where thou thyself dost air;—the queen o' the sky,
Whose watery arch and messenger am I,
Bids thee leave these; and with her sovereign grace,
Here on this grass-plot, in this very place,
To come and sport:—her peacocks fly amain:
75 Approach, rich Ceres, her to entertain.

Enter CERES.

CER. Hail, many-colour'd messenger, that ne'er
Dost disobey the wife of Jupiter;
Who, with thy saffron wings, upon my flowers
Diffusest honey-drops, refreshing showers;
80 And with each end of thy blue bow dost crown
My bosky acres and my unshrubb'd down,
Rich scarf to my proud earth;—why hath thy queen
Summon'd me hither, to this short-grass'd green?
IRIS. A contract of true love to celebrate;
85 And some donation freely to estate
On the blest lovers.
CER. Tell me, heavenly bow,
If Venus or her son, as thou dost know,
Do now attend the queen? Since they did plot
The means that dusky Dis my daughter got,

90 Her and her blind boy's scandal'd company
I have forsworn.
IRIS. Of her society
Be not afraid: I met her Deity
Cutting the clouds towards Paphos, and her son
Dove-drawn with her. Here thought they to
    have done
95 Some wanton charm upon this man and maid,
Whose vows are, that no bed-right shall be paid
Till Hymen's torch be lighted: but in vain;
Mars's hot minion is returned again;
Her waspish-headed son has broke his arrows,
100 Swears he will shoot no more, but play with
    sparrows,
And be a boy right out.
CER. High'st queen of state,
Great Juno, comes; I know her by her gait.

Enter JUNO.

JUNO. How does my bounteous sister? Go with me
To bless this twain, that they may prosperous be,
105 And honour'd in their issue. *They sing:*
JUNO. Honour, riches, marriage-blessing,
Long continuance, and increasing,
Hourly joys be still upon you!
Juno sings her blessings on you.
110 *CER.* Earth's increase, foison plenty,
Barns and garners never empty;
Vines with clustering bunches growing;
Plants with goodly burthen bowing;
Spring come to you at the farthest
115 In the very end of harvest!
Scarcity and want shall shun you;
Ceres' blessing so is on you.
FER. This is a most majestic vision, and
Harmonious charmingly. May I be bold
To think these spirits?
PROS. 120 Spirits, which by mine art
I have from their confines call'd to enact
My present fancies.
FER. Let me live here ever;
So rare a wonder'd father and a wife

Makes this place Paradise.
Juno and Ceres whisper, and send Iris on employment.
PROS. Sweet, now, silence!
125 Juno and Ceres whisper seriously;
There's something else to do: hush, and be mute,
Or else our spell is marr'd.
IRIS. You nymphs, call'd Naiads, of the windring
       brooks,
With your sedged crowns and ever-harmless looks,
130 Leave your crisp channels, and on this green land
Answer your summons; Juno does command:
Come, temperate nymphs, and help to celebrate
A contract of true love; be not too late.

Enter certain Nymphs.

You sunburnt sicklemen, of August weary,
135 Come hither from the furrow, and be merry:
Make holiday; your rye-straw hats put on,
And these fresh nymphs encounter every one
In country footing.
*Enter certain Reapers, properly habited: they join with the
       Nymphs in a graceful dance; towards the end whereof
       PROSPERO starts suddenly, and speaks; after which, to a
       strange, hollow, and confused noise, they heavily
       vanish.*
PROS. [*Aside*] I had forgot that foul conspiracy
140 Of the beast Caliban and his confederates
Against my life: the minute of their plot
Is almost come. [*To the Spirits.*] Well done! avoid; no
       more!
FER. This is strange: your father's in some passion
That works him strongly.
MIR. Never till this day
145 Saw I him touch'd with anger so distemper'd.
PROS. You do look, my son, in a moved sort,
As if you were dismay'd: be cheerful, sir.
Our revels now are ended. These our actors,
As I foretold you, were all spirits, and
150 Are melted into air, into thin air:
And, like the baseless fabric of this vision,
The cloud-capp'd towers, the gorgeous palaces,
The solemn temples, the great globe itself,

Yea, all which it inherit, shall dissolve,
155 And, like this insubstantial pageant faded,
Leave not a rack behind. We are such stuff
As dreams are made on; and our little life
Is rounded with a sleep. Sir, I am vex'd;
Bear with my weakness; my old brain is troubled:
160 Be not disturb'd with my infirmity:
If you be pleased, retire into my cell,
And there repose: a turn or two I'll walk,
To still my beating mind.
Fer. & Mir.
We wish your peace. *Exeunt.*
Pros. Come with a thought. I thank thee, Ariel: come.

Enter Ariel.

165 *Ari.* Thy thoughts I cleave to. What's thy
      pleasure?
Pros. Spirit,
We must prepare to meet with Caliban.
Ari. Ay, my commander: when I presented Ceres,
I thought to have told thee of it; but I fear'd
Lest I might anger thee.
170 *Pros.* Say again, where didst thou leave these
      varlets?
Ari. I told you, sir, they were red-hot with drinking;
So full of valour that they smote the air
For breathing in their faces; beat the ground
For kissing of their feet; yet always bending
175 Towards their project. Then I beat my tabor;
At which, like unback'd colts, they prick'd their ears,
Advanced their eyelids, lifted up their noses
As they smelt music: so I charm'd their ears,
That, calf-like, they my lowing follow'd through
180 Tooth'd briers, sharp furzes, pricking goss, and
      thorns,
Which enter'd their frail shins: at last I left them
I' the filthy-mantled pool beyond your cell,
There dancing up to the chins, that the foul lake
O'erstunk their feet.
Pros. This was well done, my bird.
185 Thy shape invisible retain thou still:
The trumpery in my house, go bring it hither,

For stale to catch these thieves.
ARI. I go, I go. *Exit.*
PROS. A devil, a born devil, on whose nature
Nurture can never stick; on whom my pains,
190 Humanely taken, all, all lost, quite lost;
And as with age his body uglier grows,
So his mind cankers. I will plague them all,
Even to roaring.

Re-enter ARIEL, loaden with glistering apparel, &c.

Come, hang them on this line.

PROSPERO and ARIEL remain, invisible. Enter CALIBAN,
STEPHANO, and TRINCULO, all wet.

CAL. Pray you, tread softly, that the blind mole
may not
195 Hear a foot fall: we now are near his cell.
STE. Monster, your fairy, which you say is a harmless
fairy, has done little better than played the Jack
with us.
TRIN. Monster, I do smell all horse-piss; at which my
nose is in great indignation.
200 *STE.* So is mine. Do you hear, monster? If I should
take a displeasure against you, look you,—
TRIN. Thou wert but a lost monster.
CAL. Good my lord, give me thy favour still.
Be patient, for the prize I'll bring thee to
205 Shall hoodwink this mischance: therefore speak
softly.
All's hush'd as midnight yet.
TRIN. Ay, but to lose our bottles in the pool,—
STE. There is not only disgrace and dishonour in that,
monster, but an infinite loss.
210 *TRIN.* That's more to me than my wetting: yet this
is your harmless fairy, monster.
STE. I will fetch off my bottle, though I be o'er ears for
my labour.
CAL. Prithee, my king, be quiet. See'st thou here,
215 This is the mouth o' the cell: no noise, and enter.
Do that good mischief which may make this island
Thine own for ever, and I, thy Caliban,

For aye thy foot-licker.

STE. Give me thy hand. I do begin to have bloody _220_ thoughts.

TRIN. O King Stephano! O peer! O worthy Stephano! look what a wardrobe here is for thee!

CAL. Let it alone, thou fool; it is but trash.

TRIN. O, ho, monster! we know what belongs to a frippery. _225_ O King Stephano!

STE. Put off that gown, Trinculo; by this hand, I'll have that gown.

TRIN. Thy Grace shall have it.

CAL. The dropsy drown this fool! what do you mean _230_ To dote thus on such luggage? Let's alone,
And do the murder first: if he awake,
From toe to crown he'll fill our skins with pinches,
Make us strange stuff.

STE. Be you quiet, monster. Mistress line, is not this _235_ my jerkin? Now is the jerkin under the line: now, jerkin, you are like to lose your hair, and prove a bald jerkin.

TRIN. Do, do: we steal by line and level, an't like your Grace.

STE. I thank thee for that jest; here's a garment for't: _240_ wit shall not go unrewarded while I am king of this country. 'Steal by line and level' is an excellent pass of pate; there's another garment for't.

TRIN. Monster, come, put some lime upon your fingers, and away with the rest.

_245_ CAL. I will have none on't: we shall lose our time,
And all be turn'd to barnacles, or to apes
With foreheads villanous low.

STE. Monster, lay-to your fingers: help to bear this away where my hogshead of wine is, or I'll turn you out _250_ of my kingdom: go to, carry this.

TRIN. And this.

STE. Ay, and this.

A noise of hunters heard. Enter divers Spirits, in shape of dogs and hounds, and hunt them about, PROSPERO and ARIEL setting them on.

PROS. Hey, Mountain, hey!

ARI. Silver! there it goes, Silver!

_255_ PROS. Fury, fury! there, Tyrant, there! hark, hark!

C<small>AL</small>., S<small>TE</small>., and T<small>RIN</small>. are driven out.

Go charge my goblins that they grind their joints
With dry convulsions; shorten up their sinews
With aged cramps; and more pinch-spotted
   make them
Then pard or cat o' mountain.
A<small>RI</small>. Hark, they roar!
₂₆₀ *P<small>ROS</small>.* Let them be hunted soundly. At this hour
Lie at my mercy all mine enemies:
Shortly shall all my labours end, and thou
Shalt have the air at freedom: for a little
Follow, and do me service. *Exeunt.*

ACT V

SCENE I. BEFORE THE CELL OF PROSPERO.

Enter PROSPERO in his magic robes, and ARIEL.

PROS. Now does my project gather to a head:
My charms crack not; my spirits obey; and time
Goes upright with his carriage. How's the day?
ARI. On the sixth hour; at which time, my lord,
You said our work should cease.
PROS. ₅ I did say so,
When first I raised the tempest. Say, my spirit,
How fares the king and's followers?
ARI. Confined together
In the same fashion as you gave in charge,
Just as you left them; all prisoners, sir,
₁₀ In the line-grove which weather-fends your cell;
They cannot budge till your release. The king,
His brother, and yours, abide all three distracted,
And the remainder mourning over them,
Brimful of sorrow and dismay; but chiefly
₁₅ Him that you term'd, sir, "The good old lord,
      Gonzalo;"
His tears run down his beard, like winter's drops
From eaves of reeds. Your charm so strongly
      works 'em,
That if you now beheld them, your affections
Would become tender.

Pros. Dost thou think so, spirit?
Ari. Mine would, sir, were I human.
Pros. 20 And mine shall.
Hast thou, which art but air, a touch, a feeling
Of their afflictions, and shall not myself,
One of their kind, that relish all as sharply,
Passion as they, be kindlier moved than thou art?
25 Though with their high wrongs I am struck to the
    quick,
Yet with my nobler reason 'gainst my fury
Do I take part: the rarer action is
In virtue than in vengeance: they being penitent,
The sole drift of my purpose doth extend
30 Not a frown further. Go release them, Ariel:
My charms I'll break, their senses I'll restore,
And they shall be themselves.
Ari. I'll fetch them, sir. *Exit.*
Pros. Ye elves of hills, brooks, standing lakes, and
    groves;
And ye that on the sands with printless foot
35 Do chase the ebbing Neptune, and do fly him
When he comes back; you demi-puppets that
By moonshine do the green sour ringlets make,
Whereof the ewe not bites; and you whose pastime
Is to make midnight mushrooms, that rejoice
40 To hear the solemn curfew; by whose aid—
Weak masters though ye be—I have bedimm'd
The noontide sun, call'd forth the mutinous winds,
And 'twixt the green sea and the azured vault
Set roaring war: to the dread rattling thunder
45 Have I given fire, and rifted Jove's stout oak
With his own bolt; the strong-based promontory
Have I made shake, and by the spurs pluck'd up
The pine and cedar: graves at my command
Have waked their sleepers, oped, and let 'em forth
50 By my so potent art. But this rough magic
I here abjure; and, when I have required
Some heavenly music,—which even now I do,—
To work mine end upon their senses, that
This airy charm is for, I'll break my staff,
55 Bury it certain fathoms in the earth,
And deeper than did ever plummet sound
I'll drown my book. *Solemn music.*

Re-enter ARIEL *before: then* ALONSO, *with a frantic gesture, attended by* GONZALO; SEBASTIAN *and* ANTONIO *in like manner, attended by* ADRIAN *and* FRANCISCO: *they all enter the circle which* PROSPERO *had made, and there stand charmed; which* PROSPERO *observing, speaks:*

A solemn air, and the best comforter
To an unsettled fancy, cure thy brains,
60 Now useless, boil'd within thy skull! There stand,
For you are spell-stopp'd.
Holy Gonzalo, honourable man,
Mine eyes, even sociable to the show of thine,
Fall fellowly drops. The charm dissolves apace;
65 And as the morning steals upon the night,
Melting the darkness, so their rising senses
Begin to chase the ignorant fumes that mantle
Their clearer reason. O good Gonzalo,
My true preserver, and a loyal sir
70 To him thou follow'st! I will pay thy graces
Home both in word and deed. Most cruelly
Didst thou, Alonso, use me and my daughter:
Thy brother was a furtherer in the act.
Thou art pinch'd for't now, Sebastian. Flesh and
    blood,
75 You, brother mine, that entertain'd ambition,
Expell'd remorse and nature; who, with Sebastian,—
Whose inward pinches therefore are most strong,—
Would here have kill'd your king; I do forgive thee,
Unnatural though thou art. Their understanding
80 Begins to swell; and the approaching tide
Will shortly fill the reasonable shore,
That now lies foul and muddy. Not one of them
That yet looks on me, or would know me: Ariel,
Fetch me the hat and rapier in my cell:
85 I will discase me, and myself present
As I was sometime Milan: quickly, spirit;
Thou shalt ere long be free.

ARIEL sings and helps to attire him.

Where the bee sucks, there suck I:
In a cowslip's bell I lie;
90 There I couch when owls do cry.

On the bat's back I do fly
After summer merrily.
Merrily, merrily shall I live now
Under the blossom that hangs on the bough.

₉₅ *Pros.* Why, that's my dainty Ariel! I shall miss
thee;
But yet thou shalt have freedom: so, so, so.
To the king's ship, invisible as thou art:
There shalt thou find the mariners asleep
Under the hatches; the master and the boatswain
₁₀₀ Being awake, enforce them to this place,
And presently, I prithee.

Ari. I drink the air before me, and return
Or ere your pulse twice beat. *Exit.*

Gon. All torment, trouble, wonder and amazement
₁₀₅ Inhabits here: some heavenly power guide us
Out of this fearful country!

Pros. Behold, sir king,
The wronged Duke of Milan, Prospero:
For more assurance that a living prince
Does now speak to thee, I embrace thy body;
₁₁₀ And to thee and thy company I bid
A hearty welcome.

Alon. Whether thou be'st he or no,
Or some enchanted trifle to abuse me,
As late I have been, I not know: thy pulse
Beats, as of flesh and blood; and, since I saw
thee,
₁₁₅ The affliction of my mind amends, with which,
I fear, a madness held me: this must crave—
An if this be at all—a most strange story.
Thy dukedom I resign, and do entreat
Thou pardon me my wrongs.—But how should
Prospero
Be living and be here?

Pros. ₁₂₀ First, noble friend,
Let me embrace thine age, whose honour cannot
Be measured or confined.

Gon. Whether this be
Or be not, I'll not swear.

Pros. You do yet taste
Some subtilties o' the isle, that will not let you
₁₂₅ Believe things certain. Welcome, my friends all!

[*Aside to* SEB. *and* ANT.] But you, my brace of lords,
    were I so minded,
I here could pluck his Highness' frown upon you,
And justify you traitors: at this time
I will tell no tales.
SEB. [*Aside*]
The devil speaks in him.
PROS. No.
130 For you, most wicked sir, whom to call brother
Would even infect my mouth, I do forgive
Thy rankest fault,—all of them; and require
My dukedom of thee, which perforce, I know,
Thou must restore.
ALON. If thou be'st Prospero,
135 Give us particulars of thy preservation;
How thou hast met us here, who three hours since
Were wreck'd upon this shore; where I have lost—
How sharp the point of this remembrance is!—
My dear son Ferdinand.
PROS. I am woe for't, sir.
140 ALON. Irreparable is the loss; and patience
Says it is past her cure.
PROS. I rather think
You have not sought her help, of whose soft grace
For the like loss I have her sovereign aid,
And rest myself content.
ALON. You the like loss!
145 PROS. As great to me as late; and, supportable
To make the dear loss, have I means much weaker
Than you may call to comfort you, for I
Have lost my daughter.
ALON. A daughter?
O heavens, that they were living both in Naples,
150 The king and queen there! that they were, I wish
Myself were mudded in that oozy bed
Where my son lies. When did you lose you daughter?
PROS. In this last tempest. I perceive, these lords
At this encounter do so much admire,
155 That they devour their reason, and scarce think
Their eyes do offices of truth, their words
Are natural breath: but, howsoe'er you have
Been justled from your senses, know for certain
That I am Prospero, and that very duke

160 Which was thrust forth of Milan; who most
    strangely
Upon this shore, where you were wreck'd, was
    landed,
To be the Lord on't. No more yet of this;
For 'tis a chronicle of day by day,
Not a relation for a breakfast, nor
165 Befitting this first meeting. Welcome, sir;
This cell's my court: here have I few attendants,
And subjects none abroad: pray you, look in.
My dukedom since you have given me again,
I will requite you with as good a thing;
170 At least bring forth a wonder, to content ye
As much as me my dukedom.

Here Prospero discovers FERDINAND *and* MIRANDA *playing at
chess.*

MIR. Sweet lord, you play me false.
FER. No, my dear'st love,
I would not for the world.
MIR. Yes, for a score of kingdoms you should
    wrangle,
And I would call it fair play.
ALON. 175 If this prove
A vision of the island, one dear son
Shall I twice lose.
SEB. A most high miracle!
FER. Though the seas threaten, they are merciful;
I have cursed them without cause. *Kneels.*
ALON. Now all the blessings
180 Of a glad father compass thee about!
Arise, and say how thou camest here.
MIR. O, wonder!
How many goodly creatures are there here!
How beauteous mankind is! O brave new world,
That has such people in't!
PROS. 'Tis new to thee.
185 ALON. What is this maid with whom thou wast at
    play?
Your eld'st acquaintance cannot be three hours:
Is she the goddess that hath sever'd us,
And brought us thus together?

Fer. Sir, she is mortal;
But by immortal Providence she's mine:
190 I chose her when I could not ask my father
For his advice, nor thought I had one. She
Is daughter to this famous Duke of Milan,
Of whom so often I have heard renown,
But never saw before; of whom I have
195 Received a second life; and second father
This lady makes him to me.
Alon. I am hers:
But, O, how oddly will it sound that I
Must ask my child forgiveness!
Pros. There, sir, stop:
Let us not burthen our remembrances with
A heaviness that's gone.
Gon. 200 I have inly wept,
Or should have spoke ere this. Look down, you gods,
And on this couple drop a blessed crown!
For it is you that have chalk'd forth the way
Which brought us hither.
Alon. I say, Amen, Gonzalo!
205 *Gon.* Was Milan thrust from Milan, that his issue
Should become kings of Naples? O, rejoice
Beyond a common joy! and set it down
With gold on lasting pillars: In one voyage
Did Claribel her husband find at Tunis,
210 And Ferdinand, her brother, found a wife
Where he himself was lost, Prospero his dukedom
In a poor isle, and all of us ourselves
When no man was his own.
Alon. [to *Fer.* and *Mir.*]
Give me your hands:
Let grief and sorrow still embrace his heart
That doth not wish you joy!
Gon. 215 Be it so! Amen!

Re-enter Ariel, *with the Master and Boatswain amazedly
following.*

O, look, sir, look, sir! here is more of us:
I prophesied, if a gallows were on land,
This fellow could not drown. Now, blasphemy,
That swear'st grace o'erboard, not an oath on shore?

₂₂₀ Hast thou no mouth by land? What is the news?
Boats. The best news is, that we have safely found
Our king and company; the next, our ship—
Which, but three glasses since, we gave out split—
Is tight and yare and bravely rigg'd, as when
We first put out to sea.
₂₂₅ *Ari.* [*Aside to Pros.*]
Sir, all this service
Have I done since I went.
Pros. [*Aside to Ari.*]
My tricksy spirit!
Alon. These are not natural events; they strengthen
From strange to stranger. Say, how came you hither?
Boats. If I did think, sir, I were well awake,
₂₃₀ I'ld strive to tell you. We were dead of sleep,
And—how we know not—all clapp'd under hatches;
Where, but even now, with strange and several
    noises
Of roaring, shrieking, howling, jingling chains,
And more diversity of sounds, all horrible,
₂₃₅ We were awaked; straightway, at liberty;
Where we, in all her trim, freshly beheld
Our royal, good, and gallant ship; our master
Capering to eye her:—on a trice, so please you,
Even in a dream, were we divided from them,
And were brought moping hither.
₂₄₀ *Ari.* [*Aside to Pros.*]
Was't well done?
Pros. [*Aside to Ari.*] Bravely, my diligence. Thou shalt
    be free.
Alon. This is as strange a maze as e'er men trod;
And there is in this business more than nature
Was ever conduct of: some oracle
Must rectify our knowledge.
Pros. ₂₄₅ Sir, my liege,
Do not infest your mind with beating on
The strangeness of this business; at pick'd leisure
Which shall be shortly, single I'll resolve you,
Which to you shall seem probable, of every
₂₅₀ These happen'd accidents; till when, be cheerful,
And think of each thing well. [*Aside to Ari.*] Come
    hither, spirit:
Set Caliban and his companions free;

Untie the spell. [*Exit Ariel.*] How fares my gracious
    sir?
There are yet missing of your company
₂₅₅ Some few odd lads that you remember not.

Re-enter ARIEL, *driving in* CALIBAN, STEPHANO, *and* TRINCULO,
in their stolen apparel.

STE. Every man shift for all the rest, and let no man
    take care for himself; for all is but fortune.—Cora-
    gio, bully-monster, coragio!
TRIN. If these be true spies which I wear in my head,
    ₂₆₀ here's a goodly sight.
CAL. O Setebos, these be brave spirits indeed!
How fine my master is! I am afraid
He will chastise me.
SEB. Ha, ha!
What things are these, my lord Antonio?
Will money buy 'em?
ANT. ₂₆₅ Very like; one of them
Is a plain fish, and, no doubt, marketable.
PROS. Mark but the badges of these men, my lords,
Then say if they be true. This mis-shapen knave,
His mother was a witch; and one so strong
₂₇₀ That could control the moon, make flows and
    ebbs,
And deal in her command, without her power.
These three have robb'd me; and this demi-devil—
For he's a bastard one—had plotted with them
To take my life. Two of these fellows you
₂₇₅ Must know and own; this thing of darkness I
Acknowledge mine.
CAL. I shall be pinch'd to death.
ALON. Is not this Stephano, my drunken butler?
SEB. He is drunk now: where had he wine?
ALON. And Trinculo is reeling ripe: where should
    they ₂₈₀
Find this grand liquor that hath gilded 'em?—
How camest thou in this pickle?
TRIN. I have been in such a pickle, since I saw you
    last, that, I fear me, will never out of my bones: I
    shall not fear fly-blowing.
₂₈₅ SEB. Why, how now, Stephano!

STE. O, touch me not;—I am not Stephano, but a
    cramp.
PROS. You'ld be king o' the isle, sirrah?
STE. I should have been a sore one, then.
ALON. This is a strange thing as e'er I look'd on.
    Pointing to Caliban.
290 PROS. He is as disproportion'd in his manners
As in his shape. Go, sirrah, to my cell;
Take with you your companions; as you look
To have my pardon, trim it handsomely.
CAL. Ay, that I will; and I'll be wise hereafter,
295 And seek for grace. What a thrice-double ass
Was I, to take this drunkard for a god,
And worship this dull fool!
PROS. Go to; away!
ALON. Hence, and bestow your luggage where you
    found it.
SEB. *Or stole it, rather. Exeunt CAL., STE., and TRIN.*
300 PROS. Sir, I invite your Highness and your train
To my poor cell, where you shall take your rest
For this one night; which, part of it, I'll waste
With such discourse as, I not doubt, shall make it
Go quick away: the story of my life,
305 And the particular accidents gone by
Since I came to this isle: and in the morn
I'll bring you to your ship, and so to Naples,
Where I have hope to see the nuptial
Of these our dear-beloved solemnized;
310 And thence retire me to my Milan, where
Every third thought shall be my grave.
ALON. I long
To hear the story of your life, which must
Take the ear strangely.
PROS. I'll deliver all;
And promise you calm seas, auspicious gales,
And sail so expeditious, that shall catch
315 Your royal fleet far off. [*Aside to ARI.*] My Ariel,
    chick,
That is thy charge: then to the elements
Be free, and fare thou well! Please you, draw near.

                               Exeunt.

EPILOGUE

SPOKEN BY PROSPERO.

Now my charms are all o'erthrown,
And what strength I have's mine own,
Which is most faint: now, 'tis true,
I must be here confined by you,
₅ Or sent to Naples. Let me not,
Since I have my dukedom got,
And pardon'd the deceiver, dwell
In this bare island by your spell;
But release me from my bands
₁₀ With the help of your good hands:
Gentle breath of yours my sails
Must fill, or else my project fails,
Which was to please. Now I want
Spirits to enforce, art to enchant;
₁₅ And my ending is despair,
Unless I be relieved by prayer,
Which pierces so, that it assaults
Mercy itself, and frees all faults.
As you from crimes would pardon'd be,
₂₀ Let your indulgence set me free.

TWELFTH NIGHT

DRAMATIS PERSONÆ

ORSINO, Duke of Illyria.
SEBASTIAN, brother to Viola.
ANTONIO, a sea captain, friend to Sebastian.
A Sea Captain, friend to Viola.
VALENTINE, GENTLEMAN ATTENDING THE DUKE
CURIO, GENTLEMAN ATTENDING THE DUKE
SIR TOBY BELCH, uncle to Olivia.
SIR ANDREW AGUECHEEK.
MALVOLIO, steward to Olivia.
FABIAN, SERVANT TO OLIVIA
FESTE a Clown, servant to Olivia
OLIVIA.
VIOLA.
MARIA, Olivia's woman.
Lords, Priests, Sailors, Officers, Musicians, and
other Attendants.

SCENE: A CITY IN ILLYRIA, AND THE SEA-COAST NEAR IT.

ACT I

SCENE I. AN APARTMENT IN THE DUKE'S PALACE.

Enter Duke, Curio, and other Lords; Musicians attending.

Duke. If music be the food of love, play on;
Give me excess of it, that, surfeiting,
The appetite may sicken, and so die.
That strain again! it had a dying fall:
₅ O, it came o'er my ear like the sweet sound,
That breathes upon a bank of violets,
Stealing and giving odour! Enough; no more:
'Tis not so sweet now as it was before.
O spirit of love, how quick and fresh art thou!
₁₀ That, notwithstanding thy capacity
Receiveth as the sea, nought enters there,
Of what validity and pitch soe'er,
But falls into abatement and low price,
Even in a minute! so full of shapes is fancy,
₁₅ That it alone is high fantastical.
Cur. Will you go hunt, my lord?
Duke. What, Curio?
Cur. The hart.
Duke. Why, so I do, the noblest that I have:
O, when mine eyes did see Olivia first,
₂₀ Methought she purged the air of pestilence!
That instant was I turn'd into a hart;

And my desires, like fell and cruel hounds,
E'er since pursue me.

Enter Valentine.

How now! what news from her?
Val. So please my lord, I might not be admitted;
25 But from her handmaid do return this answer:
The element itself, till seven years' heat,
Shall not behold her face at ample view;
But, like a cloistress, she will veiled walk
And water once a day her chamber round
30 With eye-offending brine: all this to season
A brother's dead love, which she would keep fresh
And lasting in her sad remembrance.
Duke. O, she that hath a heart of that fine frame
To pay this debt of love but to a brother,
35 How will she love, when the rich golden shaft
Hath kill'd the flock of all affections else
That live in her; when liver, brain and heart,
These sovereign thrones, are all supplied, and fill'd
Her sweet perfections with one self king!
40 Away before me to sweet beds of flowers:
Love-thoughts lie rich when canopied with bowers.
    [*Exeunt.*

SCENE II. THE SEA-COAST

Enter Viola, *a* Captain, *and* Sailors.

Vio. What country, friends, is this?
Cap. This is Illyria, lady.
Vio. And what should I do in Illyria?
My brother he is in Elysium.
5 Perchance he is not drown'd: what think you,
    sailors?
Cap. It is perchance that you yourself were saved.
Vio. O my poor brother! and so perchance may he be.
Cap. True, madam: and, to comfort you with chance,
Assure yourself, after our ship did split,
10 When you and those poor number saved with you

Hung on our driving boat, I saw your brother,
Most provident in peril, bind himself,
Courage and hope both teaching him the practice,
To a strong mast that lived upon the sea;
₁₅ Where, like Arion on the dolphin's back,
I saw him hold acquaintance with the waves
So long as I could see.
Vio. For saying so, there's gold:
Mine own escape unfoldeth to my hope,
₂₀ Whereto thy speech serves for authority,
The like of him. Know'st thou this country?
Cap. Ay, madam, well; for I was bred and born
Not three hours' travel from this very place.
Vio. Who governs here?
₂₅ *Cap.* A noble Duke, in nature as in name.
Vio. What is his name?
Cap. Orsino.
Vio. Orsino! I have heard my father name him:
He was a bachelor then.
₃₀ *Cap.* And so is now, or was so very late;
For but a month ago I went from hence,
And then 'twas fresh in murmur,—as, you know,
What great ones do the less will prattle of,—
That he did seek the love of fair Olivia.
₃₅ *Vio.* What's she?
Cap. A virtuous maid, the daughter of a count
That died some twelvemonth since; then leaving her
In the protection of his son, her brother,
Who shortly also died: for whose dear love,
₄₀ They say, she hath abjured the company
And sight of men.
Vio. O that I served that lady,
And might not be delivered to the world,
Till I had made mine own occasion mellow,
What my estate is!
Cap. That were hard to compass;
₄₅ Because she will admit no kind of suit,
No, not the Duke's.
Vio. There is a fair behaviour in thee, captain;
And though that nature with a beauteous wall
Doth oft close in pollution, yet of thee
₅₀ I will believe thou hast a mind that suits

With this thy fair and outward character.
I prithee, and I'll pay thee bounteously,
Conceal me what I am, and be my aid
For such disguise as haply shall become
55 The form of my intent. I'll serve this Duke:
Thou shalt present me as an eunuch to him:
It may be worth thy pains; for I can sing,
And speak to him in many sorts of music,
That will allow me very worth his service.
60 What else may hap to time I will commit;
Only shape thou thy silence to my wit.
Cap. Be you his eunuch, and your mute I'll be:
When my tongue blabs, then let mine eyes not see.
Vio. I thank thee: lead me on. [*Exeunt.*

SCENE III. OLIVIA'S HOUSE

Enter Sir Toby Belch *and* Maria.

Sir To. What a plague means my niece, to take the death
of her brother thus? I am sure care's an enemy to life.
Mar. By my troth, Sir Toby, you must come in earlier
o' nights: your cousin, my lady, takes great exceptions to
5 your ill hours.
Sir To. Why, let her except, before excepted.
Mar. Ay, but you must confine yourself within the
modest limits of order.
Sir To. Confine! I'll confine myself no finer than I
10 am: these clothes are good enough to drink in; and so be
these boots too: an they be not, let them hang themselves
in their own straps.
Mar. That quaffing and drinking will undo you: I
heard my lady talk of it yesterday; and of a foolish knight
15 that you brought in one night here to be her wooer.
Sir To. Who, Sir Andrew Aguecheek?
Mar. Ay, he.
Sir To. He's as tall a man as any's in Illyria.

MAR. What's that to the purpose?

20 *SIR TO.* Why, he has three thousand ducats a year.

MAR. Ay, but he'll have but a year in all these ducats: he's a very fool and a prodigal.

SIR TO. Fie, that you'll say so! he plays o' the viol-de-gamboys,

and speaks three or four languages word for word 25 without book, and hath all the good gifts of nature.

MAR. He hath indeed, almost natural: for besides that he's a fool, he's a great quarreller; and but that he hath the gift of a coward to allay the gust he hath in quarrelling,

'tis thought among the prudent he would quickly 30 have the gift of a grave.

SIR TO. By this hand, they are scoundrels and sub-stractors

that say so of him. Who are they?

MAR. They that add, moreover, he's drunk nightly in your company.

35 *SIR TO.* With drinking healths to my niece: I 'll drink

to her as long as there is a passage in my throat and drink

in Illyria: he's a coward and a coystrill that will not drink

to my niece till his brains turn o' the toe like a parish-top.

What, wench! Castiliano vulgo; for here comes Sir Andrew

40 Agueface.

ENTER SIR ANDREW AGUECHEEK.

SIR AND. Sir Toby Belch! how now, Sir Toby Belch!

SIR TO. Sweet Sir Andrew!

SIR AND. Bless you, fair shrew.

MAR. And you too, sir.

45 *SIR TO.* Accost, Sir Andrew, accost.

SIR AND. What's that?

SIR TO. My niece's chambermaid.

Sir And. Good Mistress Accost, I desire better acquaintance.

50 *MAR.* My name is Mary, sir.

SIR AND. Good Mistress Mary Accost,—

SIR TO. You mistake, knight: 'accost' is front her, board
her, woo her, assail her.

SIR AND. By my troth, I would not undertake her in
55 this company. Is that the meaning of 'accost'?

MAR. Fare you well, gentlemen.

SIR TO. An thou let part so, Sir Andrew, would thou
mightst never draw sword again.

SIR AND. An you part so, mistress, I would I might
60 never draw sword again. Fair lady, do you think you have
fools in hand?

MAR. Sir, I have not you by the hand.

SIR AND. Marry, but you shall have; and here's my
hand.

65 MAR. Now, sir, 'thought is free': I pray you, bring your
hand to the buttery-bar and let it drink.

SIR AND. Wherefore, sweet-heart? what's your
metaphor?

MAR. It's dry, sir.

70 SIR AND. Why, I think so: I am not such an ass but I
can keep my hand dry. But what's your jest?

MAR. A dry jest, sir.

SIR AND. Are you full of them?

MAR. Ay, sir, I have them at my fingers' ends: marry,
75 now I let go your hand, I am barren. [Exit.

SIR TO. O knight, thou lackest a cup of canary: when
did I see thee so put down?

SIR AND. Never in your life, I think; unless you see
canary put me down. Methinks sometimes I have no more
80 wit than a Christian or an ordinary man has: but I am a
great eater of beef and I believe that does harm to my wit.

SIR TO. No question.

SIR AND. An I thought that, I'ld forswear it. I'll ride
home to-morrow, Sir Toby.

85 SIR TO. Pourquoi, my dear knight?

SIR AND. What is 'pourquoi'? do or not do? I would
I had bestowed that time in the tongues that I have in

fencing, dancing and bear-baiting: O, had I but followed

the arts!

90 SIR TO. Then hadst thou had an excellent head of hair.

SIR AND. Why, would that have mended my hair?

SIR TO. Past question; for thou seest it will not curl by nature.

95 SIR AND. But it becomes me well enough, does't not?

SIR TO. Excellent; it hangs like flax on a distaff; and I hope to see a housewife take thee between her legs and

spin it off.

SIR AND. Faith, I'll home to-morrow, Sir Toby: your 100 niece will not be seen; or if she be, it's four to one she'll

none of me: the count himself here hard by woos her.

SIR TO. She'll none o' the count: she'll not match above her degree, neither in estate, years, nor wit; I have

heard her swear't. Tut, there's life in't, man.

105 SIR AND. I'll stay a month longer. I am a fellow o' the strangest mind i' the world; I delight in masques and

revels sometimes altogether.

SIR TO. Art thou good at these kickshawses, knight?

SIR AND. As any man in Illyria, whatsoever he be, 110 under the degree of my betters; and yet I will not compare

with an old man.

SIR TO. What is thy excellence in a galliard, knight?

SIR AND. Faith, I can cut a caper.

SIR TO. And I can cut the mutton to't.

115 SIR AND. And I think I have the back-trick simply as

strong as any man in Illyria.

SIR TO. Wherefore are these things hid? wherefore have these gifts a curtain before 'em? are they like to take

dust, like Mistress Mall's picture? why dost thou not go to

120 church in a galliard and come home in a
    coranto? My
very walk should be a jig; I would not so much
    as make
water but in a sink-a-pace. What dost thou mean? Is it
a world to hide virtues in? I did think, by the ex-
    cellent
constitution of thy leg, it was formed under the star
    of a
125 galliard.
SIR AND. Ay, 'tis strong, and it does indifferent well
in a flame-coloured stock. Shall we set about some
    revels?
SIR TO. What shall we do else? were we not born
under Taurus?
130 SIR AND. Taurus! That's sides and heart.
SIR TO. No, sir; it is legs and thighs. Let me see thee
caper: ha! higher: ha, ha! excellent! [Exeunt.

SCENE IV. THE DUKE'S PALACE

Enter VALENTINE, *and* VIOLA *in man's attire.*

VAL. If the Duke continue these favours towards you,
Cesario, you are like to be much advanced: he hath
    known
you but three days, and already you are no stranger.
VIO. You either fear his humour or my negligence,
5 that you call in question the continuance of his love:
    is he
inconstant, sir, in his favours?
VAL. No, believe me.
VIO. I thank you. Here comes the count.

Enter DUKE, CURIO, *and* Attendants.

DUKE. Who saw Cesario, ho?
10 VIO. On your attendance, my lord; here.
DUKE. Stand you a while aloof. Cesario,
Thou know'st no less but all; I have unclasp'd
To thee the book even of my secret soul:
Therefore, good youth, address thy gait unto her;

15 Be not denied access, stand at her doors,
And tell them, there thy fixed foot shall grow
Till thou have audience.
VIO. Sure, my noble lord,
If she be so abandon'd to her sorrow
As it is spoke, she never will admit me.
20 *DUKE.* Be clamorous and leap all civil bounds
Rather than make unprofited return.
VIO. Say I do speak with her, my lord, what then?
DUKE. O, then unfold the passion of my love,
Surprise her with discourse of my dear faith:
25 It shall become thee well to act my woes;
She will attend it better in thy youth
Than in a nuncio's of more grave aspect.
VIO. I think not so, my lord.
DUKE. Dear lad, believe it;
For they shall yet belie thy happy years,
30 That say thou art a man: Diana's lip
Is not more smooth and rubious; thy small pipe
Is as the maiden's organ, shrill and sound;
And all is semblative a woman's part.
I know thy constellation is right apt
35 For this affair. Some four or five attend him;
All, if you will; for I myself am best
When least in company. Prosper well in this,
And thou shalt live as freely as thy lord,
To call his fortunes thine.
VIO. I'll do my best
40 To woo your lady: [*Aside*] yet, a barful strife!
Whoe'er I woo, myself would be his wife. [*Exeunt.*

SCENE V. OLIVIA'S HOUSE

ENTER MARIA AND CLOWN.

MAR. Nay, either tell me where thou hast been, or I
will not open my lips so wide as a bristle may enter
in way
of thy excuse: my lady will hang thee for thy absence.
CLO. Let her hang me: he that is well hanged in this
5 world needs to fear no colours.
MAR. Make that good.

Clo. He shall see none to fear.

Mar. A good lenten answer: I can tell thee where that saying was born, of 'I fear no colours.'

10 *Clo.* Where, good Mistress Mary?

Mar. In the wars; and that may you be bold to say in your foolery.

Clo. Well, God give them wisdom that have it; and those that are fools, let them use their talents.

15 *Mar.* Yet you will be hanged for being so long absent;

or, to be turned away, is not that as good as a hanging to you?

Clo. Many a good hanging prevents a bad marriage; and, for turning away, let summer bear it out.

20 *Mar.* You are resolute, then?

Clo. Not so, neither; but I am resolved on two points.

Mar. That if one break, the other will hold; or, if both break, your gaskins fall.

Clo. Apt, in good faith; very apt. Well, go thy way;

25 if Sir Toby would leave drinking, thou wert as witty a

piece of Eve's flesh as any in Illyria.

Mar. Peace, you rogue, no more o' that. Here comes my lady: make your excuse wisely, you were best.

[*Exit.*

Clo. Wit, an't be thy will, put me into good fooling!

30 Those wits, that think they have thee, do very oft prove

fools; and I, that am sure I lack thee, may pass for a wise

man: for what says Quinapalus? 'Better a witty fool than

a foolish wit.'

ENTER LADY OLIVIA *WITH* MALVOLIO.

God bless thee, lady!

35 *Oli.* Take the fool away.

Clo. Do you not hear, fellows? Take away the lady.

Oli. Go to, you're a dry fool; I'll no more of you: besides,

you grow dishonest.

CLO. Two faults, madonna, that drink and good
counsel
40 will amend: for give the dry fool drink, then is the
fool not
dry: bid the dishonest man mend himself; if he mend,
he is
no longer dishonest; if he cannot, let the botcher
mend him.
Any thing that's mended is but patched: virtue that
transgresses
is but patched with sin; and sin that amends is but
45 patched with virtue. If that this simple syllogism
will serve,
so; if it will not, what remedy? As there is no true
cuckold
but calamity, so beauty's a flower. The lady bade take
away the fool; therefore, I say again, take her away.
OLI. Sir, I bade them take away you.
50 CLO. Misprision in the highest degree! Lady,
cucullus
non facit monachum; that's as much to say as I
wear not
motley in my brain. Good madonna, give me leave to
prove you a fool.
OLI. Can you do it?
55 CLO. Dexteriously, good madonna.
OLI. Make your proof.
CLO. I must catechize you for it, madonna: good my
mouse of virtue, answer me.
OLI. Well, sir, for want of other idleness, I'll
bide your
60 proof.
CLO. Good madonna, why mournest thou?
OLI. Good fool, for my brother's death.
CLO. I think his soul is in hell, madonna.
OLI. I know his soul is in heaven, fool.
65 CLO. The more fool, madonna, to mourn for your
brother's
soul being in heaven. Take away the fool,
gentlemen.
OLI. What think you of this fool, Malvolio? doth he
not mend?
70 MAL. Yes, and shall do till the pangs of death shake

him: infirmity, that decays the wise, doth ever
    make the
better fool.

Clo. God send you, sir, a speedy infirmity, for the
better increasing your folly! Sir Toby will be
    sworn that
75 I am no fox; but he will not pass his word for two
    pence
that you are no fool.

Oli. How say you to that, Malvolio?

Mal. I marvel your ladyship takes delight in such a
barren rascal: I saw him put down the other day
    with an
80 ordinary fool that has no more brain than a
    stone. Look
you now, he's out of his guard already; unless you
    laugh
and minister occasion to him, he is gagged. I protest, I
take these wise men, that crow so at these set kind of
    fools,
no better than the fools' zanies.

85 *Oli.* O, you are sick of self-love, Malvolio, and taste
with a distempered appetite. To be generous, guiltless
    and
of free disposition, is to take those things for
    bird-bolts that
you deem cannon-bullets: there is no slander in an
    allowed
fool, though he do nothing but rail; nor no railing in a
90 known discreet man, though he do nothing but
    reprove.

Clo. Now Mercury endue thee with leasing, for thou
speakest well of fools!

Re-enter MARIA.

Mar. Madam, there is at the gate a young gentleman
much desires to speak with you.

95 *Oli.* From the Count Orsino, is it?

Mar. I know not, madam: 'tis a fair young man, and
well attended.

Oli. Who of my people hold him in delay?

Mar. Sir Toby, madam, your kinsman.

100 *Oli.* Fetch him off, I pray you; he speaks
nothing but
madman: fie on him! [*Exit Maria.*] Go you, Malvolio:
if it be a suit from the count, I am sick, or not at home;
what you will, to dismiss it. [*Exit Malvolio.*] Now you
see, sir, how your fooling grows old, and people dislike it.

105 *Clo.* Thou hast spoke for us, madonna, as if thy
eldest son
should be a fool; whose skull Jove cram with brains! for,—here
he comes,—one of thy kin has a most weak pia mater.

Enter Sir Toby.

Oli. By mine honour, half drunk. What is he at the
gate, cousin?

110 *Sir To.* A gentleman.

Oli. A gentleman! what gentleman?

Sir To. 'Tis a gentleman here—a plague o' these
pickle-herring!
How now, sot!

Clo. Good Sir Toby!

115 *Oli.* Cousin, cousin, how have you come so
early by
this lethargy?

Sir To. Lechery! I defy lechery. There's one at the
gate.

Oli. Ay, marry, what is he?

Sir To. Let him be the devil, an he will, I care not:
120 give me faith, say I. Well, it's all one. [*Exit.*

Oli. What's a drunken man like, fool?

Clo. Like a drowned man, a fool and a mad man: one
draught above heat makes him a fool; the
second mads
him; and a third drowns him.

125 *Oli.* Go thou and seek the crowner, and let him
sit o'
my coz; for he's in the third degree of drink, he's
drowned:
go, look after him.

Clo. He is but mad yet, madonna; and the fool shall
look to the madman. [*Exit.*

Re-enter MALVOLIO.

₁₃₀ MAL. Madam, yond young fellow swears he will speak

with you. I told him you were sick; he takes on him to understand so much, and therefore comes to speak with

you. I told him you were asleep; he seems to have a foreknowledge of that too, and therefore comes to speak

₁₃₅ with you. What is to be said to him, lady? he's fortified

against any denial.

OLI. Tell him he shall not speak with me.

MAL. Has been told so; and he says, he'll stand at your door like a sheriff's post, and be the supporter to a

₁₄₀ bench, but he'll speak with you.

OLI. What kind o' man is he?

MAL. Why, of mankind.

OLI. What manner of man?

MAL. Of very ill manner; he'll speak with you, will ₁₄₅ you or no.

OLI. Of what personage and years is he?

MAL. Not yet old enough for a man, nor young enough

for a boy; as a squash is before 'tis a peascod, or a codling

when 'tis almost an apple: 'tis with him in standing water,

₁₅₀ between boy and man. He is very well-favoured and he

speaks very shrewishly; one would think his mother's milk

were scarce out of him.

OLI. Let him approach: call in my gentlewoman.

MAL. Gentlewoman, my lady calls. [*Exit.*

Re-enter MARIA.

₁₅₅ OLI. Give me my veil: come, throw it o'er my face.
We'll once more hear Orsino's embassy.

Enter VIOLA, *and* Attendants.

VIO. The honourable lady of the house, which is she?

OLI. Speak to me; I shall answer for her. Your will?

VIO. Most radiant, exquisite and unmatchable
  beauty,—I

₁₆₀ pray you, tell me if this be the lady of the house,
  for I

never saw her: I would be loath to cast away my
  speech,

for besides that it is excellently well penned, I have
  taken

great pains to con it. Good beauties, let me sustain no

scorn; I am very comptible, even to the least sinister
  usage.

₁₆₅ *OLI.* Whence came you, sir?

VIO. I can say little more than I have studied, and

that question's out of my part. Good gentle one,
  give me

modest assurance if you be the lady of the house,
  that I

may proceed in my speech.

₁₇₀ *OLI.* Are you a comedian?

VIO. No, my profound heart: and yet, by the very

fangs of malice I swear, I am not that I play. Are you
the lady of the house?

OLI. If I do not usurp myself, I am.

₁₇₅ *VIO.* Most certain, if you are she, you do usurp
  your-self;

for what is yours to bestow is not yours to reserve.
  But

this is from my commission: I will on with my
  speech in

your praise, and then show you the heart of my
  message.

OLI. Come to what is important in't: I forgive you the
₁₈₀ praise.

VIO. Alas, I took great pains to study it, and 'tis
poetical.

OLI. It is the more like to be feigned: I pray you, keep
it in. I heard you were saucy at my gates, and allowed
₁₈₅ your approach rather to wonder at you than to
  hear you.

If you be not mad, be gone; if you have reason, be
  brief:
'tis not that time of moon with me to make one in so
  skipping
a dialogue.
MAR. Will you hoist sail, sir? here lies your way.
190 *VIO.* No, good swabber; I am to hull here a little
longer. Some mollification for your giant, sweet lady.
Tell me your mind: I am a messenger.
OLI. Sure, you have some hideous matter to deliver,
when the courtesy of it is so fearful. Speak your office.
195 *VIO.* It alone concerns your ear. I bring no overture
of war, no taxation of homage: I hold the olive in my
hand; my words are as full of peace as matter.
OLI. Yet you began rudely. What are you? what
would you?
200 *VIO.* The rudeness that hath appeared in me have I
learned from my entertainment. What I am, and
  what I
would, are as secret as maidenhead; to your ears,
  divinity,
to any other's, profanation.
OLI. Give us the place alone: we will hear this
  divinity.
205 [*Exeunt Maria and Attendants.*] Now, sir, what is
  your text?
VIO. Most sweet lady,—
OLI. A comfortable doctrine, and much may be
  said of
it. Where lies your text?
VIO. In Orsino's bosom.
210 *OLI.* In his bosom! In what chapter of his bosom?
VIO. To answer by the method, in the first of his heart.
OLI. O, I have read it: it is heresy. Have you no more
to say?
VIO. Good madam, let me see your face.
215 *OLI.* Have you any commission from your lord to
  negotiate
with my face? You are now out of your text: but
we will draw the curtain and show you the picture.
  Look
you, sir, such a one I was this present: is't not well
  done?

[Unveiling.

Vio. Excellently done, if God did all.

220 *Oli.* 'Tis in grain, sir; 'twill endure wind and
weather.

Vio. 'Tis beauty truly blent, whose red and white
Nature's own sweet and cunning hand laid on:
Lady, you are the cruell'st she alive,
If you will lead these graces to the grave
225 And leave the world no copy.

Oli. O, sir, I will not be so hard-hearted; I will give
out divers schedules of my beauty: it shall be in-
ventoried,
and every particle and utensil labelled to my will: as,
item, two lips, indifferent red; item, two grey
eyes, with
230 lids to them; item, one neck, one chin, and so
forth. Were
you sent hither to praise me?

Vio. I see you what you are, you are too proud;
But, if you were the devil, you are fair.
My lord and master loves you: O, such love
235 Could be but recompensed, though you were
crown'd
The nonpareil of beauty!

Oli. How does he love me?

Vio. With adorations, fertile tears,
With groans that thunder love, with sighs of fire.

Oli. Your lord does know my mind; I cannot
love him:
240 Yet I suppose him virtuous, know him noble,
Of great estate, of fresh and stainless youth;
In voices well divulged, free, learn'd and valiant;
And in dimension and the shape of nature
A gracious person: but yet I cannot love him;
245 He might have took his answer long ago.

Vio. If I did love you in my master's flame,
With such a suffering, such a deadly life,
In your denial I would find no sense;
I would not understand it.

Oli. Why, what would you?

250 *Vio.* Make me a willow cabin at your gate,
And call upon my soul within the house;

409

Write loyal cantons of contemned love
And sing them loud even in the dead of night;
Halloo your name to the reverberate hills
₂₅₅ And make the babbling gossip of the air
Cry out 'Olivia!' O, you should not rest
Between the elements of air and earth,
But you should pity me!
OLI. You might do much.
What is your parentage?
₂₆₀ *VIO.* Above my fortunes, yet my state is well:
I am a gentleman.
OLI. Get you to your lord;
I cannot love him: let him send no more;
Unless, perchance, you come to me again,
To tell me how he takes it. Fare you well:
₂₆₅ I thank you for your pains: spend this for me.
VIO. I am no fee'd post, lady; keep your purse:
My master, not myself, lacks recompense.
Love make his heart of flint that you shall love;
And let your fervour, like my master's, be
₂₇₀ Placed in contempt! Farewell, fair cruelty.[*Exit.*
OLI. 'What is your parentage?'
'Above my fortunes, yet my state is well:
I am a gentleman.' I'll be sworn thou art;
Thy tongue, thy face, thy limbs, actions, and spirit,
₂₇₅ Do give thee five-fold blazon: not too fast: soft,
   soft!
Unless the master were the man. How now!
Even so quickly may one catch the plague?
Methinks I feel this youth's perfections
With an invisible and subtle stealth
₂₈₀ To creep in at mine eyes. Well, let it be.
What ho, Malvolio!

Re-enter MALVOLIO.

MAL. Here, madam, at your service.
OLI. Run after that same peevish messenger,
The county's man: he left this ring behind him,
Would I or not: tell him I'll none of it.
₂₈₅ Desire him not to flatter with his lord,
Nor hold him up with hopes; I am not for him:
If that the youth will come this way to-morrow,

I'll give him reasons for't: hie thee, Malvolio.
Mal. Madam, I will. [*Exit.*
₂₉₀ *Oli.* I do I know not what, and fear to find
Mine eye too great a flatterer for my mind.
Fate, show thy force: ourselves we do not owe;
What is decreed must be, and be this so. [*Exit.*

ACT II

SCENE I. THE SEA-COAST.

ENTER ANTONIO *AND* SEBASTIAN.

ANT. Will you stay no longer? nor will you not that
I go with you?
SEB. By your patience, no. My stars shine darkly over
me: the malignancy of my fate might perhaps
   distemper
5 yours; therefore I shall crave of you your leave that
   I may
bear my evils alone: it were a bad recompense
   for your
love, to lay any of them on you.
ANT. Let me yet know of you whither you are bound.
SEB. No, sooth, sir: my determinate voyage is mere
10 extravagancy. But I perceive in you so excellent a
   touch
of modesty, that you will not extort from me what
   I am
willing to keep in; therefore it charges me in
   manners the
rather to express myself. You must know of me then,
Antonio, my name is Sebastian, which I called
   Roderigo.
15 My father was that Sebastian of Messaline, whom
   I know

you have heard of. He left behind him myself and a
sister, both born in an hour: if the heavens had been
pleased, would we had so ended! but you, sir, altered
    that;
for some hour before you took me from the breach
    of the
20 sea was my sister drowned.

Ant. Alas the day!

Seb. A lady, sir, though it was said she much re-
    sembled
me, was yet of many accounted beautiful: but, though
I could not with such estimable wonder overfar
    believe
25 that, yet thus far I will boldly publish her; she
    bore a
mind that envy could not but call fair. She is drowned
already, sir, with salt water, though I seem to
    drown her
remembrance again with more.

Ant. Pardon me, sir, your bad entertainment.

30 *Seb.* O good Antonio, forgive me your trouble.

Ant. If you will not murder me for my love, let me
be your servant.

Seb. If you will not undo what you have done, that is,
kill him whom you have recovered, desire it not.
    Fare ye
35 well at once: my bosom is full of kindness, and I
    am yet
so near the manners of my mother, that upon the least
    occasion
more mine eyes will tell tales of me. I am bound
to the Count Orsino's court: farewell. [*Exit.*

Ant. The gentleness of all the gods go with thee!
40 I have many enemies in Orsino's court,
Else would I very shortly see thee there.
But, come what may, I do adore thee so,
That danger shall seem sport, and I will go. [*Exit.*

SCENE II. A STREET

Enter VIOLA, MALVOLIO *following.*

Mal. Were not you even now with the Countess
    Olivia?
Vio. Even now, sir; on a moderate pace I have since
arrived but hither.
Mal. She returns this ring to you, sir: you might have
₅ saved me my pains, to have taken it away yourself.
    She
adds, moreover, that you should put your lord into a
    desperate
assurance she will none of him: and one thing more,
that you be never so hardy to come again in his
    affairs,
unless it be to report your lord's taking of this.
    Receive
₁₀ it so.
Vio. She took the ring of me: I'll none of it.
Mal. Come, sir, you peevishly threw it to her; and her
will is, it should be so returned: if it be worth
    stooping
for, there it lies in your eye; if not, be it his that
    finds it.

[Exit.

₁₅ *Vio.* I left no ring with her: what means this lady?
Fortune forbid my outside have not charm'd her!
She made good view of me; indeed, so much,
That methought her eyes had lost her tongue,
For she did speak in starts distractedly.
₂₀ She loves me, sure; the cunning of her passion
Invites me in this churlish messenger.
None of my lord's ring! why, he sent her none.
I am the man: if it be so, as 'tis,
Poor lady, she were better love a dream.
₂₅ Disguise, I see, thou art a wickedness,
Wherein the pregnant enemy does much.
How easy is it for the proper-false
In women's waxen hearts to set their forms!
Alas, our frailty is the cause, not we!
₃₀ For such as we are made of, such we be.
How will this fadge? my master loves her dearly;
And I, poor monster, fond as much on him;
And she, mistaken, seems to dote on me.

What will become of this? As I am man,
35 My state is desperate for my master's love;
As I am woman,—now alas the day!—
What thriftless sighs shall poor Olivia breathe!
O time! thou must untangle this, not I;
It is too hard a knot for me to untie! [*Exit.*

SCENE III. OLIVIA'S HOUSE

Enter Sir Toby *and* Sir Andrew.

Sir To. Approach, Sir Andrew: not to be a-bed after
midnight is to be up betimes; and 'diluculo surgere,'
    thou
know'st,—
Sir An. Nay, by my troth, I know not: but I know,
5 to be up late is to be up late.
Sir To. A false conclusion: I hate it as an unfilled can.
To be up after midnight and to go to bed then, is
    early: so
that to go to bed after midnight is to go to bed
    betimes.
Does not our life consist of the four elements?
10 *Sir And.* Faith, so they say; but I think it rather
consists of eating and drinking.
Sir To. Thou'rt a scholar; let us therefore eat and
drink. Marian, I say! a stoup of wine!

Enter Clown.

Sir And. Here comes the fool, i'faith.
15 *Clo.* How now, my hearts! did you never see the
    picture
of 'we three'?
Sir To. Welcome, ass. Now let's have a catch.
Sir And. By my troth, the fool has an excellent breast.
I had rather than forty shillings I had such a leg,
    and so
20 sweet a breath to sing, as the fool has. In sooth,
    thou wast
in very gracious fooling last night, when thou
    spokest of

Pigrogromitus, of the Vapians passing the equinoctial of

Queubus: 'twas very good, i'faith. I sent thee sixpence for

thy leman: hadst it?

25 CLO. I did impeticos thy gratillity; for Malvolio's nose

is no whipstock: my lady has a white hand, and the

Myrmidons are no bottle-ale houses.

SIR AND. Excellent! why, this is the best fooling, when

all is done. Now, a song.

30 SIR TO. Come on; there is sixpence for you: let's have

a song.

SIR AND. There's a testril of me too: if one knight

give a—

CLO. Would you have a love-song, or a song of good

35 life?

SIR TO. A love-song, a love-song.

SIR AND. Ay, ay: I care not for good life.

CLO. [Sings]

O mistress mine, where are you roaming?

O, stay and hear; your true love's coming,

40 That can sing both high and low:

Trip no further, pretty sweeting;

Journeys end in lovers meeting,

Every wise man's son doth know.

SIR AND. Excellent good, i' faith.

45 SIR TO. Good, good.

CLO. [Sings]

What is love? 'tis not hereafter;

Present mirth hath present laughter;

What's to come is still unsure:

In delay there lies no plenty;

50 Then come kiss me, sweet and twenty,

Youth's a stuff will not endure.

SIR AND. A mellifluous voice, as I am true knight.

SIR TO. A contagious breath.

SIR AND. Very sweet and contagious, i'faith.

55 SIR TO. To hear by the nose, it is dulcet in contagion.

But shall we make the welkin dance indeed? shall we

rouse the night-owl in a catch that will draw three
    souls
out of one weaver? shall we do that?
SIR AND. An you love me, let's do't: I am dog at a
60 catch.
CLO. By'r lady, sir, and some dogs will catch well.
SIR AND. Most certain. Let our catch be, 'Thou
knave.'
CLO. 'Hold thy peace, thou knave,' knight? I shall be
65 constrained in't to call thee knave, knight.
SIR AND. 'Tis not the first time I have constrained one
to call me knave. Begin, fool: it begins 'Hold thy
    peace.'
CLO. I shall never begin if I hold my peace.
SIR AND. Good, i'faith. Come, begin. [Catch sung.

Enter MARIA.

70 MAR. What a caterwauling do you keep here! If my
lady have not called up her steward Malvolio and
    bid him
turn you out of doors, never trust me.
SIR TO. My lady's a Cataian, we are politicians,
    Malvolio's
a Peg-a-Ramsey, and 'Three merry men be we.' Am
75 not I consanguineous? am I not of her blood?
    Tillyvally.
Lady! [Sings] 'There dwelt a man in Babylon, lady,
    lady!'
CLO. Beshrew me, the knight's in admirable fooling.
SIR AND. Ay, he does well enough if he be disposed,
and so do I too: he does it with a better grace, but I
    do it
80 more natural.
SIR TO. [Sings] 'O, the twelfth day of December',—
MAR. For the love o' God, peace!

ENTER MALVOLIO.

MAL. My masters, are you mad? or what are you?
Have you no wit, manners, nor honesty, but to
    gabble like

₈₅ tinkers at this time of night? Do ye make an ale-
house of
my lady's house, that ye squeak out your coziers'
catches
without any mitigation or remorse of voice? Is
there no
respect of place, persons, nor time in you?
Sir To. We did keep time, sir, in our catches. Sneck
₉₀ up!
Mal. Sir Toby, I must be round with you. My lady
bade me tell you, that, though she harbours you
as her
kinsman, she's nothing allied to your disorders. If you
can separate yourself and your misdemeanours,
you are
₉₅ welcome to the house; if not, an it would please
you to
take leave of her, she is very willing to bid you
farewell.
Sir To. 'Farewell, dear heart, since I must needs be
gone.'
Mar. Nay, good Sir Toby.
Clo. 'His eyes do show his days are almost done.'
₁₀₀ *Mal.* Is't even so?
Sir To. 'But I will never die.'
Clo. Sir Toby, there you lie.
Mal. This is much credit to you.
Sir To. 'Shall I bid him go?'
₁₀₅ *Clo.* 'What an if you do?'
Sir To. 'Shall I bid him go, and spare not?'
Clo. 'O no, no, no, no, you dare not.'
Sir To. Out o' tune, sir: ye lie. Art any more than a
steward? Dost thou think, because thou art virtuous,
₁₁₀ there shall be no more cakes and ale?
Clo. Yes, by Saint Anne, and ginger shall be hot i'
the mouth too.
Sir To. Thou'rt i' the right. Go, sir, rub your chain
with crums. A stoup of wine, Maria!
₁₁₅ *Mal.* Mistress Mary, if you prized my lady's
favour at
any thing more than contempt, you would not give
means

for this uncivil rule: she shall know of it, by this hand.
    [*Exit.*
MAR. Go shake your ears.
SIR AND. 'Twere as good a deed as to drink when a
120 man's a-hungry, to challenge him the field, and
    then to
break promise with him and make a fool of him.
SIR TO. Do't, knight: I'll write thee a challenge; or
I'll deliver thy indignation to him by word of mouth.
MAR. Sweet Sir Toby, be patient for to-night: since
125 the youth of the count's was to-day with my lady,
    she is
much out of quiet. For Monsieur Malvolio, let me
    alone
with him: if I do not gull him into a nayword,
    and make
him a common recreation, do not think I have wit
    enough
to lie straight in my bed: I know I can do it.
130 *Sir To.* Possess us, possess us; tell us something of
him.
MAR. Marry, sir, sometimes he is a kind of puritan.
SIR AND. O, if I thought that, I'ld beat him like a dog!
SIR TO. What, for being a puritan? thy exquisite
    reason,
135 dear knight?
SIR AND. I have no exquisite reason for't, but I have
reason good enough.
MAR. The devil a puritan that he is, or any thing con-
    stantly,
but a time-pleaser; an affectioned ass, that cons
140 state without book and utters it by great swarths:
    the best
persuaded of himself, so crammed, as he thinks, with
    excellencies,
that it is his grounds of faith that all that look on
him love him; and on that vice in him will my
    revenge
find notable cause to work.
145 *Sir To.* What wilt thou do?
MAR. I will drop in his way some obscure epistles of
love; wherein, by the colour of his beard, the shape
    of his

420

leg, the manner of his gait, the expressure of his eye,
forehead,
and complexion, he shall find himself most feelingly
150 personated. I can write very like my lady your
niece: on
a forgotten matter we can hardly make distinction
of our
hands.

Sir To. Excellent! I smell a device.

Sir And. I have 't in my nose too.

155 *Sir To.* He shall think, by the letters that thou wilt
drop, that they come from my niece, and that she's
in love
with him.

Mar. My purpose is, indeed, a horse of that colour.

Sir And. And your horse now would make him
an ass.

160 *Mar.* Ass, I doubt not.

Sir And. O, 'twill be admirable!

Mar. Sport royal, I warrant you: I know my physic
will work with him. I will plant you two, and let
the fool
make a third, where he shall find the letter:
observe his
165 construction of it. For this night, to bed, and
dream on
the event. Farewell. [*Exit.*

Sir To. Good night, Penthesilea.

Sir And. Before me, she's a good wench.

Sir To. She's a beagle, true-bred, and one that
adores
170 me: what o' that?

Sir And. I was adored once too.

Sir To. Let's to bed, knight. Thou hadst need send
for more money.

Sir And. If I cannot recover your niece, I am a foul
175 way out.

Sir To. Send for money, knight: if thou hast her not
i' the end, call me cut.

Sir And. If I do not, never trust me, take it how you
will.

180 *Sir To.* Come, come, I'll go burn some sack;
'tis too

421

late to go to bed now: come, knight; come, knight.
[*Exeunt.*

SCENE IV. THE DUKE'S PALACE

Enter DUKE, VIOLA, CURIO, *and others.*

DUKE. Give me some music. Now, good morrow,
  friends.
Now, good Cesario, but that piece of song,
That old and antique song we heard last night:
Methought it did relieve my passion much,
₅ More than light airs and recollected terms
Of these most brisk and giddy-paced times:
Come, but one verse.
CUR. He is not here, so please your lordship, that
should sing it.
₁₀ **DUKE.** Who was it?
CUR. Feste, the jester, my lord; a fool that the lady
  Olivia's
father took much delight in. He is about the house.
DUKE. Seek him out, and play the tune the while.

[*Exit* CURIO. *Music plays.*

Come hither, boy: if ever thou shalt love,
₁₅ In the sweet pangs of it remember me;
For such as I am all true lovers are,
Unstaid and skittish in all motions else,
Save in the constant image of the creature
That is beloved. How dost thou like this tune?
₂₀ **VIO.** It gives a very echo to the seat
Where Love is throned.
DUKE. Thou dost speak masterly:
My life upon't, young though thou art, thine eye
Hath stay'd upon some favour that it loves:
Hath it not, boy?
₂₅ **VIO.** A little, by your favour.
DUKE. What kind of woman is't?
VIO. Of your complexion.
DUKE. She is not worth thee, then. What years, i'
  faith?

Vio. About your years, my lord.
Duke. Too old, by heaven: let still the woman take
₃₀ An elder than herself; so wears she to him,
So sways she level in her husband's heart:
For, boy, however we do praise ourselves,
Our fancies are more giddy and unfirm,
More longing, wavering, sooner lost and worn,
Than women's are.
₃₅ *Vio.* I think it well, my lord.
Duke. Then let thy love be younger than thyself,
Or thy affection cannot hold the bent;
For women are as roses, whose fair flower
Being once display'd, doth fall that very hour.
₄₀ *Vio.* And so they are: alas, that they are so;
To die, even when they to perfection grow!

Re-enter CURIO *and* Clown.

Duke. O, fellow, come, the song we had last night.
Mark it, Cesario, it is old and plain;
The spinsters and the knitters in the sun
₄₅ And the free maids that weave their thread with
bones
Do use to chant it: it is silly sooth,
And dallies with the innocence of love,
Like the old age.
Clo. Are you ready, sir?
₅₀ *Duke.* Ay; prithee, sing. [*Music.*

SONG.

Clo. Come away, come away, death,
And in sad cypress let me be laid;
Fly away, fly away, breath;
I am slain by a fair cruel maid.
₅₅ My shroud of white, stuck all with yew,
O, prepare it!
My part of death, no one so true
Did share it.
Not a flower, not a flower sweet,
₆₀ On my black coffin let there be strown;
Not a friend, not a friend greet
My poor corpse, where my bones shall be thrown:

A thousand thousand sighs to save,
Lay me, O, where
65 Sad true lover never find my grave,
To weep there!
Duke. There's for thy pains.
Clo. No pains, sir; I take pleasure in singing, sir.
Duke. I'll pay thy pleasure then.
70 *Clo.* Truly, sir, and pleasure will be paid, one time or
another.
Duke. Give me now leave to leave thee.
Clo. Now, the melancholy god protect thee; and the
tailor make thy doublet of changeable taffeta, for
thy mind
75 is a very opal. I would have men of such constancy put
to sea, that their business might be every thing and
their
intent every where; for that's it that always makes
a good
voyage of nothing. Farewell. [*Exit.*
*Duke. Let all the rest give place. [Curio and Attendants
retire.*
Once more, Cesario,
80 Get thee to yond same sovereign cruelty:
Tell her, my love, more noble than the world,
Prizes not quantity of dirty lands;
The parts that fortune hath bestow'd upon her,
Tell her, I hold as giddily as fortune;
85 But 'tis that miracle and queen of gems
That nature pranks her in attracts my soul.
Vio. But if she cannot love you, sir?
Duke. I cannot be so answer'd.
Vio. Sooth, but you must.
Say that some lady, as perhaps there is,
90 Hath for your love as great a pang of heart
As you have for Olivia: you cannot love her;
You tell her so; must she not then be answer'd?
Duke. There is no woman's sides
Can bide the beating of so strong a passion
95 As love doth give my heart; no woman's heart
So big, to hold so much; they lack retention.
Alas, their love may be call'd appetite,—

No motion of the liver, but the palate,—
That suffer surfeit, cloyment and revolt;
100 But mine is all as hungry as the sea,
And can digest as much: make no compare
Between that love a woman can bear me
And that I owe Olivia.
Vio. Ay, but I know,—
Duke. What dost thou know?
105 *Vio.* Too well what love women to men may owe:
In faith, they are as true of heart as we.
My father had a daughter loved a man,
As it might be, perhaps, were I a woman,
I should your lordship.
Duke. And what's her history?
110 *Vio.* A blank, my lord. She never told her love,
But let concealment, like a worm i' the bud,
Feed on her damask cheek: she pined in thought;
And with a green and yellow melancholy
She sat like patience on a monument,
115 Smiling at grief. Was not this love indeed?
We men may say more, swear more: but indeed
Our shows are more than will; for still we prove
Much in our vows, but little in our love.
Duke. But died thy sister of her love, my boy?
120 *Vio.* I am all the daughters of my father's house,
And all the brothers too: and yet I know not.
Sir, shall I to this lady?
Duke. Ay, that's the theme.
To her in haste; give her this jewel; say,
My love can give no place, bide no denay. [*Exeunt.*

SCENE V. OLIVIA'S GARDEN

Enter Sir Toby, Sir Andrew, *and* Fabian.

Sir To. Come thy ways, Signior Fabian.
Fab. Nay, I'll come: if I lose a scruple of this sport,
let me be boiled to death with melancholy.
Sir To. Wouldst thou not be glad to have the
niggardly
5 rascally sheep-biter come by some notable shame?
Fab. I would exult, man: you know, he brought me

out o' favour with my lady about a bear-baiting here.
SIR TO. To anger him we'll have the bear again; and
we will fool him black and blue: shall we not, Sir
    Andrew?
10 SIR AND. An we do not, it is pity of our lives.
SIR TO. Here comes the little villain.

Enter MARIA.

How now, my metal of India!
MAR. Get ye all three into the box-tree: Malvolio's
coming down this walk: he has been yonder i' the sun
15 practising behaviour to his own shadow this half
    hour: observe
him, for the love of mockery; for I know this letter
will make a contemplative idiot of him. Close, in the
name of jesting! Lie thou there [*throws down a letter*];
for here comes the trout that must be caught with
20 tickling.[*Exit.*

ENTER MALVOLIO.

MAL. 'Tis but fortune; all is fortune. Maria once told
me she did affect me: and I have heard herself
    come thus
near, that, should she fancy, it should be one of my
    complexion.
Besides, she uses me with a more exalted respect
25 than any one else that follows her. What should I
    think
on't?
SIR TO. Here's an overweening rogue!
FAB. O, peace! Contemplation makes a rare
    turkey-cock
of him: how he jets under his advanced plumes!
30 SIR AND. 'Slight, I could so beat the rogue!
SIR TO. Peace, I say.
MAL. To be Count Malvolio!
SIR TO. Ah, rogue!
SIR AND. Pistol him, pistol him.
35 SIR TO. Peace, peace!
MAL. There is example for't; the lady of the Strachy
married the yeoman of the wardrobe.

SIR AND. Fie on him, Jezebel!

FAB. O, peace! now he's deeply in: look how imagination

40 blows him.

MAL. Having been three months married to her,
sitting

in my state,—

SIR TO. O, for a stone-bow, to hit him in the eye!

MAL. Calling my officers about me, in my branched

45 velvet gown; having come from a day-bed, where
I have

left Olivia sleeping,—

SIR TO. Fire and brimstone!

FAB. O, peace, peace!

MAL. And then to have the humour of state; and
after a

50 demure travel of regard, telling them I know my
place as I

would they should do theirs, to ask for my kinsman
Toby,—

SIR TO. Bolts and shackles!

FAB. O, peace, peace, peace! now, now.

MAL. Seven of my people, with an obedient start,

55 make out for him: I frown the while; and perchance
wind

up my watch, or play with my—some rich
jewel. Toby

approaches; courtesies there to me,—

SIR TO. Shall this fellow live?

FAB. Though our silence be drawn from us with
cars,

60 yet peace.

MAL. I extend my hand to him thus, quenching my
familiar smile with an austere regard of control,—

SIR TO. And does not Toby take you a blow o' the
lips then?

65 MAL. Saying, 'Cousin Toby, my fortunes
having cast

me on your niece give me this prerogative of
speech,'—

SIR TO. What, what?

MAL. 'You must amend your drunkenness.'

SIR TO. Out, scab!

427

₇₀ *FAB.* Nay, patience, or we break the sinews of our
plot.

MAL. 'Besides, you waste the treasure of your time
with a foolish knight,'—

SIR AND. That's me, I warrant you.

MAL. 'One Sir Andrew,'—

₇₅ *SIR AND.* I knew 'twas I; for many do call me fool.

MAL. What employment have we here? [*Taking up the
letter.*

FAB. Now is the woodcock near the gin.

SIR TO. O, peace! and the spirit of humours intimate
reading aloud to him!

₈₀ *MAL.* By my life, this is my lady's hand: these
be her

very C's, her U's and her T's; and thus makes she her
great P's. It is, in contempt of question, her hand.

SIR AND. Her C's, her U's and her T's: why that?

MAL. [*reads*] To the unknown beloved, this, and
my good

₈₅ wishes:—her very phrases! By your leave, wax.
Soft!

and the impressure her Lucrece, with which she
uses to

seal: 'tis my lady. To whom should this be?

FAB. This wins him, liver and all.

MAL. [*reads*] Jove knows I love:

₉₀ But who?;

Lips, do not move;

No man must know.

'No man must know.' What follows? the numbers
altered!

'No man must know:' if this should be thee,
Malvolio?

₉₅ *SIR TO.* Marry, hang thee, brock!

MAL. [*reads*] I may command where I adore;

But silence, like a Lucrece knife,

With bloodless stroke my heart doth gore:

M, O, A, I, doth sway my life.

₁₀₀ *FAB.* A fustian riddle!

SIR TO. Excellent wench, say I.

MAL. 'M, O, A, I, doth sway my life.' Nay, but first,
let me see, let me see, let me see.

FAB. What dish o' poison has she dressed him!

105 *SIR TO.* And with what wing the staniel checks
at it!

MAL. 'I may command where I adore.' Why, she
may command me: I serve her; she is my lady.
Why, this
is evident to any formal capacity; there is no obstruction
in this: and the end,—what should that alphabetical
position
110 portend? If I could make that resemble something
in me,—Softly! M, O, A, I,—

SIR TO. O, ay, make up that: he is now at a cold
scent.

FAB. Sowter will cry upon't for all this, though it be
as rank as a fox.

115 *MAL.* M,—Malvolio; M,—why, that begins my
name.

FAB. Did not I say he would work it out? the cur is
excellent at faults.

MAL. M,—but then there is no consonancy in the
sequel;
that suffers under probation: A should follow, but O
does.

120 *FAB.* And O shall end, I hope.

SIR TO. Ay, or I'll cudgel him, and make him cry O!

MAL. And then I comes behind.

FAB. Ay, an you had any eye behind you, you might
see more detraction at your heels than fortunes
before you.

125 *MAL.* M, O, A, I; this simulation is not as the
former:
and yet, to crush this a little, it would bow to me, for
every
one of these letters are in my name. Soft! here follows
prose.

[*Reads*] If this fall into thy hand, revolve. In my stars I
am above
thee; but be not afraid of greatness: some are born
great, some achieve
130 greatness, and some have greatness thrust upon
'em. Thy Fates open
their hands; let thy blood and spirit embrace them;
and, to inure

thyself to what thou art like to be, cast thy humble
    slough and appear

fresh. Be opposite with a kinsman, surly with ser-
    vants; let thy

tongue tang arguments of state; put thyself into the
    trick of singularity:

135 she thus advises thee that sighs for thee. Re-
    member who

commended thy yellow stockings, and wished to see
    thee ever cross-

gartered: I say, remember. Go to, thou art made, if
    thou desirest to

be so; if not, let me see thee a steward still, the fellow
    of servants,

and not worthy to touch Fortune's fingers. Farewell.
    She that would

140 alter services with thee,

—THE FORTUNATE-UNHAPPY.

Daylight and champain discovers not more: this is
    open.

I will be proud, I will read politic authors, I will
    baffle Sir

Toby, I will wash off gross acquaintance, I will be
    point-devise

145 the very man. I do not now fool myself, to let
    imagination

jade me; for every reason excites to this, that my lady

loves me. She did commend my yellow stockings of
    late,

she did praise my leg being cross-gartered; and in
    this she

manifests herself to my love, and with a kind of in-
    junction

150 drives me to these habits of her liking. I thank my
    stars I

am happy. I will be strange, stout, in yellow stock-
    ings, and

cross-gartered, even with the swiftness of putting
    on. Jove

and my stars be praised! Here is yet a postscript.

[*Reads*] Thou canst not choose but know who I am. If
    thou entertainest

155 my love, let it appear in thy smiling; thy smiles
become
thee well; therefore in my presence still smile, dear
my sweet, I prithee.
Jove, I thank thee: I will smile; I will do every
thing that
thou wilt have me. [*Exit.*
FAB. I will not give my part of this sport for a pension
160 of thousands to be paid from the Sophy.
SIR TO. I could marry this wench for this device.
SIR AND. So could I too.
SIR TO. And ask no other dowry with her but such
another jest.
165 SIR AND. *Nor I neither.*
FAB. Here comes my noble gull-catcher.

Re-enter MARIA.

SIR TO. Wilt thou set thy foot o' my neck?
SIR AND. Or o' mine either?
SIR TO. Shall I play my freedom at tray-trip, and
become
170 thy bond-slave?
SIR AND. I' faith, or I either?
SIR TO. Why, thou hast put him in such a dream, that
when the image of it leaves him he must run mad.
MAR. Nay, but say true; does it work upon him?
175 SIR TO. Like aqua-vitæ with a midwife.
MAR. If you will then see the fruits of the sport, mark
his first approach before my lady: he will come to
her in
yellow stockings, and 'tis a colour she abhors, and
cross-gartered,
a fashion she detests; and he will smile upon her,
180 which will now be so unsuitable to her disposition,
being
addicted to a melancholy as she is, that it cannot
but turn
him into a notable contempt. If you will see it,
follow me.
SIR TO. To the gates of Tartar, thou most excellent
devil of wit!
185 SIR AND. I'll make one too. [*Exeunt.*

ACT III

SCENE I. OLIVIA'S GARDEN.

Enter VIOLA, *and Clown with a tabor.*

VIO. Save thee, friend, and thy music: dost thou live
by thy tabor?
CLO. No, sir, I live by the church.
VIO. Art thou a churchman?
5 *CLO.* No such matter, sir: I do live by the church;
  for I
do live at my house, and my house doth stand by the
  church.
VIO. So thou mayst say, the king lies by a beggar, if a
beggar dwell near him; or, the church stands by thy
  tabor,
if thy tabor stand by the church.
10 *CLO.* You have said, sir. To see this age! A sentence
is but a cheveril glove to a good wit: how quickly the
wrong side may be turned outward!
VIO. Nay, that's certain; they that dally nicely with
words may quickly make them wanton.
15 *CLO.* I would, therefore, my sister had had no
  name, sir.
VIO. Why, man?
CLO. Why, sir, her name's a word; and to dally with
that word might make my sister wanton. But indeed
words are very rascals since bonds disgraced them.

20 *Vio.* Thy reason, man?

Clo. Troth, sir, I can yield you none without words;
and words are grown so false, I am loath to prove
reason
with them.

Vio. I warrant thou art a merry fellow and carest for
25 nothing.

Clo. Not so, sir, I do care for something; but in my
conscience, sir, I do not care for you: if that be to
care for
nothing, sir, I would it would make you invisible.

Vio. Art not thou the Lady Olivia's fool?

30 *Clo.* No, indeed, sir; the Lady Olivia has no
folly: she
will keep no fool, sir, till she be married; and fools
are as
like husbands as pilchards are to herrings; the
husband's
the bigger: I am indeed not her fool, but her corrupter
of
words.

35 *Vio.* I saw thee late at the Count Orsino's.

Clo. Foolery, sir, does walk about the orb like
the sun,
it shines every where. I would be sorry, sir, but
the fool
should be as oft with your master as with my
mistress: I
think I saw your wisdom there.

40 *Vio.* Nay, an thou pass upon me, I'll no more with
thee. Hold, there's expenses for thee.

Clo. Now Jove, in his next commodity of hair, send
thee a beard!

Vio. By my troth, I'll tell thee, I am almost sick for
45 one; [*Aside*] though I would not have it grow on my
chin.
Is thy lady within?

Clo. Would not a pair of these have bred, sir?

Vio. Yes, being kept together and put to use.

Clo. I would play Lord Pandarus of Phrygia, sir, to
50 bring a Cressida to this Troilus.

Vio. I understand you, sir; 'tis well begged.

Clo. The matter, I hope, is not great, sir, begging but

a beggar: Cressida was a beggar. My lady is within,
    sir.
I will construe to them whence you come; who
    you are
55 and what you would are out of my welkin, I
    might say
'element,' but the word is over-worn. [*Exit.*
Vio. This fellow is wise enough to play the fool;
And to do that well craves a kind of wit:
He must observe their mood on whom he jests,
60 The quality of persons, and the time,
And, like the haggard, check at every feather
That comes before his eye. This is a practice
As full of labour as a wise man's art:
For folly that he wisely shows is fit;
65 But wise men, folly-fall'n, quite taint their wit.

ENTER SIR TOBY, *AND* SIR ANDREW.

Sir To. Save you, gentleman.
Vio. And you, sir.
Sir And. Dieu vous garde, monsieur.
Vio. Et vous aussi; votre serviteur.
70 *Sir And.* I hope, sir, you are; and I am yours.
Sir To. Will you encounter the house? my niece is
desirous you should enter, if your trade be to her.
Vio. I am bound to your niece, sir; I mean, she is the
list of my voyage.
75 *Sir To.* Taste your legs, sir; put them to motion.
Vio. My legs do better understand me, sir, than I un-
    derstand
what you mean by bidding me taste my legs.
Sir To. I mean, to go, sir, to enter.
Vio. I will answer you with gait and entrance. But
80 we are prevented.

Enter OLIVIA *and* MARIA.

Most excellent accomplished lady, the heavens rain
    odours
on you!
Sir And. That youth's a rare courtier: 'Rain odours;'
well.

₈₅ *Vio.* My matter hath no voice, lady, but to
your own
most pregnant and vouchsafed ear.

Sir And. 'Odours,' 'pregnant,' and 'vouchsafed:' I'll
get 'em all three all ready.

Oli. Let the garden door be shut, and leave me to my
₉₀ hearing. [*Exeunt Sir Toby, Sir Andrew, and Maria.*]
Give
me your hand, sir.

Vio. My duty, madam, and most humble service.

Oli. What is your name?

Vio. Cesario is your servant's name, fair princess.

₉₅ *Oli.* My servant, sir! 'Twas never merry world
Since lowly feigning was call'd compliment:
You're servant to the Count Orsino, youth.

Vio. And he is yours, and his must needs be yours:
Your servant's servant is your servant, madam.

₁₀₀ *Oli.* For him, I think not on him: for his thoughts,
Would they were blanks, rather than fill'd with me!

Vio. Madam, I come to whet your gentle thoughts
On his behalf.

Oli. O, by your leave, I pray you,
I bade you never speak again of him:
₁₀₅ But, would you undertake another suit,
I had rather hear you to solicit that
Than music from the spheres.

Vio. Dear lady,—

Oli. Give me leave, beseech you. I did send,
After the last enchantment you did here,
₁₁₀ A ring in chase of you: so did I abuse
Myself, my servant and, I fear me, you:
Under your hard construction must I sit,
To force that on you, in a shameful cunning,
Which you knew none of yours: what might you
think?
₁₁₅ Have you not set mine honour at the stake
And baited it with all the unmuzzled thoughts
That tyrannous heart can think? To one of your re-
ceiving
Enough is shown: a cypress, not a bosom,
Hides my heart. So, let me hear you speak.

Vio. I pity you.

₁₂₀ *Oli.* That's a degree to love.

Vio. No, not a grize; for 'tis a vulgar proof,
That very oft we pity enemies.
Oli. Why, then, methinks 'tis time to smile again.
O world, how apt the poor are to be proud!
125 If one should be a prey, how much the better
To fall before the lion than the wolf! [*Clock strikes.*
The clock upbraids me with the waste of time.
Be not afraid, good youth, I will not have you:
And yet, when wit and youth is come to harvest,
130 Your wife is like to reap a proper man:
There lies your way, due west.
Vio. Then westward-ho!
Grace and good disposition attend your ladyship!
You'll nothing, madam, to my lord by me?
Oli. Stay:
135 I prithee, tell me what thou think'st of me.
Vio. That you do think you are not what you are.
Oli. If I think so, I think the same of you.
Vio. Then think you right: I am not what I am.
Oli. I would you were as I would have you be!
140 *Vio.* Would it be better, madam, than I am?
I wish it might, for now I am your fool.
Oli. O, what a deal of scorn looks beautiful
In the contempt and anger of his lip!
A murderous guilt shows not itself more soon
145 Than love that would seem hid: love's night is
    noon.
Cesario, by the roses of the spring,
By maidhood, honour, truth and every thing,
I love thee so, that, maugre all thy pride,
Nor wit nor reason can my passion hide.
150 Do not extort thy reasons from this clause,
For that I woo, thou therefore hast no cause;
But rather reason thus with reason fetter,
Love sought is good, but given unsought is better.
Vio. By innocence I swear, and by my youth,
155 I have one heart, one bosom and one truth,
And that no woman has; nor never none
Shall mistress be of it, save I alone.
And so adieu, good madam: never more
Will I my master's tears to you deplore.
160 *Oli.* Yet come again; for thou perhaps
    mayst move

437

That heart, which now abhors, to like his love.
[*Exeunt.*

SCENE II. OLIVIA'S HOUSE

Enter SIR TOBY, SIR ANDREW, *and* FABIAN.

SIR AND. No, faith, I'll not stay a jot longer.
SIR TO. Thy reason, dear venom, give thy reason.
FAB. You must needs yield your reason, Sir Andrew.
SIR AND. Marry, I saw your niece do more
      favours to
5 the count's serving-man than ever she bestowed
      upon me;
I saw 't i' the orchard.
SIR TO. Did she see thee the while, old boy? tell me
that.
SIR AND. As plain as I see you now.
10 *FAB.* This was a great argument of love in her
      toward
you.
SIR AND. 'Slight, will you make an ass o' me?
FAB. I will prove it legitimate, sir, upon the oaths of
judgement and reason.
15 *SIR TO.* And they have been grand-jurymen since
      before
Noah was a sailor.
FAB. She did show favour to the youth in your sight
only to exasperate you, to awake your dormouse
      valour, to
put fire in your heart, and brimstone in your
      liver. You
20 should then have accosted her; and with some ex-
      cellent
jests, fire-new from the mint, you should have
      banged the
youth into dumbness. This was looked for at your
      hand,
and this was balked: the double gilt of this opportu-
      nity you
let time wash off, and you are now sailed into the
      north

$_{25}$ of my lady's opinion; where you will hang like an icicle

on a Dutchman's beard, unless you do redeem it by some

laudable attempt either of valour or policy.

SIR AND. An't be any way, it must be with valour; for

policy I hate: I had as lief be a Brownist as a politician.

$_{30}$ *SIR TO.* Why, then, build me thy fortunes upon the

basis of valour. Challenge me the count's youth to fight

with him; hurt him in eleven places: my niece shall take

note of it; and assure thyself, there is no love-broker in

the world can more prevail in man's commendation with

$_{35}$ woman than report of valour.

FAB. There is no way but this, Sir Andrew.

SIR AND. Will either of you bear me a challenge to him?

SIR TO. Go, write it in a martial hand; be curst and

$_{40}$ brief; it is no matter how witty, so it be eloquent and full

of invention: taunt him with the license of ink: if thou

thou'st him some thrice, it shall not be amiss; and as

many lies as will lie in thy sheet of paper, although the

sheet were big enough for the bed of Ware in England, set

$_{45}$ 'em down: go, about it. Let there be gall enough in thy

ink, though thou write with a goose-pen, no matter: about it.

SIR AND. Where shall I find you?

SIR TO. We'll call thee at the cubiculo: go. [*Exit Sir Andrew.*

$_{50}$ *FAB.* This is a dear manakin to you, Sir Toby.

SIR TO. I have been dear to him, lad, some two thousand

strong, or so.

FAB. We shall have a rare letter from him: but you'll not deliver't?

$_{55}$ *SIR TO.* Never trust me, then; and by all means stir

on the youth to an answer. I think oxen and
    wainropes
cannot hale them together. For Andrew, if he were
    opened,
and you find so much blood in his liver as will
    clog the
foot of a flea, I'll eat the rest of the anatomy.
₆₀ *FAB.* And his opposite, the youth, bears in his
    visage
no great presage of cruelty.

Enter MARIA.

SIR TO. Look, where the youngest wren of nine
    comes.
MAR. If you desire the spleen, and will laugh
    yourselves
into stitches, follow me. Yond gull Malvolio is
₆₅ turned heathen, a very renegado; for there is no
    Christian,
that means to be saved by believing rightly, can ever
    believe
such impossible passages of grossness. He's in yellow
stockings.
SIR TO. And cross-gartered?
₇₀ *MAR.* Most villanously; like a pedant that keeps a
school i' the church. I have dogged him, like his
    murderer.
He does obey every point of the letter that I
    dropped to
betray him: he does smile his face into more lines
    than is
in the new map with the augmentation of the
    Indies: you
₇₅ have not seen such a thing as 'tis. I can hardly
    forbear
hurling things at him. I know my lady will strike
    him: if
she do, he'll smile and take't for a great favour.
SIR TO. Come, bring us, bring us where he is. [*Exeunt.*

SCENE III. A STREET

ENTER SEBASTIAN *AND* ANTONIO.

SEB. I would not by my will have troubled you;
But, since you make your pleasure of your pains,
I will no further chide you.
ANT. I could not stay behind you: my desire,
5 More sharp than filed steel, did spur me forth;
And not all love to see you, though so much
As might have drawn one to a longer voyage,
But jealousy what might befall your travel,
Being skilless in these parts; which to a stranger,
10 Unguided and unfriended, often prove
Rough and unhospitable: my willing love,
The rather by these arguments of fear,
Set forth in your pursuit.
SEB. My kind Antonio,
I can no other answer make but thanks,
15 And thanks; and ever ... oft good turns
Are shuffled off with such uncurrent pay:
But, were my worth as is my conscience firm,
You should find better dealing. What's to do?
Shall we go see the reliques of this town?
20 *ANT.* To-morrow, sir: best first go see your lodging.
SEB. I am not weary, and 'tis long to night:
I pray you, let us satisfy our eyes
With the memorials and the things of fame
That do renown this city.
ANT. Would you'ld pardon me;
25 I do not without danger walk these streets:
Once, in a sea-fight, 'gainst the count his galleys
I did some service; of such note indeed,
That were I ta'en here it would scarce be answer'd.
SEB. Belike you slew great number of his people.
30 *ANT.* The offence is not of such a bloody nature;
Albeit the quality of the time and quarrel
Might well have given us bloody argument.
It might have since been answer'd in repaying
What we took from them; which, for traffic's sake,
35 Most of our city did: only myself stood out;
For which, if I be lapsed in this place,

I shall pay dear.

SEB. Do not then walk too open.

ANT. It doth not fit me. Hold, sir, here's my purse.
In the south suburbs, at the Elephant,
40 Is best to lodge: I will bespeak our diet,
Whiles you beguile the time and feed your
    knowledge
With viewing of the town: there shall you have me.

SEB. Why I your purse?

ANT. Haply your eye shall light upon some toy
45 You have desire to purchase; and your store,
I think, is not for idle markets, sir.

SEB. I'll be your purse-bearer and leave you
For an hour.

ANT. To the Elephant.

SEB. I do remember. [*Exeunt.*

SCENE IV. OLIVIA'S GARDEN

ENTER OLIVIA *AND* MARIA.

OLI. I have sent after him: he says he'll come;
How shall I feast him? what bestow of him?
For youth is bought more oft than begg'd or
    borrow'd.
I speak too loud.
5 Where is Malvolio? he is sad and civil,
And suits well for a servant with my fortunes:
Where is Malvolio?

MAR. He's coming, madam; but in very strange
    manner.
He is, sure, possessed, madam.

10 *OLI.* Why, what's the matter? does he rave?

MAR. No, madam, he does nothing but smile: your
ladyship were best to have some guard about you,
    if he
come; for, sure, the man is tainted in's wits.

OLI. Go call him hither. [*Exit Maria.*] I am as mad
    as he,
15 If sad and merry madness equal be.

RE-ENTER MARIA, *WITH* MALVOLIO.

How now, Malvolio!

MAL. Sweet lady, ho, ho.

OLI. Smilest thou?

I sent for thee upon a sad occasion.

₂₀ *MAL.* Sad, lady! I could be sad: this does make some

obstruction in the blood, this cross-gartering; but what of

that? if it please the eye of one, it is with me as the very

true sonnet is, 'Please one, and please all.'

Oli. Why, how dost thou, man? what is the matter

₂₅ with thee?

MAL. Not black in my mind, though yellow in my legs.

It did come to his hands, and commands shall be executed:

I think we do know the sweet Roman hand.

OLI. Wilt thou go to bed, Malvolio?

₃₀ *MAL.* To bed! ay, sweet-heart, and I'll come to thee.

OLI. God comfort thee! Why dost thou smile so and kiss thy hand so oft?

MAR. How do you, Malvolio?

MAL. At your request! yes; nightingales answer daws.

₃₅ *MAR.* Why appear you with this ridiculous boldness

before my lady?

MAL. 'Be not afraid of greatness:' 'twas well writ.

OLI. What meanest thou by that, Malvolio?

MAL. 'Some are born great,'—

₄₀ *OLI. Ha!*

MAL. 'Some achieve greatness,'—

OLI. What sayest thou?

MAL. 'And some have greatness thrust upon them.'

OLI. Heaven restore thee!

₄₅ *MAL.* 'Remember who commended thy yellow stockings,'—

OLI. Thy yellow stockings!

MAL. 'And wished to see thee cross-gartered.'

OLI. Cross-gartered!

₅₀ *MAL.* 'Go to, thou art made, if thou desirest to be so;'—

OLI. Am I made?

MAL. 'If not, let me see thee a servant still.'
OLI. Why, this is very midsummer madness.

Enter Servant.

SER. Madam, the young gentleman of the Count
    Orsino's
₅₅ is returned: I could hardly entreat him back: he
attends your ladyship's pleasure.
OLI. I'll come to him. [*Exit Servant.*] Good Maria,
let this fellow be looked to. Where's my cousin Toby?
Let some of my people have a special care of him: I
    would
₆₀ not have him miscarry for the half of my dowry.

[*Exeunt Olivia and Maria.*

MAL. O, ho! do you come near me now? no
    worse man
than Sir Toby to look to me! This concurs directly
    with
the letter: she sends him on purpose, that I may
    appear
stubborn to him; for she incites me to that in the
    letter.
₆₅ 'Cast thy humble slough,' says she; 'be opposite
    with a
kinsman, surly with servants; let thy tongue tang
    with arguments
of state; put thyself into the trick of singularity;'
and consequently sets down the manner how; as, a
    sad face,
a reverend carriage, a slow tongue, in the habit of
    some sir
₇₀ of note, and so forth. I have limed her; but it is
    Jove's
doing, and Jove make me thankful! And when
    she went
away now, 'Let this fellow be looked to:' fellow! not
    Malvolio,
nor after my degree, but fellow. Why, every thing
adheres together, that no dram of a scruple, no
    scruple of a

₇₅ scruple, no obstacle, no incredulous or unsafe cir-
    cumstance—What
can be said? Nothing that can be can come between
me and the full prospect of my hopes. Well, Jove,
not I, is the doer of this, and he is to be thanked.

RE-ENTER MARIA, *WITH* SIR TOBY *AND* FABIAN.

SIR TO. Which way is he, in the name of sanctity? If
₈₀ all the devils of hell be drawn in little, and Legion
    himself
possessed him, yet I'll speak to him.
FAB. Here he is, here he is. How is't with you, sir?
how is't with you, man?
MAL. Go off; I discard you: let me enjoy my private:
₈₅ go off.
MAR. Lo, how hollow the fiend speaks within
    him! did
not I tell you? Sir Toby, my lady prays you to have a
care of him.
MAL. Ah, ha! does she so?
₉₀ SIR TO. Go to, go to; peace, peace; we must deal
gently with him: let me alone. How do you, Malvolio?
how is't with you? What, man! defy the devil;
    consider,
he's an enemy to mankind.
MAL. Do you know what you say?
₉₅ MAR. La you, an you speak ill of the devil, how he
takes it at heart! Pray God, he be not bewitched!
FAB. Carry his water to the wise woman.
MAR. Marry, and it shall be done to-morrow morning,
if I live. My lady would not lose him for more than I'll
₁₀₀ say.
MAL. How now, mistress!
MAR. O Lord!
SIR TO. Prithee, hold thy peace; this is not the way:
do you not see you move him? let me alone with him.
₁₀₅ FAB. No way but gentleness; gently, gently: the
    fiend
is rough, and will not be roughly used.
SIR TO. Why, how now, my bawcock! how dost thou,
chuck?
MAL. Sir!

110 *SIR To.* Ay, Biddy, come with me. What, man! 'tis
not for gravity to play at cherry-pit with Satan:
hang him,
foul collier!
MAR. Get him to say his prayers, good Sir Toby, get
him to pray.
115 *MAL.* My prayers, minx!
Mar. No, I warrant you, he will not hear of godliness.
MAL. Go, hang yourselves all! you are idle shallow
things: I am not of your element: you shall
know more
hereafter. [*Exit.*
120 *SIR To.* Is't possible?
FAB. If this were played upon a stage now, I could
condemn it as an improbable fiction.
SIR To. His very genius hath taken the infection of
the device, man.
125 *MAR.* Nay, pursue him now, lest the device take air
and taint.
FAB. Why, we shall make him mad indeed.
MAR. The house will be the quieter.
SIR To. Come, we'll have him in a dark room and
130 bound. My niece is already in the belief that
he's mad:
we may carry it thus, for our pleasure and his
penance, till
our very pastime, tired out of breath, prompt us
to have
mercy on him: at which time we will bring the
device to
the bar and crown thee for a finder of madmen.
But see,
135 but see.

ENTER SIR ANDREW.

FAB. More matter for a May morning.
SIR AND. Here's the challenge, read it: I warrant
there's vinegar and pepper in't.
FAB. Is't so saucy?
140 *SIR AND.* Ay, is't, I warrant him: do but read.
SIR To. Give me. [*Reads*] Youth, whatsoever thou art,
thou art but a scurvy fellow.

Fab. Good, and valiant.

Sir To. [*reads*] Wonder not, nor admire not in thy mind, why

145 I do call thee so, for I will show thee no reason for't.

Fab. A good note; that keeps you from the blow of the law.

Sir To. [*reads*] Thou comest to the lady Olivia, and in my

sight she uses thee kindly: but thou liest in thy throat; that is not the

150 matter I challenge thee for.

Fab. Very brief, and to exceeding good sense—less.

Sir To. [*reads*] I will waylay thee going home; where if it be

thy chance to kill me,—

Fab. Good.

155 *Sir To.* [*reads*] Thou killest me like a rogue and a villain.

Fab. Still you keep o' the windy side of the law: good.

Sir To. [*reads*] Fare thee well; and God have mercy upon one

of our souls! He may have mercy upon mine; but my hope is better,

160 and so look to thyself. Thy friend, as thou usest him, and thy sworn

ENEMY, ANDREW AGUECHEEK.

If this letter move him not, his legs cannot: I'll give't him.

Mar. You may have very fit occasion for't: he is

165 now in some commerce with my lady, and will by and by

depart.

Sir To. Go, Sir Andrew; scout me for him at the corner

of the orchard like a bum-baily: so soon as ever thou

seest him, draw; and, as thou drawest, swear horrible; for

170 it comes to pass oft that a terrible oath, with a swaggering

accent sharply twanged off, gives manhood more ap-probation

447

than ever proof itself would have earned him.
Away!

Sir And. Nay, let me alone for swearing. [*Exit.*

175 Sir To. Now will not I deliver his letter: for the behaviour
of the young gentleman gives him out to be of
good capacity and breeding; his employment between his
lord and my niece confirms no less: therefore this letter,
being so excellently ignorant, will breed no terror in the
180 youth: he will find it comes from a clodpole. But, sir, I will
deliver his challenge by word of mouth; set upon Aguecheek
a notable report of valour; and drive the gentleman,
as I know his youth will aptly receive it, into a most
hideous opinion of his rage, skill, fury and impetuosity.
185 This will so fright them both, that they will kill one another
by the look, like cockatrices.

Re-enter OLIVIA, with VIOLA.

Fab. Here he comes with your niece: give them way
till he take leave, and presently after him.

Sir To. I will meditate the while upon some horrid
190 message for a challenge.

[*Exeunt Sir Toby, Fabian, and Maria.*

Oli. I have said too much unto a heart of stone
And laid mine honour too unchary out:
There's something in me that reproves my fault;
But such a headstrong potent fault it is,
195 That it but mocks reproof.

Vio. With the same 'haviour that your passion bears
Goes on my master's grief.

Oli. Here, wear this jewel for me, 'tis my picture;
Refuse it not; it hath no tongue to vex you;
200 And I beseech you come again to-morrow.

What shall you ask of me that I'll deny,
That honour saved may upon asking give?
Vio. Nothing but this;—your true love for my master.
Oli. How with mine honour may I give him that
Which I have given to you?
205 *Vio.* I will acquit you.
Oli. Well, come again to-morrow: fare thee well:
A fiend like thee might bear my soul to hell. [*Exit.*

RE-ENTER Sir Toby *AND* Fabian.

Sir To. Gentleman, God save thee.
Vio. And you, sir.
210 *Sir To.* That defence thou hast, betake thee to't: of
what nature the wrongs are thou hast done him,
    I know
not; but thy intercepter, full of despite, bloody as the
hunter, attends thee at the orchard-end: dismount thy
    tuck,
be yare in thy preparation, for thy assailant is quick,
    skilful
215 and deadly.
Vio. You mistake, sir; I am sure no man hath any
quarrel to me: my remembrance is very free and
    clear
from any image of offence done to any man.
Sir To. You'll find it otherwise, I assure you:
    therefore,
220 if you hold your life at any price, betake you
    to your
guard; for your opposite hath in him what youth,
    strength,
skill and wrath can furnish man withal.
Vio. I pray you, sir, what is he?
Sir To. He is knight, dubbed with unhatched rapier
225 and on carpet consideration; but he is a devil in
    private
brawl: souls and bodies hath he divorced three; and
    his incensement
at this moment is so implacable, that satisfaction
can be none but by pangs of death and sepulchre.
    Hob,
nob, is his word; give't or take't.

₂₃₀ *Vio.* I will return again into the house and desire some
conduct of the lady. I am no fighter. I have heard of
some kind of men that put quarrels purposely on others, to
taste their valour: belike this is a man of that quirk.
Sir To. Sir, no; his indignation derives itself out of a
₂₃₅ very competent injury: therefore, get you on and give him
his desire. Back you shall not to the house, unless you undertake
that with me which with as much safety you might
answer him: therefore, on, or strip your sword stark naked;
for meddle you must, that's certain, or forswear to wear iron
₂₄₀ about you.
Vio. This is as uncivil as strange. I beseech you, do
me this courteous office, as to know of the knight what my
offence to him is: it is something of my negligence, nothing
of my purpose.
₂₄₅ *Sir To.* I will do so. Signior Fabian, stay you by this
gentleman till my return. [*Exit.*
Vio. Pray you, sir, do you know of this matter?
Fab. I know the knight is incensed against you, even
to a mortal arbitrement; but nothing of the circumstance
₂₅₀ more.
Vio. I beseech you, what manner of man is he?
Fab. Nothing of that wonderful promise, to read him
by his form, as you are like to find him in the proof of his
valour. He is, indeed, sir, the most skilful, bloody and
₂₅₅ fatal opposite that you could possibly have found in any
part of Illyria. Will you walk towards him? I will make
your peace with him if I can.
Vio. I shall be much bound to you for't: I am one
that had rather go with sir priest than sir knight: I

care not
₂₆₀ who knows so much of my mettle. [*Exeunt.*

RE-ENTER SIR TOBY, *WITH* SIR ANDREW.

SIR TO. Why, man, he's a very devil; I have not seen
such a firago. I had a pass with him, rapier, scabbard
and
all, and he gives me the stuck in with such a mortal
motion,
that it is inevitable; and on the answer, he pays you as
₂₆₅ surely as your feet hit the ground they step on.
They say
he has been fencer to the Sophy.
SIR AND. Pox on't, I'll not meddle with him.
SIR TO. Ay, but he will not now be pacified: Fabian
can scarce hold him yonder.
₂₇₀ SIR AND. Plague on't, an I thought he had been
valiant
and so cunning in fence, I'ld have seen him damned
ere I'ld have challenged him. Let him let the matter
slip,
and I'll give him my horse, grey Capilet.
SIR TO. I'll make the motion: stand here, make a good
₂₇₅ show on't: this shall end without the perdition of
souls.
[*Aside*] Marry, I'll ride your horse as well as I ride you.

Re-enter FABIAN *and* VIOLA.

[*To Fab.*] I have his horse to take up the quarrel: I have
persuaded him the youth's a devil.
FAB. He is as horribly conceited of him; and pants and
₂₈₀ looks pale, as if a bear were at his heels.
SIR TO. [*To Vio.*] There's no remedy, sir; he will fight
with you for's oath sake: marry, he hath better
bethought
him of his quarrel, and he finds that now scarce to be
worth
talking of: therefore draw, for the supportance of
his vow;
₂₈₅ he protests he will not hurt you.
VIO. [*Aside*] Pray God defend me! A little thing

would make me tell them how much I lack of a man.

Fab. Give ground, if you see him furious.

Sir To. Come, Sir Andrew, there's no remedy; the
₂₉₀ gentleman will, for his honour's sake, have one
  bout with
you; he cannot by the duello avoid it: but he has
  promised
me, as he is a gentleman and a soldier, he will not
  hurt you.
Come on; to't.

Sir And. Pray God, he keep his oath!

₂₉₅ *Vio.* I do assure you, 'tis against my will.[*They
  draw.*

ENTER ANTONIO.

Ant. Put up your sword. If this young gentleman
Have done offence, I take the fault on me:

If you offend him, I for him defy you.

Sir To. You, sir! why, what are you?

₃₀₀ *Ant.* One, sir, that for his love dares yet do more
Than you have heard him brag to you he will.

Sir To. Nay, if you be an undertaker, I am for you.
  [*They draw.*

Enter Officers.

Fab. O good Sir Toby, hold! here come the officers.

Sir To. I'll be with you anon.

₃₀₅ *Vio.* Pray, sir, put your sword up, if you please.

Sir And. Marry, will I, sir; and, for that I promised
you, I 'll be as good as my word: he will bear you
  easily
and reins well.

First Off. This is the man; do thy office.

₃₁₀ *Sec. Off.* Antonio, I arrest thee at the suit of
  Count Orsino.

Ant. You do mistake me, sir.

First Off. No, sir, no jot; I know your favour well,
Though now you have no sea-cap on your head.

₃₁₅ Take him away: he knows I know him well.

Ant. I must obey. [*To Vio.*] This comes with seeking

you:
But there's no remedy; I shall answer it.
What will you do, now my necessity
Makes me to ask you for my purse? It grieves me
320 Much more for what I cannot do for you
Than what befalls myself. You stand amazed;
But be of comfort.
Sec. Off. Come, sir, away.
Ant. I must entreat of you some of that money.
325 *Vio.* What money, sir?
For the fair kindness you have show'd me here,
And, part, being prompted by your present trouble,
Out of my lean and low ability
I'll lend you something: my having is not much;
330 I'll make division of my present with you:
Hold, there's half my coffer.
Ant. Will you deny me now?
Is't possible that my deserts to you
Can lack persuasion? Do not tempt my misery,
Lest that it make me so unsound a man
335 As to upbraid you with those kindnesses
That I have done for you.
Vio. I know of none;
Nor know I you by voice or any feature:
I hate ingratitude more in a man
Than lying, vainness, babbling, drunkenness,
340 Or any taint of vice whose strong corruption
Inhabits our frail blood.
Ant. O heavens themselves!
Sec. Off. Come, sir, I pray you, go.
Ant. Let me speak a little. This youth that you
see here
I snatch'd one half out of the jaws of death;
345 Relieved him with such sanctity of love;
And to his image, which methought did promise
Most venerable worth, did I devotion.
First Off. What's that to us? The time goes by: away!
Ant. But O how vile an idol proves this god!
350 Thou hast, Sebastian, done good feature shame.
In nature there's no blemish but the mind;
None can be call'd deform'd but the unkind:
Virtue is beauty; but the beauteous evil
Are empty trunks, o'erflourish'd by the devil.

355 *First Off.* The man grows mad: away with him!
    Come, come, sir.

Ant. Lead me on. [*Exit with Officers.*

Vio. Methinks his words do from such passion fly,
That he believes himself: so do not I.
Prove true, imagination, O, prove true,
360 That I, dear brother, be now ta'en for you!

Sir To. Come hither, knight; come hither, Fabian:
we'll whisper o'er a couplet or two of most sage saws.

Vio. He named Sebastian: I my brother know
Yet living in my glass; even such and so
365 In favour was my brother, and he went
Still in this fashion, colour, ornament,
For him I imitate: O, if it prove,
Tempests are kind and salt waves fresh in love! [*Exit.*

Sir To. A very dishonest paltry boy, and more a
    coward
370 than a hare: his dishonesty appears in leaving his
    friend
here in necessity and denying him; and for his cow-
    ardship,
ask Fabian.

Fab. A coward, a most devout coward, religious in it.

Sir And. 'Slid, I'll after him again and beat him.

375 *Sir To.* Do; cuff him soundly, but never draw thy
sword.

Sir And. An I do not, — [*Exit.*

Fab. Come, let's see the event.

Sir To. I dare lay any money 'twill be nothing yet.
    [*Exeunt.*

ACT IV

Enter SEBASTIAN *and* Clown.

CLO. Will you make me believe that I am not sent for
you?
SEB. Go to, go to, thou art a foolish fellow:
Let me be clear of thee.
₅ *CLO.* Well held out, i' faith! No, I do not know you;
nor I am not sent to you by my lady, to bid you come
speak with her; nor your name is not Master Cesario;
    nor
this is not my nose neither. Nothing that is so is so.
SEB. I prithee, vent thy folly somewhere else:
₁₀ Thou know'st not me.
CLO. Vent my folly! he has heard that word of some
great man and now applies it to a fool. Vent my
    folly! I
am afraid this great lubber, the world, will prove a
    cockney.
I prithee now, ungird thy strangeness and tell me
    what I
₁₅ shall vent to my lady: shall I vent to her that
    thou art
coming?
SEB. I prithee, foolish Greek, depart from me:
There's money for thee: if you tarry longer,

455

I shall give worse payment.

20 *Clo.* By my troth, thou hast an open hand.
    These wise
men that give fools money get themselves a good re-
    port—after
fourteen years' purchase.

Sir And. Now, sir, have I met you again? there's for
you.

25 *Seb.* Why, there's for thee, and there, and there.
Are all the people mad?

Sir To. Hold, sir, or I'll throw your dagger o'er the
house.

Clo. This will I tell my lady straight: I would not be
30 in some of your coats for two pence [*Exit.*

Sir To. Come on, sir; hold.

Sir And. Nay, let him alone: I'll go another way to
work with him; I'll have an action of battery against
    him,
if there be any law in Illyria: though I stroke him first,
35 yet it's no matter for that.

Seb. Let go thy hand.

Sir To. Come, sir, I will not let you go. Come, my
young soldier, put up your iron: you are well fleshed;
come on.

40 *Seb.* I will be free from thee. What wouldst
    thou now?
If thou darest tempt me further, draw thy sword.

Sir To. What, what? Nay, then I must have an ounce
or two of this malapert blood from you.

Oli. Hold, Toby; on thy life, I charge thee, hold!
45 *Sir To. Madam!*

Oli. Will it be ever thus? Ungracious wretch,
Fit for the mountains and the barbarous caves,
Where manners ne'er were preach'd! out of my sight!
Be not offended, dear Cesario.
Rudesby, be gone!

[Exeunt Sir Toby, Sir Andrew, and Fabian.

50 I prithee, gentle friend,
Let thy fair wisdom, not thy passion, sway
In this uncivil and unjust extent
Against thy peace. Go with me to my house;
And hear thou there how many fruitless pranks
55 This ruffian hath botch'd up, that thou thereby
Mayst smile at this: thou shalt not choose but go:
Do not deny. Beshrew his soul for me,
He started one poor heart of mine in thee.
SEB. What relish is in this? how runs the stream?
60 Or I am mad, or else this is a dream:
Let fancy still my sense in Lethe steep;
If it be thus to dream, still let me sleep!
OLI. Nay, come, I prithee: would thou'ldst be ruled
    by me!
SEB. Madam, I will.
OLI. O, say so, and so be! [*Exeunt.*

SCENE II. OLIVIA'S HOUSE

Enter MARIA *and* CLOWN.

MAR. Nay, I prithee, put on this gown and this beard;
make him believe thou art Sir Topas the curate: do it
quickly; I'll call Sir Toby the whilst. [*Exit.*
CLO. Well, I'll put it on, and I will dissemble myself
5 in 't; and I would I were the first that ever dissem-
    bled in
such a gown. I am not tall enough to become the
    function
well, nor lean enough to be thought a good student;
    but
to be said an honest man and a good housekeeper
    goes as
fairly as to say a careful man and a great scholar. The
10 competitors enter.

ENTER SIR TOBY *AND* MARIA.

SIR TO. Jove bless thee, master Parson.

Clo. Bonos dies, Sir Toby: for, as the old hermit of
Prague, that never saw pen and ink, very wittily said
    to a
niece of King Gorboduc, 'That that is is;' so I, being
    master
15 Parson, am master Parson; for, what is 'that' but
    'that,'
and 'is' but 'is'?
Sir To. To him, Sir Topas.
Clo. What, ho, I say! peace in this prison!
Sir To. The knave counterfeits well; a good knave.
20 *Mal.* [*within*] Who calls there?
Clo. Sir Topas the curate, who comes to visit
    Malvolio
the lunatic.
Mal. Sir Topas, Sir Topas, good Sir Topas, go to my
lady.
25 *Clo.* Out, hyperbolical fiend! how vexest thou this
man! talkest thou nothing but of ladies?
Sir To. Well said, master Parson.
Mal. Sir Topas, never was man thus wronged: good
Sir Topas, do not think I am mad: they have laid
    me here
30 in hideous darkness.
Clo. Fie, thou dishonest Satan! I call thee by the most
modest terms; for I am one of those gentle ones
    that will
use the devil himself with courtesy: sayest thou that
house
is dark?
35 *Mal.* As hell, Sir Topas.
Clo. Why, it hath bay windows transparent as bar-
    ricadoes,
and the clearstores toward the south north are as
    lustrous
as ebony; and yet complainest thou of obstruction?
Mal. I am not mad, Sir Topas: I say to you, this
40 house is dark.
Clo. Madman, thou errest: I say, there is no darkness
but ignorance; in which thou art more puzzled
    than the
Egyptians in their fog.
Mal. I say, this house is as dark as ignorance, though

₄₅ ignorance were as dark as hell; and I say, there was never

man thus abused. I am no more mad than you are: make

the trial of it in any constant question.

Clo. What is the opinion of Pythagoras concerning wild fowl?

₅₀ *Mal.* That the soul of our grandam might haply inhabit

a bird.

Clo. What thinkest thou of his opinion?

Mal. I think nobly of the soul, and no way approve his opinion.

₅₅ *Clo.* Fare thee well. Remain thou still in darkness:

thou shalt hold the opinion of Pythagoras ere I will allow of

thy wits; and fear to kill a woodcock, lest thou dispossess

the soul of thy grandam. Fare thee well.

Mal. Sir Topas, Sir Topas!

₆₀ *Sir To.* My most exquisite Sir Topas!

Clo. Nay, I am for all waters.

Mar. Thou mightst have done this without thy beard and gown: he sees thee not.

Sir To. To him in thine own voice, and bring me word

₆₅ how thou findest him: I would we were well rid of this

knavery. If he may be conveniently delivered, I would he

were; for I am now so far in offence with my niece, that I

cannot pursue with any safety this sport to the upshot. Come

by and by to my chamber. [Exeunt Sir Toby and Maria.

₇₀ *Clo. [Singing]* Hey, Robin, jolly Robin,

Tell me how thy lady does.

Mal. Fool,——

Clo. My lady is unkind, perdy.

Mal. Fool,——

₇₅ *Clo.* Alas, why is she so?

Mal. Fool, I say,——

Clo. She loves another—Who calls, ha?

MAL. Good fool, as ever thou wilt deserve well at my
hand, help me to a candle, and pen, ink and paper:
as I
₈₀ am a gentleman, I will live to be thankful to thee
for't.

CLO. Master Malvolio?

MAL. Ay, good fool.

CLO. Alas, sir, how fell you besides your five wits?

MAL. Fool, there was never man so notoriously
abused:
₈₅ I am as well in my wits, fool, as thou art.

CLO. But as well? then you are mad indeed, if you be
no better in your wits than a fool.

MAL. They have here propertied me; keep me in
darkness,
send ministers to me, asses, and do all they can to
₉₀ face me out of my wits.

CLO. Advise you what you say; the minister is here.
Malvolio, Malvolio, thy wits the heavens restore! endeavour
thyself to sleep, and leave thy vain bibble babble.

MAL. Sir Topas,——

₉₅ *CLO.* Maintain no words with him, good fellow.
Who,
I, sir? not I, sir. God be wi' you, good Sir Topas.
Marry,
amen. I will, sir, I will.

MAL. Fool, fool, fool, I say,——

CLO. Alas, sir, be patient. What say you, sir? I am
₁₀₀ shent for speaking to you.

MAL. Good fool, help me to some light and some
paper: I tell thee, I am as well in my wits as any
man in
Illyria.

CLO. Well-a-day that you were, sir!

₁₀₅ *MAL.* By this hand, I am. Good fool, some ink,
paper
and light; and convey what I will set down to my
lady: it
shall advantage thee more than ever the bearing of
letter
did.

CLO. I will help you to't. But tell me true, are you

110 not mad indeed? or do you but counterfeit?

Mal. Believe me, I am not; I tell thee true.

Clo. Nay, I'll ne'er believe a madman till I see his brains. I will fetch you light and paper and ink.

Mal. Fool, I'll requite it in the highest degree: I 115 prithee, be gone.

Clo. [*Singing*] I am gone, sir,
And anon, sir,
I'll be with you again,
In a trice,
120 Like to the old vice,
Your need to sustain;
Who, with dagger of lath,
In his rage and his wrath,
Cries, ah, ha! to the devil:
125 Like a mad lad,
Pare thy nails, dad;
Adieu, goodman Drivel. [*Exit.*

SCENE III. OLIVIA'S GARDEN

Enter Sebastian.

Seb. This is the air; that is the glorious sun;
This pearl she gave me, I do feel't and see't;
And though 'tis wonder that enwraps me thus,
Yet 'tis not madness. Where's Antonio, then?
5 I could not find him at the Elephant:
Yet there he was; and there I found this credit,
That he did range the town to seek me out.
His counsel now might do me golden service;
For though my soul disputes well with my sense,
10 That this may be some error, but no madness,
Yet doth this accident and flood of fortune
So far exceed all instance, all discourse,
That I am ready to distrust mine eyes
And wrangle with my reason, that persuades me
15 To any other trust but that I am mad,
Or else the lady's mad; yet, if 'twere so,
She could not sway her house, command her
    followers,
Take and give back affairs and their dispatch

With such a smooth, discreet, and stable bearing
₂₀ As I perceive she does: there's something in't
That is deceivable. But here the lady comes.

Enter OLIVIA *and* Priest.

OLI. Blame not this haste of mine. If you mean well,
Now go with me and with this holy man
Into the chantry by: there, before him,
₂₅ And underneath that consecrated roof,
Plight me the full assurance of your faith;
That my most jealous and too doubtful soul
May live at peace. He shall conceal it
Whiles you are willing it shall come to note,
₃₀ What time we will our celebration keep
According to my birth. What do you say?
SEB. I'll follow this good man, and go with you;
And, having sworn truth, ever will be true.
OLIV. Then lead the way, good father; and heavens so
    shine,
₃₅ That they may fairly note this act of mine! [*Exeunt.*

ACT V

SCENE I. BEFORE OLIVIA'S HOUSE.

Enter Clown *and* FABIAN.

FAB. Now, as thou lovest me, let me see his letter.
CLO. Good Master Fabian, grant me another request.
FAB. Any thing.
CLO. Do not desire to see this letter.
5 FAB. This is, to give a dog, and in recompense desire
my dog again.

ENTER DUKE, VIOLA, CURIO, *AND* LORDS.

DUKE. Belong you to the Lady Olivia, friends?
CLO. Ay, sir; we are some of her trappings.
DUKE. I know thee well: how dost thou, my good
     fellow?
10 CLO. Truly, sir, the better for my foes and the worse
for my friends.
DUKE. Just the contrary; the better for thy friends.
CLO. No, sir, the worse.
DUKE. How can that be?
15 CLO. Marry, sir, they praise me and make an ass of
me; now my foes tell me plainly I am an ass: so
     that by
my foes, sir, I profit in the knowledge of myself;
     and by

my friends I am abused: so that, conclusions to be as
    kisses,
if your four negatives make your two affirmatives,
    why then,
20 the worse for my friends, and the better for my
    foes.

Duke. Why, this is excellent.

Clo. By my troth, sir, no; though it please you to be
one of my friends.

Duke. Thou shalt not be the worse for me: there's
    gold.

25 *Clo.* But that it would be double-dealing, sir, I
    would
you could make it another.

Duke. O, you give me ill counsel.

Clo. Put your grace in your pocket, sir, for this once,
and let your flesh and blood obey it.

30 *Duke.* Well, I will be so much a sinner, to be a dou-
    ble-dealer:
there's another.

Clo. Primo, secundo, tertio, is a good play; and
    the old
saying is, the third pays for all: the triplex, sir, is
    a good
tripping measure; or the bells of Saint Bennet, sir,
    may put
35 you in mind; one, two, three.

Duke. You can fool no more money out of me at this
throw: if you will let your lady know I am here to
    speak
with her, and bring her along with you, it may
    awake my
bounty further.

40 *Clo.* Marry, sir, lullaby to your bounty till I come
    again.
I go, sir; but I would not have you to think that my
    desire
of having is the sin of covetousness: but, as you say,
    sir, let
your bounty take a nap, I will awake it anon. [*Exit.*

Vio. Here comes the man, sir, that did rescue me.

Enter Antonio *and* Officers.

$_{45}$ *DUKE.* That face of his I do remember well;
Yet, when I saw it last, it was besmear'd
As black as Vulcan in the smoke of war:
A bawbling vessel was he captain of,
For shallow draught and bulk unprizable;
$_{50}$ With which such scathful grapple did he make
With the most noble bottom of our fleet,
That very envy and the tongue of loss
Cried fame and honour on him. What's the matter?
FIRST OFF. Orsino, this is that Antonio
$_{55}$ That took the Phoenix and her fraught from Candy;
And this is he that did the Tiger board,
When your young nephew Titus lost his leg:
Here in the streets, desperate of shame and state,
In private brabble did we apprehend him.
$_{60}$ *VIO.* He did me kindness, sir, drew on my side;
But in conclusion put strange speech upon me:
I know not what 'twas but distraction.
DUKE. Notable pirate! thou salt-water thief!
What foolish boldness brought thee to their mercies,
$_{65}$ Whom thou, in terms so bloody and so dear,
Hast made thine enemies?
ANT. Orsino, noble sir,
Be pleased that I shake off these names you give me:
Antonio never yet was thief or pirate,
Though I confess, on base and ground enough,
$_{70}$ Orsino's enemy. A witchcraft drew me hither:
That most ingrateful boy there by your side,
From the rude sea's enraged and foamy mouth
Did I redeem; a wreck past hope he was:
His life I gave him and did thereto add
$_{75}$ My love, without retention or restraint,
All his in dedication; for his sake
Did I expose myself, pure for his love,
Into the danger of this adverse town;
Drew to defend him when he was beset:
$_{80}$ Where being apprehended, his false cunning,
Not meaning to partake with me in danger,
Taught him to face me out of his acquaintance,
And grew a twenty years removed thing
While one would wink; denied me mine own purse,
$_{85}$ Which I had recommended to his use
Not half an hour before.

Vio. How can this be?

Duke. When came he to this town?

Ant. Today, my lord; and for three months before,
No interim, not a minute's vacancy,
90 Both day and night did we keep company.

Enter OLIVIA *and* Attendants.

Duke. Here comes the countess: now heaven walks
    on earth.
But for thee, fellow; fellow, thy words are madness:
Three months this youth hath tended upon me;
But more of that anon. Take him aside.
95 *Oli.* What would my lord, but that he may not
    have,
Wherein Olivia may seem serviceable?
Cesario, you do not keep promise with me.

Vio. Madam!

Duke. Gracious Olivia,—

100 *Oli.* What do you say, Cesario? Good my lord,—

Vio. My lord would speak; my duty hushes me.

Oli. If it be aught to the old tune, my lord,
It is as fat and fulsome to mine ear
As howling after music.

Duke. Still so cruel?

105 *Oli.* Still so constant, lord.

Duke. What, to perverseness? You uncivil lady,
To whom ingrate and unauspicious altars
My soul the faithfull'st offerings hath breathed out
That e'er devotion tender'd! What shall I do?

110 *Oli.* Even what it please my lord, that shall be-
    come him.

Duke. Why should I not, had I the heart to do it,
Like to the Egyptian thief at point of death,
Kill what I love?—a savage jealousy
That sometime savours nobly. But hear me this:
115 Since you to non-regardance cast my faith,
And that I partly know the instrument
That screws me from my true place in your favour,
Live you the marble-breasted tyrant still;
But this your minion, whom I know you love,
120 And whom, by heaven I swear, I tender dearly,
Him will I tear out of that cruel eye,

466

Where he sits crowned in his master's spite.
Come, boy, with me; my thoughts are ripe in mischief:
I'll sacrifice the lamb that I do love,
125 To spite a raven's heart within a dove.
Vio. And I, most jocund, apt and willingly,
To do you rest, a thousand deaths would die.
Oli. Where goes Cesario?
Vio. After him I love
More than I love these eyes, more than my life,
130 More, by all mores, than e'er I shall love wife.
If I do feign, you witnesses above
Punish my life for tainting of my love!
Oli. Ay me, detested! how am I beguiled!
Vio. Who does beguile you? who does do you
      wrong?
135 *Oli.* Hast thou forgot thyself? is it so long?
Call forth the holy father.
Duke. Come, away!
Oli. Whither, my lord? Cesario, husband, stay.
Duke. Husband!
Oli. Ay, husband: can he that deny?
Duke. Her husband, sirrah!
Vio. No, my lord, not I.
140 *Oli.* Alas, it is the baseness of thy fear
That makes thee strangle thy propriety:
Fear not, Cesario; take thy fortunes up;
Be that thou know'st thou art, and then thou art
As great as that thou fear'st.

Enter Priest.

O, welcome, father!
145 Father, I charge thee, by thy reverence,
Here to unfold, though lately we intended
To keep in darkness what occasion now
Reveals before 'tis ripe, what thou dost know
Hath newly pass'd between this youth and me.
150 *Priest.* A contract of eternal bond of love,
Confirm'd by mutual joinder of your hands,
Attested by the holy close of lips,
Strengthen'd by interchangement of your rings;
And all the ceremony of this compact
155 Seal'd in my function, by my testimony:

Since when, my watch hath told me, toward my grave
I have travell'd but two hours.
Duke. O thou dissembling cub! what wilt thou be
When time hath sow'd a grizzle on thy case?
160 Or will not else thy craft so quickly grow,
That thine own trip shall be thine overthrow?
Farewell, and take her; but direct thy feet
Where thou and I henceforth may never meet.
Vio. My lord, I do protest—
Oli. O, do not swear!
165 Hold little faith, though thou hast too much fear.

Enter Sir Andrew.

Sir And. For the love of God, a surgeon! Send one
presently to Sir Toby.
Oli. What's the matter?
Sir And. He has broke my head across and has given
170 Sir Toby a bloody coxcomb too: for the love of
    God, your
help! I had rather than forty pound I were at home.
Oli. Who has done this, Sir Andrew?
Sir And. The count's gentleman, one Cesario:
    we took
him for a coward, but he's the very devil incardinate.
175 *Duke.* My gentleman, Cesario?
Sir And. 'Od's lifelings, here he is! You broke my
head for nothing; and that that I did, I was set on
    to do't
by Sir Toby.
Vio. Why do you speak to me? I never hurt you:
180 You drew your sword upon me without cause;
But I bespake you fair, and hurt you not.
Sir And. If a bloody coxcomb be a hurt, you have
hurt me: I think you set nothing by a bloody
    coxcomb.

Enter Sir Toby *and* Clown.

Here comes Sir Toby halting; you shall hear more:
    but if
185 he had not been in drink, he would have tickled
    you othergates

468

than he did.

Duke. How now, gentleman! how is't with you?

Sir To. That's all one: has hurt me, and there's the end on't. Sot, didst see Dick surgeon, sot?

190 *Clo.* O, he's drunk, Sir Toby, an hour agone; his eyes

were set at eight i' the morning.

Sir To. Then he's a rogue, and a passy measures panyn:

I hate a drunken rogue.

Oli. Away with him! Who hath made this havoc with
195 them?

Sir And. I'll help you, Sir Toby, because we'll be dressed together.

Sir To. Will you help? an ass-head and a coxcomb and a knave, a thin-faced knave, a gull!

200 *Oli.* Get him to bed, and let his hurt be look'd to.

*[Exeunt Clown, Fabian, Sir Toby, and Sir Andrew.
Enter Sebastian.*

Seb. I am sorry, madam, I have hurt your kinsman;

But, had it been the brother of my blood,

I must have done no less with wit and safety.

You throw a strange regard upon me, and by that
205 I do perceive it hath offended you:

Pardon me, sweet one, even for the vows

We made each other but so late ago.

Duke. One face, one voice, one habit, and two persons,

A natural perspective, that is and is not!

210 *Seb.* Antonio, O my dear Antonio!

How have the hours rack'd and tortured me,

Since I have lost thee!

Ant. Sebastian are you?

Seb. Fear'st thou that, Antonio?

Ant. How have you made division of yourself?

215 An apple, cleft in two, is not more twin

Than these two creatures. Which is Sebastian?

Oli. Most wonderful!

Seb. Do I stand there? I never had a brother;

Nor can there be that deity in my nature,

220 Of here and every where. I had a sister,

Whom the blind waves and surges have devour'd.
Of charity, what kin are you to me?
What countryman? what name? what parentage?
Vio. Of Messaline: Sebastian was my father;
₂₂₅ Such a Sebastian was my brother too,
So went he suited to his watery tomb:
If spirits can assume both form and suit
You come to fright us.
Seb. A spirit I am indeed;
But am in that dimension grossly clad
₂₃₀ Which from the womb I did participate.
Were you a woman, as the rest goes even,
I should my tears let fall upon your cheek,
And say 'Thrice-welcome, drowned Viola!'
Vio. My father had a mole upon his brow.
₂₃₅ *Seb.* And so had mine.
Vio. And died that day when Viola from her birth
Had number'd thirteen years.
Seb. O, that record is lively in my soul!
He finished indeed his mortal act
₂₄₀ That day that made my sister thirteen years.
Vio. If nothing lets to make us happy both
But this my masculine usurp'd attire,
Do not embrace me till each circumstance
Of place, time, fortune, do cohere and jump
₂₄₅ That I am Viola: which to confirm,
I'll bring you to a captain in this town,
Where lie my maiden weeds; by whose gentle help
I was preserved to serve this noble count.
All the occurrence of my fortune since
₂₅₀ Hath been between this lady and this lord.
Seb. [*To Olivia*] So comes it, lady, you have been
  mistook:
But nature to her bias drew in that.
You would have been contracted to a maid;
Nor are you therein, by my life, deceived,
₂₅₅ You are betroth'd both to a maid and man.
Duke. Be not amazed; right noble is his blood.
If this be so, as yet the glass seems true,
I shall have share in this most happy wreck.
[*To Viola*] Boy, thou hast said to me a thousand times
₂₆₀ Thou never shouldst love woman like to me.
Vio. And all those sayings will I over-swear;

And all those swearings keep as true in soul
As doth that orbed continent the fire
That severs day from night.
Duke. Give me thy hand;
₂₆₅ And let me see thee in thy woman's weeds.
Vio. The captain that did bring me first on shore
Hath my maid's garments: he upon some action
Is now in durance, at Malvolio's suit,
A gentleman, and follower of my lady's.
₂₇₀ *Oli.* He shall enlarge him: fetch Malvolio hither:
And yet, alas, now I remember me,
They say, poor gentleman, he's much distract.

Re-enter Clown with a letter, and FABIAN.

A most extracting frenzy of mine own
From my remembrance clearly banish'd his.
₂₇₅ How does he, sirrah?
Clo. Truly, madam, he holds Belzebub at the stave's
end as well as a man in his case may do: has here
    writ a
letter to you; I should have given 't you to-day
    morning,
but as a madman's epistles are no gospels, so it
    skills not
₂₈₀ much when they are delivered.
Oli. Open 't, and read it.
Clo. Look then to be well edified when the fool
    delivers
the madman. [*Reads*] By the Lord, madam,—
Oli. How now! art thou mad?
₂₈₅ *Clo.* No, madam, I do but read madness: an your
    ladyship
will have it as it ought to be, you must allow Vox.
Oli. Prithee, read i' thy right wits.
Clo. So I do, madonna; but to read his right wits is to
read thus: therefore perpend, my princess, and
    give ear.
₂₉₀ *Oli.* Read it you, sirrah. [*To Fabian.*
Fab. [*Reads*] By the Lord, madam, you wrong
    me, and
the world shall know it: though you have put me into
    darkness and

given your drunken cousin rule over me, yet have I
the benefit of my
senses as well as your ladyship. I have your own
letter that induced
295 me to the semblance I put on; with the which I
doubt not but to do
myself much right, or you much shame. Think of me
as you please.
I leave my duty a little unthought of and speak out of
my injury.—THE MADLY-USED MALVOLIO.
Oli. Did he write this?
300 *Clo.* Ay, madam.
Duke. This savours not much of distraction.
Oli. See him deliver'd, Fabian; bring him hither. [*Exit
Fabian.*
My lord, so please you, these things further
thought on,
To think me as well a sister as a wife,
305 One day shall crown the alliance on't, so
please you,
Here at my house and at my proper cost.
Duke. Madam, I am most apt to embrace your offer.
[*To Viola*] Your master quits you; and for your service
done him,
So much against the mettle of your sex,
310 So far beneath your soft and tender breeding,
And since you call'd me master for so long,
Here is my hand: you shall from this time be
Your master's mistress.
Oli. A sister! you are she.

RE-ENTER FABIAN, WITH MALVOLIO.

Duke. Is this the madman?
Oli. Ay, my lord, this same.
How now, Malvolio!
315 *Mal.* Madam, you have done me wrong,
Notorious wrong.
Oli. Have I, Malvolio? no.
Mal. Lady, you have. Pray you, peruse that letter.
You must not now deny it is your hand:
Write from it, if you can, in hand or phrase;
320 Or say 'tis not your seal, not your invention:

You can say none of this: well, grant it then
And tell me, in the modesty of honour,
Why you have given me such clear lights of favour,
Bade me come smiling and cross-garter'd to you,
₃₂₅ To put on yellow stockings and to frown
Upon Sir Toby and the lighter people;
And, acting this in an obedient hope,
Why have you suffer'd me to be imprison'd,
Kept in a dark house, visited by the priest,
₃₃₀ And made the most notorious geek and gull
That e'er invention play'd on? tell me why.
OLI. Alas, Malvolio, this is not my writing,
Though, I confess, much like the character:
But out of question 'tis Maria's hand.
₃₃₅ And now I do bethink me, it was she
First told me thou wast mad; then camest in smiling,
And in such forms which here were presupposed
Upon thee in the letter. Prithee, be content:
This practice hath most shrewdly pass'd upon thee;
₃₄₀ But when we know the grounds and authors
   of it,
Thou shalt be both the plaintiff and the judge
Of thine own cause.
FAB. Good madam, hear me speak,
And let no quarrel nor no brawl to come
Taint the condition of this present hour,
₃₄₅ Which I have wonder'd at. In hope it shall not,
Most freely I confess, myself and Toby
Set this device against Malvolio here,
Upon some stubborn and uncourteous parts
We had conceived against him: Maria writ
₃₅₀ The letter at Sir Toby's great importance;
In recompense whereof he hath married her.
How with a sportful malice it was follow'd,
May rather pluck on laughter than revenge;
If that the injuries be justly weigh'd
₃₅₅ That have on both sides pass'd.
OLI. Alas, poor fool, how have they baffled thee!
CLO. Why, 'some are born great, some achieve
   greatness,
and some have greatness thrown upon them.' I was
one, sir, in this interlude; one Sir Topas, sir; but
   that's all

₃₆₀ one. 'By the Lord, fool, I am not mad.' But do you
   remember?
'Madam, why laugh you at such a barren rascal?
an you smile not, he's gagged:' and thus the whirligig
   of
time brings in his revenges.
MAL. I'll be revenged on the whole pack of you. [*Exit.*
₃₆₅ *OLI.* He hath been most notoriously abused.
DUKE. Pursue him, and entreat him to a peace:
He hath not told us of the captain yet:
When that is known, and golden time convents,
A solemn combination shall be made
₃₇₀ Of our dear souls. Meantime, sweet sister,
We will not part from hence. Cesario, come;
For so you shall be, while you are a man;
But when in other habits you are seen,
Orsino's mistress and his fancy's queen. [*Exeunt all,*
   except Clown.
CLO. [*Sings*]
₃₇₅ When that I was and a little tiny boy,
With hey, ho, the wind and the rain,
A foolish thing was but a toy,
For the rain it raineth every day.
But when I came to man's estate,
₃₈₀ With hey, ho, &c.
'Gainst knaves and thieves men shut their gate,
For the rain, &c.
But when I came, alas! to wive,
With hey, ho, &c.
₃₈₅ By swaggering could I never thrive,
For the rain, &c.
But when I came unto my beds,
With hey, ho, &c.
With toss-pots still had drunken heads,
₃₉₀ For the rain, &c.
A great while ago the world begun,
With hey, ho, &c.
But that's all one, our play is done,
And we'll strive to please you every day. [*Exit.*

Made in United States
North Haven, CT
26 September 2023

42023628R00286